FEAT

&

MAGAZINE ARTICLE

WRITING

FEATURE
&
MAGAZINE ARTICLE
WRITING

JANET E. RAMSEY
SUNY COLLEGE AT BUFFALO

WCB Brown & Benchmark
PUBLISHERS

Madison, Wisconsin • Dubuque, Iowa

Book Team

Executive Editor *Stan Stoga*
Managing Developmental Editor *Sue Pulvermacher-Alt*
Production Editor *Debra DeBord*
Visuals/Design Developmental Consultant *Marilyn A. Phelps*
Visuals/Design Freelance Specialist *Mary L. Christianson*
Publishing Services Specialist *Sherry Padden*
Advertising Manager *Brett Apold*

WCB Brown & Benchmark

A Division of Wm. C. Brown Communications, Inc.

Executive Vice President/General Manager *Thomas E. Doran*
Vice President/Editor in Chief *Edgar J. Laube*
Vice President/Sales and Marketing *Eric Ziegler*
Director of Production *Vickie Putman Caughron*
Director of Custom and Electronic Publishing *Chris Rogers*

 Wm. C. Brown Communications, Inc.

President and Chief Executive Officer *G. Franklin Lewis*
Corporate Senior Vice President and Chief Financial Officer *Robert Chesterman*
Corporate Senior Vice President and President of Manufacturing *Roger Meyer*

Cover and interior designs by Carol S. Joslin

Copyedited by Kathy Anderson

The credits section for this book begins on page 353 and is considered
an extension of the copyright page.

A Times Mirror Company

Library of Congress Catalog Card Number: 92–75772

ISBN 0–697–13832–1

Printed in the United States of America by Wm. C. Brown Communications, Inc.,
2460 Kerper Boulevard, Dubuque, IA 52001

10 9 8 7 6 5 4 3 2 1

CONTENTS

3   Interviews: Asking Questions of Sources and Subjects 49

4   Style: Planning a Strategy for Sending the Message 69

5 Leads: Getting Started on the Story 90

PART II   SOME BASIC FEATURE STORIES   115

---

6 Narratives: Telling What Happens Next 116

PART III SPECIAL-PURPOSE,
SPECIAL-CIRCUMSTANCE STORIES 227

---

17 Query Letters: Offering Ideas to Editors 324

18 Professional Ethics and Legal Issues: Preparing for Publication 336

PREFACE

This textbook began, as I suppose many textbooks do, with a dissatisfaction with the books currently available—in this instance, with books available for my course on feature and magazine article writing. Not that any one of the books I examined was so unsatisfactory, but no single book had all the elements I was looking for. Costs of student texts being what they are, I was not inclined to ask my students to buy two or three books simply to get everything *I* wanted. I decided, therefore, to write my own textbook.

What was I looking for, and what have I chosen to include in this, my textbook on feature and magazine article writing?

First and foremost, I wanted a text that clearly identifies and defines popular kinds of features and magazine articles. I had noticed that our department's journalism students, who work on the student newspaper as part of a reporting class and who frequently obtain first jobs working on weekly rather than daily newspapers, seemed at a loss when asked to write certain kinds of stories. If asked to write a profile, they wrote a newslike interview; if asked to write a color article, they produced a personal column; if asked to write a backgrounder, they composed an editorial.

Their inability to understand what was expected of them made me believe that students need a clearer sense of what journalists mean when they refer to and ask for certain kinds of writing. We don't use the term ''genre'' in journalism; nonetheless, genres of journalistic stories exist. I believe students should understand and be familiar with those genres. Thus, in this text, I ask students to explore, analyze, and consider (with the understanding, of course, that they will eventually write) various kinds of features and magazine articles. This book tries to be as clear as possible about structures and styles typically used to create types of stories. It strives to describe the characteristics of each story type, while at the same time reminding students that the creative nature of feature writing means the parameters of any typical story form are not fixed, but flexible.

A typological approach to the teaching of writing is currently less fashionable than a process approach, but I do not believe the two approaches to teaching writing are mutually exclusive. My students write and revise, keep diagnostic journals and portfolios, have peer evaluations and free writing experiences. Nothing in this text precludes process pedagogy, but this text concentrates on making as clear as possible the scope of what educators and professionals mean when they demand certain kinds of tried-and-true stories common to journalism.

Second, I wanted to present to students many examples of successful feature and magazine article writing, examples both short and substantial. Within the text, I wanted students to have readable examples brief enough so that they wouldn't do what I did when I skimmed those other textbooks: jump over the examples to continue reading the explanatory material. After each chapter, I wanted a full-length feature or magazine article to serve as an example of the type of story the chapter presents, and to provoke discussion about how a particular story could or should have been handled. Since duplication of materials from magazines and newspapers is one of the constant headaches of teaching feature and magazine article writing, I also hoped that including these full-length stories at the end of each chapter would save teachers from at least some duplication tasks.

The writing examples in this book were selected from among the best in feature and magazine article writing. Too often we in journalism education emphasize speed and accuracy—both extremely important objectives—at the expense of emphasizing excellence in the craft of writing. Too often we assume that students have exposure to the best in the business, when in fact they are primarily exposed to mediocre local and suburban newspapers, opinionated news magazines, and relatively superficial teen and sports magazines. Hence, in this textbook I have made an effort to emphasize writing excellence, presenting as often as possible not just *any* examples of writing, but *prize-winning* examples, excerpts from stories or complete stories that have achieved some sort of professional recognition for style and substance.

Third, I wanted to include with each chapter exercises students could do before writing a full-length story or series of stories. Students in my course write for each class meeting; however, because of the interviewing and research time involved, they don't write full-length stories for every class. The brief writing assignments in the exercises of this book can be used for in-class writing or homework between major writing assignments. The skills exercises are meant to be warm-ups for writing the longer pieces; the discussion questions are intended to encourage students to consider the choices they may make and the difficulties they may encounter when they write their longer stories.

Finally, I wanted to include in this textbook practical material on the publication process. Students study feature writing for many reasons: some want to work on newspapers, some in public relations; some hope for magazine staff positions, some to have successful free-lance careers. Practical advice on publication is available in this text for any student who wants and needs it. Chapters containing this advice are placed together at the end of the book, but this place-ment does not necessarily mean that the material must be taught at the end of a semester. Rather, these chapters can be presented at the end of the course or integrated into the teaching of other chapters, as the instructor finds most ap-propriate.

Different teachers with whom I have spoken seem to make very different choices about the most appropriate time to discuss, for example, query letters or story markets. I often wait to see the make-up of the class before I make a decision about when to present such material. Whatever time a teacher does choose for the presentation of material about story publication (or if such mate-rial is never used at all), I believe students profit from learning to consider more carefully and thoughtfully their intended audiences. Too often they write to please themselves or the teacher, rather than writing to interest readers of a newspaper or magazine that might publish their stories. The early ''Style'' chapter in this text, therefore, discusses audience and how a consideration of readers affects other decisions involved in researching and writing a story.

I should add that features and magazine articles are not, for the most part, discussed separately in this book. Rather, their differences are understood as arising from distinctions in markets and audiences. Discussion of their differ-ences, therefore, is generally included in an examination of the elements of any story affected by a consideration of its readers, elements such as voice, level of formality, difficulty of language, and tone.

I have arranged the material in this textbook into four sections. The first considers the steps students take to prepare for writing; the second and third sections consider popular kinds of feature stories and magazine articles; the final section concerns the publication process.

Section two includes those stories most identifiable by a particular writing style or structure: narratives, color stories, profiles, backgrounders, how-tos and brights. Section three includes stories derived from these basic stories, blended from several styles or structures, or written for special purposes or circum-stances. It seemed more useful to me to discuss *first* the basic stories most characterized by straight narrative, description, analysis, explanation, and comic writing, before moving on to less straightforward types of writing. I am aware, however, that my ordering is arbitrary. The intention is that any teacher using this book can choose when and how to use each chapter. While there is some interdependence among the chapters, each chapter should have value as a self-contained, independent entity, and therefore can be assigned to students without too much concern about what in the text comes before or after.

This textbook is, I hope, a teacher-friendly book, one that includes what is most needed to construct a basic one-semester college course. What I use in my teaching now has been collected from many places, over many years. How helpful it would have been to have had, from the beginning, my material in one place: explanation, exercises, examples; advice on how to find ideas, interview, and use quotations; material on how to research, publish, and subscribe to pro-fessional ethics.

Many people who teach feature and magazine article writing come to their teaching from the working world; to them, putting together a college course for the first time can be bewildering. As one new adjunct said: ''I'm beginning to think they had it backwards. The saying should be, 'Those who *do, can't* teach.' '' This textbook, I hope, can ease a transition from doing to teaching by articulating a close analysis of features and magazine articles, by providing pedagogically sound activities for students, and by presenting many fine illustrations of what some of the most talented people in the field of journalism have written.

A great many people have been invaluable in their help with the writing of this book. I wish to acknowledge especially my editors at Brown & Benchmark, who have been unfailingly professional, competent, and pleasant to work with; my reviewers (Sandy Barnard, Indiana State University; Thomas Lieb, Towson State University; Patricia Mills, Ball State University; Robert Ours, West Virginia University–Perley Isaac Reed School of Journalism; John Morano, Monmouth College; Catherine M. Stablein, College of DuPage), who offered such positive, constructive criticism about drafts of the text; the State University of New York–College at Buffalo and in particular Dr. W. Richard Whitaker, chairperson of the Communication Department, and Dr. Patricia Cummins, dean of the Faculty of Arts and Humanities, who supported my writing with a sabbatical and arrangements for released time; and my family, who endured me while I was working on ''The Book,'' especially my husband John, whose insightful criticism and intelligent comment have influenced so many of its pages.

Above all I am indebted to the many fine journalists who so generously permitted the use of their words in this text. After reading carefully again and again those pieces that they have written, I am struck as never before with what a rich and enduring resource to all Americans is their intelligence, human sympathy, and energetic determination to tell the story.

FEATURE

◇ &

MAGAZINE ARTICLE

WRITING

The Preliminary Process

The Feature
Defining That Elusive Term

People talk about the weather, but can't do anything about it; journalists, on the other hand, do feature writing, but seldom talk about it—or at least they seldom define what a feature is and how it should be written.

Consequently, if you are starting a career in journalism and beginning to write features for newspapers or magazines, you may have difficulty determining precisely how to go about it. What is a feature, anyway? How is a feature story different from a news story? from an editorial, column, or review? from a work of fiction or creative writing?

And what, if any, is the difference between writing a "feature" for a newspaper and an "article" for a magazine?

The little that professional newspaper reporters or magazine staff writers do say about feature writing is of little help. They compound the problem of definition by using the word "feature" in similar, yet distinct ways: as if it were an action—"Let's feature that story on page one"—a thing—"Are you going to write a feature on that?"—or a description of a style of writing—"I gave that story feature treatment."

Yet despite the difficulty of arriving at a definition, you will find it helpful to have a sense of the characteristics defining features, because you can expect to write many feature stories throughout your career, whether you write for newspapers, magazines, or any other of a variety of public relations or community publications.

THE POPULARITY OF FEATURES

It helps if you understand that features have increased dramatically in number and popularity in recent years. In the past, newspapers identified themselves as publications primarily offering straightforward news—''the facts, ma'am; nothing but the facts.'' Feature stories were in some respects a kind of afterthought; they were, so to speak, the icing on the cake of hard information.

Television and radio, however, eventually proved themselves capable of offering straight informational news faster, and perhaps better, than newspapers—or at least radio and television offered the news live, with sound effects and accompanying pictures. Newspapers thus were forced, and are still being forced, to offer more than just factual news. Newspapers were forced to redefine and enlarge their concept of soft news, or features.

Features could be stories with depth and breadth, stories longer and more detailed than 30-second, or even 5-minute, broadcast stories. And if hard news stories had historically emphasized ''who,'' ''what,'' ''where,'' and ''when,'' features could especially emphasize ''how'' and ''why.'' Features could offer fresh and unusual perspectives on events, analytic considerations of the past, evocative glimpses into the future, arresting presentations of options and choices, and empathetic examinations of the personal dimension to public affairs.

Of course, features could also capitalize on one advantage that newspaper stories already possessed: permanency. Stories printed on paper can be saved to be read during leisure hours (they don't have to be consumed precisely at 6 P.M.), and they can be read again and again (you don't have to set up a tape recorder or video machine to obtain a copy). They can also be shared easily, passed around to friends and relatives.

So today, newspapers compete with radio and television by offering stories which readers want to hold on to, stories telling more than just the day's news. Readers will buy newspapers to have those stories even though they have already heard the news on the radio or watched the nightly news on television.

Today's newspapers also compete with radio and television by offering a rich variety of stories. Newspapers give readers the possibility of choosing what to read—in the readers' own good time and in their own personal order—from many different kinds of presentations of information. Readers can choose not only from news and features, but also from opinion writing, that is, from editorials, political columns, reviews, and letters to the editor.

NEWSPAPER FEATURE AND MAGAZINE ARTICLE

The increase in the number and variety of feature stories, and the expansion in the length and depth of features, has often been described as the ''magazining'' of newspapers: newspapers, in the volume and variety of their feature stories (and other stories), seem more like magazines. Today's newspapers not only publish feature stories on front pages, but also publish entire daily feature sections, under section headings such as ''Lifestyle,'' ''People,'' or ''Today.'' Newspapers may also publish supplemental Sunday feature sections on topics such as travel, food, entertainment, and health and fitness; some newspapers even publish their own Sunday "magazines."

As newspapers have become magazine-like, the distinction between the definition of a "newspaper feature" and a "magazine article" has considerably blurred—if it was ever all that clear in the first place. Traditionally, a newspaper "feature" was defined as a piece of writing that was shorter, more informational and timely, and more objectively written than a "magazine article," which was longer, less information-giving, and more personal and opinionated.

This book contends, however, that the differences between the newspaper "feature" and magazine "article" have largely disappeared. For example, the writer of a profile, travel, or narrative story does not necessarily write a very different story when writing for a newspaper or magazine—except for the obvious difference of the audience the writer is writing for. So in this text, the two terms are used interchangeably: "article" and "feature" both name magazine and newspaper stories.

An additional point should be made, however. Large-circulation, general-interest magazines are on the decline; small-circulation, special-interest magazines are on the increase. To a certain extent, the newspaper business also participates in this down-sizing process: few, if any, major metropolitan dailies are being born; small-circulation, suburban newspapers are being created. Magazines, however, typically don't have the security that newspapers have if they are the only newspaper in town, and so magazines seem more affected by this trend toward specialized, smaller audiences. The result is that magazine articles continue to sound more personal and opinionated than newspaper features, as magazines address their specific readerships with "voices of authority" on particular issues. *Working Mother* magazine, for example, speaks especially to women who balance a career and motherhood; *Bird Talk* speaks particularly to owners of pets and exotic birds.

Of course, nonobjective opinion may be discovered in newspaper features, particularly overtly stated support of local teams, schools, and businesses. But newspapers, as a rule, despite their "magazining," don't *try* to be voices of authority to their readers.

We should add that magazines, which may have to *sell* themselves on newsstands or to special interest groups more than newspapers generally do, feel compelled to publish only positive stories that readers *want* to read. Negative stories that make readers feel bad about the world or themselves, may not "sell" the magazine, and therefore may never be seen in print on its pages or cover. On the other hand, large metropolitan newspapers, especially those that are the only newspaper in a one-newspaper town, have a better ability to publish features about ugly, unpleasant topics than do newspapers; newspapers can publish features readers *need* to read, even if they may not *want* to.

It could also be said, however, that since magazines depend on their stories to sell the publication, and since magazines must be sure that readers will be satisfied with what they have purchased, magazines have a clearer sense of what kind of writing satisfies readers. Newspapers, which publish features along with a great number of news stories, may not be as able to gauge the success of individual stories or types of features, or kinds of feature-writing styles.

In addition to newspapers and magazines, other publications, such as public relations newsletters and magazines, corporate newspapers, professional journals, and student newspapers, also use features extensively, capitalizing on their popularity with readers.

And interestingly, the feature cycle has come full circle. Broadcast journalism now incorporates many techniques of feature writing in its presentations. We speak of television "magazine" programs or shows like *Charles Kurault's Sunday Morning,* which offer stories researched, organized, and presented in ways similar to the ways that newspaper features and magazine articles are researched, organized, and presented. In-depth explanatory pieces on nightly news programs, such as "American Agenda," or reports on the *MacNeil/Lehrer NewsHour,* closely resemble backgrounders written for newspapers and magazines.

So if as a journalist you intend to eventually write stories for newspapers, magazines, or even broadcast news or public relations publications, you can benefit from a clear sense of what features are, and from a sense of their content, purpose, and style.

THE FEATURE AS ENTERTAINMENT

Average readers, if you asked them, would probably say feature stories are those that "entertain" readers. In a general sense, this definition is correct—though only partially accurate. Certain features, such as those which deal with the new baby giraffe at the zoo or a widow who found $1000 in her attic, are stories with the sole purpose of entertaining the reader.

Other feature stories, however, offer the reader entertainment, but in a slightly different sense; they offer more serious entertainment than that which draws a fleeting smile. A profile of the mayoral candidate, an anniversary story recalling the bombing of Pearl Harbor, a narrative about a cancer patient fighting for the right to use a controversial new drug, are also feature stories, but hardly "entertainment" in the casual humorous sense.

Generally, when we say these feature stories are entertaining, we mean that these articles are less essential reading. The basic factual information—the information most necessary to readers—has already been published in other news articles reported and published the same day on which the event occurred. For example, brief biographical material on the mayor would have been in the news story announcing his or her candidacy, information on the FDA ruling would have been in a story reporting that organization's proceedings, news of the observance of the Pearl Harbor anniversary would have been in the coverage of the ceremony held to lay the memorial wreath.

Features, then, give a supplementary way of knowing about current events, suggest a second point of view on situations. Factual information useful for daily efficiency is in news stories; feature articles seldom have information with the same degree of immediate, physical, and direct impact. Features don't tell of a traffic slow-down on the highway that will delay a return home from work, or relate when and where to vote on county real estate taxes, or announce a regulation or judicial decision.

Features are, in a certain sense, optional reading. We read features because we *choose* to, not because we *need* to, and because the feature article offers us something *more* than the initial news story. The feature article, for example, may suggest a new understanding of a situation through a clearer analysis of statistics or facts, or it may give us a heightened awareness of what a certain event means to us or to a particular group of people, or it may provide us with the simple pleasure of reading a dramatic, suspenseful, or verbally dazzling presentation of reality.

NON-DEADLINE WRITING AND CREATIVE FLEXIBILITY

Because features offer an alternative, secondary presentation of information, feature writing often lacks the sharp urgency toward publication that characterizes news writing. Features lack what journalists call "timeliness." Feature writing is thus sometimes called simply "non-deadline" writing, because features are not written under stringent deadline pressure. For example, a newspaper story about a fire on Second Avenue, if it misses today's paper, is fit only for the wastebasket: the impact on the reader is over immediately, and by tomorrow other fires will be around to report. But a feature story on the courage it takes to be a fire fighter is not timely, but timeless. An article about the bravery and character it takes to fight fires will be as satisfying to read tomorrow as it is today, and can be published next week, next year, next decade.

This lack of urgency and rigorous deadline pressure influences feature writing in all sorts of ways. The feature's relative imperishability permits it to be written through a different process from straight news, and to have a different style and different construction.

First, writers of features have more flexibility and artistic creativity than writers of news. Since readers *choose* to read features, the style and structure of an article's writing become crucial in attracting (and holding) readers' attention. The form the writer uses to tell the story is almost as important as the information it relates.

News writing, on the other hand, subjugates content to form. Information is regimented into an "inverted pyramid" structure (the most important information first, the least important information last) so that a newspaper editor can quickly cut the last paragraphs from the story if the article does not fit the number of column inches available on a page for a particular day.

Feature writing demands instead that content determine form. The most effective ordering of information must be discovered for each individual story. The feature writer must find the structure and style that will stimulate readers to sit up and take notice, choose to read, then continue to read on to the article's conclusion. As far as feature writers and their editors are concerned, "anything goes"—that is, any story structure or style is acceptable—as long as it works. And it works when readers want to read, keep reading, and value what they have read.

This range of acceptability in terms of written order and style makes it difficult to define a feature precisely in terms of its physical form. If a poet starts to write a sonnet, he or she knows the number of lines and the rhyme scheme the sonnet requires. Similarly, a news writer knows that a robbery story requires the inverted pyramid structure with the standard what-happened lead. When a feature writer goes to write a feature, however, he or she knows no such requirements or prescriptions. He or she has only general guidelines describing typical kinds of successful stories that have historically proven popular with readers and effective in entertaining them and in selling publications.

Thus, while traditional, typical feature story "types" are presented in this book, it is important that you realize these story types do not identify *required* structures; you are free to alter their way of handling information, if you feel you have a better way to tell what you want to tell. You can choose from all the standard story options. But you can also mix and match, add and delete elements, and create your own structures. The same information, for example, can be presented in a suspenseful narrative, a first-person reminiscence, a kaleidoscopic series of descriptions, or a roll-call of names or facts. Any structure appropriate to a reality you want to represent is possible, so long as readers respond positively.

In addition to creative freedom, feature writers also have slightly more freedom than news writers to negotiate with editors the timing of the publication of their stories. That is not to say that feature writers can simply finish an article any time they want to, and of course, some feature stories cannot wait indefinitely for publication. For example, a personality profile of a mayoral candidate is no good after the candidate has *lost* the election. But in general, feature writers *can* attempt to convince an editor that a later publication date, a little more writing time, would result in a superior story. They can argue for scheduling the story when it is ready, when it has been perfected and polished, researched and fact-checked, in a way that fixed deadlines never permit news stories to be.

Since the timing of the publication of feature stories is more flexible, features can usually be whatever length suits the demands of the material. An

Crossed up

That's how the Carmel (Calif.) Pine Cone termed its error of omission when, over the Fourth of July weekend, its editors forgot to run The New York Times crossword puzzle.

They did more than apologize to their readers, over 100 of whom had called to complain.

Editor Ray L. March, who blamed "some inexplicable transition of type and page formatting," wiped out most of the next issue's front page and filled the space with the missed puzzle. Under the headline "We apologize . . . ," March wrote, "May this never happen again."

In an editorial inside, March observed that the 77-year-old weekly still had a bit to learn about its readers. In "the drive to present the news," he wrote, "we forget at times that the Carmel Pine Cone is many things to many people: that it's not just the latest 'scoop' or late-breaking story that our readers are looking for. . . . In addition to information—and hopefully enlightenment—our readers want entertainment, intellectual challenge, perhaps some simple diversions."

Forgetting the puzzle, he concluded, "was a sharp reminder that while we are loved, it may be for something other than we think."

As this presstime *article makes evident, and the* Carmel Pine Cone *learned, readers turn to newspapers for more than just hard news. Editor Ray L. March points out,* ". . . *readers want entertainment, intellectual challenge, perhaps some simple diversions.*" *(*CARMEL PINE CONE *[BROWN & WILSON INC.]. Reprinted with permission of* presstime, *the journal of the Newspaper Association of America.)*

article need not fit only a given space available on a particular day. The story can be held until adequate space is available. At times the length of a story may even control the page layout, as in newspaper Sunday supplements or in magazines, where page design may be determined by article length; photos or graphics flow *around* the space which the print of the feature story occupies.

Because the length and date of publication of the feature story are, to a certain degree, flexible, when the feature article is cut, it is not necessarily cut with a single chop-off at article's end, but judiciously pruned. Feature writers and editors can determine what to preserve and delete and where; in particular, they can keep a particular ending to the story if they believe it is the best way to conclude the story.

Feature writers can thus ''point'' things in the story to a particular conclusion, since the conclusion is no more dispensable than any other section of the story. The feature article can head *toward* a final paragraph; as opposed to the news story which must descend *from* its initial paragraph. Feature writers can plan everything in the story to build, for example, to a surprise finish, a final pathetic scene, or a last somber reassessment of the facts.

Perhaps most important, because each feature is written with freedom and flexibility, each feature article is unique. The chance that any two features will be identical or even similar is unlikely—even if they are features on the same topic and of the same length. Two *news* articles of a traffic accident should be very much the same, but two feature articles about a little girl dying of leukemia on her birthday or two features on children of divorce would be very different, depending on the writers who created the stories and the choices they made about how to tell them.

Because every feature story is an exclusive, expressed through each writer's angle of vision, feature writers don't have to worry about being the first person to write on a particular topic. If a news writer doesn't break a story, that story is devalued, because each repeat account by another reporter basically duplicates the first. But if a feature writer discovers that someone else has written about a topic, the feature writer needs only to find a new perspective on the same situation, or to write with a different structure or style. With imaginative exploration of ideas and expression, he or she may write an even better version than the first.

In conclusion, then, we can say that features generally offer a secondary, supplemental understanding of occurrences and events. They entertain in the sense that readers *choose* to read them rather than *need* to read them. Feature story structures are not prescribed, and features do not follow rigid structures or patterns. Because of the slightly relaxed deadline pressure, features can be edited judiciously rather than cut from the end. Features are unique creations reflecting the individual writer's angle of vision and choice of form and expression.

RESTRICTIONS ON THE FEATURE WRITER

Feature writers, however, do not have artistic flexibility and freedom in the same sense that journalistic opinion writers or literary writers such as novelists, playwrights, or poets have.

Literary writers such as novelists, playwrights, and poets conceive characters, plot, and setting from their own imaginations. Quite simply, they are allowed to make things up. Feature writers cannot do this; as journalists, they report from the real world, not from the private world of their personal imaginations. Feature writers may be creative in handling reality, but they cannot produce characters who do not actually live—even if an article would be greatly improved by the presence of those characters. Nor can feature writers rearrange the order of events or alter the settings of their real-life dramas.

Feature writers work within the confines of the actual, physical world. Their challenge is to take reality and shape it into the most creative, appealing presentation that talent and intelligence can contrive. Feature writers are always, *always* bound by the ethics of accuracy. For a feature writer to falsify any information for the sake of creating a more emotionally satisfying story is for him or her to deceive the reader, who recognizes the journalistic ethic of telling what is true, and who expects the feature writer to report about a real, historical world.

Feature writers are thus *like* news writers in that they must value factual accuracy, not only in matters large, but in matters small. For example, if you, as a feature writer, were writing a personality profile of a famous actress, you would need to relate accurately not only information about major events in her life, but also information about such details as her address on Park Avenue. A journalistic publication—whether a newspaper or magazine—builds its credibility with readers on its accuracy; readers assume that if the publication is sloppy about little details, it cannot be trusted on large, important issues. Most journalistic publications, therefore, insist on accuracy in all material and from all writers, whether the writing be features, opinion, or news. In fact, in some ways feature writers are *more* accountable for factual accuracy than news writers, because feature writers cannot explain away inaccuracies as arising from the demands of reporting under deadline pressure.

Another restriction imposed upon feature writers, at least to a certain degree, is objectivity. Newspapers in particular like to reserve overt statements of opinion for articles clearly identified as opinion writing—that is, for editorials, reviews, and columns. Most newspapers see themselves as heirs to the journalistic tradition derived from the Bill of Rights: they believe their freedom of expression is protected by the First Amendment in order to preserve the open discussion of society and government essential to the welfare of the democracy. In that open discussion, it must be clear who is speaking and how their statements are affected by personal bias. Newspapers thus presume an ethical responsibility to identify expressions of opinion clearly and limit them to identified opinion articles and opinion pages. Newspaper feature writers, unlike opinion writers of editorials, reviews, and columns, therefore generally remove themselves from stories, keeping out their own private reactions and feelings, and rarely using the pronoun ''I.''

Magazine article writers are less likely to feel obliged to strive for this stringent objectivity, because magazines do not define their role as that of creating a forum for the exchange of ideas in a democracy. While magazines want to develop credibility with readers, that credibility is more likely to come from providing authoritative material about certain subjects, rather than from being neutral and objective about current events.

Nonetheless, whether newspaper feature or magazine article, feature stories generally tend *not* to express opinion openly. The objectivity situation has sometimes been described as a line between two opposite ends. News stories occupy one end and opinion articles the other; features fall in different places on the line between, some tending more toward objectivity, others tending more toward subjectivity. A feature such as an educational backgrounder on causes of alcoholism may be written quite neutrally and be similar to a news story; a personal narrative feature about recovering from alcoholism through attending AA meetings may be written with emotion and feeling, and be similar to an opinion column.

Feature writers do express themselves in their stories as all reporters do—as professionals who have gathered information and exercised judgment in the selection of that information. And feature writers, like opinion writers, have more freedom than news writers to determine *how* they present that information, what kind of language to use in presenting that information. They can be more descriptive, use words with richer emotional overtones, and employ language more creatively. Nonetheless, unlike opinion writers, feature writers do not use their articles as soapboxes for their own individual theories or ideas. Feature writers do not advocate, espouse, or plead for action; they do not conclude, cajole, or implore readers to feel a certain way or do a certain thing.

THE FEATURE WRITER'S PRESENCE

Certain features do require that writers be present in the story with personal, less-than-objective reactions. If a feature writer were to witness or take part in an unusual event, his or her personal account of what happened would be the honest way to tell the story. If, for example, you as feature writer witnessed the execution of a criminal, it would be better for you to write an article about your own reactions to seeing the event than to pretend that you were interviewing an "anonymous" source, who was, in fact, yourself.

Except for such special circumstances, however, a feature writer's personal presence in the article is minimized—not only because it makes the story objective, but because it makes it more powerful and effective. Readers are not all that interested in the average writer's personal opinions; instead, readers want to react to the story, to experience it for themselves. The best features allow readers to see, hear, smell, touch, and taste events. The best features capture the experience, rather than judge it or tally up its consequences.

In past years, a school of writers called "new journalists" has argued that since absolute, total objectivity is impossible, journalists—after they study their subjects for so long that they feel practically a part of them—should write like fiction writers. In other words, journalists should write like omnipresent, omniscient fiction narrators, telling what the people they are writing about are thinking, believing, and feeling, rather than identifying through direct quotations what those people *say* they are thinking, believing, and feeling.

Other journalists, however, do not agree that journalism can be "fictionalized." They argue that feature writers should *not* be omniscient narrators, but should continue to rely only on direct and indirect quotations. These journalists argue that however well-researched a new journalism article may be, its dramatic immediacy is not worth the blurring of the distinction between what is created inside a fiction writer's head and what is reported from outside a journalist's head.

If you're beginning to write features, you should probably not be too hasty to play literary journalist or personal columnist. Instead, master first the discipline of keeping your presence in the article to a minimum, learning how to gather an abundance of direct quotations and how to be precise in your use of attribution and identification. Then you won't become dependent on writing paraphrases (weak style) or, worse yet, fabricate what people have probably said (dishonest work). In addition, if you force yourself out of the story, you will learn how to *show* a scene and describe people, rather than *tell* readers your own reactions or what you think their reactions should be.

Quotations, we should note, *are* used differently by feature writers and news writers. News writers use quotations to clarify information or suggest the possible impact of a news event; feature writers use quotations to reveal character or add color. Feature writers want to relate *how* a speaker is talking, rather than limiting themselves to saying simply what the speaker has said.

THE FEATURE WRITER AS JOURNALIST

The definition of feature writing is a little clearer, then, if we expand the definition to say that while feature writing is written using some of the methods and means of creative fiction writers, and while it is more expressive of the writer's subjective feelings and opinions than news, it nonetheless preserves its objective, journalistic nature. Features are written by journalists committed to accuracy and striving to focus on real-life subjects rather than themselves.

Features also use many traditional journalistic writing techniques, writing skills particularly emphasized by journalism schools and by high-quality newspapers and magazines. These techniques are part of the historical canon of good journalism; they are tools writers have traditionally used as they strive to be clear, concise, and powerful. Some of these techniques, considered shared implements of all journalists, are:

- using simple words and simple sentences to keep meanings clear;
- placing actors close to action (subjects close to verbs), descriptions close to what they describe (adjectives close to nouns), time and sequence words close to actions (adverbs close to verbs);

- using specific, physical, factual details to convey a sense of reality and indicate degree;
- employing strong, action verbs to create a sense of energy and movement;
- finding the precise, exact word for every nuance of meaning; and
- avoiding repetition and redundancy, except where repetition creates clarity.

Particularly characteristic of journalistic writing is economy of language. While literary writing often seeks expansion, journalistic writing requires that every word fights for its right to remain in the story and on the page. Each word in a story takes away from the newspaper's or magazine's ability to publish another story, or to use the page for advertising in order to stay financially solvent. So the writer of a feature must be able to justify every word, sentence, and paragraph, to argue for the necessity of the presence of each element of the story.

You should not think, however, that feature writers feel themselves *limited* by their commitment to factual accuracy, objectivity, and economy of language. Feature writers—like all journalists—delight in the challenge of capturing current events and real people. They enjoy discovering and exploring actual daily life, immediate and physical, around them.

To journalists, feature writing is a satisfying art: it requires seeing the essence of reality clearly and sharing it fully—with sensitivity, originality, and strength. The process doesn't feel limited, but limitless. Each morning feature writers find in the world an abundance of material to write about, more subjects than they could satisfactorily present in a day, or a lifetime. Feature writers know their work is as full of variety and contradiction and complexity as the real human beings they describe, as full of change and turmoil and conflict as the real events they report.

EXERCISES

1. Which of the following situations seem to require primarily hard news coverage? Which readily suggest feature coverage? Are there any that suggest first news treatment and then feature treatment?

- Local legislature asks state to OK tax increase
- Copter crew plucks two children from raging flood waters
- President vows new efforts to solve trade imbalance with Japan
- 61 percent of children in inner city said to face lead poisoning from old paint
- AIDS cases rise in county
- 20-year-old motorist hospitalized after car crashes into house

2. Below is a short Associated Press news brief. If you were a feature writer, what other stories about this situation could you possibly write? What might the reader gain from reading your stories?

BASKETBALL STAR COLLAPSES, DIES

Hank Gathers, No.11 on the NCAA's career scoring list, died Sunday after collapsing on the court during Loyola Marymounts' West Coast Conference semifinal game against the University of Portland in Los Angeles. The cause of death was not immediately known, but officials said Gathers had suffered cardiac arrest.

Gathers collapsed in convulsions near mid-court after scoring on a dunk. He was taken to a hospital, where he was pronounced dead.

3. Features offer "a different or unusual point of view on situations," a "new perspective on statistics or facts, or a heightened awareness of what a certain event means in human terms, or the simple pleasure of reading a dramatic, suspenseful, or verbally dazzling presentation of reality." Apply this statement to the following list of titles from contemporary magazines. How would readers profit from reading these features? What would they gain from their reading? What do you think might be the content of these articles?

- Just Like Us? Toward a Notion of Animal Rights
- How Women Are Changing TV: New Power on and off the Screen
- Sample the New Zoos
- Chill: How Winter Affects Your Skin
- Drinking in America: A Sobering Report
- A Kinder, Gentler Stephen King

4. "Features are unique creations reflecting their individual writer's angle of vision and choice of form and expression." With that statement in mind, read Peter Marks' "No More Stupid Pet Tricks Here," written for *Newsday,* and Henry Mitchell's "When Breeding Is Everything," written for *The Washington Post.* Compare and contrast the "angle of vision" and "choice of form and expression" of the two writers. Discuss the relationship the two writers seem to have with their readers. What audiences do they seem to be writing for?

- What difference does it make that one writer chose to write *after* the Madison Square Garden dog show, and one writer focused on a time well beforehand?
- What would the news story covering the event have said?
- Which story did you prefer? Why?
- Would you have *chosen* to read either story if it had not been a class assignment?

NO MORE STUPID PET TRICKS HERE

By Peter Marks
Newsday, *February 10, 1992*

THAT HAIR, as luxurious as the locks of Thor. That body, sleek and muscular, with the strong, lean lines of a sprinter. Those eyes—oh those eyes!—gazing regally into the distance, dark and full of mystery.

What a *dog!*

Talk about animal magnetism: In the presence of Triumph, the top Afghan hound in the country, dog people go wild. They crowd around to watch him pose, run their hands admiringly across his flawless coat, shower him with best-of-show ribbons. They love the perfect curl of his question-mark tail, the perfect wisps of Fu Manchu under his chin. But most of all, they love his perfect aloofness: Peer into those big eyes. Mark the imperious bearing. "The Look of Eagles," some dog people call it.

It is not something a dog can pick up in obedience school, this Look of Eagles. Nature, not nurture, is what separates the great Afghan from the run-of-the-kennel. "It's like royalty," said Michael Canalizo, who raised Triumph from pup to champion in a snazzy two-story kennel on a seven-acre estate on Long Island's North Shore. "They look past you. It's like the way the Queen of England looks unapproachable."

That look has served him well. At the ripe old age of 4, Champion Triumph of Grandeur—"T.R." to his close friends—has won dozens of shows across the nation, a record that makes him a top dog by any measure. And yet, he has still not reached the pinnacle, the honor that dog people rank above all others: Best-of-Show at Westminster.

Today, at Madison Square Garden, the competition starts in the oldest and most prestigious event in all of American canine showdom, the Westminster Kennel Club Dog Show. Triumph will be one of 2,500 dogs that have attained the rank of champion, representing 144 breeds and varieties, competing in the show that dog people fantasize about the way playwrights dream of Pulitzers. The only difference is that in the world of judging dogs, the attraction is purely physical.

It sounds shallow, but there it is. Dog shows are like Miss America pageants without the talent competition. You know of a dog that fetches newspapers? Carries brandy to stranded skiers? Converses in Serbo-Croatian? Yeah, OK. But does he have the Look of Eagles? Other types of shows may test a dog's agility and mental abilities, but there is only one prestige event for dogs. And it's about beauty, not brains.

The brainy stuff is left to the handlers, the people like Canalizo, who are on an endless quest for the perfect dog, the dog that, in form, movement and temperament, embodies the ideal for its breed.

Weekend after weekend, in Winnebagos and Aerostars, the handlers, professionals and amateurs alike, ferry their dogs from show to show, to places like Waukesha and Schenectady and Johnstown. It's called campaigning the dog, because the dog has to get out and meet the voters if he's going to get anywhere in dog shows. Last year, Canalizo took out ads about his Afghan in major dog publications—a common practice among top owners and handlers—and traveled by air and highway with Triumph to about 130 shows. Not in search of cash: There is no prize money in dog shows. Not in search of publicity: The only people who notice are other dog people. For ribbons. Just ribbons.

It really isn't all that unfathomable. Dog people blow their money on entry fees and hotel rooms and dog food for the same reasons ballplayers endure season after season in the minors and actors bide their time in dinner theaters in Scranton. They're hooked on The Show.

"It's a sickness," observes Canalizo's mother, Lee, who introduced her son to his first Afghan when he was a little boy. "And Michael and I both have it."

A bone-chilling Saturday in January. The gymnasium at Orange County Community College in upstate Middletown is wall-to-wall dog. Eleven hundred dogs, to be exact, of every shape and size. A few dogs look dazzling, but the atmosphere is the opposite of glamorous. A big space filled with cages, carpeted in hair balls and thick with pet-smell.

The event is the Wallkill Kennel Club Dog Show, a dot on the dog-show map, one of 11,000 shows of various types sanctioned by the American Kennel Club. But because it occurs less than three weeks before Westminster, it attracts several important dogs, Triumph among them.

Canalizo has arrived here hours earlier to stake out a prime spot for the preparation of Triumph and two other Afghans from his kennel that are learning the ropes. "The English Springer Spaniel is here, too," he says conspiratorially. Translation: Another top, top dog. The competition is going to be keen.

The gym has been converted into a vast preening room, alive with the sounds of yipping Yorkies and howling Huskies. Feverish activity all over the place, as terriers and poodles standing on crates submit to the ministrations of their handlers, who hover over them with the intensity of surgeons, using small implements to brush, comb, chalk, cut, powder, clip and fluff.

The primping is under way, and it's like the scene in Emerald City: Snip, snip here; snip, snip there . . .

The Bichons Frises look like mutant cotton balls, the Rough Collies as if they have been under the hair dryer too long. A couple of macho Standard Schnauzers square off while a Great Dane decides to take a breather in the aisle near Ring Five, bringing pedestrian traffic to a standstill.

And there, standing atop his metal crate, unperturbed by the chaos around him, his serene highness, Ch. Triumph of Grandeur, awaits his daily ablutions. He already has that Look of Eagles—even with his head wrapped in a fancy *schmatte*. It's supposed to keep his lustrous tresses out of his mouth.

Canalizo joins the chorus of dog beauticians around the room and begins Triumph's combout. The *schmatte* comes off, and the dog shakes himself out, his hair tumbling onto his shoulders in a way that makes him look disconcertingly like Barbra Streisand. Canalizo runs his brush over the dog's coat of chocolate brown flecked with rust brown again and again, until it is as silky as the hairdos on the models in shampoo commercials.

Canalizo, who can talk with friends and apply conditioner at the same time, is Triumph's co-owner—with Long Island builder Roger Rechler—as well as handler. From the look of things, he is in reality the dog's personal valet.

"He has to see everything that's being done," Canalizo tut-tuts, as Triumph peers out on his domain majestically. The owner-handler is dressed in camel's hair jacket, brown slacks and hand-painted tie. He, too, will be appearing before the judges.

Although Canalizo, 37, knows the routine of dog shows cold—he had his first win in the ring at the age of 8—he is nervous today. Triumph's the cool customer in this partnership, Canalizo the one eternally afflicted by the old bedeviller of performers, stage jitters. "No matter how long you do this, your hand never stops shaking," he says.

Breed by breed, the dogs are marched into the rings by their handlers for the initial judging. Some handlers own their dogs; others are paid by absent owners or breeders to campaign the dog for them. The contest is run like a tennis tournament, with winning dogs moving on to successive levels of competition against winners of other breeds.

The judges treat the dogs like late-model cars, checking the undercarriage, surveying the alignment, peering into nooks and crannies. Then they step back and take in the whole dog. It's a process that is surprisingly emotional for some judges, who are mostly former handlers and owners.

Ann Clark is not ashamed to admit that she has gone misty over a Doberman. "There are dogs that I have been unable to judge without crying," said Clark, a three-time Westminster winner and one of the most knowledgeable dog-show judges in the nation. "You look at a certain dog, and you get goose-bumpy."

Canalizo hangs out for hours by Triumph's crate; the Afghans don't go on until 3:30. Across the room, Diane Wisney sprinkles tons of powder on Ch. Starlo's Guitar Man, a Rough Collie, better known as Elvis. "That makes them whiter," she says, as Elvis shakes the powder out of his coiff, kicking up a dust storm. It's OK to do this, she says, as long as the powder is out of his coat by the time he goes into the ring. There are, apparently, styling tricks for virtually every breed and also many styling no-nos. Someone whispers the allegation that terriers sometimes are dyed, but this cannot be independently confirmed.

Handlers like Canalizo have considerable resources to breed and travel. But Wisney has only a small kennel in her backyard in Malverne and limited funds. The sport is not exactly a level playing field. Still, dog people insist that once they go into the ring, the only thing that matters is the dog. In theory, judges are not even supposed to know whose dogs they are judging. But the world of dogs is small, and word about hot new dogs spreads fast. According to dog people, many judges develop favorites; as a result, some handlers avoid certain shows, concerned the judge won't "put up"—select as a winner—their dog.

"It's all ego, even at this level," says Carol Soranno, of Byram, N.J., whose tri-color Collie,

Ch. Wyndfall's Ghostbuster, is in the competition. But even so, she has a ball. The dog has a ball. "He loves it," she says. "I've had other dogs and they've hated it. You don't keep showing them."

Back in Ring Three, it's show time: best of breed, Afghans. The dogs line up, and Canalizo gives Triumph a final spritz and brush-down. In the smallish ring, Canalizo bounds gracefully in synch with Triumph, man and animal working together like figure skaters in the pairs. The judge gives the Afghans the once-over and nods almost imperceptibly at Canalizo. It is that fast and easy: Triumph has won another Best of Breed.

"Congratulations, Michael," says another handler, as valet returns champion to the haven of his crate.

Canalizo, who grew up in a middle-class family in Freeport, has always had a magic touch with the aristocratic Afghans, the royal hunting dogs of Afghanistan. The American Kennel Club says the breed came to the United States in 1931, when Zeppo Marx and his wife imported an Afghan female, or bitch, and male, or dog, from England. Prized for their beauty and gentleness, Afghans are now popular show dogs but remain a fairly exotic breed. While 6,476 new Cocker Spaniels were registered with the AKC last year, for example, only 123 Afghans entered the purebred rolls.

"In the Sixties it was great. Every hippie had an Afghan," said Lee Canalizo. "Afghans are different, not like a German Shepherd or Golden Retriever. There is something very primitive and almost mystical about them. They appealed to anybody who was free and we were. We were a bunch of hippies in the Sixties."

Her son, however, was the studious type, conservative and quiet. Except when he got in the ring with an Afghan. He was a boy competing against adults—and winning. "He and I got started out together, and he got to be very, very good," said his mom, who is now a dog-show judge.

The most important influence in Michael Canalizo's growth as a handler and breeder was a towering figure in dog shows, Sunny Shay. She ran a kennel called Grandeur in Hicksville and was one of the most flamboyant people on the circuit. Mention her or her champion, Shirkhan, to real dog people, and they come to life. She won Westminster in 1957, which was a miraculous thing at the time, for dogs has been dominated for all time by blue-bloods. A heavy-set Jewish woman who friends say had to scrape up the cash for entry fees, Shay was the first combination owner, breeder and handler—and Shirkhan the first dog from the Hound group—to win in the Garden.

"She was the most dramatic person in dogs," says Canalizo, who as a young man handled dogs owned jointly by Shay and Roger Rechler. "She came out in full riding garb and white gloves."

When Shay died in 1978—suffering a massive coronary while showing a champion Afghan at an event in Connecticut—Rechler took over Grandeur, eventually moving the kennel to his estate in Oyster Bay, and hired Canalizo to handle the dogs. They have been running Shay's kennel ever since, with Canalizo keeping up the tradition of showing Grandeur dogs as owner-breeder-handler.

"This is what you hope for—to wind up in the finals," Canalizo says after the group judging at Wallkill. Triumph has triumphed again, winning the Hound group over the Dachshund, Beagle, Whippet and 13 other Best-of-Breed hounds. "Whatever happens now, it's been a wonderful day."

The gymnasium crowds have thinned. The balls of dog hair drift across the floor, rolling under abandoned work stations like sagebrush. Even though this is the main event, nobody is left to watch. It is now 7 p.m., and the show has been under way for 12 hours. The owners and handlers of hundreds of eliminated Bullmastiffs and German Shorthaired Pointers and Gordon Setters have already disappeared.

The English Springer Spaniel, however, is still here. It won the Sporting group. The other finalists for Best-in-Show: An Akita, a Pomeranian, Norwich Terrier, Bichon Frise as well as the Collie owned by Carol Soranno.

"I can't look," Soranno says, sitting outside the ring. Her handler, Paul Capobianco of Farmingdale, L.I., a banker who shows dogs part time, pats the Collie reassuringly.

The judge sends the dogs sweeping around the oblong ring, and Triumph looks splendid, his long hair bouncing along with the pace. Canalizo, who is soft-spoken outside the ring, is a commanding presence inside, bounding athletically alongside his dog.

They come to a rest. The handlers stand at attention. The judge nods to one.

"Thank you!" Canalizo calls out.

He's won it all: Eleven hundred entrants showed up, but only he goes home on top. The handler of the English Springer Spaniel, who has beaten Triumph in other days, stops to congratulate him.

"I *adore* that dog," the judge, Carol Duffy, gushes moments later, as Triumph and his valet have their photo taken. "He has what Afghans used to have—really exquisite."

Another trophy, another show. Canalizo is pleased, but he doesn't show much emotion. Experienced dog people take these victories in stride. It's unlikely he'd be this undemonstrative if he won it all at Westminster—but that's something he won't even talk about.

It has been a good day on the campaign. In the gym, the dog obligingly enters his crate. He seems a little tired himself—the Look of Nightingales. But it is time to move to the next show, which starts in the morning 100 miles away. Canalizo rolls his equipment and dog out of the gym and into the frigid night.

. . .

When Breeding Is Everything
Champion Dogs' Day in Madison Square Garden
By Henry Mitchell
The Washington Post, *February 14, 1990*

NEW YORK—Don't you sort of like that Dane?

Such a comment at the Westminster Dog Show will always get you a snappy answer:

"Well, I must say I didn't care for the way she moved."

But if you're beautiful enough, you don't have to move.

"I guess none of those big things can move, so they don't bother about it when judging."

All the same, I thought the Dane was lovely and so (hear, hear) did the judges who gave her a high award.

Dogs come from 49 states and some from abroad to this show, which has been held every year since 1839. The Civil War and gas rationing and all kinds of things have been inconvenient or worse, but never stopped the dog show.

Madison Square Garden is a madhouse for the two days in which the dogs are benched. That is, they sit on benches and visitors wander about cooing at the itty-bitty sweethearts and occasionally making snide comments to the Akitas. Everybody wants to stop and visit with his favorite breeds, and it can take 20 minutes to get to the real dogs (depending on what "real dogs" are). You must be patient with humans here. Slow? Dear Lord. But then as Schopenhauer said, the real trouble with humanity is that it is descended from monkeys and not from dogs.

Each breed has its own place and each dog its own number, and the 432-page catalogue lists each of the 2,932 mutts—from the wee Brussels griffon that you could put in your pocket (though only a fool would try, as they are brave fellows and do not care to be trifled with) to the great mastiffs, terribly sweet beasts though the head is the size of a calf's.

No matter the size; to see with the eyes of a dog you must have the heart of a lion, as the Chinese proverb correctly puts it.

Some say dog people soon start to resemble the breed they favor, but this is far from the usual case. A tiny red-maned woman does not look at all like the huge giant schnauzer she's trotting about the ring with. She is pretty but Dreamer is gorgeous, solid black with a wonderful short back. OOOH.

Thanks to cross-town traffic you may arrive late for the basset hound judging. It is at 8:30 a.m. and probably interferes with their morning nap, yet this is one breed for whom everything is for the best in the best of all possible worlds. You might stop to visit Keystone Express and Soaring Eagle, both sound asleep after an exhausting session in the ring. These hounds often have names expressing violent motion, as that's as close as they ever come to it.

It's clear at this show that people either love terriers or have no use for them. The dividing line seems to come with the Irish terrier, an elegant dog composed largely of live wires. The Irish is (according to your taste) either brisk or intolerably aggressive.

There are no shar-peis at Westminster, as those high-fashion, over-wrinkled mandarins are not yet recognized by the American Kennel Club. Not that the club is snobbish or resistant to new things; there are 141 breeds and varieties already officially recognized and present at the show, including a sole entry for American Staffordshire. You can't win much if you win against no opposition, but then you can't lose big, either.

If you win big at Westminster, your mutt can retire to stud or to littering forever. Some will argue that the show circuit is barbarous and stressful to the dog and assaultive to the wallet. Once a fellow who inherited a good kennel, asked if he would continue the great work of breeding fine terriers, said he would certainly cut back as he did not have $300,000 to throw down that particular rat hole. (The figure of speech, rat hole, suggests he was already smitten with terriers, to whom any hole is a new world of golden treasure.)

There's no point even thinking of taking Old Rusty to this show, though you may have had him eight years and know him to be the best dog of North America. For this is a court of champions, and if your dog hasn't won his coveted 15 points against good competition (in which case he is "finished") you don't have much chance here. And if he hasn't won at least a point toward his championship, he can't even be entered.

Still, of course, it hurts—even when you have the obviously best Rhodesian ridgeback in the world—to see some spavined mutt (if one may use the vocabulary of losers) made queen of the May. Once at Westminster there was a spectacular hound who, when he entered the ring, drew small gasps from the fanciers hanging about, but he won nothing at all.

"May I say you have the most beautiful hound I've ever seen," said a man who went over to cheer him up.

"He's the most gorgeous hound *anybody* has ever seen, except that [three obscenities] judge."

Even at Westminster, there's room for daffy love. What brings the thousands here is not mainly to see dogs of perfect conformation of body. It's a ritual each year to touch base (by wandering among the muzzles) with the most ancient bond known to mankind. As Nietzsche observed, the world was conquered through the understanding of dogs; the world exists through the understanding of dogs. The older you get the less stupid it sounds.

To some people the judging setup is a mystery, but it's simple enough, really. Say your dog is entered to be judged with other black and tan coonhounds (a particularly dandy breed if one

may say so). He is entered either in a special category of limited competition (say, Open, Bitches) or else is entered for Best of Breed. The best of the various subclasses is judged a winner. Then the best opposite sex of the winner is judged Best Opposite Sex. There may be several of these limited classes, and they are then judged together to get a Best of Winners. Then in the great class of Best of Breed, both Winner's Dog and Winner's Bitch compete with the other champions, and the breed winner is chosen. All this is determined in show rings during the day. Great signs above each ring inform ordinary viewers (fanatics already know) which breed is being judged in which ring at which time.

Then at night comes a moment of great luster in which only your black and tan competes with the best of breed winners of all the other hounds—Afghans, Basenjis, bassets, bloodhounds and the rest. If all goes as it should, your dog is chosen best of all the hounds.

In the last event of the show, the best of the hound group competes against the best of all the sporting dogs, the best of all the toy dogs, best of working dogs, terriers, non-sporting dogs and herding dogs.

So at the last there are only seven dogs in the ring, one from each group, and the judge has the unenviable job of deciding if (an example of the subjective difficulty) the best of all dogs is a superb giant schnauzer, a grand Lakeland terrier, a tiny griffon, etc.

There is no known way to judge competing breeds scientifically, though judges do their best to be impartial. A judge would never say, beholding a Manchester terrier, "Call that a dog?" but would examine it with the same respect he gives a Doberman. The Best in Show winner last night was judged by Frank T. Sabella of Santa Fe who chose a toy dog, the Pekingese called Prince.

A winning dog always has some curious radiance. Not only is he relatively flawless physically, but his beautiful soul is manifest. Or at least some damned judge thinks so.

Ideas and Research
Finding Inspiration,
Gathering Information

Ideas for feature articles come alive in three places: your eyes, your brain, and your nearest library. To produce an effective story, you have to use all three—though not necessarily in that order.

No one can tell you exactly how to initiate feature stories. No one can say exactly what will make you a highly creative writer, one who easily spins off story ideas instead of one who sits chin in hand, contemplating absolutely nothing, when called upon to produce an article.

However, if you lack confidence in yourself as a creative person, if you aren't sure you can create fresh and original feature stories, you might think again about what creativity *really* means. Those who teach creative thinking say people generally misunderstand creativity. It's not a process like our stereotypical image: the wild, unconventional artist frantically daubing oil paints on canvas. True creativity, they say, springs from an openness to new ideas, a willingness to experiment, and an ability to be flexible about change and compromise. A car mechanic or a stock broker—or a journalist—can be a creative genius if he or she possesses these qualities.

So, while you may never be a Michelangelo with words, you may be a different sort of story creator: a journalistic version of television's MacGyver, someone with a positive, can-do response to the challenges of the ''bad guys'' of stale story ideas and blank computer screens. And no matter how creative you naturally are, you can enhance your ability to generate feature articles by engaging in thorough-going, wide-ranging research, and by constantly making yourself aware of ideas discussed and debated in the various media around you.

STOP, LOOK, AND LISTEN

Feature writers generally agree that one of the most important ways of generating stories is through personal observation, through constantly watching the world around you.

When you were a child, you were probably told to "stop, look, and listen, before you cross the street." It's not a bad slogan to carry around in your head as an adult journalist. Train yourself to be a careful observer, to stop what you're doing long enough to examine carefully what's before your eyes, and to listen to (and smell, feel, and taste) all the stimuli you encounter. How many times have you driven to an address and realized it's for a house you pass two or three times every day, but have never "seen"? Or been asked to recall the color of the eyes of a person you were just talking to, and not been able to say whether they were blue or brown? Journalists need to *consciously* look at everything around them (and take copious notes about what they see and hear), so their stories will be filled with vivid impressions of real life.

Alice Steinbach of *The Baltimore Sun,* for example, is one journalist who has learned to stop and look; *she* had no trouble remembering the color of someone's eyes, as this lead for her story on a blind youth (a story that won the 1985 Pulitzer Prize for Feature Writing) illustrates:

> First, the eyes: They are large and blue, a light, opaque blue, the color of a robin's egg. And if, on a sunny spring day, you look straight into those eyes—eyes that cannot look back at you—the sharp, April light turns them pale, like the thin blue of a high, cloudless sky.

As a writer, you need to train yourself not to miss things because you are only half-consciously looking at them; concentrate, concentrate, concentrate on what's before you. Physical, concrete objects around you can inspire story ideas, as Roy Peter Clark and Don Fry remind readers in their book, *Coaching Writers: Reporters and Editors Working Together* (St. Martin's):

> An old army medal in a drawer inspires a reminiscence. A piece of sheet music becomes a story on its composer. A high school yearbook becomes a window onto 20 years of educational change.

If you're not only looking, but listening as well, you may hear people say things that spark story ideas. Inspiration for a story can come from overheard, off-hand remarks: something you hear piques your curiosity or starts your thinking, and a feature is born.

You need to be aware, however, that you may miss seeing or hearing things around you if you don't *want* to see or hear them, and that omission is more insidious than a simple lack of concentration. Consider how Republicans and Democrats see and hear a presidential election debate and *both* conclude their candidate was the winner. They see and hear what they want to see and hear—what their prejudices and prejudgments have led them to believe is there.

Journalists can't afford to see only what they want to see. They must be willing to at least *consider* the possibility that they have blinders on their eyes. If you've never thought much about your own prejudices (or if you don't even believe you have any), it's worth your while to spend a little time reading up on psychology, or taking a course in sociology, psychology, or communication. Try to discover your personal blind spots, as well as your educational, economic, ethnic, and sexual biases.

Of course, it's not expected that you rid yourself totally of personal feelings or beliefs; no one wants a journalist to be the unfeeling, unthinking man or woman. But you do want to be aware of how your feelings can influence your vision and your judgment, so that when you go to report and write a particular story, you will be able to consider how to compensate for emotional conflicts of interest.

SEARCHING FOR CLUES TO A STORY: THE OFFBEAT

As you're open-mindedly observing with your eyes (and listening with your ears, etc.), use your brain to seek clues for a story you know will appeal to readers—one that will excite them, entertain them, educate them. If you can, even go one step further: think of second, future articles. Keep in mind how this present possibility could lead to another good story, sequel, or series, and so forth.

You can often find a clue to an appealing, fresh story in an offbeat, unusual aspect of a situation. In other words, when everyone else is watching the ball, you watch the kicker. When everyone else is congratulating the winners, you seek out the losers. If a dozen people look self-satisfied, interview the one who looks depressed. What makes a good feature may not be the unusualness of the story, but the unusualness of your perspective on it.

William Ruehlmann, in his *Stalking the Feature Story* (Vintage Books), advises feature writers to follow Henry James' advice: ''Be one on whom nothing is lost.'' In other words, watch *everything,* not just the obvious things. Ruehlmann uses this example to illustrate his point:

> There is a famous photograph by Jenaro Olivares that shows the spontaneous revelry subsequent to a bullfight. A cheering crowd rises to its feet in the background; in the foreground, a matador is held aloft on the shoulders of exultant spectators. In one corner a police officer gestures outward in warning, his back to the procession.
>
> A perceptive viewer will note that the bullfighter's face is twisted in pain, not triumph—the blood on his suit of lights suggests he has undergone a goring. But the writer will be the one who observes the boy at the bottom of the picture. The boy stands pressed close to the laughing man who carries the matador, and the boy is picking that man's pocket, right under the noses of the cops.

Seeing things from a different angle, considering a different part of the whole, examining cause rather than effect (or vice-versa), finding good when everyone else sees bad (or vice-versa), thinking as an outsider rather than an insider (or vice-versa), drawing parallels when no one else sees them or contrasts when everyone else sees similarities—all these approaches to a story entail looking at ordinary things in extraordinary ways and thus provide a creative approach to an article.

CLUES: THE INCONGRUOUS

A second clue to a good story can be to look for the incongruous, for what seems out of place or doesn't belong. For example, study body language and see if there's a difference between what people say they are feeling and what their body language says they are feeling. Or study actions and see if there is an incongruity between what people say they are doing and what they actually do. When you find contradictions, ask questions about what causes them. Try to discover what's behind the incongruity.

Your own reactions to a situation may also be incongruous, and a personal sense of contradiction can be a good starting point for a story. If you've attended a charity Christmas party, for example, and left the event feeling cynical and unmoved, consider the reasons for the way you felt. Why didn't you experience the mood you expected to experience? What was wrong on the surface of things, or what was wrong beneath the surface? Reconsider your observations and ask yourself what you saw that seemed out of place. When you've identified the inappropriate aspect, you probably will have identified a good starting place for an unusual story—or at least for a story different from the one your readers (and you yourself) might have expected you to write.

CLUES: HUMAN EMOTION

A third clue to a good story is human emotion. Clark and Fry also tell their readers to "find the person behind the story and the story behind the person." Stories about human emotions are good stories, stories people like to read. Try to discover what emotions underlie ordinary events; in your reporting of situations, follow the feelings of your subjects.

Sex and money are usually seen as two great arousers of human passion, and many clichés suggest that if you find where sex and money belong in a situation, you will have found the emotions of the people involved (and thus, an interesting human tale). Investigative reporters often "follow the money," because it provides the best and most conclusive trail to what's really going on; as a feature writer, you may turn up some interesting angles to otherwise dull stories if you play investigative reporter and follow the money.

Another saying about money and human emotion involves the stereotypical murder case, with detectives asking "who benefits" from the crime. When they learn who benefits, or what motivates people, they are able to start making sense of people's actions. As a feature writer, you may find that asking the question "who benefits" will help you, especially when you're involved in a situation all prettied up with a public relations presentation. If you ask yourself "who benefits," your answer may throw a dash of reality onto your perception of the event. You can then take a hard look at what's really going on, at who's doing what and why, and you'll probably come up with a good idea for a story.

A cliché dealing with sex and emotions is the French expression "cherchez la femme" (literally, "look for the woman"). This old expression specifically focused on "the other woman" (if a man is not happy with one woman, it's probably because he has his eye on another). But today, the expression has a more general, less sexist meaning: when a couple is not getting along, another person is probably lurking in the background.

As a feature writer, use this phrase to remind you to look for hidden personal emotions behind situations that on the surface don't make a lot of sense. If you start hearing reasons for certain kinds of behavior, reasons that don't add up or ring true, look for emotional connections that aren't being disclosed.

A CHILDLIKE CURIOSITY

Finally, in coming up with feature article ideas, look for what gives meaning and zest to life. Sometimes writers approach feature stories as if they have been ordered to produce the great American novel; they seem to regard finding story ideas as a heavy responsibility instead of a natural process growing from curiosity about people and life. Psychologists talk about the child within you, that part of you that wants to play and enjoy life; feature writers need to permit this inner child to respond to what they encounter in their environments. Daniel Williamson, in *Feature Writing for Newspapers* (Hastings House), advises feature writers to "follow your curiosity and let it lead you to a feature story that you will *enjoy* researching and writing."

If you want to try to remember how to follow your childlike curiosity, spend a day with some two-year-olds. Their persistence and straightforwardness in inquiring "why" or "what makes it do that" or "where does it come from" is worth imitating. Children seem to ask questions all the time because they really want to know about what's going on around them. They're not just making conversation; they want to know how things work, where they come from, what they're supposed to do. Try to have your own version of a child's persistent curiosity. Ask "what if," "why," and "how." Go where your natural, enjoyable curiosity leads you, and you'll probably find a story of interest.

STORIES FROM THE MARKETPLACE OF IDEAS

Your brain not only helps you investigate and interpret what you observe, it can suggest stories from what you read. Most good feature writers are interested, not just in journalistic writing, but in *all* writing: history, biography, fiction, poetry, drama. And most good feature writers are voracious readers. They find in other genres fresh insights into subject, style, and presentation. Clark and Fry, in discussing the role of a good editor, suggest that he or she often inspires writers by inspiring their reading.

Many feature writers say their most important written source of story ideas is the daily newspaper. There they find stories which offer further lines of inquiry, or stories revealing trends or changing attitudes which can be more fully explored.

Magazines and newsletters also present ideas which people are currently sharing and debating. Nonwritten media can also help you become aware of issues of interest. Radio and television talk shows (even the sensationalistic ones) or broadcast ''magazine'' programs can expose you to current areas of opinion and emotion.

Finding out what's current, however, isn't useful if it only sparks ideas for similar stories. By the time you get your stories into print the ideas will be stale—over-handled merchandise in the marketplace of ideas. Instead, you must consider where present events are *heading*. The stories you write need to be a jump ahead of current situations; you have to be sensitive to the winds of change and focus your articles toward what you sense future concerns will be.

If you can't afford to buy many books or subscribe to numerous newspapers and magazines, seek out your nearest library. Plant yourself in its reading room and immerse yourself in the abundance of written material around you. When you find something you think is useful, make a copy of the original to take home for later perusal. (Be sure to note publication, author, date, and page number.)

CLIPPINGS AND IDEA FILES

Whether you are using public libraries or personal newspapers and magazines to shop in the marketplace of ideas, you should make it a habit to keep a clippings file of articles of interest to you, so if you don't have the time to write something now, you can always turn to the file later, when you need inspiration. It's helpful to organize the clippings, although how you organize them depends on your personal habits as well as your purposes in writing. You might organize the material into possible story types (for example, arrange clippings for use in a how-to article, or for a profile), topics (such as AIDS or high school dropouts), or by publications you think might buy a particular article (such as *Reader's Digest, Audubon* magazine, etc.).

Some writers not only keep a clippings file, but also an idea file or a personal journal, creating for themselves a verbal sketchbook similar to sketchbooks artists make so they can remember striking images and impressions. You can use such a journal or idea file to jot down story possibilities, impressions, or details about how things work.

Now is probably the time to make the point that good feature stories usually develop from *both* library work and personal observation. If you stay in your chair—whether in a library, at the office, or at home—you won't feel the immediacy of being out in the community, watching real people in real-life situations. On the other hand, if you never take your observations beyond the state of being simply observations—if you do no research about them—you won't have much depth to your work. Your writing won't resonate off historical, literary, psychological, or scientific background. Nor will it fit into a framework of argumentation and discussion currently in the media.

NOTHING NEW UNDER THE SUN

Assuming that your observations and your explorations of material in various media have led to some tentative ideas for feature stories, you're ready to begin the more intense preliminary research phase of article writing. Some features require a good deal of library research; some almost none. If you're a freelance writer, generally the least amount of library work you must do is a survey of what else has been written on your tentative topic and where such articles have been published.

Finding an article already published on your topic, however, should not necessarily discourage you from writing your story. As we said in Chapter 1, feature stories are unique productions; two stories can be quite different if two writers use different styles and structure their stories differently.

Remember, too, that in one sense there's nothing new under the sun. Most feature articles are recycled in some sense sooner or later, because the human condition remains the same. Thus the subjects of interest always seem to basically concern the same issues: love, family, health, work, and play.

Myrick Land asserts in *Writing for Magazines* (Prentice-Hall) that most magazines deal with a basic, rather limited number of topics. He writes:

> Month after month, all over the world, the most popular magazines offer their readers articles that deal with these 21 subjects:

1. diets
2. health
3. sex
4. money
5. celebrities
6. how-to
7. self-help
8. first-person experiences
9. human behavior
10. marriage
11. children
12. travel
13. fashion
14. home furnishing
15. cooking
16. trends
17. sports
18. hobbies
19. animals
20. national problems
21. foreign news

Given time, many topics are written about again, either because circumstances have changed and a fresh look at them is useful, or because a new group of people have grown up to read about these topics. It seems that every few years a new generation wants to read what the last one read, just as every seven years a new generation of children wants to see the Disney movies the previous generation saw.

YOUR PERSONAL LIBRARY

Your very nearest library resource, of course, is the shelf of books next to your desk. Many feature writers own a small library of reference works which provide the starting point for their early research. You will probably want to develop a personal collection of reference texts as you can afford them: a dictionary, thesaurus, atlas, book of quotations, grammar handbook, and stylebook.

The following books are often suggested as useful personal reference works:

Webster's New World Dictionary of American English, Third College Edition
Webster's Collegiate Thesaurus
Roget's International Thesaurus
Goode's World Atlas
McNally Road Atlas: United States/Canada/Mexico
Familiar Quotations (known as Bartlett's *Familiar Quotations*)
The Associated Press Stylebook
When Words Collide: A Journalist's Guide to Grammar and Style
Working With Words: A Concise Handbook for Media Writers and Editors

A set of encyclopedias is a luxury, but very helpful at the beginning of any research. *World Book Encyclopedia* (22 volumes), designed for students, is considered a fairly elementary source, but is nonetheless a good investment if other family members are also using the set. *Encyclopedia Americana* (30 volumes) and *Encyclopaedia Britannica* (25 volumes) are highly regarded encyclopedic classics; the *Columbia Encyclopedia* is a one-volume encyclopedia (with over 2,000 pages) that is a less expensive substitute for a full set.

WHAT'S BEEN WRITTEN BEFORE

If you want to determine what has already been published on a topic that interests you, you will probably consult one of several sources.

Indexes of periodical literature are *Magazine Index* (published monthly, indexes American and Canadian periodicals), *Popular Periodicals Index* (indexes American periodicals), or the ever-popular *Reader's Guide to Periodical Literature* (an author/subject index to general interest magazines; published semi-monthly, then cumulated).

Major newspapers such as *The Wall St. Journal* and *The New York Times* publish their own indexes. *Newsband* is a monthly index to 100 of the largest American daily newspapers; *Newspaper Index* serves as an index to *The Los Angeles Times, San Francisco Chronicle, Washington Post, Chicago Tribune, Detroit News,* and *New Orleans Times-Picayune.*

Books in Print gives an annual listing of all books in print in a given year; listings are according to subject, author, and title. *Paperbound Books in Print* gives the same information for paperback books.

REFERENCE GUIDES

After you have finished your research to find out what's been recently published, you're ready to gather more specific information preparatory to interviewing and writing. Reference works and indexes traditionally regarded as good sources of information are listed at the end of this chapter. If these listings feel a bit overwhelming to you, consider becoming familiar with one of the following research guidebooks, written particularly for journalists:

Finding Facts by William Rivers (Prentice Hall)

Journalism: A Guide to the Reference Literature by Jo Cates (Libraries Unlimited)

Names and Numbers: A Journalist's Guide to Most Needed Information Sources and Contacts by Ron Nordland (Wiley-Interscience Publications)

Uncovering the News: A Journalist's Search for Information by Lauren Kessler and Duncan McDonald (Wadsworth)

Search Strategies in Mass Communications by Jean Ward and Kathleen Hansen (Longman)

COMPUTER RESEARCH

Perhaps one of the most exciting, if challenging, developments in library research involves the use of computers. Electronic libraries of information are now more available to average library users and independent researchers than they were five or ten years ago.

Computerized library material has several benefits. The first is that material is quickly available—you can call up on a screen what it might have taken you half an hour to find on a library shelf. Second, material stored in library computers is safe—no one can remove books from shelves, tear out pages, or "forget" to return something. Third, and perhaps most important, library material is accessible—you don't have to be in the library building to reach it. The library is as close as a computer modem, an attachment to a telephone that lets your computer talk to the library's computers.

SIBLING REVELRY

Indeed, as more powerful computers and modems become part of standard household conveniences, it seems likely that our entire sense of the library as a separate place from our personal library will inevitably change: we'll "go to the library" simply by turning on our own home computer. In professional terms, new computer accessibility to library information means that writers who are geographically close to great university libraries and large public libraries no longer have the research advantage they traditionally have had. Writers far removed from libraries are able to obtain access to the same information.

Library computer collections of information (databases) generally exist in two forms: those which help you locate material (bibliographic) and those which actually show you the material so that you can read it (full-text).

One kind of bibliographic database is simply a replacement of the library's card catalogue. You seek information on the computer's database in the traditional card-catalogue way: by author, title, or subject. You can also search for information in a new way: by "key word." You give the computer a word or group of words you expect to be in the titles of works about your topic and the computer searches for those words, then prints out a list of the titles it finds. The computer essentially shuffles through all the electronic catalogue cards to come up with the five or fifty citations that have to do with your topic. And because the computer gives you a print-out of these citations, you don't have to spend time copying the entries, as you had to do with catalogue cards.

Another kind of bibliographic database is essentially an electronic form of index information; some databases duplicate the print indexes cited at the end of this chapter as common reference sources. Computer database material is often called "CD-ROM" ("compact disk—read only memory"). The library purchases databases on compact disks, then lets library researchers use them as it would let them use any other materials. Thus, there is not usually a fee to use these CD-ROMs. You search in traditional ways or by using key words. CD-ROMs may hold full-text material as well as bibliographic material; that is, you may be able not only to find a citation for a particular article in a journal, but also to call up that article on screen and read it.

A third kind of database is a large commercial national database that identifies sources of material, including those your local library does not possess. National databases search for information, then tell you what they find. For each source they give the title, the character of the publication (article, book, pamphlet), the publisher, and a description of contents (as well as some other information). When you use a national database (called doing ''on-line databasing''), you use a telephone and its computer modem to call in to the national program. You have to pay for the time that you are logged on to its network, so a search can be expensive. You usually have to request the library's permission to do this kind of research and you will probably want a librarian monitoring your computer work, or at least helping you get your research underway. Particularly you may need help ''writing your question''—composing a research statement about what you want to know—so the computer can extract appropriate key words from your question and use them in its search.

Whether you're dealing with bibliographic or full-text databases, most information on the screen is ''read only'': you can only read it, not alter or change it. And with most databases, you are dealing primarily with contemporary materials, since libraries or commercial database services have usually found it too expensive to put very old materials in their systems.

Databases that you frequently hear mentioned include NEXIS/LEXIS, WESTLAW, MEDLINE, and DIALOG. Their contents are too enormous to detail here, but briefly, LEXIS includes legal treatises and briefs of legal cases; NEXIS includes nonlegal information, such as *The New York Times* and *The Washington Post,* the *Encyclopaedia Britannica,* business journals, and news magazines. WESTLAW incorporates a wide variety of material concerning law; MEDLINE, a wide variety of material concerning medicine; DIALOG, data from over 260 million records from a variety of disciplines.

The point to be made is that these commercial databases are not only enormous but extremely complex. Some databases provide entry into other databases. Different databases are organized in different ways, so a search process in one will not be the same as a search process in another. Unless you're fairly knowledgeable about computers, you really need the help of a qualified librarian/ researcher if you're not to come up empty-handed and waste your money.

Computer research seems scientific and straightforward, but in fact, human skill and knowledge enter into the process. Five researchers apparently will not turn up five identical sets of data. According to professors of library science Tefko Saracevic and Paul Kantor, who have studied the human element in online searching, there's still a good deal we have to learn about the role of human decision-making in computer research and about human/system interaction.

In the meantime, according to an article in *Library Journal,* computer research remains, not a science, but an art. It is a process still very governed by human impulse and intuition—in their words, ''a very imprecise art at that.'' (''Online Searching: Still an Imprecise Art,'' *Library Journal,* October 1, 1991.)

COMMON REFERENCE SOURCES

The following books are traditional reference sources. Use them . . .

. . . if you want to learn about **people:**

Almanac of Famous People—three-volume reference guide, with biographical entries for over 25,000 people from Biblical times to the present

Biography Index—quarterly, with annual cumulations; index of biographical material in books and periodicals

Current Biography—monthly, then compiled at the end of a year and titled "Current Biography Yearbook"; biographies of contemporary people

Directory of American Scholars—biographical directory, divided into specific academic areas

Index to Women of the World from Ancient to Modern Times—biographies and portraits

The New York Times Obituaries Index, 1858–1968—index of *The New York Times'* obituaries

Webster's Biographical Dictionary—brief biographies of over 40,000 noteworthy people

Who's Who in America—over 80,000 brief entries of living people (*Who's Who,* published in London, is the British equivalent)

Biographical Dictionaries Master Index—biographies for the over 750,000 Americans listed, references to other biographical compilations

Who's Who Among Black Americans—biographies of African Americans

International Who's Who—individual listings for major international figures.

. . . if you want to learn about **words and language:**

Dictionary of Foreign Phrases and Abbreviations—translations into English of common foreign expressions

Oxford English Dictionary on Historical Principles—called "the O.E.D."; a dictionary of derivations and origins of words dating back to the 13th century

A Dictionary of American English on Historic Principles—called "the D.A.E."; a dictionary similar to the O.E.D., but gives origins of American words

Webster's New International Dictionary of the English Language, Third Edition—known as "Webster's Third"; a complete dictionary, with over 3,000 pages

The New York Times Manual of Style and Usage—brief guidelines for writers and editors

The Washington Post Desk-book on Style—similar to the *New York Times* manual or the *Associated Press Stylebook*

. . . if you want to learn about **education, history, and social sciences:**

The American Book of Days—information about American holidays, festivals, anniversaries, and holy days

Blacks in America,1492–1970—African-American history and facts

Educational Index—index to periodicals on educational psychology and education

An Encyclopedia of World History: Ancient, Medieval and Modern—world history in a chronological arrangement

ERIC—"educational resources information center"; index to current journals in education, plus resources in education

Famous First Facts—records of first happenings, discoveries, and inventions

Poole's Index to Periodical Literature 1802–1906—index to periodicals for the nineteenth century

Psychological Abstracts—index to material related to psychology by subject and author

Social Sciences Index—before 1974 called the *Social Sciences and Humanities Index;* index of articles on economics, geography, law, criminology, and medical science

Who's Who in American Politics—biographies of U.S. political leaders

Who's Who in Educational Administration—a directory of American school administrators

. . . if you want to learn about **agriculture, science, medicine:**

Applied Science and Technology Index—monthly, with quarterly cumulations; an index to periodical articles on aeronautics, computers, engineering, textiles, and food

Cambridge Encyclopaedia of Astronomy—an encyclopedia of astronomical information

American Men and Women of Science—a directory of current leaders in physical, biological, and related sciences

Applied Science and Technology Index—monthly index, with quarterly and annual cumulations

Biological and Agricultural Index—index published 11 months a year, with three quarterly cumulations and one annual cumulation

The Merck Manual of Diagnosis and Therapy—a manual described as "therapeutics and materia medica"

McGraw-Hill Encyclopedia of Science and Technology—a reference work in 15 volumes

Physicians' Desk Reference—annual publication, with supplemental sheets

. . . if you want to learn about the **humanities, performing arts, art, or music:**

American Popular Music: 1875–1950—a selected list of first or early editions of American songs

Art Index—quarterly, cumulated frequently; index to periodicals on architecture, archaeology, graphic arts, painting, and sculpture

The New York Times Film Reviews—reviews from 1913–1968 in six volumes

The Filmgoer's Companion—a dictionary of motion pictures

Humanities Index—before 1974 called the *Social Sciences and Humanities Index,* quarterly, then cumulated; an index to periodicals on language, literature, performing arts, religion, theology, and philosophy

Music Index—monthly, with annual cumulations

Who's Who in American Music—biennial; biographies concerning classical music

Who's Who Among North American Authors—biographical dictionary for United States and Canada

Who's Who in Entertainment—biographical dictionary for the performing arts

. . . if you want to learn about **business and law:**

Black's Law Dictionary—definitions of terms from American and British jurisprudence, ancient and modern

Business Periodicals Index—previously called *Industrial Arts Index;* monthly, then cumulated; an index to advertising, finance, labor, taxation, and marketing

Current Law Index—monthly, with quarterly and annual cumulations; index to periodicals

Moody's Industrial Manual—annual; information about New York, American, and regional stock exchanges and international companies

Standard and Poor's Register of Corporations, Directors and Executives—annual; a listing of sales figures, names of executives, and addresses and phone numbers for over 40,000 American business organizations

. . . if you need **to look up facts:**

American Statistics Index—monthly, cumulated quarterly and then annually; index to statistical material collected by U.S. government

Countries of the World and Their Leaders Yearbook—compilation of U.S. government reports on contemporary political and economic conditions, politics, history, etc. for each nation listed

The Europa Year Book—annual; information on European politics and government for Europe and the rest of the world.

Facts on File—weekly, cumulated to ''Facts on File Yearbook''; world news digest with a cumulated index

Guinness Book of World Records—annual; compilation of world records

The World Almanac and Book of Facts—annual; almanac and encyclopedia

Information Please Almanac—annual; almanac, atlas and yearbook

Statesman's Yearbook—annual; statistics and historical data for states of the world

Statistical Yearbook—annual; statistics from the United Nations

. . . if you need to find **geographic locations:**

The Columbia Lippincott Gazetteer of the World—an older geographical dictionary

National Geographic Atlas of the World, 5th edition—produced by the National Geographic Society

Rand McNally Commercial Atlas and Marketing Guide—maps primarily of the United States and its possessions

The Times Atlas of the World—maps of the world

. . . or if you need information from the **federal government:**

CIS Index—Congressional Information Service; monthly, cumulates quarterly, then annually (then called the *CIS Annual*); index to Congressional publications and public law

Congressional Staff Directory—annual; listing of Congressional staff

Washington Information Directory—annual; directory for Washington, D.C., metropolitan area and U.S. executive departments

Monthly Catalog of U.S. Government Publications—monthly, with semi-annual and annual indexes; government's index to its publications

Statistical Abstract of the United States—a digest of statistical data collected by the U.S. government such as death and birth rates; one supplement is the *County and City Data Book,* which gives data for all counties and large cities in the United States; to look up past statistics, use *Historical Statistics of the United States,* beginning with a volume on years 1789 to 1945 and continuing with updated volumes

EXERCISES

1. Sit in an interesting place for a short period of time. From five concrete objects you see, generate five story ideas.

2. Practice your observation skills in competition with another journalist:

    a. You and another journalism student go to cover a campus event; each of you comes back with descriptions of 20 things you observed. Compare your descriptions.

    b. Attend an event (football game, speech, concert) that you know will be covered or reviewed in the media. Write down all the things you observe. Compare your items to those included in the newspaper or magazine account.

3. You're interested in doing free-lance writing on vacation travel. For your articles, what is the average temperature in Bermuda in July? And what is the average precipitation in Miami, Florida, in January?

4. For a feature story on Halloween, find the origins of the word "goblin."

5. For a profile of Dustin Hoffman, find out where, or if, he attended college.

6. H. G. Bissinger's story, "The plane that fell from the sky," was published in the *St. Paul Pioneer Press* over two years after the incident that the story describes occurred. Why do you think Bissinger decided to write the story then? What do you think were some of the things he was curious about? Find some instances in the story where Bissinger gives answers to questions that curious readers might have about how technical equipment or pilots work. How does Bissinger "follow the feelings" of the people in the story? How do readers get a sense of the depth of the emotions passengers and pilots experienced?

   (Bissinger's story made him a finalist in non-deadline writing in the American Society of Newspaper Editors 1982 competition.)

THE PLANE THAT FELL FROM THE SKY

By H. G. Bissinger

St. Paul Pioneer Press, *May 24, 1981*

On April 4, 1979, a TWA Boeing 727 bound for Minneapolis-St. Paul suddenly went out of control and rocketed nose down toward the ground at 630 miles an hour. With only precious seconds left before it would have crashed, it miraculously was brought under control. In 44 seconds of terror, the plane fell 34,000 feet. Never has a commercial plane dropped that far that fast and not crashed. For the 82 passengers and seven crew members on board, those 44 seconds became an eternity. And when the ordeal was over, few of their lives would ever be the same.

April 3, 1979
9:35 a.m.
Los Angeles International Airport

The truth was, flying commercial could be boring work. The old philosophy among pilots, starting in the days when the DC-3 was the biggest thing going, was that you didn't really get paid for all the times you flew without a hitch, but for the one time out of a thousand when everything went to hell and you still brought the airplane in. That was the test of skill, and the reason for all the other paychecks.

After 16 years of piloting for Trans World Airlines, 44-year-old Hoot Gibson didn't find his work particularly creative. Or daring. Or exhilarating. After spending 15,709 hours of flight time in the confining cockpits of 727s, DC-9s, and 747s as a flight engineer, co-pilot and captain, things were bound to become as familiar as the boring drone of a jet engine.

Gibson's excitement came when he left the lumbering commercial birds behind and climbed alone into his own planes to do acrobatic stunts and punch in and out of canyon crevices and clouds.

That kind of airmanship was more in line with his machismo reputation, which, whether it was merited or not, had become the subject of shop talk in TWA hangars and cockpits.

But whatever tidbits circulated about Hoot Gibson's lifestyle, his commercial flying abilities were difficult to fault. In the parlance of his peers, he carried a simple tag: he was a "good airman." He confined his colorful ways to the ground, not the skies.

The April 3 flight package he had drawn was hardly the stuff of glamour, taking him out of Los Angeles at 9:35 a.m. on a hop-skip-and-jump tour to Phoenix, Wichita, Kansas City, Chicago and finally Columbus, Ohio. Once there, Gibson and the other two members of his crew, first officer Scott Kennedy and flight engineer Gary Banks, bedded down for the night in a hotel.

The crew, which had never worked together before, got about eight hours sleep. The next day—April 4—they left about 3 p.m. for New York's Kennedy Airport.

There was about a two-hour layover at Kennedy as they changed equipment—to Boeing 727-100 aircraft No. N840TW—and prepared for their final hop of the evening.

The plane was old, delivered to TWA in 1965 as part of the first batch of 727s coming out of Boeing's suburban Seattle plant. The destination, considering TWA's other routes, was not the kind of place a pilot would beg for—St. Paul-Minneapolis International on TWA Flight 841.

With all his experience, Hoot Gibson probably could make the trip—a relatively short course over Lake Michigan and Green Bay—with his eyes closed. Any airline pilot could—just get the plane up to cruise altitude and set in the autopilot until it was time to land.

After 15,000 hours of flying, it certainly was not the test of skill that would make a pilot find out just how much he was really worth.

April 4, 1979
6:55 p.m.
Kennedy International Airport

Just when it seemed as if there were no alternative except to stay in New York for longer than he wanted to, Bob Reber found TWA Flight 841.

The flight he hoped to get booked on—a Northwest 6 p.m. flight out of LaGuardia—was full. So Reber, 52, walked to the TWA counter at the Sheraton Hotel and the luck there was better: A seat was available on their flight to Minneapolis, leaving at 6:55 p.m.

Typically, the plane was late taking off and did not leave the JFK gate until 7:39 p.m., prompting pilot Hoot Gibson to come on the intercom and give the 82 passengers on board one of those little speeches about being held up.

Eventually, the plane took off at 8:25 p.m. Reber settled into seat 22F, a window seat in the last row of seats in the smoking section, pulled out the copy of the *New York Times* and sipped a cocktail.

The manager of data processing for Powers department stores in the Twin Cities, he stayed wide awake throughout the flight. Falling asleep on planes was a habit he had never acquired. But he thought the trip was extremely dull as airplane flights always are, with the engines humming and the funny smell of disinfectant that tried to rid the cabin of any human smell.

In the *Minneapolis Tribune* that morning, his horoscope by Jeane Dixon had at least been topical for once: "Traveling appeals, but is not favored. Try staying close to home (Cancer. June 21–July 22)." But Reber didn't pay attention to junk like that.

April 4, 1979
8:45 p.m.
Nearing the Great Lakes
35,000 feet

First Officer Scott Kennedy, who had flown the 727 for all but six months of his 13 years at TWA, put the flaps up with effortless routine.

On takeoff, the flaps were extended to produce lift so the plane could get off the ground.

160 knots. Flaps up from 15 degrees to 5 degrees to increase speed.

190 knots. Flaps up from 5 degrees to 2 degrees.

200 knots. Flaps tucked in all the way.

Flight 841 was cleared by air traffic control to an altitude of 5,000 feet. Then up to 8,000, 23,000, and finally 35,000 feet at 8:45 p.m. The air was calm with a little turbulence—"smooth with a light chop" as the pilots referred to it. Nothing to get excited about.

Five minutes later, the four flight attendants on board, two men, two women, started serving the meal—hot and forgettable food served on plastic trays.

Headwinds of 110 knots were bearing down on Flight 841 as it maintained 35,000 feet altitude. Gibson didn't like that and figured the best way to beat the winds was to go below them—or above them.

At 9:24, Gibson got on the mike with the air traffic control center in Toronto and asked for clearance up to 39,000 feet to beat the winds.

"Centre TW841 like to try Flight Level 390."
"Roger, TW841 climb to maintain FL390."
"Out of 35 for 39."

At 9:38 p.m., Flight 841 reported that it was at 39,000 feet.

"TWA's 841 level 3 nine 0."
"841 roger."

The conditions at that altitude were clear and smooth. It was quiet up there, nice and quiet, the cockpit noise at a whisper compared to other altitudes.

A moonlit trail of clouds shimmered about 4,000 feet below the silver underbelly of the plane as it darted across Michigan in the black night. The clouds stretched for several miles to the shoreline of Lake Michigan, and from his seat in the cockpit, Hoot Gibson could see the on-and-off flicker of distant city lights across the mammoth lake.

At 39,000 feet, the serenity of the sky belonged to Flight 841.

April 4, 1979
9:47 p.m.
Near Saginaw, Michigan
39,619 feet

Dr. Peter Fehr had never particularly liked to fly. To be perfectly honest about it, Fehr used to have a horrendous fear of it, and the whole concept of motion was not something that he had ever quite gotten used to.

As a kid, when he used to go on drives with the family, the result was always the same—he got sick. And his first airplane ride, from Minneapolis to Chicago when he was interviewing to be a missionary in Africa, had left his stomach badly upset.

Fehr, an obstetrician-gynecologist, knew, of course, that it was impossible to live in the modern world without flying. So, with the help of God and large dosages of Dramamine, he had persevered. He made it to Africa as a missionary, suffering in ancient DC-3s that barely wobbled over the African swamps, making so much noise that it sounded like the metal was being sheared off.

But for the past 11 years that Fehr had lived in Minneapolis, things changed. He had been able to get on an airplane whenever it was required. For the past year, in fact, he had been flying without fear and without Dramamine.

But it still didn't take much to get unnerved. A few days earlier, when he had been on his way to New York for a convention, the woman sitting next to him, a large Italian woman, kept repeating her rosary and kissing her prayer book.

Fehr had an urge to look her straight in the eye and say, "Lady, these planes keep flying and most of'em don't go down." A timid man, he didn't have the courage to say it. But, of course, he was right. The trip to New York was without consequence.

Fehr went to his convention at the New York Hilton, and now he was returning home on Flight 841.

The seat belt sign had gone off, dinner had been served, and the food trays picked up. It was time to relax.

Fehr and the man sitting next to him, a University of Minnesota professor, chatted for a bit.

Suddenly, without warning, the plane shuddered and began to feel as though it were sliding sideways across the sky. There was the sensation that the plane was changing speed and maybe even trying to land. But at 39,000 feet?

"We can't be in Minneapolis already?" said the professor.

Fehr knew the professor was right.

April 4, 1979
9:47.57 p.m.
39,046 feet

Gary Bank's mind idled.

There wasn't much for the flight engineer to do, so he started filling out parts of his log and looked vacantly at the array of instruments and switches before him. Then he felt a high frequency vibration.

Co-pilot Kennedy was preoccupied with trying to figure out the plane's ground speed.

And Hoot Gibson, with the plane set on autopilot and flying steady, put away his charts and cleaned up the cockpit.

Then he heard a sound—a slight buzz—and saw the wheel of the airplane turning slowly to the left, about 10 degrees. The plane was turning right for some reason and the autopilot was trying to correct it.

The buzz continued, and now the plane was shaking slightly. And it was turning slightly, and still rolling to the right. And the autopilot was still turning the wheel to the left. But it wasn't doing a thing. The plane was still turning to the right.

Gibson watched for about 10 seconds. Then he disconnected the autopilot. The plane was still rolling to the right. Still rolling.

Gibson grabbed onto the wheel with both hands and turned it all the way to the left. Leaning back in his seat, he took his foot and punched down on the rudder pedal all the way to the left to try to bring the plane around.

It did nothing. The thing was still going to the right. Through 20 degrees. Then 30.

Speaking to his co-pilot, he said what was by now the inevitable truth.

"This airplane's going over."

It continued.

50 degrees.

60 degrees.

70 degrees.

And in that fraction of a section, Hoot Gibson felt stark terror. The plane was rolling over and going in. He knew it. That was it.

He was going to die. And take 88 other people down with him.

April 4, 1979
9:48.04 p.m.
Near Saginaw
36,307 feet

The tiny 2-month-old baby in Holly Wicker's lap started grasping for breath and turning blue as the plane hurtled downward at a vertical pitch, the speed increasing.

The baby's name was Asha (if means "hope" in Hindi) and this was her first experience in the United States after coming from India. She was on her way to Minneapolis to be adopted and Holly was in charge of her.

With each foot that the plane lost, the forces of gravity (G forces) increased. The pressure was forcing Wicker back into her seat, shoving her skin backwards, almost like someone had grabbed her cheeks and was trying to pull them back to see how much they would stretch.

Wicker tried to rotate Asha onto her back and pull the baby toward her. But she couldn't—the gravity was too great—and instead Wicker leaned forward.

Out of the corner of her eye, she looked across the aisle and saw the instrument panels over the passenger's heads pop down even though they weren't supposed to—forcing down oxygen masks and light bulbs and wires.

Wicker watched the knuckles of hands turning white as passengers tried to fight gravity and reach for the masks. She watched people with their mouths open as though they were trying to

scream. But there wasn't a sound, as though the gravity had frozen their cries.

Wicker bent down and gave Asha a breath. She gave another. And then another, when a searing pain ripped across her chest. She couldn't give anymore. There was nothing left. And she knew that the next breath she would take would have to be for herself—not for the tiny baby on her lap turning blue.

April 4, 1979
9:48.07 p.m.
Near Saginaw
34,459 feet

The plane went into its first roll and Gibson pulled back on the control wheel to try to apply enough downward pressure to keep the passengers in their seats. With the seat belt sign off, they all could be walking around for all he knew.

He closed off the engine throttles—shutting off some of the power to the plane's engines—and started saying "Get 'em up. Get 'em up here." Kennedy thought he was talking to the plane, as pilots often do, trying to coax it back up, pleading with it.

But what Gibson wanted was for Kennedy to grab the "spoiler" handle and pull it back so the flaps on the top of the wing would pop up and help slow the plane down.

By now the plane was into a second roll—this one almost vertical. Gibson let go of the control wheel and pulled the spoiler handle up and down himself.

Nothing happened.

He tugged on the control wheel to see if he could get the plane to reduce its pitch.

It didn't matter.

The plane was in a dive.

By this time, Gary Banks had pulled his seat in between Gibson and Kennedy and tried to get a fix on their instruments. He couldn't figure out what was going on and he needed to get a look at the artificial horizon indicator—an instrument that tells a plane's position on the horizon and where it is pointing. It is divided into two colors—blue for the sky and black for the ground.

Gibson's elbow was blocking the indicator. So Banks looked over at Kennedy's panel, which has an identical set of instruments.

The indicator was black. Pure black. Not a trace of blue in there. It was like walking into a room and finding all the furniture on the ceiling. Banks couldn't believe what he was seeing. And it meant only one thing.

The plane was heading straight for the ground nose down.

He watched as Gibson and Kennedy tried to regain control. From his days as an Air Force instructor on the supersonic T-38s, where you did spiral dives on purpose just to let the student know what the plane could and couldn't do, Banks was impressed: Gibson and Kennedy were doing everything right.

But they weren't saving the plane. They weren't doing it.

Banks glanced at Gibson. He glanced to the right at Kennedy. Then he sat back in his chair and became very calm. He knew the ending now, and in a whisper he confirmed it to himself: "It is all over. I wonder what it's gonna feel like to hit the ground."

April 4, 1979
9:48.10 p.m.
Near Saginaw
29,982 feet

The increasing gravity forces pulled Peter Fehr's glasses off his face. He tried to grab them with his arms but he couldn't—gravity had glued them to the armrests. The upper part of his body went upright against his seat like a diving board.

The plane was rattling like crazy, the vibration increasing with each foot of the plunge. The noise sounded like the B-29s that went down in the World War II movies, that horrible, moaning whine that got louder and louder. And then there was another sound, the wrenching, gnarling sound of metal being torn from the right wing.

Fehr knew there was no way the pilot—*any pilot*—was going to bring the plane back up.

The passenger in the seat in front of him kept trying to coax the plane back up. It sounded like he was talking to the pilot, "Take it easy," the man whispered. "You haven't lost it yet. You can pull it out." Fehr thought the man was a fool.

He knew he was going to die.

He became calm and objective. The scene became an abstraction, with Fehr a detached observer.

In the remaining seconds left, he began to make a checklist. He reviewed his will—it was in order and his wife should be well-cared for. He remembered what he had said to his four kids before he left for New York.

And it irked him now that one of his sons had taken out a loan to buy a new pair of tires for his car without coming to him. The interest rates were probably ridiculous . . . his son was probably getting gouged to death . . . it wasn't a good business deal . . . in fact, it was downright stupid . . . why did he do something like that . . . they should have talked about it beforehand . . . they really should have.

The roar of the plane grew louder.

April 4, 1979
9:48.16 p.m.
Near Saginaw
24,121 feet

As the descent of the plane grew faster, Scott Kennedy's mind worked faster.

He remembered the crash of a commercial plane that had been flying at 39,000 feet and dropped into Lake Michigan.

He remembered the crash of the Pacific Southwest Airlines jet in San Diego that had happened only six months ago and left close to 150 people dead.

And then he remembered a conversation he had with the flight engineer only the night before—an insider's conversation about recovering a plane from a vertical stall.

From his experience in the Air Force, Banks knew of only one way to do it—pop the drag shoot on the tail of the plane—a parachute-type piece of equipment that was normally used to slow the aircraft down during landing. Activating it during a stall would slow the plane down enough so the pilot could get control of it back, Banks had told Kennedy.

The co-pilot watched as Gibson tried just about every maneuver there was and still the plane was screaming through the sky. He was impressed by Gibson's perseverance, his reluctance to give up.

Then Kennedy's eye was drawn to something that might help—putting the landing gear down.

He suggested that to Gibson and had his hand poised and waiting on the landing gear handle. The plane continued to plummet, the altimeter unwinding so fast that no one in the cockpit could read it.

21,000 feet.

18,000 feet.

They were getting close and Gibson could see the lights of cities spinning through the fog.

15,000 feet and dropping vertical.

"Gear down," said Gibson.

Kennedy followed the command.

For a second, the two pilots fought against each other as they worked their control wheels—Gibson pushing in to get the tail into the wind current so it would fly again, Kennedy pulling his out to keep the nose of the plane up.

The gear dropped down.

The explosion was deafening, like nothing Gibson or Kennedy or Banks had ever heard in their lives.

TWA Flight 841 continued to fall.

10,000 feet.

8,000 feet.

Gibson didn't know where he was. He couldn't read the instruments. Where the hell was the ground?

And then the plane started to fly again.

And Gibson couldn't help but feel what a damn shame it was that he was getting control back just as the plane was going to crack.

He pulled back on the control wheel as if he was trying to rein a wild mustang. The nose of the plane shot up about 50 degrees. Gibson almost looped the plane he was so desperate to avoid the Michigan farmland beneath him. He

was afraid the wings might move, or snap off the plane, but he had no choice but to pull up.

The G forces were incredible—flight data showed them registering 6 at one point—meaning a person's weight was six times what it normally would be. The blood rushed downward from the brain as passengers were flattened into their seats with incredible force. Their faces were pushed sideways as though they were being held in a vise.

Gibson, the acrobatic pilot, had taken 6 Gs before and knew what they were like. Banks, as he had learned in the Air Force, tightened his stomach and tried to keep the blood from pushing down.

The nose still pointed up about 50 degrees as the plane punched through the clouds again—this time on the way up.

Banks felt a rush of panic. If Gibson pulled the nose of the plane down too fast to bring it level, the reverse force of the gravity could be enough to rip an engine off its mount.

Banks coaxed Gibson to get the wings level and gently ease the nose over. "Keep 'em level," he repeated, "Keep 'em level."

Gibson was having trouble figuring out the plane's direction. And then he saw the moon. He pinned it on the windshield, it became his compass, and he kept it in the same exact spot until he pushed the nose over and brought the plane level.

The noise and vibration in the tiny cockpit was incredible. Almost unbearable. Inside the cabin, the shaking and gravity had caused more of the overhead panels to pop open. Oxygen masks accidentally came tumbling down in some of the rows. But some of the passengers didn't realize it was an accident. They thought everyone was supposed to have a mask. And they were clawing at their closed panels with their fingers, trying to pry them open.

Gibson got on the intercom. He had to say *something*. Anything.

"We've had a slight problem, but everything seems to be under control."

April 4, 1979
9:51 p.m.
Near Saginaw
10,509 feet

Even though the plane was flying again, Atul Bhatt knew something was terribly wrong. One look at the flight attendants told him that.

They were agitated, upset, one of them was crying. And he was scared to death. Once when he was 10 years old, he was riding his bicycle on the edge of a highway when he lost control and fell under a moving truck. The driver just caught a glimpse of him, and the back wheels came to a halt right next to his body.

He had missed death by a screeching second. But he had been a kid then, and the whole thing had happened so quickly.

But this wasn't happening quickly. This was taking forever. There was time—too much time—to think again and again about what would happen. As the plane had started to plummet, the knowledge of a death that would be quick and painless had somehow been comforting.

But now the plane was going to make a crash landing, and Bhatt didn't even know where it would be. The Chicago airport maybe? Or a forest? Or a farm? It was so dark outside, he couldn't see a thing.

The fear of being paralyzed gnawed at him. Or of being maimed. Or half-burned. And Bhatt, 27, a Ph.D. candidate from India at the University of Minnesota, couldn't bear that. If the plane did crash, he wanted to die quickly. Survival at any odds, with a thousand different possible after effects, wasn't worth the risk.

But the choice wasn't his.

Bhatt was lost in his fear when an Italian woman sitting next to him, after watching his agony for a few minutes now, spoke up. "Don't be scared, young man," said the woman.

Bhatt felt a little embarrassed after that. Here he was a grown man, being admonished just like a little kid for being a coward—not even tough enough to take a bumpy little plane ride. And then he thought a little more.

And he knew in his heart exactly how he felt.

And he couldn't think of one single reason to be brave about it.

He had never been more scared in his entire life.

April 4, 1979
9:55 p.m.
60 miles from Detroit, Michigan
12,749 feet

Hoot Gibson needed to find an airport. Quickly.

He checked with air traffic control about Saginaw, where the weather was overcast with light snow and three miles visibility. Then he checked Lansing. And Detroit, where the weather was a little better but certainly not perfect—overcast skies, seven miles visibility, wind at 10 knots.

Although it was the farthest away of the three choices—about 60 miles—Detroit's Metro Airport seemed to Gibson to be the most logical choice. He was familiar with the airport and it could handle a major emergency.

And he figured he could make it.

While Gibson handled the controls of the plane, Kennedy and Banks went through a series of emergency "checklists" to pinpoint what was wrong with the plane and how to try to remedy it.

The noise and vibrating inside the cockpit was still deafening. Banks and Kennedy were shouting, and they still could barely understand each other and had to rely on reading lips.

The diagnosis was not good.

One of the plane's hydraulic power systems was out, so the flaps would have to be extended by an alternate power source. A yaw damper—an electronic device on the rudder that stops a plane from weaving uncontrollably—was apparently out of commission, too.

The landing gear indicator lights inside the cockpit were red, meaning the dropped gear was unlocked and unsafe to land on. It would have to be cranked down manually.

Banks hands shook and his body shivered as he removed a plate from the floor of the cockpit and used a lever to put the main landing gear down by hand. There was no feel on the gear at all, as though it wasn't holding. And when he was through, the indicator lights still were red.

The nose landing gear was extended manually, and the indicator light showed green—the gear was down and locked into place. Once the nose gear dropped, the terrible cockpit noise stopped. Banks couldn't believe what a relief it was to have a little quiet. That noise had almost driven him crazy.

The crew then tried to use alternate power to get the flaps to extend, so the plane would slow down and be easier to land.

The flaps were barely out before the aircraft rolled sharply to the left. Gibson couldn't believe it—he figured he had lost the plane again. But he recovered, and for the rest of the trip he had to fly with the control wheel and the rudder pedal pushed all the way to the right so the plane would not roll over.

Gibson realized that his margin for error here was very small. Below about 170 knots an hour, the plane would begin to roll. Above about 210 knots an hour, the same thing would happen. It gave him about 40 knots to work with, and the likelihood of a landing under the worst possible conditions.

When TWA Flight 841 came in to Detroit on runway 3L, it would be making its touchdown at almost twice the normal speed. And on landing gear that, for all Hoot Gibson knew, might not even be there.

April 4, 1979
10 p.m.
Near Detroit
13,000 feet
Passenger Barbara Merrill had crashed to the floor trapped in the lavatory. Stewardess Fran Schaller, walking to the liquor cart to get someone a drink, had fallen flat in the middle of the aisle. Unable to get up, a passenger cradled her head while she clung to the cart with her left hand. Others on board had blacked out.

As the plane leveled out, Merrill, 41, crawled out of the bathroom and made it as far as the right aisle seat in the last row of the plane, Row 22.

Her ribs ached, maybe one of them was cracked. Her hip had crashed against the toilet seat when she had been thrown to the floor, and she had a cut on her knee.

Merrill's 14-year-old daughter, Susan, walked to the back of the cabin to be with her mother.

She sat in seat 22E, in between her mother and Bob Reber.

Under the conditions, there couldn't have been a more reassuring figure. Reber had blacked out almost instantly after the plane had started to dive. But now he felt quite calm and not really aware that something terrible had happened—or was going to happen.

"We're gonna die!" Reber heard Mrs. Merrill repeat over and over. "We're gonna die!"

"Are we?" Mrs. Merrill's daughter asked, her mother's sense of panic becoming infectious.

Reber remained immune. "Don't worry about it," he told them. "If you get to pick your place to land, you got a 50–50 chance."

April 4, 1979
10:20 p.m.
Flying over Detroit Metro Airport
1,600 feet
Gary Banks called flight attendant Mark Moscicki into the cockpit and asked him if he remembered his training for an emergency landing.

"You have 10 minutes to get the plane ready, and you get back here in eight minutes," Banks told him.

Moscicki met briefly with the three other flight attendants in the center galley. Then they went to work.

They whipped through the cabin, instructing passengers to remove their glasses, pens, high-heeled shoes, false teeth, canes, anything that was sharp and might cause injury.

They started emptying the overhead racks, distributing available pillows and blankets. One of the stewardesses threw Catherine Rascher's leather jacket on the floor, and she winced. Even in a time of fear and crises, it was hard for her to forget the coat was brand new and cost $200.

A passenger got into an argument with a flight attendant who wanted to remove his glasses. The passenger refused. The attendant persisted, and finally just plucked the glasses off the man's face.

Another passenger willingly had her glasses removed, but gave forewarning that she was blind without them. The flight attendant immediately designated the man sitting directly behind her as her guardian: The woman's life and the lives of her two children depended upon him, the man was told.

Moscicki got on the intercom and told the passengers about the plane's evacuation procedures. He showed them the impact position— hands behind the head, the body bent forward as far as it would go, a pillow to cushion the head from the seat in front.

At 1,600 feet, Gibson flew over the Detroit airport tower so ground personnel could get a look at the landing gear. Searchlights panned the underbelly of the plane. From what they could tell, the gear looked down and locked.

Peeking out the windows from the emergency position, passengers could see a mass of fire trucks sitting on the runway, waiting to see whether TWA Flight 841 would make it. The plane swooped so low that they could see the expressions on the firemen's faces.

After the fly-by, Banks opened the cockpit door to speak to the flight attendants one more time. But when he glimpsed outside, he saw everybody bent over, ready for the plane to crash.

The action was a little premature, there was still a little time left, so Banks got on the intercom and told everybody to sit easy for a moment. He said he would tell them when it was time to assume the . . . he was about to say "crash position" but then he stopped himself and just told the passengers he would let them know when it was time to get ready.

Gibson circled on the final approach to the runway.

He turned the plane downwind, his eyes glued to the strip so he wouldn't lose track of it for a second.

Suddenly, the plane started rolling to the left again.

Gibson was losing control, the plane was getting away from him again.

The crew erupted in the cockpit. After 40 minutes of fighting to keep the aircraft up, the adrenaline was running out. Now was the perfect time to screw up.

"Don't let it roll too far!" yelled Banks, on the verge of panic, "Don't let it roll!"

Kennedy got on the control wheel and started working the engine throttles. He cut the power to the right engine and increased the power to the left.

Moments away from landing, TWA Flight 841 skidded level.

April 4, 1979
10:30 p.m.
On approach to Detroit Metro Airport
50 feet

Frederick and Catherine Rascher held hands and waited.

They had been married for 43 years, had just enjoyed a wonderful trip to Spain, and were looking forward to a life of quiet retirement in St. Paul. Whatever happened now, at least, they would be together.

They turned and looked at each other as they prepared for the crash landing.

"We've had a nice life together," said Mrs. Rascher.

"It's too bad it has to end this way," said her husband.

The plane was on its approach now. Lifting his head up slightly, Frederick Rascher peeked out the window and began the final countdown.

"Forty feet . . . thirty feet . . . twenty feet . . . ten feet . . . get ready."

They bent their heads down and waited for the last time.

April 4, 1979
10:31 p.m.
Landing at Detroit Metro Airport

Gibson bore down on the runway at 170 knots. As he was coming in, the plane started again to roll to the left. The left landing gear hit the runway first—"pretty damn smooth" Gibson thought to himself—and the gear was holding.

The plane was rolling quite a bit and Gibson had to get the right gear on the runway, although he thought the gear would probably shear off on impact.

He brought the plane level and the right gear wasn't even hitting. Maybe it already had fallen off, Gibson thought.

The gear, when it had been extended during the dive, had broken its side brace. If any substantial pressure was put on it from either side, it would collapse on impact.

Using his controls, Gibson tilted the right wing down and finally the right gear hit the runway. It was there . . . and it was holding.

A burst of applause went up from the passengers as the plane touched down. Hoot Gibson was getting a sitting ovation.

Part of the right gear dragged along the runway, causing sparks as Gibson turned left toward the emergency vehicles. As soon as the plane stopped, fire engines sped up and started spraying the aircraft with foam.

Gibson felt exhausted—more exhausted perhaps than he had ever been in his entire life. He also felt relieved and surprised. From 39,000 feet until touchdown some 43 minutes later, he had been convinced that the plane was going to crash.

The only thing he hadn't figured out was where.

April 4, 1979
10:40 p.m.
On the ground at Detroit Metro Airport

Dr. Peter Fehr thought one of the passengers on board was having a heart attack.

He got an oxygen tank for her and made sure she got to a hospital. He gave medical attention to some of the other passengers. And then, once outside the plane, Peter Fehr—the cool, detached doctor—lost control. For 20 minutes he vomited and wretched and his legs turned to water. Then he called home to tell his family he was safe.

*   *   *

Atul Bhatt looked over at the man in his row and couldn't believe what he was seeing. The plane had landed, it was probably about to blow up, there were firemen all over the place, and here was this guy whose first instinct wasn't to run for his life, or move quickly, or even to move at all. Instead he slowly took his comb out of his pocket and started combing his hair.

Bhatt had no pretentions of vanity. In his eagerness to get off the plane, he left his suit jacket on board. And when a bottle of Scotch was passed around in the shivering cold of the runway, he gladly swigged.

*   *   *

The passenger came up to Gary Banks as he and the other crew members were leaving the cockpit.

"Isn't it interesting?" the man said.

Interesting? What the hell was interesting about a plane that by all rights should have been a hole in the ground and left 89 people dead?

"God no!" said Banks, slightly stunned by the comment.

But the passenger wasn't finished.

"Isn't it interesting that it isn't anyone's time on this plane to die," said the man. And then he walked away.

.   .   .

PILOT SAYS AUTOPILOT FLAW CAUSED HIS 727 TO PLUNGE

By Eric L. Smith
Knight-Ridder

WASHINGTON—Twelve years after a near-fatal 5-mile plunge by a Boeing 727, the pilot asserted Thursday that the cause was a fault in the autopilot and not pilot error, as determined at the time.

Pointing to several similar incidents involving Boeing 727s in the past 12 years, retired TWA pilot H. G. "Hoot" Gibson called on the National Transportation Safety Board to make a fresh investigation of the incident.

Last month, the Air Line Pilots Association filed a petition asking the safety board to investigate a possible autopilot flaw that may have caused nine similar 727 incidents since 1977. Gibson said the 1979 incident had made him a "pariah in the sky."

He said he hoped to clear his name and make other pilots aware of what he believes is a recurring problem with the autopilot mechanism of the 727, one of the most widely used aircraft in the industry.

Boeing Co. released a statement Thursday saying the company "did not find anything to relate the autopilot to the 1979 . . . incident" in repeated reviews of the system's design and operation. The company noted that the safety board had rejected an earlier request to reconsider the incident.

On April 4, 1979, a TWA Boeing 727 piloted by Gibson suddenly dropped into a 5-mile spiral toward the Earth while en route from Minneapolis to New York. Gibson regained control approximately 10,000 feet from the ground.

Although Gibson was at first hailed as a hero for bringing the craft and its 82 passengers down safely, he said he was later made a scapegoat when the safety board said pilot error caused the incident. Gibson, a commercial pilot for 26 years, continued to fly for TWA until retiring in 1989.

Gibson's attorney, Landon Dowdey, accused the safety board of pinning the blame on Gibson rather than looking toward mechanical problems.

Interviews
Asking Questions of Sources and Subjects

Once you've finished your preliminary research of a story topic so that you've seen what else has been published on the topic and educated yourself about it generally, you're ready to go directly to sources of information, or to sit down with the subject or subjects of your intended story and hold interviews.

Perhaps nothing seems as challenging to you as the prospect of holding those interviews. But don't feel discouraged by your novice status; even experienced journalists can face some interviews with uncertainty, feeling that they still have a lot to learn about the interviewing process.

If journalism is frequently described as an intuitive, imprecise ''art'' rather than a rational, fixed ''science,'' interviewing is probably considered one of the most ''artistic'' aspects of journalism. A great deal has been said and written about interviewing, but little can be declared with absolute certainty, because interviewing is so conditional, so dependent on each particular situation. Interviewing requires that each individual reporter respond differently at different times—sometimes according to traditional guidelines and at other times against all ''rules'' taught in books, the classroom, or the newsroom.

A UNIQUE EXPERIENCE

Interviewing is a unique experience because the two individuals involved are unique, each bringing to the interview a personal history, personality traits, and prejudices. What happens when these two particular people interact is different from what happens when any *other* two people interact.

Further, these two individuals meet at a unique moment in time: what happens at that moment will never happen again precisely the same way. The timing of each interview contributes to its unpredictable nature. For example, a reporter may or may not reach a source just when he or she feels ready to share confidences, or ready to explode with rage and frustration.

Since interviews are affected by individual personalities and unique timing, their success depends on the journalist's ability to express his or her own personality, to "read" the personality of the subject, and to interpret best how to "seize the moment" and make the most of whatever occurs—all difficult skills to teach and learn precisely.

Reading the advice of other journalists *can* help you sharpen your interviewing skills, as can reading or listening to tapes of other reporters' interviews. Some recent guide books on interviewing are: Shirley Biagi's *Interviews That Work: A Practical Guide for Journalists* (Wadsworth), William Donaghy's *The Interview: Skills and Applications* (Scott, Foresman), Michael Sincoff and Robert Goyer's *Interviewing* (Macmillan), and Charles Stewart and William Cash Jr.'s *Interviewing: Principles and Practices* (Wm. C. Brown). Oriana Fallaci's collections of her interviews, *Interview with History* (Liveright), is considered a classic; Studs Turkel's *Working: People Talk About What They Do All Day and How They Feel About What They Do* (Pantheon) is on many interview reading lists.

Retrospectively analyzing your own interviews and talking to your subjects *after* the publication of a story is another way you can learn more about successful interviewing. Just talking to other reporters is also a help.

But don't expect to ever "master" interviewing. It is such a fascinating process because no one journalist does it perfectly. Some journalists are better than others; some occasions are better than others. But there's always room for improvement—which may make interviewing frustrating, but also makes it stimulating and fun.

Before you begin holding your interviews, you need to do serious thinking about the two personalities involved in each interview and its particular timing. What is your attitude toward the subject or source? What attitude will he or she likely have toward you? In what kind of atmosphere do you expect to conduct the interview?

You also need to consider your purpose in conducting each interview. Are you conducting a "fishing expedition"? Searching for some specific answers to specific questions? Wanting an explanation about a topic or about a subject's past behavior? Hoping for a revelation of character? Seeking confirmation or denial of a controversial accusation? Why you're doing the interview may seem obvious, but too often interviews suffer because journalists haven't been clear in their own minds beforehand about what they want to accomplish.

Depending on the answers to these questions, you will likely see your interviews as falling into one of three general categories: information-seeking, personality-focused, or investigative.

INFORMATION-SEEKING INTERVIEWS

In an information-seeking interview, the writer needs to know information— whether facts, background, or analysis—from the possessor of that information. The possessor's personality is relatively unimportant, except as it affects his or her credibility as a source. The source has no personal stake in holding on to the information, and so the interviewer's job is relatively easy: he or she needs simply to be sure to get that information accurately and completely.

The atmosphere of the information-seeking interview is comparatively neutral, and the setting of the interview fairly unimportant. Many information-seeking interviews are held over the phone. They are often short and to-the-point, involving primarily clarification and follow-up questions that ensure the subject has expanded appropriately on the topic.

PERSONALITY-FOCUSED INTERVIEWS

A personality-focused interview is much more typical of feature writing and usually results in what is called a personality "sketch" or a "profile." (See Chapter 8.) In this type of interview, the personality of the subject is more significant than any information he or she possesses. Readers want to know "what makes this person tick," what he or she is "really like"—whether the story subject is someone famous (such as an actress or politician), someone locally important (such as the new president of a business), or someone eccentric (such as a bag lady on the street corner).

While what the person says is obviously important, *how* the person says it is also important. What is said and how it is said are both studied for what they reveal about the personality behind the image.

The atmosphere of the personality-focused interview should be positive and encouraging, so the interviewer can win the subject's confidence and draw out feelings and ideas not previously shared with other reporters. The setting for this interview is significant because the subject's "natural habitat" reveals what he or she values and holds dear.

You cannot usually do a personality-focused interview successfully over the telephone; you need to do the interview in person, and it typically takes time—at least an hour. You might also choose to do a series of interviews rather than one long interview. These interviews could be held in various places, over an extended period of time—anything from one week to several months.

INVESTIGATIVE INTERVIEWS

The investigative interview is not usually done by feature writers, but by investigative reporters. In an investigative interview, the reporter is trying to extract information or confirm information from a source unwilling to communicate, a source forced to talk to the reporter for political or public relations reasons. While they don't usually do investigative interviews, feature writers can nonetheless learn something from the process, since many subjects—whether hostile or friendly—have some information they would rather not reveal.

For an investigative interview, the reporter prepares very elaborately, carefully constructing the wording and order of questions. The reporter's role has sometimes been compared to that of a prosecuting attorney's: they both attempt to lead the subject/witness in a particular direction through a complicated line of questioning. For both, the relationship to the subject/witness tends to be adversarial and the atmosphere hostile.

Most subjects are more likely to talk freely away from supervisors or someone they feel might reprimand them for speaking too openly, so a setting that helps liberate the subject is useful. Investigative interviews are usually short, because the subject is unwilling to give the reporter time. They are better done in person and not by telephone, so the reporter can "read" the facial expressions of the hostile subject.

Information-seeking and personality-focused interviews can be conducted as group interviews, that is, with more than one subject. The nature of the investigative interview, however, usually dictates that it be conducted one-on-one.

Occasionally a reporter is lucky enough to set out to do an interview and by good fortune finds a subject who speaks particularly well—either very clearly, with precise and careful language, or very colorfully. In such a case, a smart reporter discards his or her questions and lets the subject talk freely. In this fourth kind of "extended" interview the journalist functions primarily as a recorder. He or she essentially steps back so readers hear firsthand the full, exact words of the subject.

What we call a "question-and-answer" story may derive from this kind of interview, although an extended interview has very few questions and lots of "answers." But a question-and-answer story may be derived from other interview situations as well, and may or may not be edited and cut extensively.

CONTROLLING THE INTERVIEW

You need to be clear about which interview situation you are involved in. It makes no sense to spend time developing a personal relationship with a subject when you are simply seeking information, or to try to turn an interview atmosphere positive if your subject is hopelessly hostile because of some ongoing investigation.

No matter what sort of interview you are involved in, it is important to remember that you should control the interview. Do not let the person you are interviewing take control from you. Too often, beginning interviewers are overly humble and obsequious. They feel they owe the person being interviewed something for granting the interview. However, if that person has agreed to be interviewed, he or she must have believed there is some benefit involved, whether it be personal publicity, an opportunity to convince others of certain ideas, or the sheer relief of being able to speak out publicly. This benefit is the person's reward; you don't need to provide further profit or praise.

Instead, your obligation is to the people who will be reading your article. You owe them a fair and honest account of whatever the interview revealed, as far as you—with all your limitations as an imperfect human being—were able to comprehend.

Another difficulty for most beginners is the contradictory nature of the advice about interviewing. You are told to prepare rigorously, but not so much that you get stale; to stick to your questions, but not so rigidly that you lose a good train of thought; to have a sense of the angle to the intended story, but to discard it if a better angle comes along; to use a tape recorder, but not if it distracts your subject; to be human when dealing with your subject, but not so human that you harm your professional image. And so on.

All this advice is contradictory, because, again, interviewing is not an exact science. So when you are interviewing, be flexible. Follow general guidelines, but don't be afraid to think for yourself. Trust your reactions. Remember, you're the only one who's there at that exact moment with that particular person.

RESEARCH, RESEARCH, RESEARCH

While there *is* concern that too much preparation for an interview may make you stale, and that reading what others have written about your subject may cause you to be closed-minded, it is nevertheless important that you research, research, research before interviewing. John Brady in *The Craft of Interviewing* (Writer's Digest Books) says experienced writers suggest that for every one minute of interviewing you should do at least 10 minutes of research and preparation.

Your research can go in different directions, and is necessary for different reasons. As we said earlier, you do want to know what has already been published about the topic or subject by other feature writers so you can find a fresh angle for your story, thus increasing its marketability. But you also want to know what others have written because it saves you from asking questions during the interview that everyone else has already asked, questions the source or subject may be bored with or already made clear he or she won't discuss. If, on the other hand, your research has prepared you to approach your subject with sharp new questions, he or she just may be startled into new revelations or comments.

You will also need to research the general topic (or topics) you intend to discuss in the interview. If you plan to ask about national defense strategy, you had better know something about weapons; if you intend to discuss educational philosophy, you had better be familiar with the names ''Dewey'' and ''Skinner.'' Topic research is important because it tells you where the cutting edge of the issue lies and what questions to ask to uncover new information. Your knowledgeability also gives you credibility with the source or subject, who may become annoyed if he or she has to go through the basics with a beginner, and who probably prefers to share confidences with someone well-versed in his or her area of expertise.

If you're doing a personality-based interview, you'll also do a third kind of research, research about the life of your subject. Biographical research saves interview time, so that you don't waste precious moments during the interview asking purely factual material anyone could have learned from a library or from a press release. Showing ignorance about a subject's personal history is also likely to irritate him or her. If, on the other hand, you come to the interview clearly knowledgeable about the subject, he or she will probably be flattered by your research efforts and feel you are a worthy listener to opinions and ideas.

All this pre-interview research will likely give you some ideas about the kind of story you would like to write (or perhaps your editor has already suggested, or insisted upon, a particular kind of story). Getting this focus is beneficial, because it inspires and directs the actual writing of your questions, although you must remember, of course, to discard your focus, and your questions, if a fantastic new focus should develop during the interview itself.

WRITING AND ORGANIZING YOUR QUESTIONS

Before you spend a lot of time writing questions, contact the person you want to interview. Identify yourself clearly, indicate where and when you expect to publish the article, indicate the focus of the article you have in mind, and the length of time you think you will need for the interview. Discuss with your subject the best time and place for the interview.

It's usually face-saving to say at the outset that you may want to speak to the person a second time after the interview to verify information or quotes. That way, if you need to ask more questions later, it doesn't look as if you were careless the first time around.

If you intend to interview "around" the subject—talk to relatives, friends, business associates—it is wise to forewarn him or her, to mitigate the subject's surprise and possible annoyance about what otherwise might be considered just gossiping.

When you have all arrangements complete, you're ready to begin writing your questions.

Probably the best way to write questions is to start by brainstorming: simply write down as quickly as possible everything that comes to mind that you are curious about or think your readers would be curious about. Then, discard or save questions as they suit your story's probable angle. You may want to preserve the questions you discard as a kind of reservoir you can call upon during the interview, if you should use up all the questions you had planned to ask. You may even want to create subcategories of questions in this category of discarded questions, for example, "These questions I will ask if the person is willing to discuss his or her love life," "These questions I can ask if the lawsuit has been resolved," or "These questions I can ask if the children are there," etc.

After you have a set of questions written, you're ready to refine those questions and put them into some sort of sequence. Study your queries more carefully this second time around, keeping in mind the two general categories that questions fall into: "closed-ended" or "open-ended." Closed-ended questions require a simple, one- or two-word answer, such as "yes" or "no." (Will you graduate this May? Did your mother remarry?) Open-ended questions require the subject to expand the answer into at least a phrase and probably a sentence or two. (What are the requirements for graduation? How did your mother meet your new stepfather?)

You are likely to have problems in interviewing if you ask a closed-ended question when you really want an open-ended answer. If you ask "Were you angry when they told you that you couldn't graduate this year?" the answer you may get is "yes"—a reply that gives you absolutely nothing to quote in your article and reveals little about the subject's feelings or thinking. A closed-ended question may also fail to open up a follow-up line of questioning. A simple "yes" response may compel you to move on to your next set of questions—a move that may mean the interview you thought would take an hour lasts only ten minutes.

The best order in which to ask your questions can vary, depending on what you hope to gain from the interview. Generally, the very least you want to do is arrange your questions in a logical sequence, with the sense of each question leading smoothly to the sense of the next. Infrequently, however, you may want to throw the subject off guard, catch him or her unaware, deliberately disrupt the timing of the interview so that the subject answers before he or she has time to prepare a smooth response to hide the truth. In such instances, you deliberately jumble your questions so a significant one is hidden within a group of innocuous and easy queries.

INVERTED FUNNELS AND FUNNELS

According to Brady, some interviews are like an "inverted funnel." They begin with narrow, closed-ended questions that require specific answers. After the subject is comfortable, and the interview begins to flow, the interviewer widens the interview by asking open-ended questions, questions that require the subject to expand his or her responses.

Other times, Brady says, interviews are like a "funnel." In this situation, the "thoughtful, creative" subject or source likes to talk, and can take the interview in any direction. There's no problem getting the subject or source to make open-ended statements, but the interviewer will have to eventually narrow the interview by asking more specific questions.

Whatever the ''shape'' of your interview, it is important to remember to ask one question at a time. Don't combine more than one idea into a single question (for example, ''What qualifications do you have for the job and what are you getting paid to do it?''). When you ask two questions at the same time, you give the subject or source the opportunity of choosing which half of your question to answer, and unless you are alert and ask good follow-up questions, he or she can entirely escape answering half of what you wanted to know.

Be sure, too, to avoid loaded questions, questions that contain within them clear evidence of your own personal prejudices. For example, if you use intensifiers, such as ''really'' (''Do you *really* think a woman who has an abortion is not committing murder?'' ''Can you *truly* say that you believe in capital punishment?''), you indicate your own opposition to the subject's view: you can't *really* believe that he or she could feel that way about it. Questions that imply a standard, or a set of beliefs that everyone endorses, also load the question (for example,''But isn't fighting a war what patriotism is all about?''). Of course, loaded questions *can* be helpful if you are trying to goad the subject into making statements that will defend his or her unpopular views. Generally, however, if you are hoping for a straightforward answer, ask a straightforward question.

Another kind of question to be on the alert for is the silly question, one which asks the obvious. The classic is the ''How do you feel about that?'' question, as in asking the person who has just won an Olympic medal how he or she ''feels about winning.'' Is there really any answer expected other than ''I feel great''?

Also keep in mind not to make your questions too wordy. A wordy question may put too much time and attention on *you,* making *you* the focus of the interview rather than your subject. Inappropriately long questions have been frequently seen on televised presidential election debates, when reporters wanted to seem impressive on camera. They asked complicated questions meant to make themselves seem erudite, but which instead made them seem pompous. Worse yet, they used prime time for their questions rather than the candidates' answers.

Of course, questions should also not be so short that they seem brusque or rude. If you want a serious, thoughtful, complete answer, don't ask a short, breezy question (''So, how's it going?'').

FIRST IMPRESSIONS

Once you are prepared, supplied with many *more* questions than you think you will need, you're ready to undertake the interview. When you get to the interview, remember all the manners your elders taught you. Be professional and polite. Address the person with his or her proper courtesy title. Don't stroll around the room obviously looking over its contents.

The best two guidelines about what to wear are: dress so your subject will feel comfortable and have confidence in you, and dress so that the subject remains the center of attention. If you are interviewing a rock star, for example, you should not wear a three-piece suit that suggests you majored in investment banking; you should also not dress in such a wild, flashy way that you seem more like a rock star than the rock star. Similarly, you are not likely to win the confidence of the business executive if you show up for an interview wearing jeans and a tie-dyed T-shirt.

Try to study the effect you have on people when you are wearing various styles of clothing or colors, or wearing your hair a particular way. Learn the strengths and weaknesses of your personal appearance and manner of dressing. You may find, for example, that long, flowing hair and the color purple work well for you when you're interviewing teenagers, but tidy hair and navy blue work better when you're interviewing grandparents.

Advice on conduct during the interview is as contradictory as all other interviewing advice. It goes: be polite, but not subservient; be agreeable, but don't agree with absolutely everything your subject says; be human (talk about the weather, sports, the difficulty you had parking the car), but don't reveal any human frailty that you might seem unprofessional ("Gee, I forgot to bring a pen; could I borrow one?"); be in control, but don't be afraid to follow the lead of the source or subject if he or she heads off in a new, exciting direction that would appeal to your readers.

SILENCE, TIMING, AND BODY LANGUAGE

Keep the focus of your interview on the person you are interviewing and try to keep the flow of language going. Don't interrupt too often with detail questions (you can wait to ask a group of these at the end of the interview) or argue simply for the sake of argumentation.

On the other hand, learn not to be afraid of a moment or two of silence. Most journalists are verbal people; speech comes easily to them. Faced with silence, they move quickly to fill in the gap and keep the talk flowing.

But if you, the interviewer, move to fill the gap, you keep your subject from filling it for you—and you're basically wasting your breath. You can't build an article out of what *you* said. So learn to wait it out, at least a little, to see whether the other person will speak first. Often, silence suggests to the person being interviewed that his or her answer hasn't been quite satisfactory; the discomfort of that impression can cause him or her to expand further on the original answer.

Learn also to use body language effectively: lean forward when you wish to indicate agreement or intense concentration, lean away when you wish to suggest skepticism or a relaxation of your attention. Nod occasionally in support, raise your eyebrows in surprise, murmur "yes," "uh huh," or "mm-hmm" when you wish the subject or source to continue with what he or she is saying. Your reaction creates the interpersonal dynamic that is unique to your interview and your two personalities.

Don't feel that you have to accept passively whatever your source or subject says. Press him or her with follow-up questions. Indicate when you feel the answer has avoided the question or shifted the topic away from where you wanted it to be or was simply a rehash of a previous statement. You don't have to be hostile or nasty about it; simply assert quietly that you are really after something other than what has been given you. Again, however, use your common sense: don't sacrifice the entire positive tone of an interview by reacting too negatively just because the response wasn't exactly what you needed or wanted.

LISTENING AND NOTETAKING

Many reporters have a personal system for making sure they've asked all the questions that they intended to ask in the interview. You probably will want to "check off" the questions you have asked, in one way or another, perhaps using some additional sign for those you want to return to for clarification, detail, or expansion.

If you have trouble understanding what the subject or source is saying, it's usually better to state your perception—whether unclear or inaccurate—than to simply re-ask the question; then the subject or source can correct your misunderstanding rather than explain everything all over again.

It may also be helpful to write on a new page in your notebook each time the subject or source turns to a new area of interest. That way, when you're organizing your notes later, you can "deal out" the pages of your notes into different piles, ordering the piles in the story's sequence. Be careful, however, not to flip wildly through pages of your notebook while the subject or source is talking. If it's easier, write down everything as it comes, and cut and paste pieces of pages into a different order later. Just be sure not to write on both sides of the paper.

It is also usually helpful to "star" in your notes the sentences that seem most quotable. Listen discriminately: when you hear the subject or source utter something newsworthy, memorable, or quotable, somehow mark your notes so you can find the quotation readily again. Some interviewers ask "stall" questions to keep the interviewee busy talking while they carefully write down the significant statement.

Not all responses to your questions are equally important. Pay close attention to everything, and don't waste time writing down what you know you will never use—and be especially accurate about what you know you *will* use.

Tape recorders provide the best assurance of accuracy in interviewing, but the debate continues, and probably always will, concerning whether the accuracy they provide is worth the discomfort they can cause those you interview.

Anytime you are obtrusive in setting your tape recorder up, you remind the interviewee that what will be said is for public consumption. Of course, in some situations, you may *want* to send that reminder.

Also, don't use a tape recorder if it makes you lazy. A tape recorder is splendid insurance, but if it means you stop paying attention to what the subject is saying, or you don't bother jotting *anything* down, then using a tape recorder is probably a mistake. A useful question is simply this: if you had to, could you write an accurate, complete story without playing the tape? (For example, if the tape got damaged or if you didn't have time to play it frequently.)

Take a few minutes immediately after the interview to go through your notes, filling in the gaps you find there, translating your personal shorthand into something you will understand later, and rounding out quotations with words you still remember but didn't physically write down during the interview itself.

WRAPPING UP THE INTERVIEW

You can create a more positive conclusion to the interview if you prepare your source or subject for the fact that you're almost finished. A source or subject can be rattled if you rise abruptly from your chair and flip your notebook shut. Instead, say something to indicate that you have almost everything you need, or say that you have just "a couple of quick questions" or a "few details" to ask about. You might also give the subject or source an opportunity toward the end of the interview to voice something he or she feels is important but you haven't asked about; you can ask a question such as "How do you want to be remembered?" or "What do you think my readers should know about this issue?" A wrap-up question that asks the interviewee to make a final evaluation or prediction, or consider what "it all has meant," can frequently provide a satisfying quotation to use in writing the end of your story.

Be sure that you leave the interview with a courteous "thank-you," and indicate you might call for verification of details. Do *not* promise that your article can be reviewed before it is published, unless you have agreed to that privilege as a condition for the interview being held. There is no reason why you should let a nonprofessional edit your copy. The subject or source does his or her job in granting the interview and answering the questions; you do your job when you structure those answers into an article you believe will be accurate, meaningful, and helpful to your readers.

FINAL COURTESIES

How much contact you have with the subject or source after the interview depends principally on whether you wish to maintain a relationship that will allow for further interviews with that person. If you want to keep the person as a potential source or subject, you can do several things to keep your relationship positive. Before the story is published, call to indicate the publication date; after publication, send copies of the article and write a note expressing appreciation for the time the subject or source spent on the interview. If your editor has decided to severely cut the story, you might call before the story is published to forewarn the source or subject.

You can also call after the article is published to see how your subject or source reacted to what you wrote. If you do, keep in mind that most people are hypersensitive about published material; take some of the criticism of your article with a grain of salt. Remember, the perfect interview has yet to be held and the perfect interview story yet to be written.

But if you can be open-minded, consider what the criticism of your story might reveal about prejudices or preconceived ideas you had that might have hurt the quality of the interview. Research has shown that males and females react differently to being interviewed, as do blacks and whites, and adults and children. Think about what might have created a misunderstanding or false impression in your interview, about what differences in culture, education, sex, class, age, race, or ethnic background might have led to your not asking the right question, or not correctly hearing the response. Researchers say that we tend to remember what someone has said if we agree with it and forget what is said if we don't agree with it; that simple fact should cast a healthy dash of humility your way when you're about to claim "Of course I'm sure that's *exactly* what the subject said."

Perhaps the best thing about interviewing is that you don't have to be assigned a story or be working on a particular article to practice your skills. Whenever you're in a situation where you're around other people and want to learn more about them, you are in an interview situation. All kinds of events offer opportunities to discover the stories people are carrying around inside them. Any place you are, you can ask people questions. If you do, you may be surprised to discover how quickly you will learn something you never knew before.

Such casual "interviews" may help you learn something useful for a current writing project, or suggest ideas for future feature articles. But even if there's no direct professional reward, there will at least be a personal benefit. Instead of standing around wondering what to say, you'll be thinking about what to *ask*. You'll learn plenty about other people and about how you should interview them.

And you'll never be bored.

Some Guidelines for Using Quotations

1. Quote what is quotable—that is, what strongly expresses opinion or what says something particularly well or colorfully.
2. Quotation doesn't excuse libel. If a subject says something libelous, don't use it.
3. Every direct, verbatim, word-for-word quotation must be attributed. Avoid "orphan quotes," those without identifying speech tags such as "he said." The reader shouldn't have to make assumptions about who is speaking.
4. A continuous quotation of several sentences need only be attributed once, usually at the end of the first sentence. For example: "I will leave that to my assistant," the president said. "He usually handles all the details for me. He has a first-rate understanding of what is required."
5. If the attribution of a continuous quotation of several sentences comes before the quotation, the speech tag is followed by a colon. For example: The president said: "I will leave that to my assistant. He usually handles all the details for me. He has a first-rate understanding of what is required."
6. For a short quotation, the place of preference for the speech tag is after the quotation. For example: "I hate to diet," he said.
7. The speech tag is put before the quotation if it is needed to make clear to the reader that more than one person is being quoted. For example: "I hate to diet," he said.
   Mary responded, "Why don't you exercise instead?"
8. Create a new paragraph for every change in speaker.
9. Commas and periods always go inside the quotation marks.
10. Don't combine quotation of a phrase and quotation of a complete sentence. For example, don't write: He testified that he was "a little tipsy. I don't remember getting in the car." Instead, separate the partial and full quotations. Write: He testified that he was "a little tipsy" when he left the party. "I don't remember getting in the car," he said.

EXERCISES

1. The following are a group of questions students asked in an interview with a soldier who had recently returned from the Persian Gulf War. The students thought that all the questions they were asking were open-ended, but in fact, several of the questions could be answered with a simple "yes" or "no." Can you identify which questions were not open-ended questions?

    a. Did you feel proud to be an American?

    b. What's the best thing about being home?

    c. What changes did you see in the attitudes of Kuwaitis toward Americans?

    d. Were there bad things that went on that the media didn't cover?

    e. Describe how fighting in the war affected you.

    f. Did you think this war was necessary?

    g. What will you miss about being in the Army?

    h. Do you feel the conflict was good for the American people?

    i. Did you think that things would end as quickly as they did?

    j. What things that you did made you most proud?

2. Below are some questions that are "loaded" with a sense of the journalist's personal opinion or expectation about the answer. Explain what these questions reveal about the journalist's beliefs regarding the person being interviewed or the situation being discussed.

    a. Are conditions in the Bronx really as bad as the media say they are?

    b. From farm boy to big-city attorney—is that quite a difference?

    c. Are you this stubborn in arguing about everything?

    d. Has your life always been so well-ordered?

    e. What is it actually like in California?

3. Below are some "how do you feel about" questions which ask the obvious. Suggest ways you could rewrite them.

    a. How did you feel about leaving your family behind to go to college?

    b. You must read of good things about yourself in the paper. What's that like?

    c. How do you feel about being the number-one-ranked tennis player in the state?

4. Suppose a new president arrived at your local university. Write a set of questions for an interview story that would be published in:

    a. your local campus student newspaper

    b. the local city newspaper Sunday lifestyle section

    c. the alumni magazine of the university the president attended for his bachelor's degree

5. Margo Huston's Pulitzer Prize-winning story, "I'll Never Leave My Home. Would You?" from *The Milwaukee Journal* is structured by the presentation of a series of interviews identified by nursery rhyme lines. How many interviews does the story relate? How does the interview that "this stranger" has with Bertha seem to be different from the interview "a reporter" has with Bertha's daughter? Why does Huston include in her story the social worker and judge if she was not able to interview them?

I'LL NEVER LEAVE MY HOME. WOULD YOU?

Margo Huston
The Milwaukee Journal, *October 31, 1976*

This is the house that Bertha built: Shabby bungalow, shades drawn, dark. You've seen this house, somewhere. When you were a kid, you called it haunted and raced past, screaming.

This is the woman who lived in the house that Bertha built: Urine soaks through her wheelchair, trickles down her swollen legs, into open sores, over her bleeding bare feet and lands in a pool on the warped wood floor.

At 91, her blue eyes still twinkle, her smile beckons and she manages, ever so slowly, to raise her saggy arms and motion, come here, with her fingertips.

Her stringy hair matted, she cocks her head coyly and, smiling like a contented but shriveling babe, softly pleads to this stranger, "Come here, lady, and give Bertha a little kiss."

She puts her shaky arms around the reporter who had only been doing her job: Asking questions, listening and taking notes. She hugs and hugs, hanging on, happily. Her stomach, looking like a volleyball, peeks out of her black dress. It quivers some. Then the woman purrs, like the cat she alternately pets and paddles.

But she doesn't budge; for four years she hasn't, not under her own power. It was a fall, four years ago, but 20 years before that arthritis had been crippling her body and spirit.

Even so, Bertha is some character. A visit, if you let it, can be a trip back in time and deep into all of our human fears and frailties.

Talk is constant; if flows from lively narratives about days in old Milwaukee to latter day parables that are presented, of course, as fact.

One goes like this:

Three suave gentlemen knocked at her door, proposing that if she signed her home over to them, they would take care of her forever in a beautiful new home built by a new church in Chicago. If she got ill, she would move up to the fourth floor infirmary.

"So I said, 'Don't you think they'd be forgotten up there?' These boys, they were sharp, they said (now she raises her pitch), 'You are all alone here.'

(Natural, lower pitch.) "So, what of it, what if I am? I have my own life to live. You go around like low-down thieves. Don't you know, that's robbing the rights of every human being?' So, they could see I was disgusted and they never came back."

As the story goes, she had a cousin who broke her knees, couldn't stand, couldn't cook, couldn't go to the bathroom, just sat there all day, blabbing like a child. Her cousin's husband, Carl, is a man who gets disgusted easily; her cousin's daughter works, so soon her cousin was placed in this new church infirmary in Chicago.

"Now what business does a husband have to sign a wife in anywhere—like a dog?" she asks.

As it came to pass, that was the same Chicago nursing home where fire killed 113 patients earlier this year. "So when this fire was, my cousin burned to death. Now she haunts me, and I say to her husband (now there's venom in her voice), 'You killed her. That fire that burned her is your trick.'

"Why did they make that church place? I call that a murder den. How can a new building burn like that?"

Parable ended, Bertha smiles across the dark stench between her post at the cluttered dining room table and her husband's creaky chair near the broken front door, 10 feet away. She recalls how, in his younger days, he looked exactly like J. Edgar Hoover. He smiles back, fondly, and she says of her husband, "He has a heart. He's a man. He's a human being."

Bertha has been afraid to go to a doctor, so she hasn't gone to one since she came down with pneumonia in the 1920s. But she loves TV's "Medical center," along with "The Waltons" and "Little House on the Prairie"—programs that depict "the nice life."

Bertha's parable has a lesson, and she states it slowly, softly, but most of all deliberately.

"Leave each one live—you want to live," she says. "I mean, leave each one have their life."

This is the man who married the woman who . . .: Hanging on to the wall, the gas space heater, the wood burning stove, he shuffles wearily, through this dark, dreary, smelly house that has no bathtub, no refrigerator. Since his wife's fall, he has wiped up her every bowel movement, as best he could.

This man doesn't talk much; his wife doesn't let him. She screams at him, "What are you crabbin' about?" And he replies quietly, "I'm not crabbin,' " Then he puffs his pipe.

When he does talk, crabbin' it ain't:

"When you get married, you take a vow for better, for worse, in sickness and in health. So I try to live up to the vow as good as I can.

He speaks in raspy spurts, politely, gentlemanly and, but for his filthy T-shirt and urine soaked trousers, has the classy demeanor of Chief Ironside.

"I was dead in love with her when I married her, and I'm still dead in love with her," he almost shouts. "But I made up my mind, this nagging can't go on. What's the use of her sitting in that chair all night, all day, all night?"

He holds out his sad arms and laments, "They've lost their strength. I can't lift her anymore.

"When the police were here last, she said I deliberately pushed her off the chair."

His wife coughs, sputters, purses her lips then shouts, "There you go. Are you going to shut up? Are you going to let me talk to the lady?"

This time, he doesn't let her.

"You know yourself," he explains, "when you're wet, it smarts and burns. She can't stand it, so she wiggles and wiggles and gets on the edge of her chair and then she goes over. That's the God's truth, as I swear on a stack of Bibles."

Silence, a rare moment.

His wife looks up with all the dignity she can muster. "I have been all my life a self-standing person."

"And that's the trouble," concluded the husband.

These are the firemen who helped the man who . . .: First the fire truck, then a squad, then another squad, sirens blaring, park in front of this dying house. Some of the men run in, others wait outside.

Inside, there's Bertha indelicately plopped on the floor at the base of her wheelchair, its sides solid with dusty cobwebs, its seat rotten with human waste. Facing her is a shiny new wheelchair, having a commode instead of a seat and a foam rubber ring to make sitting on a toilet all day comfortable.

"How you doing, Bertha?" asks fireman Gerald Fink in his friendliest, liveliest, most enthusiastic manner.

"Here I am again," she says, picking up the jovial mood. "I can't help myself, but I'll not complain. You're my boys. You're so good."

Meanwhile, the husband instructs the firemen to put Bertha in the shiny new chair he has just bought.

No, no, no, insists Bertha, alternately friendly to the firemen and ferocious toward her husband.

"I'm not used to that, no, no," she shouts.

Now she screams with pain, two firemen are lifting her, as gently as possible, with pads and practice as cushions. Settling back into the old rancid chair, she whimpers quietly as she slowly regains her composure.

Fireman Fink steps out to the porch, his expression now pained, and asks the reporter, "Can't you do something? Isn't there some kind of social agency that could step in? Why should people live under conditions like that—for crying out loud?"

Sounding exasperated, he adds, "Helping her into her chair, that's as far as we can go."

Turning to a police officer standing outside, Fink asks, "Shouldn't somebody step in and see what can be done?"

With a cocky smile, the officer replies, "Anybody can step in there who wants to."

These are the neighbors who watched the fireman who . . .: Three widowers, in their 70s and 80s, are standing halfway down the block, chatting, watching, one wearing a straw hat, another chewing on a cigar, the third standing still as a statue.

This is what they tell a stranger about the people in the shabby bungalow:

"Ornery. That's what they are. Ornery."

"She's supposed to have 13 kids, but you never see them over there. Maybe her own children can't get along with her either."

"Something could happen to him, then they'd both sit there, who knows how long."

"Haven't seen her in 10, 11 years."

"She ain't got no funds at all. The tax man's always after them."

"The law should get after them."

"It sure don't pay to get old."

The man in the straw hat says Bertha called asking for a can opener in spring, so he took over a beer can opener. That wasn't the kind of opener they needed, Bertha's husband told the neighbor, who left in a huff, taking his possession with him, never to return, until . . .

After the fire truck leaves, the reporter stays in the shabby bungalow to interview its people. Time passes. Soon, there's a knock. It's that same straw hat.

"Is everything all right?" asks the neighbor.

Smiling sweetly, the old woman soaked with her own urine and caked with own feces, replies, "Everything's all right; just me sitting in a chair and I can't help myself. You're a nice man."

"Well, I just was getting concerned about the young lady. She was in here so long. I thought something might have happened," replies the neighbor, peeking his head just far enough to see the reporter sitting there at the dining room table with Bertha.

Out on the sidewalk a little voice stage-whispers, "Is it spooky in there?"

This is the nurse who criticized the neighbors who . . .: "The neighbors watch everything. They watch the police and the nurse and they start asking us questions," says public health nurse Carol Szymczak, "I get very upset with neighbors like that, with the fact that nobody helped her. Where were the neighbors, like 10 years ago?

"People don't want to get involved. There must have been a time, a time before they dug themselves in there and sealed out the rest of the world."

There are more Berthas, Ms. Szymczak, is convinced. Helping or trying to help neglected adults is routine work for the bulk of the city's 126 public health nurses, says Carol Graham, superintendent of the Bureau of Public Health Nursing.

"No, this is not unusual, not really," muses nurse Szymczak, a 10 year veteran of public health nursing. "And I'm sure, if there's one case we know about, there's three or four more we don't know about. Behind all those closed shades, what's going on? I know people who haven't stepped outside in 20 years. If only, if only the community could get a little bit involved. If only the family could care a little bit. If."

This is the daughter who ignored the nurse who . . .: A data processor for the Job Service, at 60, she definitely is her mother's daughter. Her house, a small bungalow; her legs, ankles and feet, swollen; her propensity, to talk a lot; her social life, nil; her relationship with her own daughter, sad; her obsession, never to go on welfare; her spending habits, miserly, selfish and greedy; her personality, set in its ways.

But she's determined not to end up like her mother so she bought herself an exercise bike and two books, one on psycho-cybernetics to keep her mind active, the other on charted knitting designs to keep her fingers active. Old people are so sad and lonely; she doesn't want to become one of them.

Usually after work she starts digging in her garden. Then when it gets dark, she sits with a TV tray, eats a meal of all green beans or all of something else she harvested, watches TV without turning on any lights and soon thereafter, goes to bed. On weekends lately, she paints the trim on her house and putties the windows on her garage. She wears grubbies, T-shirts, tennies.

Though certainly not warm or emotional, she seemed to enjoy talking to a reporter, but when she spoke of her mother it was if she were talking about someone she had seen on TV long ago.

Does a daughter have some responsibility to help an aging, desperate, mother?

"If it's at all possible for a daughter, I think it's a wonderful thing," she replies, sitting back in her living room chair.

What do you mean, if it's possible?

"I mean, if you have a solution on how it can be done, I'd like to hear it," she shoots back, now leaning forward. "I've got all this painting to do. I've already used six gallons of paint and five tubes of caulking and I'm still not through with the garage. And at work, we're being pushed all the time, to do more."

The next question is: What's more important, your painting or your mother?

"You can say that but if I didn't do my painting, I'd have it up to my ears and in the end I'd have nothing for my investment. I've got my car to take care of. And I have leg problems, too. We've all got problems. Do you want to see me become a county charge?"

There's only 24 hours in a day, she keeps saying, and besides, "My mother won't have any part of being helped because she's afraid. She's afraid of doctors, she's afraid of hospitals, she's afraid of nursing homes, she's afraid of anything she doesn't know about."

A few years ago, she says, she tried to help her mother. She gave her an immersible electric coil for heating a cup of water. "And I'm sorry I ever gave it to her, because she never used it." Her mother's house has no hot water heater.

Besides this, besides that: "Besides I have trouble breathing over there. I get physically sick. . . . She just wants somebody to feel sorry for her, to sympathize for her . . . I don't have any money to throw away.

"Besides, she's still able to make her own choices. Nobody can make decisions about what's right for someone else. That's the trouble with these welfare workers. There has to be a point where they stop interfering."

This is the social worker who filled in for the daughter who . . . : Her name is Nancy Woedall, but county social workers don't talk to reporters and, anyway, it was her boss' boss who made the decision that Bertha would be Milwaukee's first person to receive emergency services under a new law.

This is the law that prompted the social worker who . . . : Called simply Chapter 55 in the biz, this 1973 protective services law and in particular its 1975 emergency services amendments have the potential of revolutionizing social work in Wisconsin.

The desperate person who refuses to accept help (Bertha) has long frustrated social workers and public health nurses. The new law says emergency services (including hospitalization) may be provided for not more than 72 hours where there is reason to believe that if the services are not provided, the person entitled to the services or others will incur a substantial risk of serious physical harm."

To provide such services, social workers are to get a court order, but they may go ahead without one if "the time required to obtain such an order would result in greater risk of physical harm."

This month, an eight-member Adult Protective Services team begins a concerted effort of carrying out this law.

Eugene Paykel, director of the Welfare Department's Adult Services Division, envisions "a great amount of precedent setting starting very quickly as to where are the boundaries of Chapter 55." He sees Chapter 55 as "a whole new tool—not a tool to do to people but to do for them. It's a whole new arsenal."

But, he predicts, this arsenal will not interfere with a person's right to die at home. It will focus, he says, "on people who are not committable, but whose judgment is impaired." (Bertha was Paykel's choice for a first candidate.)

Further, Paykel predicts that the very existence of the team will help the community get a handle on the extent of need—on how many Berthas live in how many dark bungalows in Milwaukee. (The Health Systems Agency speculates that as many as 150,000 persons could be in need of home care. For the sake of comparison, that represents the combined populations of Fond du Lac, Oshkosh and Appleton.)

This is the judge who interpreted the law that . . .: Judge Thomas O'Brien, a reserve judge from Hudson, Wis., declined to talk to a reporter. He had also declined, in an informal hearing, to hear the case seeking a court order to permit the social worker and nurse, with help from the police or fire departments, to take Bertha to County General Hospital.

Assistant county corporation counsel Frank Putz, who drew up the papers seeking the court order, said the judge explained he would not issue an order for forced entry because he believed it would violate the person's (Bertha's) constitutional rights—since no one ever claimed she was incompetent.

This is the crisis that followed the judge who . . .: First, as Bertha's husband sees it. "For 10 days, she wouldn't listen to no reason. She laid back in the wheelchair like this," he drops his head back, way back, as if his neck were broken, and drops his hands, limply, at his sides.

"She was right out of her mind delirious, hollering do this, do that, weird visions. Finally, the hollering got so bad, I said, 'What the devil am I going to do?'

"So I called Mr. Steve Carner, the police in the district, and he said, 'We can't do nothing for you or your wife unless she consents to go to the hospital.' But she's not about to consent. So he says there's one salvation, call in the board of health and they'll get a court order. And I say, 'For God's sake, do something.'

"So, all right it was then—to tell you the truth—served fast. I didn't know what was going on. They just picked her up and off with her. They don't monkey around. Oh, and they did a good job of it."

Did Bertha finally consent?

"Oh, no, no, no," he replies. "She didn't give her permission and my permission didn't count. Law is law. That was the court order, that was the judge."

As nurse Szymczak sees it, the husband's permission did count and Bertha's own consent came that afternoon anyway. No court order was ever issued. If Bertha had protested, the nurse had planned to acquiesce—not to evoke the new emergency protective services law. "Nobody's aware of that law—at the hospital or the police department."

Everyone was painfully aware of Bertha's condition. Because her head was hanging back, her husband had been afraid to give her anything to drink, for fear she would choke. She asked the nurse for milk, but no clean glass could be found to even give her a sip of water. They tried to lift her, but her skin had adhered to that foam rubber pad and her body was stuck through the hole in the seat of that new wheelchair she had so feared.

So through all this filth, the police picked up Bertha once again, this time chair and all. By the time she reached County General, she was quieter.

"Right when we got there she let Patty (her longtime public health nurse, from whom she previously would accept no help) give her some milk," recalls nurse Szymczak. "It was a moving experience."

Yes the rubber ring had to be peeled off. "But just imagine," the nurse says, "how good it must have felt to lie down in a clean bed."

This is the death that ended the crisis
That followed the judge
Who interpreted the law
That moved the social worker
Who filled in for the daughter
Who ignored the nurse
Who criticized the neighbors
Who watched the firemen

Who helped the man
Who married the woman
Who lived in the house that Bertha built.

Because she died within 24 hours of being admitted to County General Hospital, a report was filed with the medical examiner's office telling the basics:

Bertha, seamstress, lived with her husband, born Sept. 15, 1885, died Aug. 12, 1976, of kidney failure brought on by a blood infection, also hardening of the arteries.

At 5:45 P.M. on the afternoon after the crisis, Bertha was found dead in her hospital bed.

Now her husband sits shirtless, washing himself in a bed at the Veterans Administration— where years ago he met his bride Bertha. He puts down the washcloth, apologizes for his looks, then recalls how the phone rang for him that day at the Ambassador Hotel, where the social worker had found him a room.

"The doctor said, 'I have bad news for you. Your wife passed on this afternoon.'" The widower winces, his face flushes.

"And there I was all alone. I didn't see it. I didn't know it." He drops his head and raises a single hand to cover his eyes, and he sobs.

"So now here I am. This is the end of it." He shields his eyes again, wincing, holding back. "I loved her too much."

Style

Planning a Strategy for Sending the Message

After you have done your research and completed your interviews, you need to take one final step of preparation before you put pen to paper (or fingers to computer keyboard). This step concerns a consideration of what we call style—the style of writing you choose for the audience and content of the particular article you are creating.

This consideration of your style is largely cerebral: there's not so much to do as there is so much to think about. With experienced writers, this thought process is so ingrained that they don't even notice they are engaged in it. Their decisions about how to write are made almost subconsciously. But if you are just beginning to write, you need to be conscious of some of the style decisions you must make. And you need to make those decisions *before* writing, rather than *as* you are writing.

It's not a question of choosing whether or not to consider style. The writing decisions that affect style—decisions about audience, point of view, level of formality, focus, pacing, emphasis, and unity—are in fact made for everything written. The question is whether or not you will make those decisions with an awareness of what you are doing or through some kind of unconsidered process, like a machine on the "default" setting.

Most beginners have a very negative attitude about the planning part of the writing process—an attitude encouraged by the stereotype of the gifted writer who through intense concentration and a brief bout of feverish energy turns out a terrific article two minutes before deadline. Also perhaps lurking in the memories of beginning writers is the requirement of former English teachers who demanded elaborate outlines of such careful balancing of categories and subcategories that after preparing them, the writer didn't have much enthusiasm for the actual writing.

What we're talking about here, however, is no such elaborate, rigid planning. We're talking about thought that elicits "strategy." A general doesn't begin a battle by marching off soldiers in the vague hope that they'll do something effective somewhere. An architect doesn't create a house by picking up mortar and brick, hoping a design will emerge as the building goes along. A journalist shouldn't start typing words until he or she has considered what strategy will control the writing style of the message he or she wants to send.

AUDIENCE

Basically, when you think about the strategy of your style, you're thinking about the relationship between you and your readers—your sense of them, your sense of yourself, and your sense of how best to send a message they will be willing to receive. Of course, it's also important that you know what message you want to send.

Even saying that style concerns your relationship to your "readers" reveals a style decision, because "readers" is plural, and in fact, not all writers choose to write as if they were speaking to many people. While their writing may actually be read by a great number of people, they prefer to write their material as if they were talking to just one person. Their style is intimate and personal, seemingly addressed to a singular "reader."

Considering the possible readers for your story, how can you write to them and how can you put yourself in their heads and sense what they want to know? Readers are generally most interested in what affects them, and what affects them is very likely to be something *close* to them. If you keep foremost in your mind a consideration of how close your article is to readers and how its content has impact on their lives, you'll know what questions to answer, what information to present, and how to present it.

For example, if you were writing an article on child abuse, the focus of your article (and the questions you would ask to suit that focus) would differ greatly if you were writing for *Sassy* magazine (for teenage girls), *Parents Magazine* (for parents of young children), *Ladies' Home Journal* (for mature homemakers), or for the readers of a large metropolitan newspaper. In the first case, you might have readers in your audience who are current victims; in the second, readers who worry about being abusive; in the third, readers who are uncovering abusive parts of their lives; and in the fourth, all three kinds of readers. Each set of readers would have different needs for you to address and different questions for you to answer, though all would have a psychological proximity to the subject.

On the other hand, your article might speak not only to those readers, but primarily to other readers who have more distance from the problem of child abuse, readers upon whom child abuse has less effect. What issues would readers with *little* proximity to child abuse still need to consider?

Would they be connected to the issue because they vote on programs that help abused and abusive people? Do they need to learn enough about child abuse to report it when they see it?

Depending on which audience you are writing for—those close or those distant, those more strongly affected or those less affected, or both—you must deal with issues in different ways. Your sense of the identity of your audience affects several style decisions, including the focus or angle of the story, the level of formality of your relationship to your readers, your article's point of view or perspective, and the structure you choose.

LANGUAGE USE

You reveal your sense of your audience primarily through your understanding of who they are, through your asking questions appropriate to their interests. But you also reveal a sense of your audience by your choice of language. The level of the reading difficulty of your story should match your audience's education and reading ability. If you use vocabulary that less educated readers can't understand, you'll put them off; they'll either set aside the article because it's "boring," or disregard your words because you seem to be a "know-it-all." On the other hand, if you're writing for a highly knowledgeable audience, easy generalities will make your article seem unsophisticated and amateurish, and your readers will set the article aside because it's "too simplistic."

In general, the wider your audience, the more simple your vocabulary. Newspaper feature writers, for example, who typically write for a broad, diverse audience, usually avoid difficult and specialized vocabulary.

In addition, the more general your audience, the less likely you'll use language with very subtle shades of meaning: certain kinds of sarcasm, understatement, and overstatement may be understood or appreciated by only a small group of the readers.

You also show your awareness of audience by your attitude toward controversial information. Do you exclude anything that might offend readers? Present certain information tentatively, with several "mights" and "maybes"? Challenge readers by stimulating them, but also risking their anger? Present opposing sides of an issue in a reasonable, rational manner, as if you were a neutral outside authority?

Finally, a sense of audience affects the kinds of physical details you include in your descriptions. It's silly, for example, to write a description of a room with details about delicate fabrics and designer wall coverings if the article is to be read by uninformed readers; yet the same details of decor might be quite appropriate for the readers of *Architectural Digest* or *House Beautiful*.

A good "test" of the suitability of your feature for its audience is to have someone from its intended audience read what you've written. If you've written for teenagers, have a teenager read your work; if you've written for coin collectors, have a coin collector read it. Reactions from people typical of your audience give you a good sense of how well you have addressed their concerns, while asking your best friend or a relative to evaluate your writing isn't likely to be all that helpful; he or she is probably only going to like what you like anyway.

LEVEL OF FORMALITY

When you decide how you are going to write to your audience, you are also making decisions about the level of formality that characterizes your style. The level of formality means the distance between you and your reader. Are you close, intimate friends? Mere acquaintances who are nonetheless cordial? Two (or more) people formally connected, like a teacher and student? People who are distant and impersonal, like a bureaucratic insurance company and its clients? Each level of formality is established and maintained through different expressions of language.

The first expression of formality or informality is your use of personal pronouns. If you, the writer, call yourself ''I'' and the reader ''you,'' you have a low level of formality. You and your reader are good friends having a casual conversation. If you address the reader as ''you,'' but refrain from mentioning yourself (for example, you say ''the sunsets are rosy in Mexico; you would enjoy them,'' instead of ''I saw rosy sunsets in Mexico; you would enjoy them'') you are moving up a step in formality; you are addressing the reader directly, but refraining from exposing yourself, or sharing with the reader your own thoughts. If you don't mention yourself directly, and you don't mention the reader directly (''Visitors will love the rosy sunsets of Mexico''), you are distancing yourself another step from your reader. And if you move up to the extremely formal ''one'' (''One should see the sunsets in Mexico; they are very rosy''), you almost eradicate your reader's personal identity as well as your own and are writing instead to the abstract everyman/anywoman that ''one'' suggests.

Level of formality is also indicated by language choice. Generally, we use slang, nicknames, funny abbreviations, and obscenities and swear words around our close friends and family. We also use simple words to express our feelings; we say things like ''I just *hate* that,'' ''This book is *stupid*,'' or ''I'm too *tired* to do it.'' As the level of formality rises, we avoid obscenities and foul language (not being too sure whether or not they might offend someone), and we drop slang and private expressions like nicknames (not being too sure they will be understood). We also move toward the use of polysyllabic words, words that are less fierce and elemental in their emotional thrust. ''I just *hate* that'' becomes ''I find that to be *offensive*''; ''This book is *stupid*'' becomes ''This book is not *intellectually stimulating*''; ''I'm too *tired* to do it'' becomes ''That task is just too *exhausting.*''

Sentence patterns also indicate the level of formality. When we speak with friends and family, we use single words, phrases, and fragments of sentences. We don't always complete our thoughts. And the sentences we construct are usually in "conversational order"; that is, we put the subject (the doer of the action) first, then the verb (the action), and then the direct object (the receiver of the action). We put modifiers after the subject and verb rather than at the beginning of the sentence or between the subject and the verb. We speak in simple sentences with a single subject-verb relationship, rather than in complex sentences with secondary subject-verb relationships (dependent clauses).

When we become more formal, when we deal with more complicated, abstract topics, or when we write down our words, our language tends to become more complicated. We write things we would never say face-to-face.

Compare the writing of columnists Ellen Goodman and William F. Buckley Jr.; Goodman is known for her straightforward, simple, conversational style:

> The vast majority of teen-agers do come to a parent for help. These girls can get abortions. But only the most sophisticated of estranged teen-agers can find their way through the system. Only the savviest can find the money, travel to the clinic, or stand up before a judge, and therefore make their own decisions.
>
> The ones who are not savvy or sophisticated get to be the mothers.

Buckley is known for his elitist, formal writing style:

> One is presumptively skeptical about great theater coming from the White House having to do with such questions as national security. As a rule, it's better to inch up on such matters as unilateral disarmament, but the case for the initiatives of George Bush is somewhere between plausible and compelling.

When writing formally, we also tend to use what is called the "passive" voice verb. "Active" verbs show the subject performing the action: "John read the book." Passive verbs reverse this pattern and put the receiver of the action first: "The book was read by John." The subject is passive, acted upon, rather than acting. You can usually recognize the passive voice because the sentence frequently includes a "by" phrase giving the identity of the actor: "The book was read *by* John."

We rarely use the passive voice when we speak. It's difficult to imagine family members sitting around a dinner table saying "Television will be watched by me tonight" or "Class was attended by me today." Yet when we write, especially when we write formally, we frequently use the passive, intentionally or unintentionally.

The passive might be used, for example, in a sentence such as "Silence will be observed today by all Army veterans to honor the war dead." Its difference from the way we talk seems fitting when we are honoring war dead. At other times the passive is used because we simply don't know who did the action: "School was closed today because of bad weather." (Note that in this passive sentence, when we don't know who did the action, there is no "by" phrase.)

But, if you want to speak to your readers informally, avoid the passive. Since it is rarely used in casual speech, it has a tendency to sound stiff and sometimes pompous.

INAPPROPRIATE INFORMALITY

Most features are characterized by a low level of formality because conversational language is simple and direct and, therefore, easily understood. But not all features work best when they are written as if you and your readers were close, intimate friends. Informality may create an impression of insincerity. Anytime you and your readers are not, in fact, intimate friends, to write as if you were creates some element of artificiality. After all, bureaucracies, such as telephone companies, also talk in advertisements as if they were dear friends of the readers, and readers are rightfully suspicious of such communication or of anyone who acts like a close friend when he or she is not. Many people resent and are suspicious of any presumption of instant intimacy.

So consider whether a friendly, informal relationship with readers best suits the content of your article and your intentions in writing it. Backgrounders, for example, are feature articles that teach, that emphasize the information they give readers. What matters most is that readers have confidence that the writer has done credible information-gathering. If you were to write a backgrounder in a breezy, confidential, intimate style, you would lessen its believability; it would seem only a single person's gossipy point of view rather than a solid body of information.

Of course, within the various levels of formality appropriate to your article, there are still possible differences in tone. Intimate, personal friendship, for example, can mean different things. Sometimes close friends are exclusive, sharing ideas while laughing at others too doltish and thick to see what they see; sometimes friends have a secretive, protective attitude toward one another; sometimes they have an open friendship inviting others to join in their good time. These differences in meaning, and others, can be expressed by a range of tones, all within any one level of formality. Your consideration of level of formality is only the initial step in suggesting the relationship you have with your readers.

POINT OF VIEW

Another aspect of style is point of view. Point of view refers to the feature's perspective, or the eyes through which events in the story are seen.

Of course since we know that the feature writer selects the material for his or her story, at the very basic level of story creation there is only one point of view, the writer's.

If you write a feature using the pronoun "I," you openly declare this personal point of view. You emphasize that this is your story and your message. While it may seem honest to thus proclaim your control over the story, there are definite drawbacks: you may be oversimplifying the situation, and your single point of view may make your story seem too limited and subjective. The "I" tells readers they are going to see things only the way you see them and be presented with only one opinion, your opinion.

As we said in Chapter 1, some feature stories demand this personal point of view, because the writer has participated in a particular and individual way in certain events. But most feature stories don't demand that the writer relate personal experiences, and most feature writers don't see their control of stories—their selectivity—as all-encompassing. They prefer to develop the story's meaning through a point of view other than their own.

If you want to suggest an external rather than a personal point of view, several options are available.

You can relay another person's perspective by letting that person primarily tell his or her own story. You quote extensively, permitting the individual to narrate events and explore them through his or her own point of view.

Or, instead of quoting just one person, you can extensively quote many people, so the story is presented through their many points of view.

You can also use the "new journalism" technique of writing what extensive research and interviewing has led you to believe a character must be thinking. The story is seen through his or her eyes, with the help of omniscient narration (See Chapter 1).

Or you can encourage readers to see and hear things through their own eyes and ears. You try to be an invisible, "fly on the wall" observer. Rather than saying "I entered the room and saw a mahogany chair," you write, "A mahogany chair stands in the corner of the room," thus avoiding stating specifically from whose perception it is seen. This presentation of point of view "shows," rather than "tells," because it reveals to readers what is there, letting readers see for themselves. Notice how *Washington Post* writer David Jay Remnick downplays his personal presence in this feature on the damage in Armenia following an earthquake:

> SPITAK, U.S.S.R.—A young woman, wrapped in a torn, dank blanket, wandered the streets of this ruined town the other day, by shattered factories and schools, past the coffins of her friends and families. "We Armenians," she said, "we have always lived under a black cross."
>
> To visit Armenia now is to meet with a people who are often on the brink of despair. "Sometimes we feel as though even the heavens are against us," said Larissa Margachyan, a woman whose children were killed when a nursery school in Spitak collapsed.

Clearly the journalist is the "visitor"; Remnick is the person to whom these statements are made. But he prefers to de-emphasize his presence, creating the sense that readers would have heard the same thing as he did if they were on the scene.

But whether the point of view is your own, a person's in your story, or that of readers themselves, the important stylistic concept is that point of view influences your relationship with your readers. Any individual point of view is concrete, and appealing; it is also subjective and suspect. A point of view that lets readers feel they are viewing things independently may be less dramatic, but also is stronger because readers trust their own perceptions more than they do another person's (or yours).

FOCUS

By "focus" we generally mean the article's angle, its particular slant into the topic. Some people call this the article's "theme"; others, the article's "message." It is definitely not the article's "lesson" in any moralistic sense; feature writers don't preach to their readers.

A feature story can, of course, have a message that makes the reader feel like eliminating evil and striving for good: a pathetic story about homeless families in soup kitchens may influence readers to believe something should be done to help the homeless. But most feature writers would say that they haven't created such a story's moral; life has.

Such a statement may oversimplify things a bit. As we said, a journalist's selectivity can shape the message. Writers can give a tone to a story's presentation of reality. But for many writers, what's crucial is that their story's focus has grown from their open-minded questions and observations, rather than from any *preconceived* opinions. They've been willing to receive whatever impression circumstances present, and to see all sides of the question before their story's focus is determined.

Being open-minded doesn't mean you can ignore choosing an angle to meet the interests of your audience. On the contrary, after you've received your impressions, your sense of your audience is essential in shaping the story: you choose to write about what best serves your readers. You also choose the focus most suitable for the times when your story is to be published.

Once the focus is determined, you write the story so that it stays focused, limited to its single message. Any time your writing wanders off in unrelated directions, you risk readers' becoming uninterested.

Of course, some literary writers like James Joyce and William Faulkner have made highly successful writing careers out of being extremely unfocused. It's a delight to figure out where they're going and to puzzle over the connections they create among apparently unrelated ideas. But the audience which enjoys these sorts of puzzles is limited. So the best advice is: digress only as much as you feel readers will tolerate.

To keep focused, you can use several techniques. You can place in front of you a single-sentence statement of your message or of the emotional reaction you want your article to elicit. Test each paragraph you write to see that it is relevant to this statement. Or as an alternative, since the lead usually indicates or suggests the focus of the article, keep it before you as you write the rest of the story. Another possibility is to write your story's conclusion first, keeping it in front of you as you write so that everything builds toward that conclusion. Focus your article toward arriving at its final paragraph.

Some writers think of each paragraph as developing the focus; they test what they've written to see that it carries the meaning of the article forward. Other writers go so far as to say that at least one sentence in each paragraph should restate the article's theme.

Repetition of key words and phrases can link an article together and provide a way of keeping the reader focused on important ideas. Be careful, however, about getting too carried away with repetition. Repetition of words, phrases, and ideas can hold a story together, but empty repetition can bore readers. Writing that repeats information to no purpose takes *away* from the article's focus. Wordy phrases like "due to the fact that" or inflated clauses such as "the following considerations compel belief in the idea that" simply slow down the text, without adding to its focus.

LOGICAL FLOW OF IDEAS

Your goal is to write an article that flows like a river held together by its banks (that is, focused), but also moving, going somewhere. Your feature may meander like the lazy Mississippi or fiercely rush like the Snake, but it should flow forward. Each paragraph should lead into the next in a logical sequence of ideas: the meaning of each paragraph should follow from the sense of the previous paragraph.

Crucial to the logical sequence of your work are transitions, words that serve as connectors of phrases, sentences, or paragraphs. Transitions control the flow of ideas. Grammatically, some of them are categorized as "conjunctions," others as "conjunctive adverbs"; what matters is not so much their category as the relationships they suggest. Is the relationship cause and effect? Then your transition word may be "because" or "therefore." Is the relationship one of time? Then your transition word may be "first," "next," or "finally." Are you adding new ideas? Then your transition word could be "also," "in addition," or "moreover."

Good writers labor long and hard to perfect their use of transitions, making sure they have chosen words that precisely suggest the relationships they want to express.

Of course, like any good thing, transitions can be overused. Particularly if you are constantly pointing out conclusions to readers—"*Therefore,* more work is needed at City Hall" or "*Thus,* a successful career came to an end"—readers can begin to feel, not so much that your article is flowing forward, but that it is drowning them. If you point out conclusions too frequently, readers may resent your addressing them as if they were children.

RHYTHM AND PACING

Whether the flow of your ideas is meandering or rushing has a lot to do with what, in terms of style, we call "pacing." Pacing refers to the rhythm of sentences and paragraphs, a rhythm not unlike musical rhythm. You no doubt have studied rhythm as it applies to poetry and counted the series of downbeats in, for example, an iambic pentameter line. Journalistic writing also has rhythm, though nothing as prescriptive as poetry's.

In journalism, the rhythm or pacing is usually described only as fast or slow. Sports stories, for example, are usually paced quickly, because they reflect the fast action of the games they are describing (golf might be an exception). Editorials tend to be paced slowly, because they require a feeling of dignity and seriousness.

Sentence length and structure are the two most common ways of setting the pace of a story. Short, staccato sentences create fast pacing; complex, convoluted sentences create slow pacing. Putting lengthy modifying phrases or clauses between subject and verb slows the pace, while putting subjects next to verbs quickens the pace. Sometimes repetition of phrases can create a pace that is either fast or slow. The following lead by Jere Longman for *The Philadelphia Inquirer* feels as if it is building up cumulative speed in the same way a train, to which it compares an athlete's mind, chugs progressively faster:

> BARCELONA—Melvin Stewart, the world's greatest butterfly swimmer, is sitting at a cafe table and his mind is hurtling along like a Lionel train, darting through tunnels, sweeping over bridges, streaming around curves, switching tracks, curling through figure-eights, racing, racing, powered by some internal current that always seems on the verge of overload.

Contrast Longman's writing with Truman Capote's; in his journalistic novel *In Cold Blood* (Random House), Capote slows the pace in order to describe the passing of three years' time in one paragraph:

> Another three years passed, and during those years two exceptionally skillful Kansas City lawyers, Joseph P. Jenkins and Robert Bingham, replaced Shultz, the latter having resigned from the case. Appointed by a Federal judge, and working without compensation (but motivated by a hard-held opinion that the defendants had been the victims of a "nightmarishly unfair trial"), Jenkins and Bingham filed numerous appeals within the framework of the Federal court system, thereby avoiding three execution dates: October 25, 1962, August 8, 1963, and February 18, 1965. The attorneys contended that their clients had been unjustly convicted because legal counsel had not been appointed them until after they had confessed and had waived preliminary hearings; and because they were not competently represented at their trial, were convicted with the help of evidence seized without a search warrant (the shotgun and knife taken from the Hickock home), were not granted a change of venue even though the environs of the trial had been "saturated" with publicity prejudicial to the accused.

Language also contributes to the pacing of the story. Words of few syllables, words ending with hard sounds like "t" or "k," or words with short vowel sounds like the soft "i" in "hit," create sentences with fast rhythm, while words with many syllables, words with consonant sounds like "th" or "w," or words with long vowel sounds such as the "o" in "swallow," make sentences which read more slowly.

You can create a strong rhythmic quality to your writing with alliteration and onomatopoeia. Alliteration is the use of words that all start with the same initial sound ("The fiery red fox fled his fierce hunting foes"); onomatopoeia is the use of words that sound like what they mean ("KaBoom," "pzzt," "rrring"). Alliteration intensifies the feeling of a strong, beating rhythm; onomatopoeia creates the rhythm of the sound represented.

You want to pace your story according to its meaning: use a fast pace for quick events, a slow pace for events with more decorum. But your story does not have to be paced absolutely similarly throughout. Stories can change their rhythms when rhythmic change correlates to a change in action described.

EMPHASIS

The drumbeat effect of rhythm and pacing also affects another characteristic of style: emphasis, or the force you put on language in order to tell readers something is important.

Emphasis is achieved when you break the drum's rhythm. For example, if you have written several long sentences (or paragraphs) and then you write a sentence (or paragraph) with just five or six words, the short piece of writing will be emphasized, because it breaks rhythm. It surprises readers and forces them to take notice.

Emphasis can also be created by inverting normal sentence word order. If the rhythm of natural speech is characterized by sentences in subject-verb-object order, then when you write a sentence reversing that order, you create emphasis. For example, if normal order is, "I was sorry to hear that your dog died," a sentence reversing that order, "Sorry I was to hear that your dog died," seems strange and unusual, and hence calls attention to itself. Short story writer Edgar Allan Poe created a fantastic atmosphere for much of his fiction by writing many sentences with inverted order.

Notice also that in the sentence "Sorry I was to hear that your dog died," the word "sorry" receives emphasis because it is the first word in the sentence. Beginnings and ends of sentences, paragraphs, and stories, are places of emphasis—beginnings, because they first catch our attention, and endings, because they leave the final impression we carry away. When you wish to emphasize something—a word, a sentence, a paragraph—put it in either the first or last position. For example, notice how this Associated Press lead puts the most unexpected words in the position of emphasis.

> NEW YORK—(AP)—The first thing the Chicago Bulls did after winning the NBA championship was not to pour champagne over each other's head, but to gather to say The Lord's Prayer.

PARALLELISM

A stylistic device we call "parallelism" also influences emphasis and rhythm. Parallelism occurs when we structurally match grammatical elements in sentences. The most familiar instance of parallelism is probably the conclusion of Lincoln's Gettysburg address, which presents a trio of prepositional phrases: ". . . *government of the people, by the people, for the people* shall not perish from this earth."

Parallelism creates order because a given element seems to balance a similar one. For example, in the sentence, "I don't know how to get there or what to take," one infinitive phrase ("how to get there") is balanced by another ("what to take"). The same sentence would seem much less orderly if it were written "I don't know about getting there or what to take."

When you create a string of parallel elements, you create rhythm: "I'd like to walk into his room, give him a piece of my mind, slam the door in his face, and toss my resignation on the desk." The beat falls on the similar elements (the four present-tense verbs "walk," "give," "slam," and "toss"). Parallelism, through this rhythm, creates reader expectation. After hearing the first three phrases, the reader expects the fourth to match it. If it doesn't, emphasis is created through contrast, just as when a short sentence comes after a series of long ones.

Consider, for example, how Jeff Legwold uses multiple instances of parallel structure, particularly repetition of simple verbs, to create a dull, angry beat to his writing of a personal column for the (Danville, Illinois) *Commercial News,* a column that was a 1990 prize-winner in a Gannett newspaper competition:

> My 38-year-old sister died of a drug overdose. My sister died because she couldn't quit, couldn't stop and wouldn't listen. . . .
>
> We all had tried everything. We drove her to therapy, sat with her in the hospital, gave her money, gave her a place to live.
>
> But she always left. She always went away. She found friends that would tell her the things she wanted to hear, give her the things she wanted. . . .
>
> In the end, we shopped for a blouse she could wear in the casket. Watched guys we didn't know throw dirt on her ...
>
> I didn't cry at the visitation, not the funeral, probably not ever. I was too angry, mad at my sister. I still am. Maybe I always will be.

The point, then, is that you can use parallelism to create order and rhythm, or lack of parallelism to provide contrast. Unmatched, dissimilar elements receive emphasis, but they also disturb harmony.

You should also remember that the elements you choose to match in language should match in meaning. It sounds silly to say "I love my mother, my father, my Uncle George, and ice cream." Reading that sentence is a little like playing "which one of these things doesn't belong here." There is a grammatical match which comes from putting together four nouns, but no match in terms of sense, since the kinds of love are not equal or similar.

UNITY

A final element of style has to do with consistency, with your ability to control all the other elements of style, and style rules regarding punctuation and usage, to create unity in any article. Whether you want to unify your style beyond that single article is up to you. Some writers pride themselves on having a unique, distinctive style, a style that is consistent throughout their work. Other writers pride themselves on their ability to master many styles. They like to show off the range of their versatility.

But no matter how distinctive or various you want to make the style of your entire body of work, within a single article you should create stylistic unity. Your sense of your audience, your point of view, your focus, your level of formality, your way of pacing, and your mode of emphasis should remain the same—unless, of course, style inconsistency serves a purpose.

One style element that especially stands out when it is not consistent is level of formality—for example, if you change from referring to the reader as "you" to the formal abstract "one," or the neutral, objective "people." Generally, you should choose one level of formality and stay with it.

Another important unity within an article involves the use of the same verb tense, unless a change in tense reflects an actual shift in time. Verbs in speech tags are frequently difficult in this regard, because you forget where you are and write "he said," then later "he says," then again "he said." You should choose either present or past verb tense for your speech tags and stick to your choice, checking copy carefully to see that you haven't inadvertently switched tenses.

Feature stories are also unified in their use of another kind of "style," that is, style according to a magazine's or newspaper's stylebook. A stylebook, as you know if you've studied news writing, deals not with the concepts we've been discussing, but with punctuation and the use of certain words and phrases. Publications like to be consistent in word usage and in the way such things as numbers and abbreviations are presented. All articles written for a given publication conform to its stylebook.

If you write features as a newspaper staff writer, you conform to your newspaper's style. If you write on a free-lance basis, you should show an awareness of standard style such as that of the Associated Press *Stylebook* or *The New York Times Style Book for Writers and Editors.*

Your use of technical style must be consistent throughout any story. You can't, for example, sometimes call a person in the feature "Bob" and at other times "Mr. Smith." Inconsistency makes the article seem sloppy. Unity in usage of courtesy titles, abbreviations, punctuation, capitalization, numbers, and names gives your article professional polish.

Unity is both a first and final style consideration—the end of writing and the beginning of rewriting. Plan for a unified article before you write, then edit your first draft to see if you have fulfilled the plan which you originally determined. Ask yourself: have I bored the audience with material that doesn't concern them? Slipped out of my chosen level of formality? Confused points of view? Lost my focus? Led the reader astray by using the wrong transitions? Unintentionally slowed the pace with wordy, irrelevant material? Emphasized the wrong things?

No matter how well you have planned your style strategy before writing, you will likely want to reconsider some style choices. If you've planned consciously, however, it shouldn't be all that hard to recognize what needs fine-tuning; nor should it be too difficult to make changes.

EXERCISES

1. Look at the writing of this chapter. What is its level of formality? How do you know? Next look at a couple of other textbooks you own. Is the level of formality the same in all the textbooks? Why might textbooks all have the same level of formality? Why might their levels of formality be different?

2. Write a description of a family holiday gathering from the viewpoints of two of the people attending the event.

3. Write a description of your immediate surroundings for two different audiences (for example, for your parents and for your best friend).

4. Read the following editorial, ''Yes, the chair,'' by Richard Aregood of the *Philadelphia Daily News.* Discuss how its style differs from that of most editorials. What are the strengths and weaknesses of Aregood's style? (Aregood's editorial was one of several that won him first place for editorial writing in the 1975 American Society of Newspaper Editors' competition.)

YES, THE CHAIR
Richard Aregood, *Philadelphia Daily News,* **Nov. 21, 1975**

It's about time for Leonard Edwards to take the Hot Squat.

Edwards, for those who haven't been following his worthless career, has been convicted of two murders. He's awaiting trial on another murder and the rape of a 14-year-old girl.

He's 29 years old. Hope of rehabilitating this piece of human crud is doubtful. It's even wildly optimistic to use the word doubtful.

The last time Edwards was freed, it was on bail pending appeal of an overly generous third-degree murder conviction. He had just stabbed somebody to death and justice, in all its majesty, had found him guilty.

Edwards then went out and killed somebody else.

His second murder jury was right. He's not worth the upkeep.

Fry him.

5. Discuss ''point of view'' as it applies to part one of Sheryl James' series, ''A Gift Abandoned,'' published by the *St. Petersburg Times.* From whose eyes are events seen? How many times does point of view shift? Why do you think James shifts points of view? What do the italics in the last paragraphs of the story suggest? When does the reporter's ''voice'' seem clearest? (James's series won the 1991 Pulitzer Prize for Feature Writing.)

DAY ONE: JACK-IN-THE-BOX
From the series A GIFT ABANDONED
By Sheryl James
St. Petersburg Times, *February 18, 1990*

Temple Terrace

That day, Ryan Nawrocki was just an ordinary sixth-grader living an ordinary life. He was 11 years old, with blond hair that hung straight and heavy on his forehead. He was a stocky kid, and it was easy to imagine him carrying a baseball mitt or playing video games after dinner. That day, Thursday, April 27, Ryan strode across the street from his house in Wildwood Acres, a complex of shoe-box-shaped duplexes on streets that curl into other streets lined with more shoe boxes. He headed toward a small courtyard where his 16-year-old sister, Melissa, was doing laundry in a small community building. Walking along a worn foot path, he passed the dumpster and a large oak tree.

He heard something. A kitten?

His eyes followed the sound to a videocassette recorder box lying on the ground beneath the oak tree about 10 feet from the dumpster. The flaps of the box were closed but unsecured. Ryan walked over to the box. He opened the flaps.

It was a painful, jolting sight: a newborn baby marked with dried blood and a cheesy substance, lying on a bloody towel. The baby gnawed on its fist and cried again.

Ryan tore over to the laundry room.

"There's a baby in a box over there!" he told his sister.

"You're lyin'," she replied.

"No, I'm not!"

His sister peered at Ryan, unsure. Then she stopped stuffing clothes into the washer. "If you're lyin', I'm gonna kill you," she announced, walking out the door.

Moments later, she reached the box. "*Oh, my God.*"

Melissa rushed across the street to her apartment. Inside, her mother, Lisa Nawrocki, was watching *Night Court* on television. She looked up as her daughter ran in. The girl was almost hysterical. Melissa told her mother what they had found.

Call 911, Lisa Nawrocki said. She told Ryan to bring the box over, but Ryan said. "I can't look at it! I can't look at it!"

His mother walked across the street, brought the box back and laid it on her living room floor. A licensed practical nurse, she checked the baby's vital signs. Melissa was too upset to speak plainly on the phone. Her mother took the receiver.

The baby was a boy, she told the 911 operator. His color was good, and he didn't seem to have any respiratory problems. His mother, whoever she was, must have cut his umbilical cord and tied the end off with blue thread or fishing line.

An ambulance was on the way, and Melissa ran next door to borrow a diaper from their neighbor, who had 1-year-old twins. Lisa carefully wrapped the child in it; the diaper nearly swallowed him, reaching from his kneecaps to his chest. It made him look even more pitiful, Lisa thought, as she picked him up and wrapped him in a plaid blanket.

She rocked and talked softly to the baby. The ambulance arrived within minutes—too soon for Lisa. She felt as if she could have held that baby forever.

The emergency services technicians, a man and a woman, came in. They checked the baby and fired off questions: Who delivered the baby? Did you name him? They seemed a little cold, Lisa thought. She placed the baby on the stretcher. He was sucking his thumb. The technicians put the stretcher into the ambulance and then drove off to Tampa General Hospital.

By then, things were hectic. Police lights flashed outside. Officers came in to interview the Nawrockis. Reporters and television cameras swarmed around with lights, microphones and notebooks. Neighbors streamed in. Everybody was asking questions. The same questions:

Who was the mother? The University of South Florida was nearby; was she a student, afraid to tell her parents, deserted by her boyfriend? How could any mother do such a thing? She oughta be strung up, someone said.

God only knows what was going on in her mind, Lisa Nawrocki thought. *I hope she gets help because she needs it. I'm going to wonder about this baby for the rest of my life. I hope whoever adopts him never tells him he was found by a dumpster. That's a heck of way to start life. Your mother threw you away.*

. . .

Detective Dennis Hallberg of the Hillsborough County Sheriff's Office got to the scene soon after the baby was found. After talking to the Nawrockis, he and other deputies swung into action. Speed was important. A woman has just given birth. She was most vulnerable, most likely to be found, right now.

Hillsborough County Health Department clinics were asked to look out for any white, female walk-ins. Meanwhile, officers knocked on neighborhood doors. Have you seen any pregnant women recently? they asked. Do you know any women who are expecting?

One person said there was a pregnant woman who lived over on Marta Drive. The officers found her; she was still pregnant. Someone else saw a young woman holding a baby on the corner earlier in the day. The deputies found her—and her baby.

Detective Hallberg studied the scene, trying to reconstruct what may have happened: A white woman had a baby. She cut and tied its umbilical cord, preventing the baby from bleeding to death. She placed the baby in a box. In broad daylight, she put the box under a tree, alongside a path that people used to go to the laundry room, about 50 yards away in a courtyard.

Did she walk here? Drive? Was she alone? Was she a scared, young kid? A cold, selfish woman? Was she locked in a terrible relationship with the father? Did she plan all this? Did she panic? Was she somewhere watching right at this moment?

. . .

At Tampa General Hospital, they called him Jack-in-the-box. They put him under a warmer to stabilize him, fed him and gave him routine injections. They dressed him up. The nurses fell in love with him, all 7 pounds, 7 ounces of him, especially Tina Davis. She helped care for him that night and the next day. She had worked with infants there for three years, but she felt different about this one.

He was such a *gift!* She just couldn't believe it. She and her husband had been trying to conceive a child for a long time. And here, she thought, some woman had this baby and just walked away.

. . .

Later that Thursday night, around the corner from where the baby was found, at 5812 Mar-Jo Drive, Judy Pemberton, 42, quietly watched television. Cats and kittens played here and there in the two-bedroom duplex apartment.

At 10:30 p.m., Judy's live-in boyfriend, Russell Hayes, 28, came home from his job at a nearby restaurant. He was a big, red-headed fellow with a ruddy, boyish face and small, serious eyes. He asked Judy how she was feeling. She looked better than she had that morning. Her blond, shoulder-length hair was softly curled, and she wore her normal, loose-fitting clothes. But there were circles under her deep-set, blue eyes.

Judy said she was feeling much better. "I finally started my period," she said. The cramps were gone. She got up to fix Russell dinner.

Russell was relieved. For the past 24 hours or so, Judy had been suffering terrible cramps. She even called in sick to work, the first time she had done that in nearly a year. She told Russell she was going through menopause. She hadn't had a period in 11 months. This was all part of it. You missed periods, then you had one, then you missed more. Don't worry.

People had been worried about Judy, though. Russell knew that. A few people had even wondered if Judy were pregnant. One of Russell's outspoken aunts had asked Judy outright. Judy said no. About three weeks earlier, Russell's other aunt, Mary Duncan, who had raised Russell from the time he was 5, talked to Russell about Judy's condition.

"Russell, something is wrong with Judy. Is she pregnant?" Mrs. Duncan said.

"No, not that I know of," Russell said.

"Well there's somethin' wrong with her. She needs to go to the doctor. Would you please talk to her?"

When Russell talked to Judy, she said, "No, I'm gettin' tired of people askin' me that, no I'm not pregnant."

Then, last night, Judy was in terrible pain at the bowling alley. Her friends were worried about her because she could hardly bowl. One woman found Judy in the bathroom doubled over in pain. Judy was worried, too, and asked her sister-in-law, Marcie Gilbert, who was also the bowling alley manager, to take her to the hospital if she got worse.

"I'm cramping so bad I can't hardly stand it," Judy told her. "I feel like I want to start (my period), but I can't."

"Judy, *quit bowling*," Marcie said. "If you're trying to start and having major problems, don't bowl." Marcie knew Judy had not had a period in months. She had asked Marcie often about menopause.

"Maybe it's a cyst," Marcie said. "Judy, let's go to the doctor tomorrow."

"I can't afford it," Judy said. "I can't afford to skip work."

"You can't afford to be dead, either. If you've got something going on inside your body, nobody can see it but a doctor."

When Russell picked up Judy that night, Marcie made him promise to take Judy to the hospital if she didn't feel better.

But Judy said she was all right. And now, as she fixed dinner, she seemed fine. The couple ate, and then fell into bed by 11:30 p.m. Both of them were dog tired.

Friday morning, Judy went to work. For the past year, she had been a general receptionist at Hallmark Packaging Corp., on nearby 39th Avenue N. She wore one of the same outfits she had worn often in the past year—a striped blouse worn out over a pair of slacks. When she got to the office, everyone was talking about the baby that was found by a dumpster in Wildwood Acres. They were outraged. Personnel manager Kim Clark and Hallmark president Vincent Tifer stood by Judy's desk, and they all discussed it.

"They should hang the woman by the damn neck," Tifer said.

"How could any mother do this?" said Kim Clark, personnel director.

Judy loved children. She had recently brought to work the cute clothes she bought for her little granddaughter. Judy agreed with Clark and Tifer. How could any mother do this?

.   .   .

The news about this baby was distressing not just because it was a disturbing crime, but also because it was getting to be such a common one. In the previous two years, news stories about babies left in boxes, garbage cans, trash bins, cars and baskets have popped up with numbing frequency. In the 10 months since this baby was found, five others have been abandoned in the Tampa Bay area, including a baby dubbed "Seminole Sam" who was left on the doorstep of a Seminole Catholic Church last week. Each case is tragically unique, and yet part of a phenomenon, ugly and terrifying, that people simply do not understand.

Last March, a baby was found dead next to a Tampa trash bin. The previous fall, a baby was left outside an apartment complex; he survived. Before that, another dead infant was found near a dumpster. The year before, a baby was found dead in a motel trash can. Across the state, near Fort Lauderdale, a police officer saved a baby thrown in a dumpster by sucking mucus out of its mouth; the same man had saved another baby a year before.

Some mothers have seemed more caring, leaving their babies in places where they would be found. One baby boy was left, wrapped in a quilt, in a Sarasota hospital parking garage. Another was left in a north Naples sheriff's department substation. One boy was left in an unlocked car in Fort Pierce. He was wrapped in a sweatshirt sleeve and blanket, and his mother left a note: "My husband is on drugs and because of it I became on drugs, too. I don't want to give my baby away, but he won't be brought up right. I cleaned him up. May God forgive me."

Across the country, it's the same thing. Mothers leaving babies in odd places, or just tossing them away. How many? No one knows. No one keeps count. No federal or state agencies keep track of how many babies are abandoned. Such cases are usually included in child abuse and neglect figures.

Only one organization—the Denver-based American Humane Association—has studied child abandonment to any degree.

The Association estimates that abandoned children make up about 1 percent of all child abuse and neglect cases. Using that measure and survey results from 20 states, the Association estimates that 17,185 children were reported abandoned in 1986. That figures includes all children up to age 18 abandoned by their parents in one way or another. In Florida, 2,226 children through age 17 were abandoned from June 1988 to July 1989.

Since reports of child abuse and neglect have risen 225 percent since 1976, the Association assumes that child abandonment parallels that increase. How many of these are newborn infants? That is impossible to guess. In a March 1987 article on baby abandonment, writer Jo Coudert found 600 newspaper accounts of babies who were thrown into dumpsters, toilets and other such places in 1986.

This was just a "pieced together" survey by one writer. How many other abandoned babies are not reported or written about? How many are never found at all and end up ignominiously in the nation's landfills?

. . .

At 10 a.m. Friday, April 28, the day after the baby was found, detectives Larry Lingo, Albert Frost and Michael Marino decided to search the dumpster. The garbage pickup was late that day. The dumpster had not been taped off as part of a crime scene. It had yet to occur to the detectives there was a connection between the baby, placed 6 to 10 feet from the dumpster under the tree, and the dumpster. If garbage trucks had come at their customary time, the dumpster would have been empty.

Instead, it was half full. Detective Marino, dressed in a suit, put on rubber yellow gloves and climbed in. He handed items of trash to the other detectives, who laid them carefully on the ground. For half an hour, they found nothing unusual. Then Marino found a box. It contained a clear plastic garbage bag. Inside the bag were two bloody towels, bloody tissue paper, bloody sanitary napkins, cat food cans, an empty Banquet Salisbury Steak TV dinner box, and directions for blond hair dye.

The box was a xerographic paper box with a half-square cut out on one side. On another side was an address label.

The address was Hallmark Packaging, 1212 39th Ave. N, Tampa.

The box provided one more piece, and many more questions, to the puzzle: The mother brought *two* boxes to the dumpster. She put one in the dumpster and the other on the ground. Did that mean she randomly left the box with the baby on the ground as part of the trash? Or did she make a conscious decision to distance the baby from the dumpster? After all, isn't it likely trash pickup workers would have grabbed the box on the ground? Or would they have *looked inside first,* to make sure someone wasn't throwing away a perfectly good videocassette recorder?

Why did she throw away the possibly incriminating box of trash? Didn't she realize someone might find it?

Detective Frost followed the first solid lead: Hallmark Packaging.

■　■　■

Hallmark Packaging is in a small, narrow office in a row of matching offices. It manufactures trash can liners and grocery sacks. Detective Frost arrived about 10:45 a.m. He walked into the small reception office and approached the window that separated the reception room from the rest of the company. Sitting at a desk behind the window was a blond woman with deep-set blue eyes. She looked to be in her 40s. Frost introduced himself and told the woman he was investigating the baby that was abandoned the day before at Wildwood Acres Apartments. He asked her what her name was.

Judy Pemberton, she replied.

Frost asked where the company put their empty boxes.

"I don't know," Ms. Pemberton said. "You'll have to ask the guys in the back, but most of us throw them out front, in the dumpster."

"Do you know if there are any pregnant women at the company?"

"None that I know of," she said. "There was one woman in the back who was expecting, but she already had her baby."

"*You're* not pregnant, are you?" Frost joked.

Ms. Pemberton laughed. "No."

They talked about 15 minutes. Halfway through the interview, Frost started to wonder about this woman, and noted in his report she should be interviewed again. Something wasn't right. It was the way she was answering his questions. Too fast, for one thing, or with another question. She avoided eye contact. She looked off across the warehouse or at her desk, especially when he mentioned the baby.

Plus, she didn't react the way most people might when a cop comes out of nowhere to ask about a baby abandoned so nearby. She didn't seem surprised, or particularly interested, or kind of excited the way people who aren't involved are. She didn't ask gossipy questions, like, Gee, what did it look like? Was it really in the trash? Any idea who the mother is?

She asked only one question, as Frost left his card, and turned to leave.

"How's the baby?"

In the corner office, Vincent Tifer, president of Hallmark, agonized over what he had to do that afternoon: fire Judy Pemberton. The company was automating, putting in computers, and Judy just didn't take to them. It was a shame. Tifer hated to let her go. She had been a reliable, punctual, hard-working employee, always willing if she didn't do something right to do it again. She was well-liked around the office. Tifer was so relieved the day before, Thursday, when she called in sick, which she had never done before. He was interviewing several candidates to replace her, and it would have been awkward with her sitting there. She had no idea that she was going to lose her job.

Tifer knew this would be hard on Judy. She had had some tough times. Two years before, she had left her husband of 21 years and her home in Colorado. She came with her 20-year-old daughter to Tampa, where she was born and raised. She soon learned her daughter was pregnant. Judy supported the family, and for a time, the father of the baby, on low wages she made working for a temporary office services company. Since her office skills were limited, Hallmark did not pay much either; about $5 an hour.

Later, Judy's daughter broke up with the boyfriend and then moved with her baby back to Colorado. They left behind a lot of unpaid bills.

At the same time, Tifer knew Judy was having health problems. She discussed it with the women there. She had missed a lot of periods and said she was going through menopause.

Not that Judy was one of these chronic complainers. She really kept to herself until she got to know you. Then, she opened up and talked about her life—especially about Russell.

Russell! When it came to Russell Hayes, Judy was a love-struck teen-ager. They had been dating about a year, living together since January. An 8-by-10 picture of him in his National Guard uniform dominated one corner of her desk. Sometimes, Tifer saw her staring at it,

all lovey-eyed, as he described it. When she and Russell went to a carnival or fair, she would bring in a stuffed animal he won for her. At night, she would put all her stuffed animals near the picture and say good night to them.

It was obvious to everyone at Hallmark that Russell was good for Judy. They had fun. They bowled. They went out to eat often, which, she said, was why they both were gaining weight. Tifer got the impression it was the first time Judy had felt relatively carefree in a long while.

The last thing she needed, Tifer thought, as the work day drew to a close, was to lose her job. But he had no choice. After paychecks were passed out, Tifer asked Judy to come into his office. As gently as he could, he told her they had to let her go. He explained why.

Judy listened quietly. Tears trickled down her face. But, so like Judy, she didn't get emotional. She said she understood, and that it had been a pleasure working for him and the company. Then she left.

Tifer felt rotten.

. . .

In those first crucial days after the baby was found, progress on the police investigation was sluggish. The VCR box had an old serial number, so it would take time to trace where it was purchased. A couple of people called saying they had seen pregnant women near Wildwood Acres, one near a traffic accident, to no avail.

Human hair had been found, there were fingerprints on the items found in the dumpster. DNA testing and other lab tests on these items would also take time. The baby had been fea-

tured on television and in newspapers in an attempt to solicit public involvement. The detectives knew that's what usually cracked these cases. Someone who knows the mother finally makes an anonymous call. Someone with a conscience. Someone who despite other loyalties cannot ignore that baby.

Hallberg, Lingo and the other detectives working the case waited for the call. The more time that passed, the less likely it would come.

. . .

Friday night, Judy Pemberton and Russell Hayes visited Raymond and Mary Duncan. The couple are Russell's aunt and uncle, but Russell thought of them as Mom and Dad. They had raised him since he was a little boy. He was very close to them. Judy had grown close to

them, too. They were an affectionate family, and she seemed to soak in that affection, as if she had never known it before. The four spent a lot of time together at the Duncan's cozy, two-bedroom Tampa apartment.

In the year or so Russell and Judy had been dating, Mrs. Duncan had grown fond of Judy. At first, the 15-year age difference between Russell and Judy seemed more important, but the two seemed so well-suited. Russell enjoyed Judy's tomboyishness, her sarcastic wit, her interest in sports. Judy seemed both mother and girlfriend to Russell, dependent on him at times, lending her own shoulder at others. Russell seemed to understand her and accept her as she was. She had quite a temper sometimes. When she lashed out, cursing and saying things she didn't mean, Russell just let it bounce off.

This night, Mrs. Duncan was quieter than usual as Judy, Russell and one of Russell's aunts watched the 11 o'clock news. Mrs. Duncan put up a good front, but something was bothering her, deep. When the report about the baby was shown, Mrs. Duncan's eyes shifted from the TV to Judy. Judy was undeniably thinner than she was 24 hours before, Mrs. Duncan thought.

It's like she had a pin stuck in her. Her feet isn't swollen. Her hands isn't swollen. I'm a listener and a looker. And I can guess things. I just know.

What am I gonna do? I read every little thing about the baby, what they found. I never have seen anything that could connect me with it. All I can go by is a picture of the baby on television, and the circumstances what happened, and the weight loss. You don't lose that much weight overnight, see. I can tell.

Maybe I should go to her, but how would I do this? What if I'm wrong? I know in my heart I'm not wrong. I really in my heart know that's my grandbaby.

The baby looked rosy and chubby on television. The reporter was describing where and how the baby was found.

"I don't see how a mother could do that," Russell's other aunt said. "They oughta take and shoot that person."

Mary watched Judy. Judy was looking away from the television, and she was humming very softly.

Leads
Getting Started on the Story

Feature leads should draw readers into stories. Your goal, in writing a feature lead, is to motivate readers to read your article. Whatever lead you write is appropriate, if it accomplishes this goal. While certain leads may be considered typical for certain kinds of feature stories, no one type of lead is *required* for any story. The best lead is the one that convinces readers to begin reading.

The goal of writing a lead that compels readers to read can be pursued too vigorously, however. While we speak of feature leads as "arousing" the reader's interest, "grabbing" the reader's attention, "attracting" the reader to the story, or "hooking" the reader into reading, we don't mean that feature leads should do so if they misrepresent the nature of the article. A feature lead should be honest, suggesting clearly the nature of the story that follows. A light-hearted feature should begin with a simple, cheerful lead; a poignant, serious feature with a dignified, formal lead. In a sense, what the reader "sees" in the lead should be what the reader "gets" in the story.

The feature lead also should not scream to get the reader's attention or show off simply for the sake of showing off. A wild, shocking lead, unless it is appropriate to the story, is like the sensationalistic headline on the front page of a supermarket tabloid: it titillates the reader to look inside, but the story there never measures up to what the headline has promised.

The best feature leads reflect the message of the story. They are not only honest advertisements of what is to come, but also, in some sense, they *make possible* what is to come: they set the tone and provide direction. They are signposts pointing to paths readers will follow.

Leonard Witt, in *The Complete Book of Feature Writing* (Writer's Digest Books), argues that feature writers ought not to think of writing leads as flashy, showy, separate entities, but rather of writing leads as *beginnings* to stories, leads that are integral parts of entire articles. His point is a good one. When you write a feature lead to an article, you should have some sense of what you want to say **after** the lead, and then what you want to say after that, and after that—that is, you should have some sense of the whole story's *raison d'être*. You need to know what you want to accomplish in telling the tale.

You also need to think of how you're going to end a story. If your lead is to be a signpost directing readers, you should be clear about what destination you are directing readers to. What is the story's final impact? How will readers feel when they finish reading? How do you expect them to react? What would you expect them to think or do?

Liz Sly of the *Chicago Tribune* seems to have had a very clear idea of the story she wanted to tell about the starvation she witnessed in Somalia. Her article portrays that country's tragic struggle for food; her lead describes an incident that characterizes the essence of that struggle and, thus, the essence of her entire story. She begins:

> BAIDOA, Somalia—The Bikini Restaurant is widely regarded as the best in town. It is packed at lunchtime, mostly by local gunmen, and although the menu is limited—camel's liver with rice or spaghetti—the portions are generous.
>
> Outside, swarms of skeletal children throng the street in the hope of receiving scraps, but they are routinely chased away by a waiter with a big stick.
>
> On one occasion last week, a particularly emaciated boy was knocked down and—too weak to rise on his matchstick limbs—he broke into heart-wrenching sobs as he flailed helplessly on the ground.
>
> A bitterly cruel struggle for survival is being played out in this starving town, in which those with guns and money eat reasonably well, while others are left to die.

The lead suggests to readers a way of approaching the rest of the information to follow; the body of the story explores the information; the conclusion returns to the lead's description of the boy with matchstick legs by telling readers what happens to him:

> The reality is that it is too late to save many victims. A young boy who had been begging with the other orphans outside the Bikini Restaurant was found later that afternoon crumpled in the gutter, too weak to beg any longer.

The ending thus returns readers to the starting point; it comes full circle to emphasize the story's sense of futility: nothing has been done, and nothing can be done, to save these victims of starvation and human cruelty.

SHARED CHARACTERISTICS

While any lead is an appropriate lead for a feature story, most feature leads do share some common characteristics, and certain types of feature leads are written so frequently that they have earned "names" which describe the particular characteristics of their language or approach to a story.

In general, we can say that one characteristic most feature leads share is length. Feature leads are typically longer than news leads. News leads, often restricted in length to one sentence and/or paragraph, are written to present significant information quickly: the very first words of the first sentence give the most important facts. Feature leads, on the other hand, do not necessarily rush out with information; they may take a little more time to build an emotional response, to create a sense of curiosity, or arouse readers' interest.

When we discuss the lead of a feature story, we don't necessarily mean one paragraph or even two; we mean a rhetorical entity, a complete unit of written thought controlled by a single kind of writing or subject matter; for example, an entire description, an entire riddle, an entire quotation, an entire statement of a problem. The lead is finished when the story turns in another direction or turns from a more specific focus to a more general focus. That turn may or may not be expressed overtly in a transition word, phrase, or sentence. (The sentence that turns the lead to the body of the story is frequently called the "nut graph.")

The rhetorical entity that is a feature lead may be very short, as is Bill Montague's lead for a *USA Today* feature:

When it comes to life-insurance companies, big doesn't automatically mean better.*

Or it can be as long (or even longer) as this lead written by Bob Drury and Marnie Inskip for a *Vanity Fair* article on Lawrencia Bembenek:

She had barely bounded the prison wall and bolted across the Canadian border before the rallies began, before the Hollywood agents faxed in, before Lawrencia "Bambi" Bembenek's name was once again on the tip of Tom Brokaw's tongue. BEMBENEK ON BOARD! the bumper stickers proclaimed, and the T-shirt industry urged her to RUN, BAMBI, RUN! For three sweet months the alluring convicted murderess did just that, eluding a nationwide womanhunt, fleeing the law with the lover who fell for her when he saw her in the prison visiting room, and rekindling the backdraft of publicity that had engulfed her trial nearly a decade before.

Perhaps the best guideline to the length of the lead is that it should be proportional to the story. A six-paragraph lead, for example, would overwhelm a 10-paragraph story; a one-sentence lead would seem inadequate to a 40-paragraph story.

Most feature leads are informal and conversational, for the obvious reason that feature *stories* are generally informal and conversational. Feature leads frequently contain sentence fragments; they may use slang, jargon, or brand names; they commonly speak to readers directly as "you"; and they often use the present tense "says" rather than the past tense "said," in order to create the sense that the writer and reader are engaged in a current, ongoing discussion.

Finally, most feature leads are, to one degree or another, written creatively. Writers try to write feature leads in fresh, original ways. Writers

---

*Copyright 1991, USA Today. Reprinted with permission.

may have fun playing with sound and sense or experimenting with unusual or unlikely ways of expressing or signifying meaning—as in this Associated Press lead:

> LAS VEGAS—It took 14 years, but Chip Beck finally gave the PGA Tour another 59 Friday.
> That's 59, as in 29-30, as in the second sub-60 round in tour history, as in 13 under par, as in 13 birdies and five pars.

Feature writers generally avoid writing leads which use stale, hackneyed expressions or cliches, unless the writer can devise a new, creative twist for the worn-out phrase.

THE SUMMARY STATEMENT LEAD

While feature leads are different from news leads, feature writers shouldn't necessarily forget everything they learned about writing the straight news lead that punches out the facts. A summary statement about the circumstances of a story can be an effective lead for a feature, especially when the events, information, or people in the story have self-evident, inherent interest to readers. The article may be about something so extraordinary, or of such impact on readers, that the lead has no need to enhance the situation; instead it simply presents information boldly and succinctly, getting the idea across to readers as fast as possible.

USA Today, which has promoted the use of the minimum number of words in leads for *news* stories, predictably uses very brief summary statement leads frequently in feature stories, like these two leads written by Pat Ordovensky and Mike Snider, respectively:

> State-supported public colleges, the traditional low-cost way to earn a degree, aren't so low-cost anymore.*

> Family medical histories should join deeds to the house and certificates of birth and marriage as valued family documents, genetics experts say.*

Linnet Myers begins her story on Cook County Court for the *Chicago Tribune* with this series of succinct, summarizing statements:

> Murderers walk these halls, and the mothers of murderers, and the mothers of the murdered too.
> This is 26th [Street] and California.
> Step through the metal detectors and enter the multicolored stream of humanity that flows through the Criminal Court building each day. It is the largest

---

*Copyright 1991, USA Today. Reprinted with permission.

felony-trial system under one roof in the United States. In 34 courtrooms, nothing but felonies are heard: murders, manslaughters, sexual assaults, armed robberies, burglaries, drug cases. Last year, 19,632 cases were heard here.

THE NARRATIVE LEAD

The narrative lead is so named because it starts the feature in the middle of a chronological story-telling, or narrative. Classical rhetoricians have a term for such beginnings; the action is said to begin *in medias res,* or "in the middle of things." The narrative lead requires that the writer, who knows the action of the story from beginning to end, hide the knowledge of the conclusion from readers and begin the story either at the very beginning of the chronology (a sort of a "once upon a time" lead) or at a point in time when the outcome of events is uncertain. The lead draws readers into the story because they want to find out what happens next, how it all works out, and whether the subjects of the story succeed or fail.

Maud Beelman of the Associated Press, for example, begins her story about a Bosnian refugee's "exodus" with a narrative lead that makes readers feel both compassionate and curious:

> IN THE MOUNTAINS OF CENTRAL BOSNIA—Old and young, fit and disabled alike, they trekked by night over rubble, blood and human remains to the streak of tracer rounds and the boom of mortars.
>
> The more than 1,500 refugees were mainly Muslims, forced from their homes as part of a Serbian "ethnic cleansing" campaign to create a "pure" homeland in Bosnia.
>
> To reach safety, the refugees had to endure a terrifying nighttime journey between battle lines to the Bosnian town of Travnik. To three Western reporters with them, it looked and felt like a biblical exodus.
>
> Women with babies, old men with canes and wheezing grandmothers climbed a barrier of rocks and walked past minefields, and through pools of blood and chunks of human flesh.
>
> The refugees had set out in nine buses, one truck and about 50 cars at noon Tuesday from the northwestern Bosnian town of Sanski Most, where Muslims had long lived peacefully with Serbs.
>
> It was pure chance that we joined them. Serbian police escorting us out of Prijedor and Omarska, sites of two notorious Serbian detention camps, unwittingly dropped us at the end of the convoy.

THE DESCRIPTIVE LEAD

A "descriptive," "scene-setting," or "atmospheric" lead begins the article by placing readers at a scene, apparently watching events happening there. The lead describes what readers would see, hear, smell, and touch if they were present. The readers' "view" of the scene may be simply a random glance or a more organized vision—a look from left to right, far to near, near to far, or around in a circle. The view can also be panoramic, bird's-eye, or telescopic.

Descriptive leads are appropriately used when the location of the story or the atmosphere of a story is relatively important, as it is in this *Yankee* magazine article on a man's dedication to reconstructing a house built during the 1700s:

> It's almost too perfect, as if a Hollywood director needed a typical 18th century saltbox in an idyllic country setting in order to film a romantic movie about a family living in Colonial times. The old gray-boarded barn, the stone walls, the two-and-a-half-acre pond, the perennial flower garden, the open land, and surrounding forests are all placed perfectly in relationship to the two-story, center-chimney house built around 1730. Like a painting. Ducks and geese swim about in the reflections of the buildings. An orange cat sits on the doorstep. This just can't be *real.*

Descriptive leads are also appropriately used to give clues to the character of a subject of a feature story, as does this lead for a *Redbook* profile of actress Mel Harris, written by Ellen Byron:

> Mel Harris' thirtysomething trailer looks more like a rumpus room than the dressing room of a star. Toys and games cram every nook and cranny. Framed photographs of her children—one-year-old daughter Madeline and six-year-old Byron—crowd all available shelf space. Still more photos are taped to the walls, including one of Harris and her husband, 41-year-old actor Cotter Smith, locked in a passionate kiss.

A descriptive lead should include details of physical objects at the scene and use rich words that suggest *exact* color, texture, sound, and smell. A descriptive lead should also be relatively short; descriptive writing that continues on paragraph after paragraph can become boring. A good descriptive lead makes the description come alive by putting people on the scene or by using strong action verbs to suggest dynamic movement of physical objects.

THE IRONIC LEAD

One of the most common feature leads is a lead that prepares readers to expect one thing and then gives them something else. This type of lead has been called various names: a "surprise" lead, a "zapper," or an "ironic" lead. (Irony occurs when what happens is the opposite of what is expected.) Whatever the name, you can recognize the ironic lead by the appearance of unexpected information, usually at the end of the lead, after readers have been thoroughly "set up" by the presentation of normal, "expected" information.

For example, Harvey Araton's lead for a *New York Times'* feature on tennis player Debbie Graham puts the unexpected word as the last word:

> After four years of high school in Fountain Valley, Calif., and three years at Stanford University in Palo Alto, Debbie Graham has decided to begin her career as a professional tennis player, hoping for a shot at the top of an increasingly lucrative sport. But she has a problem with her age. At 21, she may be too old.

Christopher Knowlton's lead in *Fortune* magazine also presents an unexpected word at the end of the lead, after setting up reader expectations:

> Sir Peter Holmes has a way of brushing death aside. He stepped on a land mine while serving with the British Army in Korea 40 years ago but escaped with minor injuries. Last summer he walked away from the crash of a small plane on a riverbank in Zambia, then fended off crocodiles and lions by lighting fires until help came 16 hours later. A good resume for a stunt man? Sir Peter, 58, is in an even more dangerous business—oil.

A variation on the ironic lead is a lead which gives readers not only what is not expected, but also a secondary message about the prejudicial nature of their expectations. For example, in this lead from *The Seattle Times,* Carey Quan Gelernter sets up readers so they see inconsistencies in their own beliefs about education:

> SEATTLE—From now on, there will be no more free public school. If you have the money, your kids can get an education. If not, tough luck.
> What? No way! Not in America!
> That's what we'd say, wouldn't we, if suddenly such an announcement were made? After all, Americans believe that every child, no matter what his background, has the right to an education—and with it, the chance to make it in the world.
> But how deep is that belief, really? Author Jonathan Kozol, whose new book is "Savage Inequalities: Children in America's Schools" (Crown, $20), argues that it amounts to mere lip service.

THE OPPOSITION LEAD

Another lead is the "opposition" lead, a lead that introduces two viewpoints representing opposing sides of a controversy, or two contrasting positions in a situation.

Margaret Hammersley's lead feature in *The Buffalo News* on an honors high school class presents an opposition and then a middle position:

> On one side, education and business leaders are calling on American schools to emphasize science and math to produce a generation that can compete with the rest of the world.
> On the other, a member of the Buffalo Board of Education, James W. Comerford Jr., condemns the schools for teaching the theory of evolution without teaching creationism as a valid alternative.

In the middle, Buffalo's City Honors offers the only course in New York State's public schools that examines both the theory of evolution and the fundamentalist belief that God created and populated the world as described in Genesis.

Kathleen Halloran's lead for the *Fort Collins Coloradoan* also presents an opposition, but about a different educational situation:

> The young sit in classrooms and stifle yawns. They learn so they can pass a test so they can finish a course so they can get out of school so they can get on with their lives.
>
> The old, on the other hand, learn because it keeps them young.
>
> At least the people who are enrolled in Elderhostel do. They share something called "the Elderhostel spirit."

You can usually recognize an opposition lead by its use of transitions such as "on the one side/on the other" and "on the other hand," as in the two previous examples. Obviously, for an opposition lead, your topic should have two identifiable sides; you wouldn't force opposition on a situation that has little clear-cut contrast.

THE PHYSICAL DETAIL LEAD

Another feature lead is the "physical detail" lead, sometimes called a "symbolic detail" lead. This lead emphasizes a particular physical object (or objects) which represents the message of the entire situation; the detail is a symbol for the article's entire meaning. Michael L. Rozansky, for example, focuses on a physical object for his lead to a *Philadelphia Inquirer* story about a new Disabilities Act :

> Barbara Jeanne Eigenbrood remembers the doors, the thick, glass double doors with metal trim that led to the employment office at The Boeing Co. in Ridley Township, where she once worked as a personnel assistant.
>
> The doors were one of the obstacles she encountered in her wheelchair. Then last fall, she heard that company managers had drafted plans to improve access to the plant for disabled people. One of their priorities: the doors.
>
> "My heart just leapt with joy when I heard they were going to make the employment doors push-button so they would open automatically. They were big, heavy doors," said Eigenbrood, her eyes growing misty.
>
> "It was symbolic to me," she said. "It was so exciting."
>
> The automatic doors, part of a $250,000 renovation plan, will not be installed at Boeing until later this year. But in a broader sense, the doors to the employment office there and at businesses across the nation were opened to disabled people today when Title I of the Disabilities Act (ADA) of 1990 took effect.

THE PARADIGMATIC LEAD

A "paradigmatic" lead is very similar to the physical detail lead, in that something stands for more than itself. But in this lead, rather than a physical object symbolizing a greater meaning, one thing represents many things.

A paradigm is a pattern, a model containing elements that all units have in common. For example, Lassie is a paradigm for all dogs that are faithful, intelligent, and protective. The previous lead, which focused on the physical object, could also be said to be a paradigmatic lead in that Eigenbrood's difficulties with an obstacle represent *many* handicapped people's difficulties with obstacles. Liz Sly's lead about starvation in Somalia could also be said to be paradigmatic, because the incident happening to one boy represents similar incidents happening to many children.

Sara Terry begins a *Christian Science Monitor* story about many children from the world's poorest countries with this paradigmatic lead about one child:

> Kham Suk is 13 years old. She is a small child, with a delicate face. When she giggles, she sounds like any little girl at play. But Kham Suk doesn't have much time for fun. Three months ago, her mother walked her across the border from Burma into Thailand and sold her to a brothel for $80.
>
> Kham Suk's family desperately needed the money. Kham Suk is still paying the price: $4 a customer.

THE ANECDOTAL LEAD

In an "anecdotal" lead, an anecdote, or little story, illustrates the crux of some problem or reveals a central characteristic of someone's personality. The anecdote is usually brief and told in straightforward chronological order, as is this lead by Richard Johnson of *The Denver Post:*

> COLORADO SPRINGS—One day 12 years ago, Sandy Nieman suddenly realized how challenging life can be when you're a mother of twins.
>
> Nieman, of Crystal, Minn., was holding her infant twin boys, Adam and Andy—one in the crook of each arm. She sat down in a deep recliner chair and soon realized she couldn't stand up.
>
> "The chair arms were too high to put one baby down on the carpet," she explained, "and I couldn't push myself up without running a risk of hurting one of them. I just wasn't able to get enough momentum to stand up."
>
> What did she do?
>
> "I sat there an hour and a half till my husband came home." It wasn't funny at the time, but Nieman can't talk about it now without smiling. "Believe me, I never sat down again when I was holding both twins."

THE TEASER LEAD

A teaser lead encourages readers to read by arousing their curiosity: the lead makes some sense, but not complete sense. Readers must keep reading if they want to figure out what the lead means. This lead from the *Los Angeles Times* is a good example:

> KAMPEHL, Germany—The fight between the mayor and the preacher was bizarre to begin with, but the invasion this summer of the six would-be body-snatchers definitely pushed it into the Twilight Zone.

Teaser leads should not make readers wait too long to satisfy their curiosity. Reading on and on, trying to make sense of a writer's gobbledegook, is annoying; readers can quickly resent being teased. Also, the lead should not be too artificial; its information shouldn't have to be twisted like a pretzel so it can be cryptic or puzzling.

A lead similar to a teaser lead is one that makes a mind-boggling statement. Such a lead has been called an ''astonisher,'' or ''brand-new-bit-of-information,'' ''surprising statement'' or ''shocker'' lead. It is straightforward, written in a style similar to that of the summary lead.

CONVERSATIONAL LEADS

Leads that particularly emphasize the apparent conversation writers are having with readers are among the most common of feature leads. To identify a lead as ''conversational,'' however, is somewhat tricky, since many leads are not only conversational, but also something else—ironic, teasing, anecdotal, or whatever.

Most common of the conversational leads is the ''direct-address'' lead, in which the writer addresses, or speaks to, the reader directly, using the pronoun ''you''—as Debra Kent does in this lead for a *Seventeen* article:

> The first thing you have to know about PMS is that it's real. It's not in your head. You're not crazy. It is *not* just a phase you're going through. It's a condition that affects one third to one half of all American women of reproductive age.

A ''command'' or ''request'' lead uses phrases such as ''consider this,'' or ''wait a minute.'' Often, the pronoun ''you'' is not stated but implied (called ''you understood'' by traditional grammarians).

Another variation of the direct-address lead asks readers a question, as in this lead from the *St. Louis Post-Dispatch:*

> At what age do you send Johnny and Judy to the gym, riding stable, tennis court, ice rink, or ball yard, to develop the skills that just might make them a household name?

Sometimes, the conversational lead doesn't address readers as "you" but includes them in a group to which the writer also belongs, as does this lead by Roy Hoopes from *Modern Maturity* magazine:

> For millions of us, the American Dream means going into business for ourselves; becoming our own boss. It's a daring midlife venture, a game played for real stakes. For those who win, it may be as easy as moving from "Go" to "Collect $200." For those who lose, however, the consequences can be real—and grim.

LANGUAGE LEADS

A variety of feature leads can be grouped generally under the concept of language emphasis. The pleasure they give to readers comes from the writer's dazzling performance with words; the lead suggests further entertainment to readers wise enough to keep reading.

Leads that play with sound effects are language leads. The "staccato" lead creates a short, abrupt sense of the situation because the words themselves are short and end with harsh sounds such as "t" and "k."

Language leads can also simply play with images they create, as Betsy Wade does by personifying the travel industry in this lead for *The New York Times*:

> When the travel industry bites a lemon, luggage makers pucker; since fewer people are taking vacations, luggage sales are expected to be down 5 percent for 1991.

Leads also play with language when they make allusions to familiar sayings readers recognize. For example, this lead from a Knight-Ridder story on a local bar serving goldfish as hors d'oeuvres capitalizes on an expression that most readers already know:

> FORT LAUDERDALE, Fla.—Talk about the fish that got away.
> Just hours from being swallowed alive, two goldfish swam merrily at the Everglades Bar on Wednesday, thanks to a reprieve from the County Health Department.

Allusion leads can also refer to literary sources, quoting something either familiar or obscure. When a literary allusion is well-known, the lead may use the saying in an unusual way or in a different context, one the original writer never intended. When the allusion is obscure, the source is commonly identified immediately, as it is in Michelle Osborn's lead for *USA Today*:

> "Books are the treasured wealth of the world," Thoreau wrote in *Walden*—and that was even before the superstores.*

---

*Copyright 1991, USA Today. Reprinted with permission.

THE QUOTATION LEAD

A quotation lead offers readers the pleasure of reading something particularly well-said, and thus can also be considered a kind of language lead. The quotation in the lead should be quotable (colorful or eloquent), relevant to the story, and capable of making sense without other explanation. Readers shouldn't have to read several paragraphs before they understand what the quotation means. Michael Maxtone-Graham begins a travel article for the *Miami Herald* by effectively using quotations:

> ELBA, Italy—Never known for his modesty, Napoleon once said to his secretary, Bourienne, "You too will be immortal."
>
> "Why?" came the response.
>
> "Well," said the Emperor, "are you not my secretary?"
>
> "Tell me the name of Alexander the Great's secretary," was Bourienne's laconic return.
>
> Although Napoleon's immortality did not rub off on his prescient aide, it did bring enduring fame to this small island to which he was exiled in 1814.

Of course even a bland quotation can be considered language well-said if it summarizes perfectly the focus of an article. For example, this lead, in which Michael Janofsky of *The New York Times* quotes an ecstatic Mike Powell *asking* reporters to interview him, perfectly expresses Powell's exuberant mood:

> TOKYO, Aug. 31—On the day after, his pride was still much in evidence. "Ask me more questions, some fun questions," Mike Powell said during a news conference today, the next-to-last day of the world track and field championships.
>
> His smile was nearly as wide as the landing pit that caught his world-record long jump of 29 feet 4 1/2 inches on Friday night.

FINAL GUIDELINES

Feature leads, as we've said, will not always fit neatly into categories. They may have multiple personalities, combining characteristics of two or more "types" of leads. The leads mentioned in this chapter represent only some of the possible ways of drawing readers into feature stories. You can create innumerable new and different leads with a free hand. You might, however, keep the following thoughts in mind.

First, be sure every word in your lead counts. Don't let the ability to write longer leads lull you into writing empty leads. Test every word to make sure it needs to be in the lead. Eliminate redundancies like "currently is" or "start a plan" and windy phrases like "due to the fact that." Try to think of yourself as paying for every word you use, just as you would if you were buying a classified ad. Discard anything that isn't worth paying for.

Second, choose the words of your lead carefully. Look for the precise word with the precise tone and meaning you want. The words of your lead set the mood for, and begin the message of, the entire story.

Third, concentrate on your audience. The best leads reflect the interests of the people who will be reading. Feature leads work as "advertisements" for the story because they appeal to their chosen audiences.

Finally, reconsider your lead after you've written the entire story. Most of us have trouble getting started and do a certain amount of written stuttering before we get to the point. Sometimes your best lead is buried in later paragraphs, the ones you wrote after you were warmed up.

You may also find that sometimes your best lead lies in your conclusion. A final image, final quote, final statistic, or final irony that you saved for your last paragraph may, after all, be more effective in the lead. If the lead sets the tone and direction of the story, and the conclusion leaves the reader with its most significant meaning and emotion, then the beginning and ending of a story should be, to some extent, similar. Both are intense and important. Both have an impact on the reader. The question is: which more effectively leaves a final feeling or a memorable parting idea, and which one arouses interest and is more likely to draw readers into your story?

EXERCISES

1. How would you categorize the following leads according to the types of leads described in this chapter:

   a. Behold the world's greatest tomato. It is the color of old bubble gum, creased with scabby brown streaks. There's a green protuberance on one side, and the other side is a rumple of lumps and ridges. No matter how you slice it (and slicing it is no easy matter), the Giant Belgium is one ugly vegetable. (*The New York Times*)

   b. QIAPUQIA, China, Aug. 30—While the newly prosperous residents of China's coastal towns build lavish brick homes and dream of sending their children to graduate school abroad, the still-poor inhabitants of western China patch their mud huts and sometimes think of an education as merely an optional extra that in any case ends in the fifth or sixth grade. (*The New York Times*)

   c. Magic Johnson discovered early what too many prime-time athletes learn too late: In these media-saturated times, scoring with the public is just as crucial as scoring for the Los Angeles Lakers. (*USA Today*)

   d. North Florida deputies say it was a serious crime: A group of vandals broke into a vacant home, poured a gallon of motor oil on the carpets and into the dishwasher, smeared their greasy black palm prints on the walls, smashed the light fixtures.

Deputies moved in swiftly last week and made four felony arrests for burglary and criminal mischief. The suspects: Neighborhood playmates—three 6-year-olds and a 4-year-old. (Knight-Ridder)

e. WHY, Ariz.—It was the sweetest and gentlest of desert evenings, pitch-black except for a sliver of new moon and the light from a hundred thousand stars. Nearby, a coyote scampered among the stately organ pipe cactuses, its occasional mournful howl slicing the silence like a jagged knife. (*The New York Times*)

2. Write feature leads for the following news stories:

a. URBANA, Ill. (AP)—Scientists have created rats that produce twice as much sperm as normal—an idea they hope to transfer to livestock to save farmers millions of dollars in breeding costs.

The technique, which involves briefly reducing the level of thyroid hormone, was developed by researchers at the University of Illinois. It next will be tested on cattle and sheep.

b. MACK, Colo. (AP)—Scientists digging in a dusty quarry in western Colorado say they have uncovered remains of what they believe may be a new species of dinosaur—and the largest ever found.

Harley Armstrong of the Museum of Western Colorado and Mike Perry of Dinamation International Corp., which produces dinosaur shows, said they were excavating an apatosaurus' vertebra that weighs at least a ton, is almost 6 feet on one side and 5 feet on the other.

c. WASHINGTON (AP)—Federal health officials announced Friday the largest anti-smoking program in the nation's history, saying it will help 17 states, including New York, counter the "sinister marketing strategies" of tobacco companies.

Health departments in the selected states will receive a total of $115 million over seven years for community-based coalitions. The coalitions will target population groups that are most likely to smoke and will apply proven anti-smoking strategies. . . .

Officials think that the project will help about 4.5 million adults stop smoking, prevent about 2 million young people from starting, and save 1.2 million people from dying prematurely from smoking-related problems.

d. NEW YORK (AP)—A gun-wielding burglar who burst into a family birthday party in Brooklyn was shot and killed when the gathering's host wrestled the weapon away, police said Saturday.

An accomplice was stabbed during the struggle Friday night and arrested. Two partygoers were also stabbed during the fight: both were treated in a local hospital, said Sgt. Ed Burns, a police spokesman.

About 10 people, including children as young as 11 years old, were celebrating a family birthday party in the Flatbush section when the two would-be robbers showed up at 10:15 P.M., Burns said.

3. Write a narrative lead for a front-page sidebar about the experiences of the men mentioned in the article below:

> ANCHORAGE, Alaska (AP)—Five fishermen who spent 11 days adrift in a life raft after their boat sank in the Pacific caught and ate a sea gull and rationed packets of water before they were rescued, one of them said Saturday.
>
> "We took it day by day, night by night," Keith Pendleton, 23, of Lake Stevens, Wash., said by telephone from Sitka Community Hospital.
>
> The five drifted in their raft after their 97-foot crab boat took on water and went down 250 miles off British Columbia. They were rescued by another fishing boat Saturday and were in good condition, the Coast Guard said.

4. Find a lead you find weak, confusing, or stale, and a lead you think is excellent. Share both leads with members of your class for discussion; explain your judgments.

5. On a scale of 1–5 rate five feature leads from features in magazines. Ask others in your class to rate the same leads, without knowing your evaluations. Then match the ratings. Did you agree or disagree about which leads were effective? Discuss why.

6. Below is the lead for William Blundell's "The fatal fraternity of Northwest loggers," a story about loggers and the logging industry written for *The Wall Street Journal.* How does his lead draw his audience into the story? How does it make the story relevant to them? How does the lead "suggest to readers how to approach the entire article"? (Blundell's story was one of several recognized in the 1982 American Society of Newspaper Editors' writing competition; he received first place for non-deadline writing.)

> KALAMA, Wash.—Let us say that you work in an office building with 1,000 people and that every day at least two are hurt on the job. Some suffer such ghastly wounds—multiple compound fractures, deep cuts severing muscle, sinew and nerve, shattered pelvises—that they may never return to their old posts. And every six months or so, a body is taken to the morgue.
>
> Almost anywhere, this would be called carnage, and a hue and cry would be raised. But in the big-tree logging woods of the Pacific Northwest, it is simply endured with what logger-writer Stan Hager has called "proud fatalism," and few outside the loggers' trade even know of it. Miners trapped behind a cave-in draw national media attention, but in the dim rain forests men fall singly and suddenly. There aren't any TV cameras.
>
> Increased stress on training and safety in recent years has helped. But death and injury rates still are extraordinarily high in part because loggers are an almost suicidally prideful and tradition-bound group, hooked on danger and suspicious of new equipment and techniques.

7. Read ''The Love That Saved Birdie Africa,'' written by Michael Capuzzo for the *Inquirer* magazine of *The Philadelphia Inquirer.* Why do you think Capuzzo decided to begin his story with a lead that emphasized present time (''Michael Moses is riding down Main Street. . . .'')? In the lead section, why are two paragraphs italicized? What in the lead shows Capuzzo's awareness of what his concluding paragraphs will say?

(Capuzzo's story won First Place/Feature in the 1989 Sunday Best competition of the Sunday Magazine Editors Association.)

THE LOVE THAT SAVED BIRDIE AFRICA

By Michael Capuzzo
Inquirer Magazine/The Philadelphia Inquirer, *May 8, 1988*

Note:

On Mother's Day, 1985, the Philadelphia police dropped a bomb on the house at 6221 Osage Ave. Inside were followers of radical leader John Africa, founder of the group MOVE, who had been harassing their neighbors, blaring political diatribes over loudspeakers, building barricades and, police believed, stockpiling weapons. Birdie Africa, born Oyewolffe Momer Puim Ward to parents who separated shortly after his birth, was the only child survivor of the fire that engulfed the house. Reunited with his father, Andino Ward, Michael Moses Ward made the transition over the next three years from wild child to modern teenage boy.

Michael Moses Ward is riding down Main Street in a blue Reliant wagon, past the old railroad station and Sally Anne's soda shop. It is an October Friday in a small suburban town outside Philadelphia. School is out, the weekend has arrived. The Pennsylvania sky is wide and streaked with purple and gold. Brown and yellow leaves swirl over the street on a gusting wind.

Autumn is when leaves fall from the trees, his father has told him, *and you feel cooler and you go to school.*

Michael scowls as his stepmother drives past storefront windows full of big pumpkins, Magic Marker signs for the Jaycees Haunted House, wood stacked for the winter.

This is where you live, his father has said. *You have to know the names of the streets. What if you get lost?*

Michael is almost 16, a student who gets A's and B's in math, English, science and social studies, plays linebacker on the Blue Knights, spends Saturdays biking with his friends, and every day rubs his chin wondering if it's time to shave. He smiles shyly at the girls who like him, but can't think of exactly what he should say.

"Your father is mad at you," his stepmother says.

Michael wears a bleached-demin jacket and a never-ending frown. "I don't understand," he protests, his voice cracking from low to high. "Lots of the kids didn't do their homework."

Amal is firm. "Your father says you're grounded."

Amal turns right at the 7-Eleven and parks two blocks down, before a small white house with a pine tree in the front yard. Michael retreats quickly to the living room, where the setting sun comes through golden curtains. While the Knights practice without him, Michael takes refuge in television.

He watches as Dan Rather, Cybill Shepherd, Weaver's Chicken Nuggets and Michael J. Fox flash before his eyes. Then *Family Ties* is interrupted by a commercial, paid for by mayoral candidate Frank Rizzo. "May 13, 1985" appears on a black screen. A voiceover intones, "Wilson Goode tells us not to judge him on the events of one day. . . ."

Michael watches without expression as the commercial flickers before him, then he smiles when *Family Ties* comes back on, the story of a normal American family, his story now. No visible trace remains of the wild child he was raised to be, no vestige of Birdie Africa, except for the scars, scars whose surface smoothness belies their depth and angry origin. . . .

. . . In the gray light before dawn on May 13, 1985, Birdie Africa awakened on the floor of 6221 Osage Ave. to the bullhorn voice of Gregore Sambor. Birdie was 13 years old, but he knew few words and could write only one— MOVE. Even so, he understood what the police commissioner meant when he called for "surrender."

Now, the confrontation—the one the Big People had said was coming, the one he had been keeping strong for by boxing with the other children and eating raw garlic—was beginning. Shots were fired, bullet after bullet. The children and women took refuge in the basement. With his mother, Rhonda, and Phil, his best friend, Birdie huddled under a wool blanket that had been soaked in water. The basement was dark. Fortifications blocked the windows. Hours passed, hours of pounding footsteps, breaking glass, gunfire and tense silences. Water dripped from the ceiling, spurted through the windows and rushed down the drain.

Explosions shook the house. Tear gas stung Birdie's eyes. He was small and he was afraid.

Then there was a big blast. The men ran downstairs. The basement got hotter. Burning debris fell from overhead. The house was on fire.

Rad ran downstairs and told the children they were going to have to leave. They didn't want to go. They were afraid of the police. They were afraid they would never see the grown-ups again. But the men started screaming, "The kids coming out! The kids coming out!"

Birdie saw Rad unbolt the cellar door and stick his head out, but there were shots, and he said the kids couldn't go yet. Black smoke filled the room and made it hard to breathe. The children started screaming, "We wanna come out! We wanna come out!" Rad tried one more time. The grown-ups were hollering, "The kids coming out!"

Rhonda was holding Tomasa in her arms. He was 9, the youngest one in the house. Suddenly Tomasa became quiet, and Birdie saw Rhonda slap him on the back, trying to revive him. Tomasa cried just one more time, but then he stopped altogether and made no more noise.

All the children were weeping now. The basement was noisy and chaotic. They were crying, "We wanna come out!" The heat grew unbearable, and Birdie got ready to die.

The children lined up to leave. Birdie was the last. Phil was in front of him. Phil's skin was melting. Rhonda was behind Birdie, and she pushed him out. He ran from the house into the alley behind, stumbling through the tongues of flame. All around him were snapping electrical wires, burning trees and swirling clouds of smoke. The ground scorched Birdie's bare feet. It was so hot, he couldn't walk and he fell.

Shadowy forms moved in the dusk. Birdie pulled himself weakly to his feet, but he could only walk in a daze.

Ramona was up a walkway, and she reached down for him. "C'mon, Birdie," she cried, "c'mon Birdie!" A police officer nearby hollered. "C'mon c'mon c'mon, kid, c'mon, son, run," but all Birdie could see was Ramona, telling him to climb up, calling him, he was moving so slowly, but when he put one foot on the wall, he lost his grip and fell straight back on the concrete. When he got up, he wobbled and began to fall again, into the deep puddled water from fire hoses.

"C'mon, son! C'mon, son!"

Then the police officer was there. He grabbed him, pulling him like a helpless puppy away from the treacherous water, and ran with him down the street. Birdie's pants fell off his burned body, and as he was carried to safety he begged, "Don't shoot me, don't shoot me!"

On Wednesday, Richard Ward, a salesman at Brooks Brothers, called his son, Andino. He'd gotten a tip from one of his customers who was a police officer. "Dino," he said "the boy in the hospital is your son."

Andino ran home to tell Amal, and together they prayed and cried. "Our prayers have been answered," Andino said.

That afternoon, Andino found Oyewolffe's birth certificate, met with a city Human Services official to prove he was the father, then rushed to Children's Hospital. He raged at police officers who frisked him, but when he saw his small, bandaged son, surrounded by nurses, Andino started to cry.

One nurse said to Birdie, "Do you know who that is?"

As Andino watched, full of emotion, Birdie looked up. "Yeah," he said. "That's my father."

Andino couldn't believe it. He ran over and kissed and hugged and held his long-lost son. "I love you," he kept repeating. "I'm so glad to see you. You have nothing to be afraid of anymore. This time everything is going to be OK."

Birdie seemed happy. But Andino realized the boy still thought his mother was alive. Holding his son, drinking in the very sight of him, he silently promised to devote the rest of his life to the boy. He would heal him and help him and never, never would they lose one another again.

At their home, Amal needed to tell her little girls about MOVE, so she drew crayon pictures on a napkin at the kitchen table.

"There was a house," she explained. "A helicopter came over and dropped a bomb. Then the house was on fire. Eleven people died in the fire, but one little boy lived. He was Daddy's son from another marriage, and now he's coming to live with us. It's like a fairy tale."

That night Andino met with Ramona Shannon, Birdie's grandmother. For years Shannon had visited her daughter and grandson in MOVE, bringing food and clothes and begging Rhonda to leave. For years Shannon had cherished the idea of having her grandson safe and with her. But now she agreed that Andino could offer the boy more energy and family support. The next day they went together to tell Birdie that his mother was dead.

"Birdie," Shannon said gently, "Rhonda didn't make it. If you want to cry, go ahead and cry."

"But she was right behind me!" the boy protested. "She was right behind me!" He burst into tears.

Shannon said what she could to comfort him. "God saved you, Birdie, and your mother's gone to heaven. And now you have your father. Your father loves you. And you have me."

But the tears "just kept pouring out of his eyes," Shannon remembered later. "It was so sad, I couldn't watch anymore."

Nurses monitored Birdie Africa as if he had come from another planet. How little he knew!

"When opening anything, using anything, allow Birdie to see it first," a nurse wrote in her notes, "and always explain what you are doing in very simple concrete terms. . . . Birdie is very bright in some areas, but is like a newborn."

"Needs to learn how to brush his own teeth. Never attended school," she wrote, although Birdie said he had been taught "to be good."

Andino Takes Birdie Home

At 7 the next morning, Andino carried his heavily bandaged son to a warm tub and gently sponged him clean. Kneeling, he peeled a single bandage off—and dead skin with it—and his son began to scream. With wet gauze, Andino rubbed off the remaining dead skin, medicated salve and white puss. He rubbed hard, as the nurses had taught him, until the wounds bled.

"He was screaming and hollering, and he looked so terrible to begin with, it was just terrible to see," Andino said. "I had to be as strong as I possibly could. I couldn't let him know how I felt about it."

Debriding had to be repeated, three to four hours each time, twice a day, every day for four months. In a windowless bathroom in the small suburban apartment, from summer into fall, Birdie Africa cried with the pain of healing and the pain of loss.

"It was excruciating for him every day, but I had to be the bad guy," said Andino. "I'd tell him he'd lose an arm or a leg from infection, you have to endure this. . . . I'd give him a break for 10 or 15 minutes, get some juice, rub his head and try to let him know, keep telling him, 'This too shall pass.'"

Sometimes it was more than even Andino could stand. He'd get up quietly, leaving Birdie in the tub, and go out of the bathroom to cry by himself, where the boy wouldn't see him. "I kept telling him, 'It won't always be like this, son. What's happening now, you'll remember as a bad dream. This too shall pass.'"

Between burn sessions, Birdie would never leave his father's side.

The boy's needs soon overwhelmed the two-bedroom apartment and the young family of five. Finances were tight. Andino took Sophia out of private school and stopped her piano lessons. The family quickly exhausted their small savings, which had been set aside for their new house. That dream now seemed like a fantasy from ages ago. Amal took in sewing and went to work at a pretzel bakery, on the midnight shift.

Andino and Amal gave up their bedroom to Birdie and slept in the living room on a sofa bed. They sold their double bed, their stereo system, their dining room furniture. They sold almost everything they had.

Richard Ward was worried. He wondered about the wisdom of Andino's giving up his job. So he drove to his son's house to find out what was going on.

"Andino was in the bathroom," the grandfather said, and the boy "was hollering out and crying for his mother . . . 'Mommy, Mommy, Mommy.' And I couldn't watch anymore. I walked out of the bathroom into the bedroom where Amal was changing [the bed] and I started to help her and she just broke down crying. She said, 'Andino goes through this every single day,' and she just cried. I embraced her, but she just kept crying. In fact, it almost made me cry to hear her cry and hearing him scream, 'Mommy, Mommy' five, 10 minutes straight for two hours."

When they had a moment to talk, Andino explained to his father, "I quit my job because I couldn't ask my wife to do what I had to do. I can't ask anybody else to do what I have to do."

Two years later, sitting over a cup of coffee in a local restaurant, Andino burst into tears. Oblivious to the stares of patrons and waitresses, he described those early awful days, how the shared pain of scrubbing his son's burns became a bond.

"I think I showed him, if nothing else, that I'm a man of my word," Andino said, tears streaming down his cheeks. "If nothing else, I told him, it will get better. All he has to be is strong enough to deal with this. This too shall pass."

Birdie had lost 17 1/2 pounds, down to 77 1/2, in the hospital. Amal let him snack on raw vege-tables. Putting weight on him seemed too important to quibble about how it got there.

But to Andino, uncooked food was his son's strongest connection to MOVE. So on Sunday, June 2, when Amal took the girls to church, Andino stayed home. He was running the bathwater when Birdie asked for a sweet potato.

"I thought, There's no time like the present to start rearranging his thought processes," Andino said. "I told him, 'No, you cannot have a raw sweet potato. That's over. You did that in MOVE. . . . You're going to have to eat normal foods like everyone else.' "

Andino was astonished at his son's reaction. Bandaged and weak, hobbling on burned feet, unable because of scar tissue to move his left arm, Birdie attacked.

"He became violent, trying to hit me, and I had to restrain him," Andino said. "He tried to run out of the room and I grabbed him and we went down on the floor. We wrestled hard for 20 minutes."

Andino felt as if he were wrestling with a dead John Africa for the very soul of his son.

"I held him and I pinned him and I said, 'There's going to be no more raw sweet potatoes.' I tried not to hurt his burns. I said, 'I can fight you all you want, but you're going to get tired before I do.' "

Birdie tried to go out the front door. Andino stopped him. He hobbled into his bedroom and started to climb out the window. Andino stopped him again. He said he was going to leave and "walk back to MOVE."

"No, you're not going back to MOVE," Andino said. "MOVE is gone and you're here now and you're going to eat normal foods like everyone else."

When the fight was over, Andino gave his son time to cool down. Birdie watched television in the living room. "It's a new life now," Andino told him, "and this is the way it's going to be. There'll be no raw food."

Birdie stared stonily at the TV. When Andino called him for his bath, the boy refused to come.

"I let him sit there and watch the Three Stooges," said Andino, "and suddenly he was crying and I said . . . 'It's OK for you to cry, but I want you to understand I'm your father, and this is the first thing on a list of things we're going to deal with.' "

Birdie looked up. "I don't care if you hate me at this point," Andino said. "I still love you and, the reason I'm doing this is I love you. I don't care how much we fight, I'll still love you."

Birdie said nothing. He just looked at his father and kept crying.

Forty-five minutes later, Andino got the bandages ready and freshened the bathwater.

"I was frightened," he said. "I was taking a calculated risk and praying to God it would work. I came up to him and said, 'OK, son, it's time for your bath.' I was ready to pick him up physically and put him in the tub, pajamas and all, if he resisted. I thought, here goes the next fight."

Andino was surprised once again.

"He got up. I was thrilled."

In the bathtub, Birdie "screamed more than usual that day. His rage and grief came out . . . It was like a large child crying and ranting—throwing a temper tantrum. When the tantrum was over, I told him, 'Now that you're done, I want you to know I still love you. It's going to be this way. It's a new world.' "

Birdie Africa never asked for uncooked food again.

In July, Birdie stood only 4 feet, 7 inches tall and weighed less than 80 pounds when his father took him, shy and frightened, to visit Solomon Katz, a biological anthropologist and child growth expert at the University of Pennsylvania. Katz, an authority on primitive diets and culture, was astonished at the 13-year-old's size.

"He was much closer in development to a Third World child than a normal Philadelphia child," Katz said. "He was so thin and frail . . . and very shy, like he hadn't had contact with people. . . . He reminded me of a feral child."

In his office, Katz charted the tragic result of MOVE philosophy. Birdie's diet, even more primitive than that of hunting and gathering tribes, had delayed his physical and intellectual development. He would never recover fully what he had lost.

In one sense, Katz said, Birdie had remained remarkably pure, as John Africa had intended. He had no cavities. Without exposure to junk food, his teeth were perfect.

Katz was concerned about the isolation from society Birdie had suffered. He lacked the skills of other children. His closest friends were all dead. Would he be able to relate to normal children his age? Birdie seemed worried himself. In a voice so meek that Katz had to bend closer to hear it, Birdie asked, "Who will I be playing with?"

By the end of June, Andino's strategy had begun to take shape: To prepare Birdie for school in September, he would have to remake his son's social and personal habits—deprogramming 11 1/2 years of MOVE in two months.

One of Andino's biggest challenges was convincing his wild child he was wild. In MOVE, the children were considered the "pure ones," and Birdie thought he knew everything he needed to know. "I kept telling him," Andino said, "you have to realize your deficiencies."

In early July, Andino told Birdie that in a new life, he needed a new name and asked if he wanted to be called Junior. Birdie shook his head, no. So Andino read names from the Bible. Birdie chose Michael, the Archangel, the fighter. Andino gave his son the middle name Moses, "because you are like Moses. You were saved, you were drawn from water."

In mid-August Andino trimmed Michael's three-quarter-inch fingernails. In MOVE, cutting fingernails, like combing hair, was a corruption of natural growth. When Michael resisted, Andino promised him a toy. Michael flinched at every clip. Afterward, they went to Toys R Us, and Michael picked out a Transformer.

As his burns healed, Andino said, Michael needed to learn how to take a shower. "He said showers weren't necessary—he would go down to the creek and swim and that would be his bath," Andino said. He taught his son how to wash, and every day for three weeks he would inspect the boy to make sure he had showered properly.

Slowly Michael Moses Ward began to look like a suburban teenager, with short hair and sports shirts and sneakers, "but he was still holding on as much as possible to the ideologies of MOVE," Andino said.

In late July, Richard Ward took Michael and Sophia to *My Bodyguard,* Michael's first movie. The grandfather didn't notice the PG rating.

"Suddenly it's all these young kids cursing, and they're half dressed . . . ," Richard Ward said. "So I said to Michael, 'This isn't the kind of movie we should be seeing.' . . . I must have had to say to him three times, 'Let's go.' And he pouted and he didn't make any effort to get up because now I'm standing and my granddaughter is standing, and that's when I picked him up."

To the astonishment of Richard Ward—and movie-goers nearby—Michael unleashed a stream of MOVE obscenities. Ward was enraged. He dragged his grandson home.

At home, Andino said, "This is the last time you'll go anywhere until you get your act together. You better not open your mouth ever again like that or let words like that come out."

"He fought hard to preserve who he was," Andino said, "until he realized who he was wasn't very pleasant."

Over dinner one night, Andino explained to Michael that he would be going to school soon and would have to be tested to see what he knew. Michael was disconsolate. "I don't know anything," he said.

Andino asked Jules Abrams, director of psychology at Hahnemann University, to evaluate his son to determine what schooling and tutoring he would need.

In a series of tests, Michael couldn't do math, spell or even recognize letters. He couldn't name which month came after March, who discovered America or in what direction the sun set. He couldn't count, "His scores were all below first-grade level," Abrams said. The average IQ of the general population ranges from 90 to 109. Michael's IQ was 57, generally the level of profoundly retarded people who will never be able to care for themselves.

Abrams held out some hope, since Michael came from intelligent parents and the tests measured what he had absorbed from his environment. "In MOVE, he hadn't had the opportunity to acquire anything," Abrams said. "He was suffering from cognitive deprivation, a lack of exposure to society. He had learned absolutely nothing."

The question was, how much of his intellectual functions would the boy ever recover?

On Oct. 12, Andino took his son to Philadelphia. In an office sat William H. Brown 3d, chairman of the MOVE special investigation commission. Speaking gently, Brown interviewed Michael for two hours about the Osage fire. Michael, obedient but terrified, talked about the location of MOVE houses, John Africa and other MOVE members.

"He was a frightened little child, and he didn't want to do it," Andino said. "He had a fear MOVE was going to hurt him if he talked about things MOVE normally never talked about."

Three months later, in January 1986, Michael was called as a defense witness for Ramona Africa, the only other survivor of the MOVE fire. She was accused of aggravated assault, conspiracy and other charges stemming from the May 13, 1985, disaster. David Shrager, the Wards' attorney, had made elaborate plans to conceal Michael's appearance at the trial, but when he, Andino and Michael got off the elevator in City Hall, they were confronted by TV cameras and lights and people behind a barricade, some of them MOVE sympathizers, some just followers of the case.

"They were whispering, 'It's Birdie,' " said Shrager, "and all of a sudden they were yelling, 'It's Birdie! Birdie!' They were treating him like a folk hero almost."

Michael was petrified. Andino rushed him into the courtroom.

When security people brought Ramona in, she caught Michael's eye. "A deep and sincere smile came across her face," said Shrager, "a very warm smile. To me it was very poignant . . . as though he'd come into the presence of a loving aunt who hadn't seen him. I thought I saw a tear in her eye." Michael averted his eyes.

Ramona was acting as her own attorney. In the presence of Andino and Shrager, she spoke to Michael in a quiet voice, very soothingly, for a few minutes, explaining, "It'll be all right. I'm just going to ask you a few questions."

Michael nodded but never looked up.

Then Ramona quickly began speaking in MOVE jargon, an attempt, it seemed to Shrager, to rekindle their old ties.

"OK, that's it," the attorney said, and he broke off the conversation.

On the witness stand Michael answered in a small childish voice while looking down. Only once did he raise his voice, when talking about the fire.

"Did you think somebody was trying to hurt you?" Ramona asked.

"Yeah!" said Michael.

"Did you think they were trying to kill you?"

"YEAH!" he said.

After the long testimony, Shrager and Andino steered Michael through a side door, past a police officer and guard dog, into the early evening air. A light snow was falling, and as they led Michael under the city, along the concourse to Suburban Station, he was totally quiet, deep in his own thoughts.

A few months later, Michael had to testify yet again, before the state grand jury. Before each legal appearance, before each visit to the doctor, Michael's nights would be a torment of nightmares. He and Phil, Tree, Rad and his mother were running, "running and running and running, and a fire was chasing us." Searing flames would trap him and his family, leaving no escape. He and his father would run into a burning house filled with monsters. The world and all its buildings and all its people were on fire.

It's over, his father would tell him, you're safe, you're all right. Every night, Michael knelt by his bed and said the Lord's Prayer, asking God to make his nightmares go away.

By the end of his first school year, Michael had advanced to almost a third-grade level. His IQ had leaped to 74, with a nonverbal IQ of 82, close to average. "It was just remarkable," Abrams, the psychologist, said. "He was a blank slate. With just an ordinary amount of stimulation, he made tremendous gains."

In his second year of school, Michael began to notice something wrong with the other students. He wondered why they weren't as sharp as the kids he played with on weekends. He asked Kathy, his new teacher, why they still couldn't read and write.

Even among these educable mentally retarded (EMR) students, though, Michael struggled to keep up. He was flustered when they knew "Mary Had a Little Lamb" and he had never heard it. He was angry when he couldn't understand how to read a thermometer and they could. "I never had that," he'd say. "Give me a break."

Andino met with Michael's teachers every three months. At the next meeting, Kathy said Michael was having problems. Maybe there was a limit to what he could learn, she said gently. Maybe he would never catch up.

Andino was furious.

He is GOING to learn this," he answered. "I don't want to set up a failure. I don't want you to baby him. I don't want to hear about limits and neither does my son. Push him as far as he can go!"

A new set of rules was imposed: Homework would have to be completed before Michael went out to play. After dinner, Michael would read two chapters of a Hardy boys novel and then start on Bible verses. At bedtime, he'd read them back to his father. Television would be restricted.

"It was so difficult for him to learn things," Andino said. "His concentration was so intense, he'd give himself a headache. He'd jerk up his body and frown his face up so hard and want to get up and walk away, and I'd have to calm him down: 'Look, you can't fall apart like this. This is what it's all about. But have no fear. You will get this.' "

Michael was having trouble with division. He'd come home from school with 10 homework problems. Once he'd done those, his father would say, "Fine, now here's 20 more." Every night, Andino would stay up late, making up math problems.

Once, Michael came down, near tears, saying he just couldn't do it.

"You can do it," said Andino. "You will do it. You're going to do it.

"I'd send him back to his room five times. I'd say, 'This is the principle you use for this problem, now go back, go back, go back, go back, go back. You like riding bikes, Mike, you like video games, you like swimming and football, but football isn't going to feed you. This is going to feed you.'

"Every new thing the teacher taught, he'd fret and fuss, bang his head against the wall for two weeks, and then he'd finally get it," Andino said. It was then that Andino noticed something special about his son. Every time Michael mastered a problem, he would move on to the next as though he'd never been frustrated before. Michael seemed to have the gift of forgetting pain.

By June 1987, Michael was writing three- or four-paragraph stories. The child who hadn't been able to recognize letters was reading 135 words a minute, slightly behind the 150–200 words a minute a normal 15-year-old reads.

"You could see his new confidence," said Kathy, his teacher. ". . . All of a sudden he became a warm, friendly person and would get this big glowing smile on his face. And I started to see the true Michael emerge."

Andino began to think that in MOVE his son had developed remarkable character. "He's vehement, frenzied, hungry. He has incentive. . . . He's amazed his teachers, he's amazed me. All of a sudden he hurtled out of nowhere."

A few days before Christmas 1987, Andino takes Michael shopping in the mall. He has just turned 16. It will be his third Christmas home. He seems happy.

In less than three years, the imprint of MOVE's indoctrination seems to have vanished. Tiny, malnourished Birdie Africa has grown almost a foot and gained 40 pounds. Every time he gets in the car now, he says, "Dad, when are you going to teach me to drive?" He wants a Corvette; he wants a summer job at McDonald's; he wants to go to normal school. He is still shy around strangers, but he is a "chatterbox" at home, and he has the savvy of any 16-year-old around his friends. His last five report cards have put him on the honor roll. In the last year, he has become impeccably groomed. He is now in EMR eighth grade.

Andino already talks to his son about college and marriage, about safe sex. People who are happy for the boy stop him in the mall. Some send him gifts. One woman has named her baby Michael after him. "He is a miracle," Amal believes. "He is a miracle from God."

Michael dreams of being a carpenter, a stunt bicycle racer, a professional football player. "You can be anything you want to be," his father always says.

But Andino still worries. At what age will Michael be able to take care of himself? How will he come to view MOVE, the bombing of his house, the death of his mother? What wounds lie below the surface?

"This is always going to be with him, always, throughout his life," says Andino. "Whenever he looks at his body, whenever he looks in a mirror and thinks, 'I don't have a mother'. . . . If he doesn't have the proper perspective, he could return to his origins," become isolated and embittered.

Michael will live with the physical scars of MOVE until the 1990s. After three operations, he faces at least six more to remove his scars. As daunting, perhaps, will be his testimony in the future in the case of Michael Moses Ward vs. the City of Philadelphia. The Wards' lawsuit contends that the city violated Michael's civil rights in the Osage Avenue disaster.

"When he smiles he can light up a room," says David Shrager, "but he still has a look on him sometimes like a guy who's been on the narrow edge and wondering, Could it happen again?"

Rhonda Harris Ward's burned remains lie buried near the middle of St. Albans Cemetery in West Oak Lane, in a circle of trees, far from the sounds of Cheltenham Avenue. Every Mother's Day, Michael Moses Ward stands quietly by his mother's grave. He does not cry, does not show emotion. Andino has worried that trips to Michael's former world will depress or even cripple his son. But again and again, he discovers his son's strength of character.

"I encourage him always to go talk to his mother, to tell his mother how he's doing and how he feels, that he misses her," Andino says. "I walk away and let him talk privately."

After last year's visit, Andino walked his son back to the Plymouth wagon for the long drive home. They drove past shiny new office buildings, church steeples and grassy hills, on a highway Michael doesn't know to a place he can't easily find on a map.

You have to know the names of the streets, his father tells him. What if you get lost?

I'll just go to the street sign and read it, Michael says now. And I'll go to a phone and call you.

Some Basic Feature Stories

CHAPTER

Narratives
Telling What Happens Next

Generally speaking, narratives are stories of action. They describe something happening. When we say someone is telling a narrative, or narrating, we usually mean that person is telling a story that flows chronologically: this happened, then that happened, and then this happened.

As we listen to a story, we want to know what happens next. The plot pulls us on as the story moves to its climax and eventually its conclusion. A narrative lead, we said earlier, is one that starts at the beginning or in the middle of the action and creates in readers the desire to read on to see what happens next. So too, the narrative story pulls readers on because primarily they want to know what happens and how the situation described in the story works out.

BEGINNING IN THE MIDDLE

Jane Schorer of *The Des Moines Register* won the 1991 Pulitzer Prize for Meritorious Public Service with a dramatic five-part series on a woman who was raped; Part I leads with the beginning of what promises to be an ordinary day for that woman:

> She would have to allow extra driving time because of the fog.

A few paragraphs later the action begins:

> She had 25 minutes to sit in the car and review her notes.
> Suddenly the driver's door opened. She turned to see a man, probably in his late 20s, wearing a navy pin-striped suit. He smelled of alcohol.
> "Move over," the man ordered, grabbing her neck. She instinctively reached up to scratch him, but he was stronger than she was. He pushed a

white dish towel into her face and shoved her into the front passenger seat, reclining it to a nearly horizontal position. Then he took her denim jacket from the back seat and covered her head.

Is there a reader alive who could stop reading Schorer's narrative at this point and not continue to find out what happens next? Her writing is a perfect example of how a narrative starts in the middle of dramatic action and hooks readers, compelling them to stay with the story until their curiosity is satisfied. (Part I in its entirety appears at the end of this chapter.)

NARRATIVES IN OTHER FEATURES

Almost any journalistic story that begins with people caught in some kind of predicament and then resolves their difficulties, either pleasantly or unpleasantly, can be considered a narrative. An abundance of such stories are published; many of them have won the Pulitzer Prize for Feature Writing. Storytelling, after all, has been popular with mankind for a very long time, so long that no one can be sure who told the first narrative—probably a cave man around a fire. The Bible is filled with narratives that are a well-established part of our culture, and narratives are connected to our earliest personal memories, memories of being told stories by our parents before we went to bed.

Many kinds of feature stories rely on narrative writing, so the category of "narratives" does not have clear-cut boundaries. A story known as a "human interest" article may be written in a narrative structure, for example, but in referring to that story, we identify it as "human interest," because it appeals to our interest in human beings.

Some longer feature stories, such as backgrounders, rely on short narratives interspersed with factual writing or analysis to keep the reader interested and compelled to read on. Regular news stories also use narratives occasionally to explain events: For example, the play-by-play information in the middle of a sports game coverage story is a narrative, as is the long account in a news crime story of the police chase after a suspect.

THE HOURGLASS

A combination narrative/inverted pyramid story form, called "the hourglass" by Roy Peter Clark ("A New Shape for the News," *Washington Journalism Review*), can be used for either news or features. The hourglass begins with an inverted pyramid summary of events ("the top"), which gives readers all the pertinent information about the event, then moves through a narrow "turn," a sentence which shifts the story's direction, and then to a fuller narrative.

In a story about a cat frozen to the underside of a station wagon fender, Dave Condren of *The Buffalo News* uses the hourglass structure. He summarizes the basic facts of the story in the second paragraph of his top:

> It's a tale with a semi-happy ending about a stray that survived more than 36 hours of incarceration inside a block of ice. The ordeal is going to cost the 4-month-old tom the tip of his tail but in exchange he has gained a name and found a home.

Further summary information continues, and readers could end the story if they chose at paragraph seven (or even paragraph two), with all the pertinent knowledge of the event related. If, however, readers would like to learn more about the chain of events leading to the belated discovery of the cat and his rehabilitation, they can be led by a "turn" into an 18-paragraph narrative. The turn basically says something like "it all began this way," or as Condren writes it:

> Miss Horner, director of the Cattaraugus County Department of the Aging, saw Morris for the first time one morning when. . . .

LINEAR TIME

There are certain feature stories, however, for which the primary "feel," or entire appeal, is narrative. These stories are dominated by a sense of time. Time is a constant throughout, whether the events in the story unfold in strict chronological order or through a series of flashbacks or other time manipulations. Narratives are usually recognizable by the fact that so many of the article's paragraphs begin with or contain words that suggest a point in time or a movement in time. For example, *New York Times* reporter Chris Hedges' personal narrative on being held captive by Iraqi soldiers, which won the 1992 Scripps Howard Foundation National Journalism Award for Human Interest Writing, uses such phrases as "for the first few moments," "one by one we were taken," "after our interrogation," and "the next morning, at first light," to begin paragraphs and to move the action straightforward chronologically.

Sometimes the "time" words dominating the article don't suggest a single continuous flow of action so much as action that jumps back and forth between various scenes—a sort of "meanwhile, back at the ranch" approach. Relman Morin won a Pulitzer Prize for National Reporting for his 1957 Associated Press news color coverage of the integration of Central High School in Little Rock, Arkansas. The story depicts several scenes of action, which particularly contrast the atmosphere inside the school and "the howling, shrieking crowd of men and women" outside the school. His article is controlled by transition time phrases, such as "Inside, meanwhile, students reported seeing Negroes with blood on their clothes," and "Suddenly, on a street leading toward the school" or "Inside, it was reported, the eight Negro students were in the office of the principal" and "Meanwhile, on the streets."

The simplest and in some ways the most natural way to write the narrative story is as straightforward, linear time; that is, as a series of events happening chronologically through time from beginning to end. Real-life events that already have a great deal of drama and suspense are particularly suitable for this kind of start-to-finish narration—stories telling about such events as a plane almost crashing, a climber reaching the top of a mountain, or a victim escaping from the clutches of a would-be murderer. These stories virtually tell themselves, and the clever feature writer simply moves the action forward as smoothly as possible.

THE RACE AGAINST THE CLOCK

A particular kind of linear narrative especially popular is known as the ''race against the clock'' story. This feature portrays human beings racing to reach a particular goal or to accomplish a certain action before time runs out; for instance, a story about a medical worker who has to locate a kidney for a transplant before the patient dies. The article, along the way of telling about the race, may reveal interesting characteristics of human behavior under pressure, or take time to explain why the system works the way it does, or why time is crucial to success or failure.

George Weller of the Chicago *Daily News* won a 1943 Pulitzer Prize for Reporting for a race-against-the-clock story, an account of an emergency appendectomy performed in a submarine during World War II by a pharmacist's mate. Complete with happy ending, the story details the step-by-step surgical procedure that saved the life of a young sailor whose bad appendix couldn't wait to reach safe hospital surgery ashore. The article makes satisfying reading, partly because sympathetic readers want to find out if the young sailor survives the procedure, but also because readers get to see the resourcefulness of the other shipmates, who use their ingenuity to ''find'' the appropriate surgical instruments:

> When you are going to have an operation, you must have some kind of antiseptic agent. Rummaging in the medicine chest, they found sulfanilamide tablets and ground them into powder. One thing was lacking: there was no means of holding open the wound after the incision had been made. Surgical tools used for this are called ''muscular retractors.'' What would they use for retractors? There was nothing in the medicine chest that gave the answer, so they went as usual to the cook's galley.
>
> In the galley they found tablespoons made of Monel metal. They bent these at right angles and had their retractors.
>
> Sterilizers? They went to one of the greasy copper-colored torpedoes waiting beside the tubes. They milked alcohol from the torpedo mechanism and used it as well as boiling water.

The light in the wardroom seemed insufficient; operating rooms always have big lamps. So they brought one of the big floods used for night loading and rigged it inside the wardroom's sloping ceiling.

Not every narrative feature article, however, lends itself to straightforward linear narration; or perhaps the writer has a secondary purpose for writing the story that makes another ordering of time, a different sequencing of events, more desirable. For example, if you want to emphasize the contrast between conditions in the present and conditions in the past, you might want to start the narrative in the present, then flash back to the beginning of the chain of events. That way your readers see everything about the past through the lens of what they know the present to be; their knowledge of the present colors their understanding and changes their perspective as they read.

Sometimes a narrative has not one flashback, but several, so that the story moves forward through time in a pattern that is more like two steps forward, one step back. This sort of sequence is useful if you want to mimic human thought more closely, which deals constantly with many separate memories of the past as it deals with present sorrows or joys. Such a pattern is also useful for heightening suspense: you tease readers by giving them just enough forward action to keep them hooked, enough action to keep them reading on to see how it all comes out. Meanwhile, you use flashbacks to flesh out the characters of people in the story or give background information or factual details that enhance the story's meaning.

A popular mystery story narrative technique, also widely used by journalists, is frequently employed when the story concerns several people who begin not knowing one another and end coming together by chance at a particular dramatic moment—a story, for example about the rescue of a swimmer attacked by a shark or the saving of someone who falls into the fast-moving river just above Niagara Falls. In this technique, several narrative lines run through the story. The writer first tells what happens to person X from time A to time B, then flashes back to begin the story again as person Y experiences the same time period, and so on for all the people. After all the people have passed from time A to B, the writer starts over again for all the characters, this time bringing them from time C to time D—and so on, and so on, as the people move closer and closer to the moment in time when their lives intersect. Usually, as the writer moves toward the dramatic moment, the time periods shorten so that there is a spiraling effect as the action tightens and the pace of events quickens.

CONDENSING AND EXPANDING TIME

When you're writing narratives, it's important to remember that there is more flexibility in using time as a dominant story element than you might have previously thought; that is, time can be changed and manipulated in several ways to enhance meaning and reinforce the emotional appeal of the message.

For example, we're all familiar with the phrase "time stood still" or with the concept of "my whole life passed before my eyes in a matter of seconds" when someone has a near-death experience. What we understand by these phrases is, simply, that time seems to condense or expand in our human perception. When we're bored, an afternoon drags on interminably; when we're having fun, a week flashes by. And in moments of intense emotion, time is experienced in a special way: 60 seconds of humiliation can seem to last forever. Narrative writers work with the condensation and expansion of time, slowing or quickening the pace of their writing to create in readers the sense that the way they experience time as they read matches the emotional passing of time in the story's historical events.

CIRCULAR TIME

We tend most often to think of time, whether condensed or expanded, as linear, because our lives are linear; we go from birth to death. But human beings also have a strong sense of circular time; that is, of time returning in a circle to the point where things began. We experience this circularity each day of our linear lives as we greet 7 A.M. and dawn yet again. And the seasons of the year return faithfully in this circular pattern: spring, summer, fall, winter, then spring once more. Religions and mythology emphasize, to a greater or lesser degree, this circular sense of human life—birth, death, and rebirth.

Stories that are dominated primarily by the passage of time, then, deal not only with linear time but also circular time. When newspapers and magazines fill their pages with anniversary stories, or how-to articles about fertilizing the lawn in the spring, or holiday features, they are capitalizing on the appeal of stories that remind us of circular time.

A DAY IN THE LIFE OF

One popular feature article that deals with the circular time of daily routine is the "day-in-the-life-of" feature. To write this story, a journalist literally follows his or her subject around for a day, observing what that person does, taking notes all the while, asking questions about why something is done a certain way, or how the subject feels about what he or she is doing each and every day. The story usually is written as straight linear time, sometimes with diary-type entries for each section (e.g., Tuesday, 9 A.M.), but the implication is strong that after the "today" which the journalist observes will come many similar tomorrows in a pattern of circular time.

To some extent, the title "day in the life of" is a misnomer, because the story can be written about any time period the journalist cares to observe. It can be "a night in the life of," an "afternoon in the life of" or "a week in the life of." The story relies heavily on the journalist's ability to expand and condense time. For example, if you were writing about a day in the life of a politician, you might write only briefly about a two-hour meeting in which he or she plays a minor role, but devote more time and space in your story to the politician's 20-minute chat with constituents, in order to demonstrate his or her ability to work the crowd and gain votes.

The day-in-the-life-of story can offer readers many kinds of understandings about a typical day and its relevance to readers' lives. For example, an article about the 36-hour shift of a young internist at a local hospital can interest readers because it explains why the attention and service they receive in emergency rooms is the quality it is, or the story can raise questions about the medical profession's insistence on this kind of rigorous tour of duty before one becomes a doctor, or it can present in human terms the sacrifice the young medical intern makes by not having time to spend with his or her family.

Many day-in-the-life-of stories deal with public servants—police, fire officials, ambulance crew members—in part because these people do have more interesting days than normal, run-of-the-mill workers, but also because the articles help readers understand and appreciate the services performed for them, services for which the reader is usually paying tax dollars or fees.

The day-in-the-life-of story, however, can also be about people who lead less exciting lives. Articles about ''invisible'' people around us, people who do things for us that we don't appreciate, are also subjects of day-in-the-life-of stories. The woman who cleans the office building after everyone leaves, the teenager who carries around hot dogs and beer at the baseball game, the man who takes tickets at the county fair—these would all be fitting subjects for day-in-the-life-of stories.

From reading these articles, readers should gain a clearer sense of others around them and an appreciation that comes from experiencing almost firsthand someone else's life. Understanding how someone else uses up the minutes of the days allotted him or her can help readers understand that person better and, perhaps, themselves as well.

WALK-A-MILE-IN-MY-SHOES AND OTHER PERSONAL NARRATIVES

An understanding of someone else's life can come from the day-in-the-life-of story that a journalist writes by *observing* a person, but it can also come from the journalist's literally *living* a day in that person's life and writing a story that could be called a ''walk-a-mile-in-my-shoes'' narrative. For example, if a journalist wants to understand what it's like to be handicapped, he or she may spend a day in a wheelchair, then write an account of what happened during that day—how it felt, what he or she experienced, how people treated him or her differently. That account is usually written as a personal narrative, that is, a story in the first-person (using the pronoun ''I''), and it usually deals only with that single journalist's experience.

Another term for this way of gathering information about the reality of other people's lives is "participatory journalism," or "participant observation." Participant observation can involve hard investigative reporting and full-blown deception: the reporter pretends to be a criminal in order to experience a night in jail, or to be someone insane in order to find out how inmates of the state mental hospital are treated, or to be a migrant laborer in order to learn whether those workers are exploited by farmers.

When playing roles to gather information for these stories, journalists, rather than identifying themselves as reporters, usually assert that their deceptions are necessary to reach the truth. If they appeared as reporters, the truth would be covered up. While many reporters are uncomfortable with this end-justifies-the-means argument, they remain motivated to gather information this way because they feel their firsthand accounts have greater credibility and stronger emotional impact on readers—thus a better chance of exposing wrong-doing—than straight news articles.

Walk-a-mile-in-my-shoes feature stories, however, are not usually investigative, but kinder and gentler. The aim of such writing is not so much to expose wrongdoing as it is to increase sympathy or awareness for someone's difficult position.

In a sidebar for a *Bangor Daily News* feature on scientists who go 70 feet under water to do research on the bottom of Penobscot Bay, senior writer Tom Weber participates in, as well as observes, a descent to the bottom of the sea and writes a lighthearted walk-a-mile-in-my-shoes personal narrative to share the underwater experience:

> When everything is ready, Slater tells me to hop in. The little yellow craft hangs over the sea, suspended by cables attached to a big white crane. It looks alarmingly like a toy designed by Jules Verne.
>
> I step off the deck and squeeze through the top hatch. After a day of diving, the insides of the sub drip with condensation. . . . Looking out one of the three small ports to my left, I can see the storm clouds gathering in the distance.
>
> Slater slides in and takes his seat at the controls, which are surprisingly few. As he seals the hatch over his head, he explains what would happen if we somehow got tangled up in lobster trap lines or other obstructions on the bottom: first, the big lead weight would be dropped from the bottom of the sub. Then the ballast chambers would be filled with air, which would send the tiny sub soaring to the surface like a steel balloon. If that didn't work, each of us would have 72 hours of air to breathe until help arrives.
>
> Now I feel better.

It's important for beginning feature writers to remember that personal narrative stories should not be done frequently. Too often new writers want to do personal narratives because they are easier to write: it's so much simpler to put down their own thoughts than go out and interview or observe other people. However, personal narrative stories really should be written only when the writer is experiencing something significant, when he or she is doing something or being somewhere no one else happens to be or can be.

Of course, magazines and newspapers are also full of other popular personal narratives, those told to a journalist by people who are not reporters but who have unusual or otherwise newsworthy experiences. For example in *Redbook's* "Rescued by Love: Forgotten Romanian Babies," three women narrate their experiences adopting children from Romania, after the conditions of abandoned children there were publicized following the downfall of the Communist government.

Walking a mile in other people's shoes, hearing their personal stories, can be a way of understanding them. Narratives help us do that.

HOW IT CAME TO BE

Narratives, however, also help our understanding in other ways: they enable us to grasp more clearly how past and future play into our present. We can read a narrative that brings us from a past moment up to a particular moment so that we understand how things got to be the way they are; we can read another narrative that projects time forward from a particular moment to a later moment so that we can see the consequences of decisions made and the effects of actions taken at earlier points in time.

In 1986, the Challenger space shuttle exploded, killing the seven astronauts aboard, including teacher-astronaut Christa McAuliffe. Associated Press reporters put together a story that reconstructed the last 100 minutes before the disaster. The narrative, dominated by time—nearly every paragraph begins with an abbreviated dateline—retraces the steps of the astronauts, their relatives, and average people before the explosion:

10:00 a.m.—A voice crackles over the public address system at Concord High School, reminding the 1,200 students that launch time is nearing for teacher Christa McAuliffe. After an hour's delay to finish fueling, liftoff is set for 10:38. TV sets are on in almost every classroom, the cafeteria, the library and the auditorium. Party horns and hats are waiting. . . .

10:00—While pumping gas into a customer's tank at his Titusville service station, R.G. Tucker squints across the mile-wide Indian River toward the east, where the 122-foot high Challenger and its rockets look no bigger than an ant. Although the distance is nearly eight miles, he knows he has a perfect spot to see the launch. . . .

10:45—In the VIP viewing stands atop the launch control center, the astronauts' spouses and children are getting restless after an hour and 45 minutes in the cold. There is grumbling about the latest delay, and NASA workers offer coffee and cocoa. . . .

11:32—Smith gets the order from Mission Control to ready the auxiliary power units that steer the shuttle's movable surfaces, such as the wings and rudder. The on-board flight recorders are switched on. . . .

11:37—250 students in the auditorium at Concord High count down, too ". . . 4–3–2–1!" The students cheer and blow their horns.

11:38—Liftoff. . . .

11:40—The faces of Christa McAuliffe's parents go slack as a voice on the loudspeaker announces there has been a malfunction. Overhead they can see a ball of fire in the sky. . . .

11:41—Dr. Marvin Resnick, father of astronaut Judith Resnick, is standing in the special viewing area, gaping skyward. In the background he can hear the voices of Smith's children. They are screaming: "Daddy! Daddy! We want our daddy—you said you wouldn't leave us."

The Resnick entry is the last in the article, which emphasizes the past events before liftoff and the shock of the moment of disaster, rather than consequences and after-effects of the explosion. In this article, the purpose of the how-it-came-to-be narrative is not to explain precisely *how* it happened—that information was not available until investigations concluded months after the explosion—but to satisfy readers' emotional needs in dealing with this news, needs that are hard to define exactly. But surely one emotional need the story satisfies is the readers' need to face the reality of what just happened. By pacing through the steps that others took up to the moment of catastrophe, readers come to grips with the fact that this tragic event really did occur. In addition, readers feel a sense of emotional community with the astronauts and their loved ones and with other people, like themselves, who also experienced this tremendous shock.

UBI SUNT QUI ANTE NOS FUERUNT

A kind of mourning process occurs when we go through the steps of how a thing happened, or when we consider past actions. In literary criticism there is a term for describing this looking at present ruins and mourning the lost past, visualizing past time: it is called *ubi sunt,* a reduction of the Latin phrase *ubi sunt qui ante nos fuerunt.* The meaning of the phrase is "where are those who have been before us"; in the *ubi sunt* literary tradition, a hero looks on the ruins of a battlefield, fortress, or castle, and asks where are the glories that once were there, where are the fallen comrades, where are the mighty steeds and glistening arms of war.

The *ubi sunt* phrase was revived popularly in the 1960s, when the song "Where have all the Flowers Gone" was part of the anti-Vietnam War protest movement. Peter Arnett, while covering that war for the Associated Press, wrote a short, straightforward narrative that won the 1966 Pulitzer Prize for International Reporting. Despite its modern simplicity, the story participates in the ancient *ubi sunt* tradition; Arnett's article reveals how a narrative concerning past action provides a vehicle for mourning death.

The story begins with two simple statements:

VAN TUONG, Vietnam—The mission of U.S. Marine Supply Column 21 yesterday was simple: Get to the beachhead, resupply a line company and return to the 7th Fleet mother ship anchored a mile out in the bay.

It never found the line company. And it never returned.

In a step-by-step recreation of events, Arnett's story continues narrating what happened to the supply column, from the Vietcong rising "from hedgerows and swamps," to 35-ton amphibious vehicles called "amtraks" getting mired in rice paddies, from men taking turns as sharpshooters knocking off the enemy while suffering heat exhaustion in the sweltering temperatures of their steel-shod vehicles, to the final rescue of the few survivors by army helicopters.

Like all *ubi sunt* narratives, the story contemplates ruins. It ends:

> The fate of Supply Column 21 was sealed at noon.
> The men thought the disabled vehicles might be carted off and repaired. But an officer of the relief force told them:
> "Take your personal belongings out of the vehicles. We're going to blow them up."
> The remains of the amtraks at Van Tuong will be a reminder of Supply Column 21.

The ruins at Van Tuong may be a reminder of the men who died there, but Arnett's narrative writing *also* serves as a reminder and a memorial to their deaths. By allowing readers to re-create, through reading, the actions that led to their demise, the story lets readers mourn the soldiers' deaths.

TIME-AFTER CONSEQUENCES

Narratives can also focus on the time *after* a major event as well as the time before. Probably the most famous time-after narrative, emphasizing the consequences of an event, is John Hershey's journalistic novel *Hiroshima,* which narrates the stories of several Japanese citizens who were working at various distances from Hiroshima when the atomic bomb was dropped on that city. Hershey's novel has been regarded as remarkable for the emotional and intellectual reaction it creates in readers. Hershey does not need to argue that nuclear energy wreaks a terrible destruction; he simply narrates how these people dealt with the collapse of their homes and lives, with grotesque physical deformations, and with painful, bizarre injuries. That narration is enough. Any reader can understand the effects on human beings of the power that has been unleashed.

Time-after stories are often written after catastrophes, whether emotional or physical. In newspapers, such features are frequently concerned with the minutes or hours following floods, explosions, plane crashes, or fires. In magazines, they are often about the time after a crises. Recovery stories are very popular stories about "my life after" a mastectomy, for example, or "learning to live with" the loss of a baby, or "recovering from" alcoholism. These stories could perhaps be defined as how-to stories (see Chapter 11), because they provide a set of directions, a kind of emotional road map for others who need to go the same way, but their popularity also arises from the emotional appeal of their narrative story lines, from the reader's desire to see how it all works out.

Reliving the time after an event may create in readers an emotional identification with the person undergoing the experience, even if readers do not expect to follow in the same footsteps. A female reader does not have to be an abused wife to identify with a woman trying to rebuild her life after an abusive relationship, nor does the average American need to be homeless to identify with people from California trying to rebuild their homes after an earthquake.

NARRATIVE PROCESS

At other times, however, the time-after narrative can emphasize a process, creating knowledge and understanding rather than simply an emotional response. Time-after stories focus particularly on process, educating the reader about what that process entails. The reader may thus be forewarned about something or perhaps encouraged to think about making changes regarding that process. For example, Schorer's article on rape mentioned at the beginning of this chapter contains five parts; Part I presents primarily the rape experience, but Parts II through V emphasize how various systems—criminal, legal, sociological, psychological—respond to rape and the rape victim. *The Washington Post* ran a similar story on date rape, again, with emphasis on *process,* on how the victim worked through the system, in that particular case, the justice system.

Both stories forewarn women about problems in participating in the process of reporting a rape. In each case a woman reader might be more or less willing to report a case of rape after reading the narrative. Another reader might be outraged enough at certain miscarriages of justice in processing rape to lobby for changes in the judicial system.

A *New York Times Magazine* narrative by Nan Robertson, which won the 1983 Pulitzer for Feature Writing, is a time-after story focusing on process in order to educate readers about the recovery process from toxic shock, and to get women to understand the severity of the disease and its consequences.

The story is filled with medical details and statistics, yet it is propelled forward by a forceful personal narrative. By the end of the article, the narrative has itself become incorporated into the medical recovery. The feature ends with Robertson's fear of being paralyzed resolved this way:

> My story is almost over except for one crucial detail: My deepest fear did not materialize.
>
> I have typed the thousands of words of this article, slowly and with difficulty, once again, able to practice my craft as a reporter. I have written it—at last—with my own hands.

IRONIC TIME AND THE WHEEL OF FORTUNE

Much of the impact of Robertson's story, the moving quality of its narrative, comes from its use of words and phrases in a way typical of many of the emotionally strongest narratives. These narratives emphasize what could be called, for lack of a better term, the ironic quality of time.

Irony, we said earlier, occurs when what happens is the opposite of what is expected to happen (in literary terms, irony occurs when what is said is the opposite of what is meant). Life is full of irony. We frequently get caught off guard, humbled by our sense that events are beyond our control, and made aware that we don't always have power over the events in our lives, or anyone else's.

Robertson directly suggests this human sense of ironic time in her first two paragraphs:

> I went dancing the night before in a black velvet Paris gown on one of those evenings that was the glamour of New York epitomized. I was blissfully asleep at 3 a.m.
>
> Twenty-four hours later, I lay dying, my fingers and legs darkening with gangrene. I was in shock, had no pulse and my blood pressure was lethally low.

Her story is laced with references to a past time when she failed to appreciate the many good things in her life. And her story is also filled with references to the many times when she almost died, when a split-second decision on the part of a doctor or other caretaker just barely saved her life.

Some of the most effective narratives carry this sense of irony, this sense of life's unexpectedness. Medieval culture emphasized the turns that life can take in the symbol of Fortune's wheel; no matter where you were on the wheel—either up or down—your fate would inevitably change as the wheel inexorably turned. Our modern culture preserves some of this sense of things. We read the narratives of other people's experiences with the sense of the fragility of our own lives and times.

One of the earliest Pulitzer Prize–winning stories is a moment-by-moment report by Magner White of Scripps Howard describing a 1923 solar eclipse. The story exquisitely captures the feeling of the fragility of human time against the cosmic time. The article constantly keeps before readers the idea that those Indians who saw the eclipse 120 years earlier in California are now dead, as all those who are reading the article will be when the next solar eclipse comes. The story ends this way:

> The spell is gone, gone for 120 years.
>
> When the shadow returns, we shall not see it. We shall be with the Pala Indians of 1806.
>
> And the event will be the all-absorbing topic then to those strange creatures whom we may never meet except in our imaginations—our children's grandchildren.

EXERCISES

1. Creating stories from your imagination is not usually the best way to learn to be a feature writer, but the following two exercises will help develop your narrative writing skill. If you can find similar situations in real life happening around you and write your stories about them, the exercise would be even better.

a. Write a middle-of-the-action lead for this short, human interest narrative with a happy ending. Choose a point in time in the "middle" of what is happening to either the father or the police officers. Your first sentence should make the readers want to see what happens next:

Officers Joe Smith and Jennifer Jones almost arrested someone for reckless speeding today. The man was swerving down the road and going at speeds of up to 60 miles an hour (in a 35 mph zone). It turns out, however, that the man was upset and speeding because he was rushing his child to the hospital. The child had been playing Little League baseball, ran to catch a high-fly ball, and fallen on a piece of glass, cutting his hand.

His missed catch meant the other team won the game. His hand was bleeding profusely, so instead of giving the man a ticket, officers turned on their sirens and accompanied him to the hospital. His son is fine now, after receiving five stitches.

The man's name is Bill Clarke; his son's name is Tom.

b. You're writing a feature on a local runner who competed in the state finals for the mile race. You were at the race, watching the runner, Sally Swift; you want to give some sense to your readers of how long the race seemed to take, even though it only lasted a few minutes. You also want to describe the quick burst of energy Swift showed as she crossed the finish line. Write two paragraphs, the first describing the runners circling the track, the second describing Swift at the finish line. Change the language and sentence structure in the two paragraphs so that the first expands time (it seems long and slow to the reader), and the second condenses time (it seems quick and fast).

2. The success of a day-in-the-life-of story depends not only on the journalist's observing what the person does, but also on the journalist's asking questions about the person's credentials, feelings, aspirations, and experiences connected with his or her work. If you were doing a day-in-the-life-of story about a social worker who deals with abused children and abusive parents, what would you ask that person while you were accompanying him or her through the day at work?

3. Part I of Jane Schorer's series, "It Couldn't Happen to Me: One Woman's Story," from *The Des Moines Register* is, for the most part, a straight, linear narration of events. When does Schorer interrupt that narrative? For what reason? Why did Schorer decide to choose that particular point in the story to break the sequence of events? What did she write as a transition back to her retelling of the chronology?

4. Shorer's story begins with action perceived from the viewpoint of the rape victim, but Schorer changes the story so that the reader sees two other people perceiving different events happening. Who are they? Why do you think Schorer changed the point of view of her narration?

5. How does Schorer's ending to Part I help keep the reader waiting to see what happens next, so that they want to read Part II of the series?

PART I: A VICTIM'S STRUGGLE: STARING DOWN THE CRUEL STIGMA OF RAPE
From the series IT COULDN'T HAPPEN TO ME: ONE WOMAN'S STORY
By Jane Schorer
The Des Moines Register, *February 25, 1990*

She would have to allow extra driving time because of the fog.

A heavy gray veil had enveloped Grinnell overnight, and Nancy Ziegenmeyer—always methodical, always in control—decided to leave home early for her 7:30 A.M. appointment at Grand View College in Des Moines.

It was Nov. 19, 1988, a day Ziegenmeyer had awaited eagerly, because she knew that whatever happened during those morning hours in Des Moines would determine her future. If she passed the state real-estate licensing exam that Saturday morning, she would begin a new career. If she failed the test, she would continue the child-care service she provided in her home.

At 6 A.M., Ziegenmeyer unlocked the door of her 1988 Pontiac Grand Am and tossed her long denim jacket in the back seat. The weather was mild for mid-November, and her Gloria Vanderbilt denim jumper, red turtleneck sweater and red wool tights would keep her warm enough without a coat.

Arrived Early

The fog lifted as Ziegenmeyer drove west on Interstate Highway 80, and she made good time after all. The digital clock on the dashboard read 7:05 as she pulled into a parking lot near Grand View's Science Building. She had 25 minutes to sit in the car and review her notes before test time.

Suddenly the driver's door opened. She turned to see a man, probably in his late 20s, wearing a navy pin-striped suit. He smelled of alcohol.

"Move over," the man ordered, grabbing her neck. She instinctively reached up to scratch him, but he was stronger than she was. He pushed a white dish towel into her face and shoved her into the front passenger seat, reclin-

ing it to a nearly horizontal position. Then he took her denim jacket from the back seat and covered her head.

He wasn't going to hurt her, the man said; he wanted money. She reached toward the console for the only cash she had with her—$3 or $4—and gave it to him. He slid the driver's seat back to make room for his long legs, started the car and drove out of the parking lot.

"Is this guy going to kill me?" Ziegenmeyer wondered. "Is he going to rape me? Does he just want my money? Does he want my car?" She thought about her three children—ages 4, 5 and 7—and realized she might never see them again.

Barrage of Questions

The man talked constantly. He asked what she was doing in the parking lot. He asked where she worked. When she said she didn't have a job, he asked how she paid for a such a nice car. He noticed cigarette butts in the ashtray and said, "You must smoke like a chimney."

Ziegenmeyer wriggled under the coat, trying to see out, and the man pushed her down.

"Don't look at me!" he yelled.

They drove for a few minutes and pulled into a driveway—it sounded like gravel beneath the tires—and the man honked the horn twice, as if to signal someone. Ziegenmeyer peeked from under the coat and saw a large, older, light-green house. They waited maybe 45 seconds, then backed out of the driveway, and she saw another house with the number 1320 on a porch pillar.

The man kept talking. He talked about white people, and about how his father had been killed by a white man. He talked about how his sister had been raped by a white man. He talked about slavery and the things that white people did to black slaves.

Then he told Ziegenmeyer he would not kill her, because he knew what it was like to grow up without a parent.

And More Questions

The sky was growing lighter, but few cars were on the streets at that hour on a Saturday morning. Nov. 19, 1988—just two weeks past the presidential election.

"Did you vote?" the man asked.

"No," she lied. She knew never to discuss politics or religion with temperamental people.

"Well, if you had voted, who would you have voted for?" he asked.

She hesitated. A staunch Democrat, she tried to think which candidate this man would favor.

"Bush," she lied again.

"It figures, because you're a white bitch," he said.

The man pulled into a deserted parking lot and stopped the car. Ziegenmeyer caught a glimpse of a building in the distance—a church, perhaps—and noticed its unusual crooked eavespouts.

The man unzipped his trousers, grasped his penis and ordered Ziegenmeyer to put it in her mouth. If she hurt him, he said, he would kill her.

After a while, the man rolled her over so that her abdomen was on the console between the two front seats and attempted anal intercourse. Then he rolled her over to her back, and forced himself into her.

"Does that feel good?" he asked her. "Have you ever made love with a black man before?"

Ziegenmeyer's mind was blank, except for one thought: "This isn't really happening to me."

After he had ejaculated, he moved back to the driver's seat and pulled up his trousers.

"I hope you didn't give me AIDS, you white bitch," he said.

He began driving again. Eventually he returned to the parking lot of the church with the crooked eavespouts.

"Are these real?" the rapist asked, removing Ziegenmeyer's wedding band and diamond engagement ring.

She told him they were. He slipped them in his shirt pocket, and wiped her fingers, hands and arms with the white dish towel. Then he thoroughly wiped everything he might have touched in the vehicle.

"You'll Be OK; You Can Afford It"

The man told Ziegenmeyer he had a car in the neighborhood, and he would follow her to the interstate to make sure she left Des Moines without going to the police. "I should tie you up and throw you in the trunk," he said. "I should tie you up and throw you in the river."

He grabbed her book bag containing her real estate books, notebooks, purse and glasses. Now he had her address, and he said he'd come after her family if she went to the police. He ordered her to lie down across the floor of the front seat, then covered her with the denim coat.

"You'll be OK," the man told her. "You're white, and you can go home to your husband and you can afford to get a counselor. You'll get through this and be just fine."

He ordered her to stay on the floor for 10 minutes. "If you do go to the police," he said, "tell them you were attacked by a white man, and that's all you know."

He left her then, but Ziegenmeyer didn't wait 10 minutes to get up.

As soon as she heard the car door slam, she stretched her arm as far as she could reach and pushed down the lock of the driver's door.

∎ ∎ ∎

132

She wanted to go home.

Nancy Ziegenmeyer, rape victim, wanted just to get out of that place and go home. But she was lost in an unfamiliar city.

The clock on the car's dashboard read approximately 7:35. Only half an hour had passed.

She began to drive, turning here and there, until she recognized Mercy Hospital Medical Center, where her children had been for doctors' appointments. She parked her car in the lot and ran into the emergency room—not for medical attention, but just to be safe from a world that suddenly had turned on her.

Once inside, she became hysterical.

"I've just been raped," she cried. A nurse whisked her away from a waiting room of shocked, nameless faces. Within minutes, hospital workers called Polk County Victim Services, and sexual assault counselor Dee Ann Wolfe was on her way.

"Don't Call the Police"
Aunt Doris lived in Des Moines, Ziegenmeyer told the nurse, but her phone number was in the purse that the rapist had stolen. The nurse pa-

tiently scoured the phone book until she found the number. Aunt Doris would be there shortly.

There were more calls to make, the nurse suggested.

"No," Ziegenmeyer protested. "Don't call the police. I've seen this kind of thing on TV." She knew that people often assumed rape victims provoked the attack themselves.

The nurse's voice was calm and gentle. After a while, she persuaded Ziegenmeyer to report the crime.

They took her clothes away; Dee Ann Wolfe brought a shapeless gray sweatsuit for her to wear home. They combed her hair and clipped her nails and labeled everything as evidence. They examined her from head to toe. Two vaginal swabs were marked "A" and "B."

Des Moines police officer Nancy LaMasters-Kappel dusted Ziegenmeyer's car for fingerprints, and officer Richard Brewer took her statement, noting that she was enormously upset. Detective Ralph Roth was called to assist.

"Nancy," Roth said softly during the questioning, "you don't have to keep telling us that he made you do it. We know he made you do it."

. . .

Saturday was Steve Ziegenmeyer's day off from his job as a mechanic at Grinnell Implement. He fixed breakfast for the kids and wondered how Nancy was doing on her real-estate exam in Des Moines.

The phone rang. Aunt Doris? Why on Earth would she be calling?

Nancy was at the hospital, Doris said, and needed to talk to him.

There's been a car accident, Steve thought.

Then Nancy was on the phone, crying and asking him not to blame her, please not to hate her. She wanted him to stay home in Grinnell with their kids, because that man had her purse and her address book and he threatened to come after them if she went to the police.

It was not yet 9 o'clock on a Saturday morning. It was his day off. The kids were giggling and eating Cheerios, and a voice on the telephone was telling him that the woman he loved had just been raped.

. . .

Steve and Nancy Ziegenmeyer have lived around Grinnell their entire lives. Theirs is a peaceful central Iowa community of 7,600. Grinnell College, an exclusive private school, boosts the population by 1,270 and employs a host of

respected educators and internationally known figures.

Still, most of the citizens of Grinnell could be termed average folks. The Ziegenmeyers aren't college professors, civic leaders or even regular church-goers. The parents of three young children, their world includes a mortgaged home, a juggling act of kids' activities at school and frequent tired arguments, more often than not over in-laws.

Man of Few Words

Steve Ziegenmeyer, 34, is a man of few words; the few he uses aren't always genteel. He's fond of cold beer, denim clothes and Western boots. He hasn't worn a suit since he was a pallbearer at a funeral several years ago.

Nancy Jo Ziegenmeyer, 29, previously worked as manager of the lounge at Motel Grinnell just off Interstate 80.

"She was probably one of the best managers we ever had," said Darlene Campbell, co-owner of the motel. "If there was a problem, she handled it. We never had to worry about getting called."

An attractive woman, Nancy always dressed in the latest fashion, her former employer said.

She had an outgoing personality and a bubbly charm that made her immediately likable. She was great for that type of business.

But she quit her job at the bar. The things most important to her, she decided, were Steve, her children and building a satisfying career. She started a child-care service, but what she really wanted was to become a licensed real-estate sales agent.

A Pampered Life

Fine, Steve said. If that was what she wanted, that's what she would have. Nancy had been raised by her grandparents, and Steve always told her she was too pampered. There had never been anything bad happen in her life, Steve said, that Grandpa couldn't make all better for her.

That was until Nov. 19, 1988—the day Nancy Ziegenmeyer went to Des Moines to take the real-estate licensing exam. The day Grandpa's outgoing, bubbly little Nancy Jo was raped.

. . .

Dec. 1, 1988. Bingo.

Detective Roth had been keeping an eye on area pawn shops, and, sure enough, the stolen wedding rings had surfaced.

Two days after the attack, they were pawned for $30 at Des Moines Gold and Silver Buyers Inc. by a woman named Lisa Davis. Roth went to Davis' home to talk about the rings. He was greeted by a man in his late 20s. Roth would learn the man was Bobby Lee Smith, Davis' common-law husband and a counselor for troubled youth with the Iowa Department of Human Services. Davis wasn't home, Smith said.

Roth did a check on Bobby Lee Smith. In 1982, the record showed, he had pleaded guilty of third-degree theft and was sentenced to two years' probation. In 1985, he pleaded guilty to a charge of carrying weapons and was fined $200.

In June 1987, he pleaded guilty of second-degree robbery and was sentenced to a 10-year prison term but was granted parole.

100 Percent Certain

Roth drove to Grinnell and showed Ziegenmeyer photographs of six suspects. She was 50 percent sure, she said, that one of the photos was the man who had assaulted her, but she needed a better picture. Accusing a man of rape is a serious matter, and she wanted to be sure.

Roth prepared another set of photos, and Nancy and Steve drove to Des Moines to view them. In that batch, the middle photo, bottom row, was the man who had raped her, she said. She was 100 percent sure.

Nancy Ziegenmeyer had twice identified photos of Bobby Lee Smith.

. . .

Dec. 8, 1988. Smith was arrested, and two navy pinstriped suits were confiscated at his home. He was charged with two counts of kidnapping in the first degree, one involving Ziegenmeyer and one involving an Indianola woman who was assaulted two days earlier.

First-degree kidnapping charges include sexual assault, and conviction carries a mandatory sentence of life in prison without parole.

Smith pleaded innocent to both counts.

Lisa Davis was arrested on a preliminary complaint of accessory after the fact in connection with the theft of the rings. She later was charged with third-degree theft, and she pleaded innocent.

Now there would be a trial. Criminal case No. 41733, the State of Iowa vs. Bobby Lee Smith.

Nancy Ziegenmeyer would be called as a witness. The trial was expected to begin within 90 days. In the meantime, the Polk County attorney's office said it would keep in touch.

CHAPTER

Color Stories
Creating a You-Are-There Feeling

If narrative stories are dominated by a sense of time, color stories are dominated by a sense of place. When feature writers speak of color stories, they mean stories that describe locations so clearly and precisely that those who read the descriptions feel as if they are there. Color stories are rich in the description of physical things and rich in the description of atmosphere; they convey mood, as well as matter.

WHAT THE COLOR STORY OFFERS

When is a sense of place important enough to dominate a story? Why would readers want to get a sense of ''being'' somewhere?

One reason might be that readers want a firsthand impression of a place where a news event is happening. Readers may want to know what it feels like to be in a city when it is bombed, near a tornado when it touches down, or in a courtroom when an accused person is pronounced guilty of murder. Color articles help readers ''see'' places written about in news stories.

Color articles may describe places where somber and serious news events occur, or places where news events such as rock concerts and Superbowl games occur. Mike Bartell, for example, describes a shuttle launch in his color article, ''They're Off! Joining the crowd on the ground at a shuttle launch,'' in the *Toledo Magazine* of the *Toledo Blade*. His story begins:

> A cool breeze blew in off the Atlantic Ocean, and an ominous-looking cloud cover moved in with it. The December day had been a good one, sunny and warm, everything Florida edging toward winter should be. But the night was beginning to look disappointingly dismal.

Guarded optimism began to give way to a sense of stoic resignation—a familiar feeling—when a voice boomed over the loudspeakers in front of the bleachers crowded with people eagerly awaiting the long-anticipated, but too-often-delayed event.

Another reason why readers may want to read a color article is for the enjoyment of ''being'' at an event with little news value but of great human interest. The first day of school, a night at the bingo hall, an afternoon at the circus—all are suitable subjects for color stories. Readers can enjoy ''being at'' the location of the stories because they identify with fellow human beings there. Most of us enjoy reading about people like ourselves, or about events that we have attended or participated in at one time or another.

Readers can also enjoy matching their perceptions of an event against the perceptions of the journalist. They can agree, for example, that the food at the church bazaar did smell delicious, or disagree that the aroma at the horse show was overwhelming.

A color story that describes an old familiar place can also give readers enjoyment, a nostalgic pleasure akin to looking at a photo album or watching old family movies. Such a color story, in its retrospective look at the past, permits readers to consider past events in the context of present reality; present reality, too, can be measured against past experience and perception.

In such a nostalgic color feature, Paul Hendrickson of *The Washington Post* describes Baltimore's old stadium and its surrounding neighborhood in the context of the present knowledge that Baltimore will soon have a new, modern stadium:

> One of its smaller glories is that you can look out from deep inside the park, deep inside the drift of the game, and get hints of:
> Real life.
> It was always and ever a neighborhood ballyard, plopped down in and amid the people. There are several neighborhoods actually, and one of them, just glimpsable from inside, is called Ednor Gardens-Lakeside. It's on the hill beyond the green center field wall. Out there, past the lights and the scoreboards, in a middle rising distance, are whitewashed Tudor houses; are sloping lawns; are chirping birds; are mailmen on their routes; are buses; are pear trees in blossom; are retirees walking their dachshunds; are carpenters from Local 101 coming home bone-exhausted from the day's labors; are accountants for law firms who play rugby on weekends and hold Opening Day bashes with bushels of oysters and gallons of beer; are sun rooms filled with white wicker furniture; are assistant managers at General Cinema; are men who crew-chiefed for Air American during Nam; are marbled front stoops and enclosed porches and striped canvas awnings and high-peaked blue-trimmed roofs; and oh yes not least out there, in a spotless house on East 36th Street, are two demure Baltimore ladies who find themselves terribly aggrieved—who in fact are brave enough to break down and cry in front of a stranger—at the thought of what tomorrow really means, at least for them:
> The last lullaby in Birdland.
> Or at least the last Opening Day in hulky, old, ungainly Memorial Stadium.

A third reason why readers may want to read color articles is to learn about exotic foreign locations. Travel stories are a special kind of feature with a good deal of "colorful" writing (see Chapter 13); they are popular not only with readers who expect to visit a particular place, but also with readers who may never go there but want to fantasize about it.

Color stories may also describe "exotic" places that are "distant" and "foreign" because they are emotionally far away and separate from ordinary life—places such as a prison, a migrant labor camp, or a Park Avenue fur salon. Readers enjoy reading stories about exotic places because such stories reveal other dimensions of experience, or give readers a heightened awareness of their own blessings.

PRETTY OR NOT

Most of us have an idea of color stories as pleasant stories—pleasurable to read—probably because color stories are descriptive, and therefore we assume they are "scenic," like lovely landscape paintings.

But just as scenic paintings are not always lovely, color stories don't always present pretty pictures. They can make us cry as readily as they can make us laugh; they can cause us to recoil in horror as easily as they can cause us to rhapsodize over the beauty of a sunset.

They can sometimes be ironic or bitingly funny, as is this description of people on New York-to-Miami plane flights, in a story written for Knight-Ridder by John Arnold:

> These days among flight attendants, the New York-Palm Beach is called the Miracle Worker Flight. That's because a huge squadron of wheelchair-bound elderly women will board in New York, where wheelchair passengers are boarded first. And then when the flight lands at Palm Beach International, where passengers needing wheelchairs must wait to leave last, the same invalids will rise from their seats to race for the door ahead of everyone else.

The principal measure of the excellence of a color story is not the attractiveness or unattractiveness of what it portrays, but the vividness of the experience it re-creates for readers. Do readers feel they have been there? Can they smell what it's like . . . taste it, hear it, see it? Does the article create a sense of witnessing what's happening? This feeling of *being there* brings readers satisfaction from reading, whether the color story portrays the pleasant or the unpleasant. If the readers' emotional connection to the world of the color article is strong, then the story is a success.

A SLICE OF TRUTH

Color features are unusual in that, unlike most journalistic stories, they don't rely on quotes from expert sources, or on outside research. Primarily, the writer's eyes, ears, nose, and hands are the "sources" of information. While these "sources" are clearly limited, readers of color stories accept such limitations because they understand that color articles tell not the full truth, but a slice of the truth, a small bit of reality perceived by a solitary journalist.

Journalists, in writing all kinds of feature articles, act like human cameras, taking pictures of all they see. But color writers also act, more than most journalists, like movie directors. Because color writers concentrate on a scene, and not on a particular event or person, they can decide from a wider variety of choices where the camera will "look." They can also decide how the camera will look. Should it gaze rapidly around an entire scene, or linger over a portion of it? Focus on the faraway horizon, or zoom in on a nearby flower? Follow the actions of people, or study the motions of a spider in its web?

Color writers can also choose the time period which the article describes; that is, the time when the camera is turned "on." The chosen moment or moments may or may not be what most people would consider the most newsworthy. A color writer, for example, might choose to focus on the melancholy night after a flood has hit town, rather than on the more newsworthy moment when the flooding actually occurred, as Dan Luzadder did in a story that was part of disaster coverage that won the 1983 Pulitzer Prize for General Spot News Reporting for the staff of The (Fort Wayne) News-Sentinel:

> It is midnight Sunday, at the moment of this dispatch, and the streets are quiet. But in the heart of the city, hearts are breaking.
> Homes sit under water. Cars have been swallowed up. Houses sit dark and empty of occupants as furniture floats on the floors.
> The lapping, slowly rising waters make an insidious sound on clapboard wall. But otherwise the evacuated areas are quiet. And all is calm.

Color writers can also arbitrarily choose the moment when their stories begin, when the movie film starts rolling and "viewers" see the scene. Color stories don't have to start at the beginning of an event or narrative, or conclude at its ending. Their leads simply describe a scene; then "actors" begin to move on it.

Todd C. Smith of The Tampa Tribune begins his story on Colombia and its drug traffickers by describing a funeral:

> MEDILLIN, Colombia—At the center of a throng of mourners is young Frank Libardo Escobar's coffin, gliding eerily on a stretcher along the walkway of the Itagui crypt.
> Leading the cortege are about two dozen drunk young men, some weeping, some with eyes bulging in stupor. They have brought along three guitarists—one of them a blind man in sunglasses—singing old Colombian ballads. More than 100 town residents gather to watch.

The group hesitates as it approaches the wall where Escobar will be entombed in the top row. A hefty man waits atop a ladder, trowel in hand, to seal off the latest victim of Colombia's cocaine-fed killing machine.

Mary Anne Weaver, writing for *Smithsonian* magazine, begins a story about a ship's graveyard by describing a beach in Pakistan:

> Fifty men, fine-boned and thin as teenage boys, stand on the beach, expectation on their faces. Some huddle together silently; others only stare out to sea, where the Greek passenger vessel *Teera* is bucking and rolling toward them, its vast 13,665-ton bulk pushed toward the land by one remaining engine, a tricky tide and crashing waves.

In their stories, color writers can use their camera ''shots'' to create a certain impression, so that the material in the story makes sense in a certain way. Color writers, through fairly arbitrary choices, can thus influence the effect their story, their slice of truth, has on readers.

Because arbitrary choice can influence color stories, news writers sometimes use the phrase ''color a story'' derogatively, meaning that a news writer has deliberately slanted an article.

SENSORY AND METAPHORIC LANGUAGE

Of course, readers need to do more than simply *see* the scene if they are going to feel they are there. They must also have their other senses, besides sight, addressed.

When, as a feature writer, you are observing a scene, trying to capture its essence for your color article, you need to pay careful attention to what *all* your senses tell you. What do you hear? Smell? Taste? Feel? Include all your sense perceptions in your story so readers can hear, smell, taste, and feel too.

Notice how Richard Ben Cramer of *The Philadelphia Inquirer* presents not only what he *sees* on a strip of no-man's land in occupied Lebanon, but also includes what he hears, feels, and smells, in a story that won him the 1979 Pulitzer Prize for International Reporting:

> A BMW sedan with a flat tire is pulled to one side of the road. Except for the tire, the car is intact. There is no explanation for its presence, until a door is opened to reveal upholstery spattered with blood.
>
> Farther along, five cars are burning. Their stink testifies to the accuracy of the Israeli aerial assault. The blistered hulks sit on bare wheels, tires burned off in the explosions that halted the cars.
>
> In the back of a Mazda, a burnt skeleton of a machine gun lies in the open trunk. When the machine gun is moved, two lizards dart out of their new home for the bushes at the side of the road.
>
> There are daisies growing in the bushes, and the air holds the scent of honeysuckle. Birds sing in the intervals between explosions on a hillside to the east.
>
> Suddenly, around a bend, the squawk of a shortwave radio cuts through the air.

Because color stories appeal to readers' senses, color articles frequently need to describe the unknown through the known. When we describe the unfamiliar through the familiar, we use what are called "similes" and "metaphors." Similes are comparisons of two unlike things using the words "like" or "as" ("soft as silk," "red as a rose"); metaphors are comparisons of two unlike things not using the words "like" or "as" ("the king, a lion in winter, roared at his serfs"). When we say the things that are compared are "unlike," we mean that while they are *essentially* unlike, they are also alike in some significant respect, the point of comparison. For example, in the simile, "her complexion is like peaches and cream," the two items, her skin and peaches/cream, are not similar in most respects, but they are alike in one significant respect, the aspect of color.

We usually associate similes and metaphors, called "figures of speech," with literature, since they are used so frequently in creative writing and we discuss them so often in the analysis of poetry, short stories, and novels. But the basic purpose of similes and metaphors is to convey the unknown through the known, and that purpose is also quite typical of journalism, especially color article writing.

If, for example, you were writing a color story about an out-of the-way Pacific island and were attempting to describe some lovely red flowers covering the mountain sides, you might use a simile, saying they were "as red as Burgundy wine." Your comparison would help readers visualize what they would not otherwise be able to see. Many shades of red exist: readers would know the unknown shade of red in the flowers through the known shade of red burgundy wine.

You could also have said that the flowers were "as red as pepperoni on a pizza" and your message about the shade of the color red would have been equally clear; however, the tone of the simile would have been jarring. While the two items in similes (and metaphors) can be unlike, the basic sense of the nature of each cannot fight with the other. A pepperoni pizza conjures up in readers' eyes an ordinary, oily image; Burgundy wine is more pleasant and pure and, therefore, a more fitting comparison for the flowers.

DENOTATIVE AND CONNOTATIVE LANGUAGE

In saying Burgundy wine is a better match to flowers than pepperoni pizza, we are dealing with the connotative versus the denotative meanings of words; color writers are particularly sensitive to the difference. The denotative meaning of a word is its literal meaning. For example, both "slender" and "skinny" literally indicate a person who is underweight; the words have similar denotative meanings. But the connotative meanings of the words are not the same. The connotative meaning includes all the emotional overtones the words carry with them: "skinny" has the negative connotation of "underweight in an unattractive way''; ''slender'' has the positive connotation of ''underweight in an attractive way.'' Color writers are careful to choose words that not only have the correct denotation but also the appropriate connotation.

In addition to using language precisely, color writers try to use language originally, especially to create fresh similes and metaphors, ones unusual as well as appropriate. A stale simile fails to conjure up an image in our mind's eye. We don't ''see'' how anyone could be ''like a red, red rose'' because we've heard that phrase so many times before. If, however, we read that ''my love is like the cherry perched on top of a hot fudge sundae,'' we might not appreciate the comparison, but we would notice it, because it's new. We stop to visualize the image, to consider the two things the writer is comparing.

In his article ''Changes in Paradise'' for *Modern Maturity* magazine, Charles N. Barnard uses an original simile to explain his feelings for the two Mauis—the present island and the one he remembers from World War II:

> Whenever I go back I look for the two faces of the island, one I knew long ago, one that is the slick prosperity of today. It's like watching your children grow up. You see them striving for success, maturing, making more money, driving better cars. But you can also still see the youngsters you remember—and you may wish for those simpler, dearer days.

Color writers must remember, however, that no matter how creatively they use figurative language, their descriptions must reflect real-life places and not places created in their imaginations. Color writers cannot alter reality, cannot change what's literally at the scene or what happens there.

A more typical problem, however, concerns whether or not color writers must include certain physical details in a description. When writing a color description, you may find yourself in a situation something like this:

You want to portray the sense of a particularly elegant room but in that room is a desk made of formica. If you include the physical detail of what material composes the desk, you may damage the mood you are trying to create (and that you feel is actually there.) ''Formica'' is not connotatively as rich a word as ''mahogany'' or ''oak.'' If you were a creative writer, you could simply change that detail in your story, choosing to make it whatever material you thought appropriate. But you're a journalist, so you can't alter reality.

Since you can't change the factual detail of the formica, should you even mention it? Is it irrelevant and therefore something you can eliminate, or is it significant and therefore something you must include? If you mention it, can readers sort through the complexity of conflicting impressions, as you did when you entered the room? If the impression of an elegant atmosphere prevailed with you, will it also prevail with readers?

Deciding whether to include a detail or details that don't ''belong'' is difficult.

In a series on Africa which won him a prize for non-deadline writing in 1988 from the American Society of Newspaper Editors, Blaine Harden of *The Washington Post* describes the Zaire River in a series of exotic and terrible pictures. Two details seem out of place, seem to be details the writer should have omitted:

> ON THE ZAIRE RIVER—The captain, dressed in crisply pressed white pajamas, stalked back and forth on the bridge. As his boat growled downriver through a green-black rain forest, he shouted and whistled and pointed to the deck below.
>
> There, the beasts that had arrived in the night were being auctioned. Glaring white morning light poured over heaps of mottled fur and squirming legs. It was hot and some of the carcasses were ripening.
>
> The night's harvest was mostly monkeys—hundreds of them, some smoked, some rotting, some freshly trapped and twitching. They were tied together by their long tails in easy-carrying bundles. There also were antelope, bushbuck, and a couple of giant forest hogs. A well-muscled sailor with a sharp knife and bloodstained sneakers was methodically cutting throats.

The detail of "crisply pressed white pajamas" seems out of place in the predatory jungle scene: the pajamas are too fine, too clean and citified. And the sailor's "sneakers" are also not in harmony with the location; they belong to 20th century American malls, not African riverboats.

Yet, Harden's inclusion of these jarring details makes his story more effective. A detail like the sneakers makes the reader confident that Harden has, in fact, been at the scene. It's not the sort of detail a writer would make up if he or she were working from imagination rather than reality. The white pajamas are also a detail that enriches the story, providing an ironic contrast between the superior, distant captain and the squalor that contributes to his livelihood.

Providing observed physical details is one of the easiest ways to add color to any story; but using them successfully, knowing when to leave a detail out and when to put it in, can be tricky for color writers.

CHARACTERS ON THE SCENE

Similes, metaphors, connotative meanings, observed details—all these have to do with description, with describing the scene before the reader's eyes. But no scene, however real, can hold a reader's attention long unless something happens there. We human beings seem to be, first and foremost, interested in other creatures and in action. So, as you describe a scene, try to show movement on it: describe people who move or animals or things that move.

When no people or creatures are available, you can create a sense of their being there through another figure of speech: "personification." Personification is ascribing human attributes to inanimate natural objects; for example, saying "the tree waved his arms" or the "sea gave a mocking roar." Trees don't have arms to wave and seas can't mock, but describing them that way makes them seem to come alive, to be like familiar people or animals.

When, however, you do observe real people moving about a scene, you should try to capture their movements as part of your description. Watch what they do and listen to the snatches of conversation that you can overhear. Observe how people or animals interact with each other; record their gestures, words or sounds, and facial expressions. The people are not ''experts'' about anything, not ''sources'' in the traditional journalistic sense, but, as ordinary human beings, they help readers ''see'' the scene through their actions and reactions.

Color writers often preserve the anonymous identities of the people they observe. They usually don't go up to them and ask them their names, ages, and addresses. Color writers identify the observed people in the story by noticeable physical features, such as hair color (''the red-head''), or what they are wearing (''the man in the red plaid shirt''), or what they are doing (''the bartender''). Names are not important because the people are not significant as unique individuals, but rather as typical human beings, or as recognizable ''types'' of human beings.

MINI-DRAMAS

Human mini-dramas that the writer observes also enliven a color story.

Perhaps in preparing to write a color story, you spend an afternoon at the zoo and find two sweethearts quarreling: if they argue, stalk away from one another, and then, after laughing at a monkey's antics, decide to kiss and make up, you have a mini-drama that readers will enjoy. Most readers can identify with a silly lovers' quarrel.

In such an afternoon at the zoo, you may also observe and record other human dramas: children whining on a nursery school field trip, a teenager illegally sneaking away from school, a lonely retiree talking to the animals. Because readers are interested in people, it's the people in a color story, with all their human faults and fickleness, that give it movement and life.

As you fill your story with mini-dramas concerning the people you observe, remember that you don't have to resolve those dramas; the color story is not a narrative and does not require a climactic resolution. People can wander on and off your ''screen'' in the way you observe them.

For example, in an article on the Soviet Union for *Buffalo Magazine of The Buffalo News*, Michael Beebe describes the black market, then tells about two youths who sold Soviet goods to him and other Americans. The young men enter the story momentarily, then leave it:

> In Moscow, the black market ranges from pin boys—adolescent kids who trade cheap Russian lapel pins for American pins or sticks of gum—to their older brothers who have a few cheap lacquer boxes, to smooth operators such as Yuri and his friend Mikhail, who came back to trade with us the following day.
>
> They showed up dressed more like Americans than we were. Both had on L. L. Bean duck boots, stone-washed Levi's denims and American warm-up jackets—Yuri

wore a Nike nylon shell. Both men, in their early 20s, were dressed for trading: Each had three or four Soviet army shirts on underneath their jackets and they wore a half-dozen Soviet army and navy belts. . . .

After nearly an hour of open trading a block away from our hotel with no interference from authorities, Yuri and Mikhail left with a new collection of American jeans, oxford cloth shirts and sweat shirts. The Americans had lacquer boxes, Soviet military garb and athletic shirts to take home, along with a suspicious feeling that they got the worst end of the deal.

If a particular drama resolves itself before your eyes, such as the lovers' quarrel we discussed earlier, then that dramatic resolution gives a nice sense of completeness to your color story. But narrative completeness isn't necessary. Color stories frequently begin nowhere and end nowhere. They are, as said earlier, simply a bit of reality the writer arbitrarily chooses to present.

UNIFYING THE ARTICLE

The color writer's artistry, however, can unify the color story and give it a limited sense of completeness.

Sometimes the color writer will tie the story together through a dominance of words having to do with a particular sense perception. For example, the inclusion of many words describing noise may create an emphasis on sound that unifies the article, as in a story describing Addis Ababa, Ethiopia, written for the *Chicago Tribune* by Will Barber—a story that won the 1936 Pulitzer Prize for Correspondence:

Typewriters are clicking in the rooms next door and beyond in the darkness hyenas are howling. There is the answering bark of a dog—a friendly, homely bark—and the screech of a house cat. It is an unearthly screech—the sort of screech that used to send shivers down your back when you were a boy hunting wild cats and you raised one. Someone whistles softly. It is the corporal of the night watch of the Hotel Imperial. From a cabin down the hill within the big compound comes a voice. A late comer is returning home. To his greeting the bearded, brown skinned guard huddled in a blanketlike poncho and carrying an old Russo-Japanese war rifle that couldn't shoot on a bet, replies in Ethiopian: "Thank you— may God give you as much."

The gasoline engine that supplies electricity for this hotel—it is one of the half dozen houses having electricity—has stopped puttering. Another hyena howls. More hyenas take up the wail, and soon, if old residents can be believed, the animals will sneak into the streets of the Ethiopian capital of Addis Ababa—the new flower—to make the nightly picking of refuse.

The reader senses, perhaps only subconsciously, that the writer has chosen to focus on sound as a way of emphasizing the absence of sight, and of revealing the spooky loneliness of the primitive city at night.

Sometimes articles are unified through a sustained metaphor or a personification repeated throughout the article. For example, the metaphor of a teacher compared to an army general could be sustained through the entire story if words keep reminding readers of the initial metaphor, words in such phrases as "he *commands* that papers be handed in on time" or "no one had better be *AWOL* from her class."

Sometimes words unify an article in a way that makes sense only when readers have finished reading the entire story, when they can consider individual images in the context of the whole article's message (what American novelist Henry James used to call seeing the "pattern in the carpet"). This unification is achieved through the repetition of words or objects throughout the story. The first time the word appears or the object is mentioned, it has its usual, rather neutral meaning. As it reappears in different contexts, however, its meaning gains symbolic value, as it is read with all its previous uses in mind. By the time the article ends, the word or object is loaded with an emotional value far beyond its initial sense, and the full meaning emerges as a pattern unifying the entire article.

New journalist Tom Wolfe, for example, uses such a technique in the opening chapter of his book about pilot astronauts, *The Right Stuff.* Wolfe wants to emphasize the high number of Navy test pilots who die, so he tells the story of a small unit of men. When the first one dies, he describes other pilots attending the funeral in their Navy bridge coats, singing the Navy hymn. He repeats this description for each funeral he mentions, as over 10 men die. By the time the survivors pull out their coats for the last funeral and sing the Navy hymn for the last time, both bridge coats and hymn have lost their nobility and have become instead terrible symbols of death and destruction.

The color writer, of course, knows the significance of these repeated words or objects from the first moment he or she uses them. William Reuhlmann, in *Stalking the Feature Story,* calls such repeated words "plants," because the writer plants them for readers in the story. They are like good clues in a detective tale. Readers respond to these plants with the same kind of pleasure they feel when they read a well-written mystery: they admire the cleverness of the work's construction, the way it creates a meaningful way of looking at something, the way repetition makes the story seem complete.

In a color story in the *New York Times* about visiting a Nazi extermination camp, a story which won the 1960 Pulitzer Prize for International Reporting, A.M. Rosenthal also uses words which take on a new, emotionally charged meaning when readers come to the story's end. Rosenthal, however, does not repeat particular words or objects throughout the story, but rather uses them to frame it. The horrors of the camp are surrounded by pleasant normalcy.

The story begins describing sun, trees, and children playing:

> BRZEZINKA, Poland—The most terrible of all, somehow, was that at Brzezinka the sun was bright and warm, the rows of graceful poplars were lovely to look upon, and on the grass near the gates children played.

It ends describing sun, trees, and children playing:

> There is nothing new to report about Auschwitz. It was a sunny day and the trees were green and at the gates the children played.

Somehow, however, what seemed pleasant at the story's beginning, seems horrible and unnatural at the story's end.

THE PRESENT TENSE

Color articles, then, may be unified and seem complete. They do not, however, achieve a sense of completeness by being a certain length. They can be either long or short. Generally, color stories are not *overly* long, because it is difficult to maintain the story's mood over an extended reading time, or over a reading period so long that reading is likely to be interrupted.

One thing that does seem to apply consistently to most color stories is their use of present tense verbs. The present tense is preferred because it gives the illusion that things are occurring at a particular instant right before the readers' eyes. Present tense verbs create the desired effect of making readers feel they are at the scene. The ongoing action or right-at-the-minute perception keeps readers emotionally drawn to the story.

Notice how Ann Banks, in a feature about the Guantanamo Bay military base written for *The New York Times Magazine,* creates a you-are-there feeling through the use of the present tense:

> Subtract the props, and the face on the T-shirt could be Milton Berle. But with the fatigue cap, wooly beard and jumbo Havana cigar, it's clearly Fidel Castro, the man who rules all Cuba—except, that is, for the 45-square-mile stronghold on the shore of Oriente Province where the T-shirt is sold. For more than 90 years, ever since the Spanish-American War, this tip of the island has been under the jurisdiction of the United States military—which is the point of the T-shirt. In the caption under the caricature, Fidel demands indignantly, "Where the hell is Guantanamo Bay, Cuba?"

AN OPEN-MINDED LOOK, AN HONEST PICTURE

Color stories are usually fun to write. They allow the writer considerable freedom with organization of material, with selection of time and place, and in the use of language. There are, however, some cautions about writing color stories.

Though color stories are rarely dull, they can be dull if the writer thinks—and writes—only in terms of life's cliches. Color descriptions are frequently written about popular events: sports spectaculars, holiday festivities, open-air concerts, fairs. In writing about these popular events that "everybody" loves, color writers can easily slip into all the familiar, worn-out, and dull observations. The cheerleaders are always pretty and enthusiastic, the Santa Clauses always plump and cheerful, the concert audiences always beating out the rhythm or swaying with the music. Good color writers try to look beyond the cliches. If they're present, of course, the writer can't ignore them; the cheerleaders, after all, *are* at the sports event. But good color writers also look for less-typical figures, for the sulking bench-warmer or the cheerleader casting spiteful looks at one of the players, or the parent who watches son or daughter with rueful amazement.

Other cautions about writing color articles have to do with the writer's honesty. Because color writers have the ability to cut and paste scenes together to create their articles, they have to work harder for journalistic integrity. The temptation always exists to recreate the order of events in a way other than the way they happened.

There's also a temptation to be dishonest about what was found on a scene if it doesn't fit what the color writer expected to find. Color writers have to be open-minded and should avoid going someplace with a mind-set that says "I am going to the zoo for a light-hearted, fun-filled article" and then insists on fitting everything seen there into that preconceived notion. There's a fine line between realizing that a particular detail is not especially important and doesn't need to be included, and deliberately leaving out a significant detail because it fights with the impression you had decided beforehand you wanted to create.

Be faithful to the truth of what you find. Don't fake a story to make it fit your objectives.

Color writers also need to have faith in the power of honest writing and reading. They don't have to instruct readers about how to react to the place they're describing, giving a benediction ("Everyone had a great time at the fair") or a judgment ("Seeing St. Paul's is an uplifting experience"). Color writers should believe in the intelligence of readers. If the description is written well, the reader will understand clearly that everyone had a great time at the fair, or that visiting St. Paul's is an uplifting experience. Furthermore, the reader's impression is stronger when earned rather than ordered.

There would be no point, for example, to adding comment to color writing as strong as Greta Tilley's. Part III of her six-part series describing Dorothea Dix Hospital, a mental institution in Raleigh, North Carolina, follows this chapter. Read "On Dix Hill life moves with the mood," and you'll have *been there*. She doesn't have to tell you how to react; you can't help it.

EXERCISES

1. The following exercises will help improve your use of figurative language and imagery:

   a. Describe the music of your favorite rock group by writing four similes, each having to do with a sense other than sound (that is, with the senses of sight, taste, feeling, and smell). For example: "Madonna's singing tastes like a frosty drink of Kool-aid and gin."

b. Sustain a simile or metaphor over two or three paragraphs comparing your life to an old or current television program. For example: "Some days my life feels like an episode of Murphy Brown. . . ." Be sure you make several points of comparison between your world and the world of the television show.

c. Find a room that elicits a strong emotional reaction from you, one that disgusts you or makes you feel sunny and cheerful, or cool and serene. Write a few paragraphs describing that room. Then have another person read your description and tell you what feelings the description elicits from him or her. Do the two sets of feelings match?

d. Go to a room particularly associated with someone you know. Describe the room, filling your description with physical details about items in the room that represent the personality of the person who occupies it. Then ask someone to read your description and tell you what kind of person he or she thinks lives there.

2. Read the following description of the dropping of an atomic bomb on Nagasaki, an excerpt from an article written by a William L. Laurence of *The New York Times*. Laurence accompanied the planes on their mission. (His story won the 1946 Pulitzer Prize for Reporting.) Why are there so *many* similes in his description? We usually say that a simile should be appropriate to its subject. Why, then, does this writer compare the terrible bomb to such positive things as "Old Faithful" and a rose-colored blossom? How can that be appropriate?

3. Greta Tilley's color story about Dorothea Dix Hospital is full of observed physical details. What are some of these details, and what do they suggest about the quality of life at Dix Hill? Besides being rich in descriptive writing, Tilley's story is full of human drama. Discuss some of the people she presents. How does she describe them? Why are they memorable? (The Dorothea Dix Hospital Series helped Tilley, of the *Greensboro News and Record*, win a 1985 writing award for non-deadline writing from the American Society of Newspaper Editors.)

Excerpt from *Reporter Saw Atomic Bomb Dropped on Nagasaki*

by William L. Laurence

The New York Times, *September 9, 1945*

Out of the belly of *The Great Artiste* what looked like a black object went downward.

Captain Bock swung around to get out of range; but even though we were turning away in the opposite direction, and despite the fact that it was broad daylight in our cabin, all of us became aware of a giant flash that broke through the dark barrier of our arc welder's lenses and flooded our cabin with intense light.

We removed our glasses after the first flash, but the light still lingered on, a bluish-green light that illuminated the entire sky all around. A tremendous blast wave struck our ship and made it tremble from nose to tail. This was followed by four more blasts in rapid succession, each resounding like the boom of cannon fire hitting our plane from all directions.

Observers in the tail of our ship saw a giant ball of fire arise as though from the bowels of the earth, belching forth enormous white smoke rings. Next they saw a giant pillar of purple fire, ten thousand feet high, shooting skyward with enormous speed.

By the time our ship had made another turn in the direction of the atomic explosion the pillar of purple fire had reached the level of our altitude. Only about forty-five seconds had passed. Awe-struck, we watched it shoot upward like a meteor coming from the earth instead of from outer space, becoming ever more alive as it climbed skyward through the white clouds. It was no longer smoke, or dust, or even a cloud of fire. It was a living thing, a new species of being, born right before our incredulous eyes.

At one stage of its evolution, covering millions of years in terms of seconds, the entity assumed the form of a giant square totem pole, with its base about three miles long, tapering off to about a mile at the top. Its bottom was brown, its center was amber, its top white. But it was a living totem pole, carved with many grotesque masks grimacing at the earth.

Then, just when it appeared as though the thing had settled down into a state of permanence, there came shooting out of the top a giant mushroom that increased the height of the pillar to a total of forty-five thousand feet. The mushroom top was even more alive than the pillar, seething and boiling in a white fury of creamy foam, sizzling upward and then descending earthward, a thousand Old Faithful geysers rolled into one.

It kept struggling in an elemental fury, like a creature in the act of breaking the bonds that held it down. In a few seconds it had freed itself from its gigantic stem and floated upward with tremendous speed, its momentum carrying it into the stratosphere to a height of about sixty thousand feet.

But no sooner did this happen when another mushroom, smaller in size than the first one, began emerging out of the pillar. It was as though the decapitated monster was growing a new head.

As the first mushroom floated off into the blue it changed its shape into a flowerlike form, its giant petals curving downward, creamy white outside, rose-colored inside. It still remained that shape when we last gazed at it from a distance of about two hundred miles. The boiling pillar of many colors could also be seen at that distance, a giant mountain of jumbled rainbows, in travail. Much living substance had gone into those rainbows. The quivering top of the pillar was protruding to a great height through the white clouds, giving the appearance of a monstrous prehistoric creature with a ruff around its neck, a fleecy ruff extending in all directions, as far as the eye could see.

. . .

PART III: ON DIX HILL LIFE MOVES WITH THE MOOD
From the DOROTHEA DIX HOSPITAL SERIES
by Greta Tilley
Greensboro News & Record, *May 1, 1984*

Raleigh—The lobby of Hoey Building smells of institutional cleaner and early lunch.

People still able to do some things for themselves live here in the largest of the three geriatric units at Dorothea Dix Hospital.

A technician in white pants and jacket waits at the first-floor elevator, and turns a key to start it toward the second floor. Locks clicking open and closed make some of the hospital's less haunting music. Uniforms are optional on Dix Hill. Staff members are the people carrying the keys.

Sarah Stevens is a friendly woman who has been drawing a paycheck at the hospital for 28 years. Right now, she says, it's time to take the patients to eat.

Curses invade the elevator before it stops.

The doors open to a tall, reedy man in a state-issued green shirt and pants and a long white beard a shade paler than his skin. He is waving long arms in all directions and stomping black shoes against the floor. He looks as if he will hit anyone in his way.

"Damn it, I ain't gonna do it, I told you. You'll have to knock me across the floor. He already took all my blood. They're trying to kill me."

People wearing an assortment of garments and expressions are standing around the man someone calls John. Some stare at him. Some shout back. Some don't seem to see him at all.

Stevens moves toward them. She takes the arm of a woman jerking and crying hoarsely, leads her to the elevator and tells her it's almost time for lunch.

The woman's pink dress hangs unevenly around her knees. Her hair is white with streaks the color of nicotine. Whiskers grow from her chin. Blood is clotted on a small piece of adhesive tape above one eye.

Before the scene jells, two men in white uniforms have calmly and without force convinced John to move down the hall.

Stevens says he will be locked in a seclusion room until he can compose himself. Someone will look in on him every 15 minutes.

All patients know about seclusion. When they become abusive and can't control themselves, they are isolated in a room stripped bare of temptation.

The only furnishing is a thin mattress on the floor. The single overhead lightbulb has been wrapped in metal braces. The high window is protected by an inverted screen thick with wire. Electrical sockets have been sealed.

Disturbed people can still find targets. In one seclusion room, the black baseboards have been ripped from the wall.

If patients become too violent or try to turn on themselves, their hands and feet are buckled to a stretcher. Some of the leather restraints are scarred by teeth marks.

Stevens says the staff can tell when John starts losing his grip. He paces the floor, plays the radio too loud and dances.

Everyone was frightened of John when he came to Dix from Central Prison, she says. He was charged with killing three people and had a long record of assaults. He couldn't seem to stay out of seclusion in the months after he arrived. Slowly, he is adjusting.

Stevens hasn't stopped moving. She is directing patients on to the elevator for a ride to the cafeteria downstairs.

They walk with small, jerky, shuffle steps. They talk with tongues that roll lazily around their mouths as if they are going to swallow or bite them. Their clothes may or may not match, their skin is thin and mottled. They seem to be looking someplace far away.

Ramie, the woman in the pink housedress, has become hysterical.

"I ain't hungry," she cries. "I'm not going to lunch."

She runs from the elevator, sits on the floor and pulls up her dress. She has on white socks and no shoes.

"Nurse, nurse, don't make me eat, nurse. I don't want to eat."

In the dining room, some of the 52 people who belong to Ward B get their own trays, others have them carried. Patients push friends in wheelchairs and give away food they don't want. A technician rescues a man choking on phlegm.

Food is eaten by fork, spoon and fingers. Some meals disappear quickly. Some are only tasted. One woman chews the same bite of chicken over and over without closing her mouth.

"Hey, you work in a department store," yells a slender man with gray state clothes and more gums than teeth, "or in the cotton mill?"

Ramie sits down, eats a few bites and walks to the door still chewing. "You ready to go? Come on, Sarah, let's go."

She sits on the floor, gets up, races over to a woman drooping over her food, and pats her on the back.

"Don't touch me," the woman says.

A patient with short silver and black hair walks up. She's wearing a blue sweater, blue jogging shoes and white athletic socks with orange stripes.

"What's your name," she asks.

"I ain't got no name," she says.

"Where are you from?"

"I'm from nowhere," she says.

"That's where I'm from. Nowhere."

Ramie and the man in gray, now rocking on his haunches by the door, exchange hard slaps.

"You're gonna have to go back to your room," he says.

"Ready to go, doctor?" Ramie asks a male technician. "What ya'll waitin' on?"

She takes a coffee cup from the tray of a man quietly eating in a wheelchair and carries it off. He says nothing.

"Hey, put that man's cup back where it belongs," yells a man in a blue flannel shirt and brogans.

Ramie obeys. Her hand convulses against her stomach, a tradeoff for years of medication. Without the medicine she wouldn't be as calm.

"You ready to go? Ready to go, nurse? Ready to go, sir? Ready to go?"

She takes a cup of coffee from the hand of the woman from nowhere. The woman lets her drink.

"Nurse, I want to spit," says the man sitting in the wheelchair with a tray attached. These are the first words he has spoken. He doesn't seem as restless as the other patients.

Stevens explains that Bennett's wheelchair is a geri-chair, used as a restraint. Without it, she says, he would be violent.

"Hey, how about moving Ramie from upstairs," the woman from nowhere asks Stevens. "I can't stand this fuss. How about giving her extra medicine like they gave me."

Stevens doesn't answer. Ramie is pulling her to the door.

"You have your ups and downs," Stevens says. "You can see good changes and you can see bad changes. It's not like going to the same job every day. I can have a week off and I'm ready to come back."

The patients have been escorted back upstairs to the day room. They are watching television, sleeping, bickering, wandering, talking to themselves, and rocking in chairs. A woman sings "Jesus Loves Me."

Stevens has ducked into a tiny storage room so she won't be interrupted. She reaches into her smock pocket for a cigarette. Cigarette manufacturers would be delighted to see the amount of tobacco burned on Dix Hill.

"Right now our ward is louder than normal," she says. "Our manic-depressives are up. We seem to have about three or four to cycle at a time. It's good because if we had them all at once. . . . The other patients that aren't manic-depressives, it gets on their nerves and they get very nervous and upset."

Stevens was hired before doctors found that drugs can ease a troubled mind. The wards were full of anxious patients in the 1940s. Training didn't come with the job.

"You were just slapped on the floor to learn the best you could," she says. "There's a difference in working with a schizophrenic and manic-depressive. It helps to know how to deal with them."

Stevens has made the rounds of jobs in the hospital. She was moved up to supervisor, but missed the patients and asked to be a technician again. In the last month she has been demoted from a shift leader to "Tech I" because there were too many shift leaders.

Like cards in a poker game, positions are frequently shuffled to adjust to the latest mandate from downtown. Rules are made by state, federal and hospital regulatory agencies.

Threats don't come only from outside. A patient threw a tray at Stevens' head. She had stitches and came back the next day. Another patient knocked her against a metal door. She cut her head again.

"You have to be cautious," she says, "You cannot be afraid. You have to tell yourself that they are mental patients and that you are there to help them."

Many patients come into the geriatric units with chronic brain syndrome such as Alzheimer's disease, or with organic brain syndrome, or as manic-depressives, whose moods swing from hysterically high to dangerously low, even catatonic.

"There are a lot of manic-depressives in these two buildings," says Kay Thornton, nurse in charge, "and they kind of cycle. We try to even them out between two buildings so they don't get too wild."

Fifteen manic-depressives live upstairs in Ward B.

"You can't stop a cycle," Thornton says. "Once they go from their manic to depressed state you can't stop it. Carol'll tell me, 'It's a full moon outside, I'm fixing' to blow.'

"They can't take too much medicine either. If you give more than the usual dose, their blood pressure hits rock bottom. You have to keep them comfortable and dry and let them holler.

"When they get in their hyper cycle they try to rearrange the ward for you. Drag furniture all over the room. That's where seclusion comes in."

Patients usually stay on geriatric wards about five years, until they die or move somewhere else. One has lived at Dix 62 years; two others for 20. There aren't many places for them to go. Nursing homes, already crowded, don't want them because they can be too aggressive or wander off.

"In Wilson, a TB sanitorium was turned into a state nursing home," Thornton says. "The Dobbin Building used to have room for 160 patients here. Well, Dobbin closed and sent all those people to Wilson. So as Wilson has one to die we send one from here over there."

Thornton has worked with older patients 20 years. It's hard.

"They don't tell you about themselves. You have to be able to tell about them by the look on their face or the way they walk. Constipation is a big problem. If they are constipated they walk leaning to one side.

"They steal from one another. Borrow each other's clothes and swear up and down, 'It's mine.' They go to the dining room and put a slice of bread in their pocket and forget about it. It gets molded and draws roaches."

A person who doesn't like the job doesn't last long in Hoey.

Attachments form. Some patients have no one; some have relatives who don't care. Some families are uncomfortable with mental illness and visit no more than one or two times a year.

So the staff becomes family. Dependency intensifies the hold. Thornton doesn't believe she would be happy anyplace else.

At lunch two weeks later, Ramie is upset again in the dining room. Somebody hit her in the eye, she says, and it's her only good eye, and she's blind and can't see, and doesn't know what to do.

She is wearing the same pink housedress with a white sweater and scuffs. A tear drops into her food, which she has been putting on John's plate.

John looks better than the day of his scene near the elevator, when his rage put him into seclusion. Jake Lane, the campus barber, has trimmed his white beard and shortened the hair around his ears. He's again wearing a lime green shirt and pants, courtesy of the state.

"Maybe I'll look pretty nice when I'm laid away," he says after a compliment on his appearance. "What I'm worried about is whether I'll be pretty in a box."

John tries to console Ramie during the meal. He asks her to eat. She doesn't.

He takes her hand, holds it, and softly tells her everything will be all right.

She can't be comforted.

"I'm blind, John, I'm blind," she says. "I'm blind," she shouts across the table. "It's my good eye, and I'll never be able to see."

John empties their trays, puts his arm around Ramie and leads her to the elevator.

Upstairs in the day room, she sits down on the floor and screams.

John stoops and talks to her in a low voice. She lets him lift her up and take her to a chair in the corner. He sits next to her and pats her on the shoulder while she talks and cries.

"Hush, Ramie, hush," William yells from across the room.

"I will, William," Ramie calls back, sobbing.

"You will, Ramie, or I'll knock the hell out of you," Martha says.

Garland Guion, a young technician with soft brown eyes, unlocks a door and comes back with a box filled with packs of labeled cigarettes. The schedule says it's time to smoke. Guion disappears behind a rush of patients pressing around the box.

Thornton nods toward a wizened little woman wearing a plain cotton dress. She is slumped in a chair. Her mouth is open.

"When she cycles," Thornton says, "she puts on all of her makeup and every strand of jewelry she owns and a purple dress. The other day, we caught her and Mr. Edwards in the bushes next to the canteen."

She points down the row of seats to a man in a red flannel shirt and glasses. He's asleep.

"We had to put their pass cards on different times," she says. "It's kind of hard to explain to him why he was wrong. She's so embarrassed when she realizes what she does. She says, 'Oh, why did you let me do it?'

"That's the way it is around here. Sad and funny at the same time. That's the way you have to look at it, anyway. You can see why."

John and Ramie haven't moved from the chairs pulled side by side. Ramie's crossed leg is swinging back and forth. John's yellowed fingers hold a cigarette.

. . .

Profiles
Capturing the Essence of Personality

A personality profile is in many ways like a color story, except that it focuses not on a place, but on a person. Just as color stories make readers feel that they've *been* at a particular scene, profile stories make readers feel they have *been* at the scene of the journalist's interview with a particular subject. Readers feel connected and close to the person profiled, just as they feel connected and close to the location of the color story.

The profile, however, goes beyond the color story in that it tries not only to present personality, but to examine it closely. Daniel Williamson in *Feature Writing for Newspapers* (Hastings House) writes that a personality profile is an in-depth story that "captures the essence of his personality"; it is a story that captures "a human being on paper."

Helene Barnhart, in *How to Write and Sell the 8 Easiest Article Types* (Writer's Digest Books) has a more limited definition, suggesting the importance of the original meaning of the word "profile" in the phrase "personality profile":

> When a portrait photographer or an artist wants to capture one side of a person's face only, he has that person sit so as to let the light fall on just one side of the face—the profile.
>
> In the same way, a writer can *highlight* a particular area of a person's life. The profile article is not a cradle-to-grave account; the writer zeros in on his subject in relation to a specific activity or circumstance.

These definitions may at first seem contradictory: if the story highlights one area of a person's life, how can it capture the essence of a whole human being? But both ideas about the personality profile are correct.

When you write a profile, you exercise selectivity over the massive amount of material you have learned about your subject. You highlight what will interest or affect your particular audience. Your selectivity means your article will ignore large areas of your subject's life. Nonetheless, what you *do* choose to write about will be presented in depth. Readers should be able to sense ambiguities and complexities of character that make the human being seem real, and not a flat stereotype or a simplistic creation of celebrity promotion. Your profile should study the person inside and out, look at image and reality, so readers feel rewarded for their reading because the profile subject's character becomes clearer, is better understood, than it was before.

THE SUBJECT OF THE PROFILE

Typically, the subject of a personality profile is someone newsworthy—that is, someone in the news because he or she is a celebrity, has the power to have an impact on readers' lives, is involved in a controversy, is the first to do something in a particular field, or is engaged in an interesting activity. While most profile subjects are newsworthy simply because of who they are, some profile subjects have a secondary newsworthiness because they are connected to a recent news event—for example, they have just published a new book or performed in a new movie or play.

However, the subject of the profile does not *have* to be newsworthy in the usual way; the subject can also be an eccentric character you believe to be particularly intriguing, such as a cleaning lady who was once a millionaire, or a horse racing aficionado who has been around the local racetrack for the last forty years. Virtually any person you meet or observe can be the subject of a profile. If you find someone interesting and enjoy listening to his or her stories, then it is likely your readers will also find this person interesting and will enjoy reading about him or her—unless, that is, your curiosity has grown from a special interest particular to you.

Locations such as small towns or religious communities, and organizations such as new businesses can also be profiled. In such profile stories, the character of the place or the organization is described and examined. The article considers the nature of the place, tries to understand what makes it succeed or fail, why things occur there that might not occur quite the same way any place else.

PROFILES, SKETCHES AND THUMBNAILS

Personality profiles, while all having generally the same intent, do come in different shapes and sizes, so to speak. When we use the word "profile," technically we mean a magazine article of substantial length, anywhere from 2,000 to 10,000 words. Newspaper profiles, called "sketches," are generally from 750 to 2,000 words. "Thumbnails," profiles of a few hundred words, can be presented individually, as boxed stories accompanying major news stories, or grouped together in a series, for example, in an article about candidates for public office or actors in a play just opening.

The process through which the profile story is written can also vary. At one end of the spectrum is the profile written following an interview with just one person, the subject. At the other end of the spectrum is the profile written following interviews with everyone *but* the subject, who has refused to cooperate with the journalist and be interviewed at all. Between the two ends of the spectrum lie more typical profiles, based primarily on an interview with the subject, but also containing some information from interviews with other people who are able to explain the subject's personal history or describe his or her performance at work or play.

Another thing that can vary is the number of interviews done with any one profile subject. For a sketch, a single interview is probably sufficient; for a longer magazine profile, it's not unusual to do several interviews, sometimes in different locations, so the journalist can observe the subject in different moods and different environments.

The journalist's attitude toward the subject of the profile also varies. Ideally, of course, the journalist comes to the interview with a simple desire to honestly discover the nature of the individual being profiled. In reality, however, profile writers may be less than open-minded; they may come to an interview already "knowing" what they will find. Public relations practitioners, for example, may see their subjects only in a favorable light. Investigative reporters may come looking for flaws. Magazine writers may come seeking only material readers will want to read.

It may be impossible to escape from some of this intentionality in the profile interview situation. But to the best of your ability, you should approach the profile subject with as open a mind as possible. The great thing about profiles is that they result from intense one-to-one interviews, and so represent a unique mix of two personalities. If your subject is newsworthy, he or she will be interviewed and profiled many, many times. So you don't need to worry about writing the profile-story-to-end-all-profile-stories. Other profile stories will give different perspectives and different perceptions of the subject. You can write from your own experience and impressions, having approached the subject with honest curiosity, having reacted to what you alone saw and heard.

RESEARCHING THE PROFILE

Before you do your profile interview, however, you should do considerable research. Chapter 3 discussed general ways of doing research for personality-focused interviews, but two things are worth emphasizing again here. The first is, don't wait until the interview itself to ask the subject about biographical information, such as where he or she was born and where he or she went to school. Assuming the information is available, as it usually is for anyone newsworthy, do your historical research before you arrive for the interview. Learn the date and place of the subject's birth, his or her education, first job and early work experience, identity of parents and other family members, military service, travel experience, and marital status. Don't rely on public relations biographies to be completely accurate; they may color or omit material unfavorable to the person.

Second, try to do some research on any topic that is of special interest to your profile subject, particularly if the topic concerns offbeat material other interviewers might ignore. Your subject may be much more willing to talk about a particular hobby or interest than to answer the same old questions. If possible, see if this special interest could provide an unusual angle to your story. Particularly if you're a free-lancer, you might be able to follow an unusual line of questioning to create a fresh story, one that might be saleable to a publication which normally wouldn't use it. For example, *Dog World* magazine might not normally publish a profile of Bill Cosby, but it might publish a profile about him, if that article focused on his interest in champion terriers.

INTERVIEWING FOR THE PROFILE

Of all feature interviews, the personality profile probably requires the greatest observation skills. When you go for the interview, all your antennae need to be functioning at peak efficiency. You should observe and take notes about the subject's physical size, facial features, complexion, hair coloring, and voice. Watch for patterns—for the way the person consistently moves or stands, for nervous mannerisms the person possesses, for phrases or words that he or she keeps using, for ideas or topics he or she keeps bringing up or avoiding. All create a sense of who that person is beyond the concerns likely to be articulated in the interviewee's answers to your questions.

Note what the person wears, since style preference reveals personality, and note the memorabilia and other objects in the subject's environment; they too give clues to character. Note how the subject interacts with other people who interrupt your interview or wander onto the scene. Interaction with others, especially with people of little status or significance, can show a private side to your subject that he or she may prefer to hide.

When it comes to what you ask in profile interviews, two kinds of questions are used more often than in straight information-seeking interviews. The first is the quirky question, something like ''What has been your worst nightmare?'' a question designed to reveal thoughts below the surface. If the question is bizarre enough, it can startle the subject into an immediate response that is unrehearsed and, therefore, more likely to be character-revealing.

However, if the subject of your interview is someone newsworthy for some serious reason, someone like the new conductor of the orchestra, asking that person whether he or she received valentine chocolates may be taking the idea of the quirky question too far. You will seem frivolous and silly. You could, however, ask the conductor which musician of another century he or she would choose to be, if he/she could live the life of someone else. The answer to that question might tell you more about the new directions in which the conductor will move the symphony than the stock question: "What are your plans for the future?"

The other kind of question used in profile interviews is the question forcing the subject to tell anecdotes or little stories of the past. Such stories help illumine the subject's character. Questions that elicit anecdotes usually start with "tell me about" or "describe"; they often deal with "first" and "most" situations—for example, "Tell me about the first game you played as a professional athlete" or "Describe your most embarrassing experience as a new teacher." Questions producing anecdotes require skillful wording, so you need to work extensively on them beforehand. But they are well worth the effort, because they produce narrative material which can provide a break from the standard responses used as straight quotes in the profile article.

WRITING THE PROFILE

When it comes to writing the profile story, you'll find that, as usual, there are few hard and fast rules. The one minimum requirement seems to be that the article include some background information about the person's past—unless the background information is unavailable, or is so well known that it really doesn't bear repeating. The article should also include some physical description of the person being profiled. How much physical description it should include varies, depending on how well known the appearance of the subject already is and how significant the subject's appearance is to an understanding of his or her character.

Generally speaking, profiles contain more description than most other features; they are very much like color stories in that respect. Like color stories, profiles use a great deal of sensory language and many figures of speech, not only in describing the subject, but also in describing his or her surroundings.

The profile, in addition to using description, uses factual material about personal background and the achievements of the subject. It uses direct and indirect quotations to relate what the subject and other people have said in interviews. It uses narrative for relating personal anecdotes that the subject or other people have related. It may also use a bit of personal narrative, if the journalist describes the dynamic interaction of the interview situation.

The profile requires that these writing modes blend together smoothly, so that the reader moves effortlessly and naturally from one kind of writing to the next, without readers' consciously noticing, "Now I'm reading description; now I'm listening to a story." Transitions are terribly important, as is the story's timing. You need to keep the article flowing and be sensitive to when the reader is ready for a change—when you've written enough factual biographical material, for example, or when a narrative anecdote has gone on long enough.

THE PROFILE LEAD

The lead for the profile story should make the reader sit up and take notice, get him or her interested in finding out more about this fascinating person. The less well known your subject is, the more your lead needs to arouse reader interest. At the same time, however, you should make sure that the lead reflects the character of the person you're profiling, and is a small but typical fragment of the whole picture.

So, as you're writing the lead for your story, think long and hard about your subject. Sort through your impressions, all that you saw and heard at the interview, and decide what element stands out. What seems memorable? What is the first picture, story, or quote that comes to your mind? When all is said and done, what one word or phrase seems to sum up all you've just learned about this person? Use that image, quote, or anecdote as the touchstone/lead for your entire article.

For many writers, a narrative anecdote, a bit of personal history, is the best way into the story. For example, Cynthia Gorney, in her *Washington Post* profile celebrating the 75th birthday of Dr. Seuss, begins her profile with an anecdote that illustrates his creative process:

> LA JOLLA, Calif.—One afternoon in 1957, as he bent over the big drawing board in his California studio, Theodor Seuss Geisel found himself drawing a turtle.
>
> He was not sure why.
>
> He drew another turtle and saw that it was underneath the first turtle, holding him up.
>
> He drew another, and another, until he had an enormous pileup of turtles, each standing on the back of the turtle below it and hanging its turtle head, looking pained.
>
> Geisel looked at his turtle pile. He asked himself, not unreasonably, What does this mean? Who is the turtle on top?
>
> Then he understood that the turtle on top was Adolf Hitler.
>
> "I couldn't draw Hitler as a turtle," Geisel says, now hunched over the same drawing board, making a pencil scribble of the original Yertle the Turtle drawings as he remembers them. "So I drew him a King What-ever-his-name-was, King" (scribble) "of the Pond." (Scribble) "He wanted to be king as far as he could see. So he kept piling them up. He conquered Central Europe and France, and there it was."
>
> (Scribble)
>
> "Then I had this great pileup, and I said, 'How do you get rid of this impostor?' "
>
> "Believe it or not, I said, 'The voice of the people.' I said, 'Well, I'll just simply have the guy on the bottom burp.' "
>
> Geisel looks up from his drawing board and smiles—just a little, because a man is taking his picture and he has never gotten used to people who want to take his picture.
>
> Dr. Seuss, American institution, wild orchestrator of plausible nonsense, booster of things that matter (like fair play, kindness, Drum Tummied Snumms, Hooded

Koopfers, and infinite winding spools of birthday hot dogs), detractor of things that don't (like bullying, snobbery, condescension, gravity and walls), is 75 years old this year.

Gorney's lead narrates a historical event in time (an afternoon in 1957), at the same time suggesting to readers Geisel's relaxed openness to ideas and inspiration. Notice that not only is the lead located in a past historical moment, but also in a present moment, that is, the moment when Geisel faces the journalist and the photographer who accompanies her (''he says, now hunched over the same drawing board''). (Gorney's profile helped her win first place in non-features in the 1980 American Society of Newspaper Editors competition.)

Some writers construct a narrative lead so it has a more suspenseful quality; the profile subject is caught in the middle of a dramatic action, and the reader keeps reading to see what happens. Barton Gellman's *Washington Post* profile of two federal prosecutors in the Mayor Marion Barry drug trial begins with such a narrative, with prosecutor Judith Retchin in the middle of high courtroom drama:

> She was about to pull the kind of move that prosecutors dream about, but no smile gave her away. No strut marked her walk to the well of the court, no tiny concession to triumph breached her reserve. At one of the biggest moments in the biggest case in town, Judith E. Retchin examined her witness as though she were asking directions to the bus.

Gellman's lead is at the same time suspenseful and revelatory of the character of his subject. Interestingly, Retchin's reserve and self-control are revealed, not in terms of the actions the journalist sees, but rather in terms of those he does not.

A very common lead for feature writers is a description of the location of the interview. Such a lead grabs the reader's attention by emphasizing the feeling that he or she is there, in the room, observing the subject right along with the journalist. Free-lancer Deborah Solomon begins her profile of artist Elizabeth Murray for *The New York Times Magazine* with this description:

> As she often does, Elizabeth Murray sits at a table in her studio, sipping coffee from an oversize cup and thinking about her work. She lives in a loft in lower Manhattan, and her studio, a long, bright room, occupies the front half. There isn't much in it beyond the usual trappings of an artist's work place. Brushes in all sizes and crumpled tubes of oil paint are heaped on wooden carts, and the air is thick with their greasy scent. A miniature easel, complete with a picture by one of the artist's children, stands in a corner.
>
> While the room is ringed with paintings and pastel drawings in various stages of completion, the wall in front of the table is reserved for postcards. They are images of the artist's favorite paintings, and have been here for years. Several are Cezannes, one of them a portrait of his wife, Hortense, a stout matron in a blue dress, her lips locked into a frown.

"It's funny," Murray says, standing up to remove the postcard from the wall for closer inspection. "Cezanne painted apples and kitchens and his wife in an easy chair, but no one ever called him a painter of domestic scenes. No one would ever call a man that. Why do people say I paint domestic dramas?"

Not only does Solomon's lead make the reader feel he or she is sitting in that New York loft listening to Murray, but the question Murray raises as she examines her postcard is a central issue concerning her art, and thus, a central issue of the profile concerning this woman.

Notice that Solomon does not directly mention that she is in the room with Murray, though it's obvious she is there. Many profile writers at least mention their presence in the room with the subject. Such references to the self, however, are usually kept to a minimum, so that the article focuses on the subject, not the journalist.

A descriptive lead can also be written when a subject is absent, as occurs in Greta Tilley's profile for the *Greensboro News & Record* of a young woman who committed suicide at age 16. After the teenager's death, Tilley sought to reveal the young girl's personality, to see what led her to shoot herself. The story begins in the teenager's bedroom, as Tilley turns her eyes (and the reader's) to all that the room contains, in hopes of finding clues to what happened:

Seven weeks have passed, yet the dim lavender room with the striped window curtains has been kept as Tonja left it.

Haphazardly positioned on top of the white French provincial-style dresser are staples of teen-age life: Sure deodorant, Enjoli cologne, an electric curling wand.

A white jewelry box opens to a ballerina dancing before a mirror. Inside, among watches and bracelets, is a gold Dudley High School ring with a softball player etched into one side and a Panther on the other. Also inside is a mimeographed reminder that a $9 balance must be paid in Mrs. Johnson's room for the 1982 yearbook. The deadline was Jan. 15.

Next to a junior high honor society certificate is a plaque inscribed to the winner of the first Terry McClured Citizenship Award, given in memory of the late Gillespie Junior High School principal who died two years ago after a courageous fight against Hodgkin's disease. Tonja was in the ninth grade when she was chosen by her teachers to receive it.

Tilley's description fails in its attempt to offer clues about the girl's suicide, but it succeeds in grabbing the reader, because it suggests that any apparently normal teenage girl—your friend, your daughter, your sister—might similarly be silently contemplating taking her own life, while participating in all the usual teenage activities. (Tilley won first place in non-deadline writing in the 1983 American Society of Newspaper Editors competition.)

Sometimes the simplest way to lead into a profile is by writing a statement that summarizes the significance of the subject, as David Germain does in his Associated Press profile of Huddie Ledbetter:

> He came out of the post-Reconstruction South, a defiant black troubadour who slung a gun as well as he plucked his oversized 12-string guitar. He went to prison for killing a man in a quarrel over a woman, and legend has it he sang his way to a pardon by enthralling the Texas governor with a plaintive blues appeal.
>
> He was sprung from another Southern prison by a genteel white folklorist who brought him north, where he dressed as a convict and played the blues for white audiences at colleges and nightclubs.
>
> Huddie Ledbetter, better known as Leadbelly, was the quintessential blues man, who lived what he sang and died on the fringes of stardom.

Sometimes a physical detail will serve to summarize the subject's significance, symbolizing the unique quality of his or her life. A profile written by Angela Wright for *The Burr,* Kent State University's student magazine, begins by presenting a person through a physical object:

> A close friend once gave Carol Cartwright, Kent State University's new president, a papier-mache statue of a clown juggling five balls. He said it symbolized her ability to balance everything she is involved in.
>
> As the first woman to head a state college or university in Ohio, Cartwright, 49, will continue the balancing act. She'll be juggling in her first months the issues of building her administration, dealing with the budget and reassessing the mission of the university.

At other times, what will most stand out is not the subject himself, but how others react to him, as illustrated by David Margolick's ironic lead for a *New York Times* profile of lawyer Thomas Barr:

> For 13 years during the epic antitrust battle that made his name, Thomas D. Barr of Cravath, Swaine & Moore waged total war against the United States Government. He clashed with several generations of antitrust lawyers from the Justice Department who were trying to break up his client, the International Business Machines Corporation. And he repeatedly attacked Federal District Court Judge David Edelstein, whom he accused of bias against I.B.M. and Cravath, and tried to take off the case. Judge Edelstein once accused Mr. Barr of "threatening" and "bullying" him by gesticulating with a red pen. At other times, the Judge called him "a very spoiled brat," "a bad boy," and "a baby"; charged him with trying to turn the trial into "a stevedore's brawl," and conducting himself in a fashion that he variously described as "unprofessional," "undignified," "intolerable," "slippery" and "absurd."
>
> But in litigation, affiliations and loyalties can shift as often as Middle Eastern alliances. So who is Mr. Barr's latest client and most enthusiastic booster? The United States Government, this time in the form of the Federal Deposit Insurance Corporation.

Margolick's lead manages to reveal a good deal about Barr's reputation, at the same time zapping the reader with the irony of the government's turn-about toward Barr—an unexpected change of events and attitudes that reveals much about the milieu in which Barr earns his living.

You might note, from the examples given above, that the lead of a profile is long even by feature standards. Usually several paragraphs are used to tell the anecdote, or complete the description, or summarize the subject's life. Such long leads work for the profile in part because the story itself is so long. In an article of twenty-five or more paragraphs, it doesn't seem inappropriate to take two or three paragraphs to begin. The lead is in proportion to the body of the story.

SPEECH TAGS AND ACCOMPANYING MATERIAL

As we said, a profile uses many quotations but is laced with other writing, particularly description. The description can be worked into the story through the speech tags: when you write what the person said, you also write how he or she said it, what he or she was doing while speaking, and where he or she was.

In your speech tags, you add phrases, clauses, or sentences, revealing more information. For example, Dana Kennedy of Associated Press describes actress Kathleen Turner's manner of speaking:

> Even when she bends over to allow a makeup artist to minister to her mane of blond hair before the photo shoot, Turner remains the center of attention.
>
> "You want me to stand where, here? Or a leetle over there?" Turner asks the photographer in her trademark flirtatious growl, affecting one of many accents in her repertoire.

Barry Paris, in a profile of Mozart biographer Marcia Davenport for *The New Yorker,* describes her physical reactions before giving her response to a question:

> The softness in the voice disappears instantly when she is asked her opinion of the popular play and film "Amadeus." A small scream is heard, and Marcia Davenport is released from her momentary melancholy.
>
> "God! It enraged me first of all because Peter Shaffer, that playwright, is a person who is obsessed with abnormal psychology. . . . So he took what he thought was sufficient material on Mozart and Salieri and turned out this play that is a tissue of lies, one lie after another."

The two-word "he/she said" speech tag, so preferred in news writing, is not necessarily preferred in profile stories. Instead, you can say things like the subject "sneered" or "said, chuckling" or "said with a grin"—words that reveal the subject's internal feelings. However, not every speech tag in a profile should be an unusual phrase replacing "he/she said." If it were, readers would soon grow weary of such excessive variety, and the effect would be spoiled. You would also run the risk of drawing so much attention to speech tags that the reader would focus on them, and not on what the subject is saying. Nevertheless, speech tags—provided you don't overdo it—offer an opportunity to use words with richer connotative meaning than "said," words that can help reveal the nature of your subject.

Speech tags and their accompanying material can also be used to reveal physical mannerisms you observe in your interview. And just as a color story can be unified by repetition in the description of certain symbolic details, a profile can be unified by the repetition throughout the story of certain significant actions.

For example, if your perception during the interview is that the subject is extremely nervous and high-strung, you would consider what you physically saw to create that impression. Did he or she get out of the chair and walk around the room at least 10 times? Or constantly drum fingers on the table? Or repeat a phrase like "you know" over and over again? After you've identified what you saw that created the impression, you write that physical action into the story, including it with the speech tags so that the reader "sees" it too. The actions are repeated in your story just as they were repeated throughout your interview.

You can also describe in your profile how the subject handled interruptions or dealt with other people who came on the scene during the interview. Consider how, for example, free-lancer Jeff Rovin describes the last few minutes of his interview with Jane Pauley for a profile in *Ladies' Home Journal:*

> Suddenly, the phone rings. Jane takes a call from a Very Important Editor who wants an interview for her trendy magazine. Explaining that she's flattered, Jane insists that she simply hasn't got the time. She's getting ready to head to East Germany tonight to tape her second special.
>
> The editor is irritated, and Jane apologizes. But when she hangs up, Jane's obviously a little miffed herself. After sitting and looking at the phone for a moment, she sticks out her tongue—and blows a raspberry.
>
> Purged, Jane smiles. As she begins to gather up papers, she overhears an NBC staffer saying that Jane has spent the last few months walking on air. In typical Pauley fashion, Jane just can't let that hyperbole pass. She shoots one last zinger over her shoulder: "Bye! Gotta float!"

The first interaction reveals how Pauley handles anger and self-important people, the second how she keeps herself in perspective. Rovin uses things that happened by chance, to show readers a part of the personality of the subject that might not be revealed through standard interview questions. In addition, he uses one action for a snappy ending to his story.

REVEALING CHARACTER

Rovin's ending shows a private side of Pauley, a side that wasn't always revealed on the *Today* show. Most writers of profiles try to show the difference between the subject's public persona and his or her private self. Descriptions, background, and anecdotes—as well as quotations—reveal the subject's intelligence, expressiveness, confidence, ambition, energy, humor, likeability, and general temperament.

For example, Matthew Purdy of Knight-Ridder chose to include in his profile of Colin L. Powell, chairman of the Joint Chiefs of Staff, this background detail:

> One Energy Department co-worker remembers that when Powell signed out of the department garage at night, his black-inked signature took up two lines.

The only reason for Purdy to include such an otherwise negligible detail is that he wants to share with readers a clue about Powell that suggests that even in as ordinary a place as a parking garage, Powell reveals himself as confident (he writes with black ink) and ambitious (large handwriting is generally believed to reveal egotism).

In a *Washington Post* profile of Cindi Lamb Manns, the founder of Mothers Against Drunk Driving, Fern Shen uses a quote rather than a physical detail to reveal Manns' positive temperament and enduring sense of humor. Manns' daughter had been paralyzed in a traffic accident caused by a drunk driver and had died by the time of Shen's interview. Shen describes the daughter's last days:

> Laura's condition was growing worse as well—she had nerve damage, her epileptic seizures worsened, she had to be put on a respirator and she had a tracheotomy. Lamb Manns remembered trying to help her daughter and herself through those final days.
>
> "I was suctioning her every 20 minutes, you had to drain this stuff out and you had to examine it and the tears were streaming down her face and I just sang a little song to her about 'sucking up the boogers, boogers boogers,'" she said, laughing. "You've got all this death and destruction around you and you need some relief."

The speech tag "laughing" seems inappropriate, until you realize that Lamb Manns is still laughing at death and destruction. Her description of herself making a soothing song out of "boogers" testifies to a gallantry, an ability to cope, that she reveals as she speaks.

Anecdotes also work particularly well to reveal the character of the profile subject. Little stories from the subject's past give an understanding of where he or she is coming from, or has been through. Readers can then understand how the subject changed to be the way he or she is today. Of course, anecdotes also illuminate character traits displayed in the past that are *still* very much a part of the subject's personality. Either way, such stories enliven the profile because they are concrete—telling of real events, real people, and real behavior—and because they show the subject in action.

PAINTING A REALISTIC PICTURE

It's important to understand that as you are showing the subject, you don't have to present only the pleasant side of that person. A too positive profile has a phony, unreal quality; it does the subject little service, because no one believes it. It's like the airbrushed photographs of cosmetic ads, or the simpering prettiness of shepherdesses in romantic paintings: no one believes those images either. If you present the subject in all his or her complexity, the reader can sort through the mixed messages and decide independently what to conclude about the character you're presenting.

For example, Gary Graff, in a Knight-Ridder sketch of Bruce Springsteen, written during Springsteen's 1992 New Jersey tour, describes how positively Springsteen's concerts have been received (''More than 200,000 fans snatched up tickets. . . . the shows have been rapturously received''). Graff also relates what critics of Springsteen have been saying:

> Since the release last March of his latest albums, ''Human Touch,'' and ''Lucky Town,'' Springsteen has been caught in a crossfire of skepticism and anticipation. A longtime workingman's hero who became a full-fledged pop culture icon with 1984's multimillion-selling ''Born in the U.S.A.'' album, Springsteen has been criticized for losing touch with his roots and with the ideals of faith and loyalty that are the bedrocks of his music.
>
> His detractors, far more numerous now than at any time in his 20-year career, point to Springsteen's move to California—where he lives in a $13 million estate with his second wife, former E Street singer Patti Scialfa, and their children, Evan James, 2, and Jessica Rae, 8 months. Detractors also point to his sacking of the E Streeters as proof of this detachment.
>
> They say that's why ticket sales are slow in cities such as Detroit, Cleveland and Los Angeles, and why his new albums, ''Human Touch'' and ''Lucky Town,'' have faltered on the charts relative to his previous outings, even though they've sold more than 3 1/2 million copies each.

Including such criticism, of course, also means that you can allow your subject to respond, as Graff allows Springsteen to do:

> ''Yeah, everybody likes to be at the top of the charts . . . but that has never been my fundamental reason for being on that stage at night and having to perform the way I've performed over the years. For me, it's a bit of a sideshow.
>
> ''People just forget that everything recycles itself, even all of the criticisms. . . . After 'Born to Run' (in 1975), I remember reading all of the 'What happened to?' articles, and it just kind of goes around and around and around . . . every time you do something different or go into a big change.''

When you have a subject about which much negative material has been written, it's more effective to deal with the negative accusations than to ignore them. Ignoring them only makes readers conclude you are either too gullible and impressed by the subject to confront the criticism, or you are deliberately trying to put one over on readers by pretending the criticism doesn't exist.

Of course, you can also be *too* negative in your portrayal of your subject and commit overkill by writing a story that overstates the case. *Washington Post* writer Martha Sherrill's profile of Sonny Bono, in town to promote a new book, captures perfectly the negatives of Bono's personality, but also leaves the reader feeling slightly uneasy and skeptical of the story's presentation of character:

> He's the ultimate ex-husband—irritating in every possible way. You know he's angry, but he acts nicey-nicey instead. When he strains to hide the bitterness, his voice gets even more nasal, as though his sinuses are tightening way inside his head. His smile grows huge.
>
> "In my heart I have disconnected from Sonny & Cher," says Sonny Bono, "and I feel great about that."
>
> But wait . . . he seems tired, downtrodden, slightly depressed. The poor guy. Imagine talking about your ex-wife—who left you in the dust big time—in five major U.S. cities. He's got a book now, "And the Beat Goes on," which is mostly about their time together. He may still be the mayor of Palm Springs, but you can't help feeling sort of bad for him—Cher's so famous, so hip, she's got all those cute guys, and there he is . . . with his nasal voice, his forced niceness, his gigantic capped teeth. *The heartbeat goes on.* He's still the same old Sonny. Emphasis on old. What long teeth! His lips have some trouble.

WHAT IT'S ALL ABOUT

Because journalists avoid passing judgment on people, finding an appropriate ending for your profile can be difficult. You don't want a last benediction which rhapsodizes about the wonders of the subject, or a final prediction about what evils will befall the subject if sinful ways aren't mended. Yet you want an ending that wraps up the story with a succinct suggestion of the general, overall character of the subject—something that seems to say, when all is said and done, what he or she is all about.

Usually journalists let other people say what they can't or would prefer not to say. So, typically, in ending the profile, they quote another person's conclusions rather than voicing their own. By far the most common profile ending is a quotation, either by the subject or by someone else about the subject. The quotation offers an assessment of the quality or meaning of the subject's life.

For example, Judy L. Thomas' profile for Knight-Ridder of anti-abortion advocate Randall Terry ends with his own defense of his work:

> He shrugs off complaints from critics that he is trying to force his religious beliefs and morals on others.
>
> "Every law we have is an imposition of someone's morality on someone else," he said. "I'm sure that all the rapists are going, 'Now you non-rapists are pushing your morals on us, and uh, we don't like it.' "

Shen's profile of MADD founder Lamb Manns, mentioned earlier, ends with this sobering assessment:

> In the end it all comes back to Laura. At the end of a day of speeches, interviews, morning talk shows, speaking cheerfully about what she wrought from her daughter's death, Lamb Manns predicted, "I'll go home and cry."

Other writers use the judgments of those who know the subject to wrap up their profiles. The profile of Tom Barr cited previously concludes with a colleague's comment that "He [Barr] is as happy now as I've seen him in a long time." Purdy's profile of Colin Powell, also mentioned earlier, concludes with a friend's judgment: "Underneath this tremendous record of achievement is not a person who meticulously planned out all those moves."

A second common way of ending the profile is to return to whatever idea the lead emphasized—a conclusion that obviously works best if you have written an appropriate lead, one that indeed captures the essence of the person you're profiling.

If the profile has been unified by frequent references to something, another way to end the profile is by referring one last time to that object, word, or image.

Another way of ending the profile may simply be to describe the end of the interview. The subject concludes the conversation with the journalist, and the article concludes its "conversation" with readers.

ANYTHING GOES

Some of the best profiles use creative approaches which particularly suit their subjects.

For example, Rick Reilly uses excerpts from the columns of sports writer Tom Murray, a journalist himself, in the profile of Murray which Reilly wrote for *Sports Illustrated.* The quotations interspersed throughout the article illuminate aspects of Murray's personal writing style, illustrating as well the attitudes and intelligence that Reilly describes.

Marcia Froelke Coburn uses extended dialogue and an emphasis on the interview situation to show, not tell, how difficult she found it to emotionally connect with her subject. Her *Rolling Stone* profile of Annette Bening reveals how Bening refused to reveal her character:

> Learning about Annette:
> "What do you think men should know about women?" I ask.
> "Gee, I'm supposed to be an expert on this?" responds Bening.
> "Well, you can be one of many experts."
> She bites her lower lip. "I'm really too shy to try to answer that question."
> "Well, let's try to answer it together."
> "I'm really hesitant to try to answer that question because, you know, why am I being asked it?"

I tick off the reasons: "You're a woman, you date men, you're playing all kinds of different roles, roles that to some degree are women defined in terms of their men. And isn't this man-woman stuff a universal concern?"

Bening sighs: "You're asking me for views on the world and relationships and things—that's what I feel uncomfortable with. I don't know how to talk about—I mean, I have opinions about things, but . . . I mean, to just generally start talking about what men should know about women . . ."

"Let's try it the other way. What should women know about men?"

"I think issues of love are fascinating," says Bening. "I'm interested in the subject. I read a lot about it. But I don't consider myself enough of an expert to sit and talk about that. I mean, I can't. God, it's too private."

"Are you a romantic?"

"Sometimes very, very much so."

"And what is romantic to you?"

Bening just smiles as she lets several beats of silence skip by.

I try again: "It could be dancing? Flowers? It could be feeling that someone truly knows you?"

"I just feel like this is too personal," she says. "Why? Why should I answer that?"

"I'm just trying to get a little idea of you," I say. "I don't mean to pry."

"I know," she says. "But I feel like this is my business. These are very personal questions, and I will only talk about this with my very dearest friends. Matters of the heart are very precious to me."

"All right."

"I'm sorry," she says. "I don't mean to be difficult."

Apparently Marcia Froelke Coburn is not the only one who had difficulty with an interview with Annette Bening. In this instance, feature writer and profile subject didn't agree about which detail was significant in revealing character.

Not too proud of Rambler

Knight-Ridder, July 26, 1991

It's beginning to look unlikely that **Annette Bening,** mother of **Warren Beatty's** child-in-progress, will appear during her pregnancy nude on the cover of Vanity Fair as did **Demi Moore.** After an interview by Glamour magazine, Bening objected to the magazine's intention to disclose the make of her car, because it was too personal. "I had included the fact that she drives a Rambler because it made her seem like a down-to-earth person, instead of some Hollywood type who drives around in a white Mercedes," Glamour's entertainment editor, **Charla Krupp,** told New York magazine. "Her spokeswoman said Annette wanted it out," and I said, "No way. Look if she's going to do an interview, she has to reveal something about herself."

One of the most famous columns written by World War II war correspondent Ernie Pyle is a Pulitzer Prize-winning profile of a Captain Waskow, an unusual profile because it includes nothing said to Pyle by the subject or anyone else in any profile interview. The article is basically Pyle's observations of reactions of the men the captain commanded when they first realized he was dead. The worth of the captain—the respect and affection his personality earned—is revealed by *their* actions, creating a sort of ultimate show-don't-tell feature article. (Pyle's story follows this chapter.)

ORGANIZATION OR PLACE, PORTRAIT OR GALLERY

As we mentioned before, you can also consider profiling a place or an organization. *The Pittsburgh Press,* for example, profiled Jehovah's Witnesses when that religious organization held a gathering at Three Rivers Stadium in Pittsburgh. The article included a description of the stadium meeting, a history of the organization, information about the size and structure of the organization, quotations from spokespeople defending the Witnesses and from critics attacking them, and information about significant court cases involving the religious group. Like most profiles, Ann Rodgers-Melnick's article ends with a quote:

> But Brumley [Phil Brumley, a staff attorney] said, "All we are telling parents is not to get the two things confused.
> "At Witness conventions we want to show the theocratic aspects of our lives, but in court we want to show the judge the whole picture. Witness children play ball, go to parties, things like that. We don't want to leave the impression that the only thing in their life is going door-to-door talking about the Bible."

Finally, your profile does not have to be limited to a single person. You can do a pair of people, as Barton Gellman did in *The Washington Post* feature mentioned earlier profiling government prosecutors. In that feature, the two subjects are quite different, one naturally restrained and cool, the other more political and passionate. Generally, profiling a pair of people works best if the people are not alike. The personalities seem sharper in contrast to each other. However, if the point is that the characters are almost identical, then profiling a similar pair is also appropriate.

A group profile can be effective when it serves a particular purpose. Michael Stone did a series of brief profiles for his article "What Really Happened in Central Park," a story for *New York* magazine about the teenage "wilding" spree in Central Park that led to the group rape and beating of a young female investment analyst. At the time of the article (August 1989), New York City was in an uproar about the brutality of the incident and general racial violence in the city. Stone's article profiled the seven teenagers arrested in connection with the incident. He wrote their portraits seemingly to answer the unspoken questions on readers' minds at that time: Are these teenagers guilty? What sort of person would do this? What happens in the inner city to make a person do this? What sort of parents raise a child who does this? Those unspoken questions, which lie behind each profile, serve to unify all the profiles into one cohesive story.

The major difficulty in writing a group profile is being sure you are even-handed. You can't ask one person easy questions, then blast the next person with difficult queries. You can't write lots of physical description of the subject of one profile, then omit any reference to physical appearance about the subject of the next. You want all the profiles to be roughly similar, and at the same time different enough so they don't seem all written to formula.

A PORTRAIT IN A PACKAGE

A last consideration is whether the single profile is enough said about the subject, or the subject's milieu. For the majority of cases, a substantial profile, with its intense scrutiny of the individual, presents all that the reader needs or wants to know. But occasionally a profile is best presented as part of a package, a package giving other insights into the context in which that person exists. For example, Stone's profiles of the Central Park "wilding" gang are part of a larger package, one that includes a narrative of what happened, a minute-by-minute timeline, pictures of the subjects and of places where events occurred, and a map of Central Park.

You might want to consider doing this kind of package. Ask yourself if there are related questions the reader might want you to answer. Does your profile make readers curious about any other topics? Is there factual background material that might be better explained through infographics or other visual material?

Ron Davis of the Springfield, Missouri, *News-Leader* won a first place for feature writing in a Gannett newspaper competition for a profile package he created about Clayton Fountain, a convicted killer considered so dangerous he lives in isolation in a custom-built, two-cell unit of the Medical Center of the U.S. Penitentiary at Marion, Illinois. Davis recognized that such an individual, and the various sides of the question of how he is incarcerated, were too big for one story.

So, after interviewing Fountain and 40 other people, as well as examining military and court records and Fountain's personal correspondence, Davis wrote several stories which were then presented in a single package in the Sunday edition of the newspaper: a profile of Fountain ("The Most Dangerous Man: Med Center's maze holds cold killer"), an examination of Fountain's relationship with his father ("Abusive Army father at root of would-be warrior's rages"), a story describing Fountain's cell ("'Suite' assures strictest security at $180,124 bill"), a listing of Fountain's convictions ("Fountain killed men as soldier, as prison mate"), an interview with a guard Fountain stabbed ("Former guard haunted by stabbing"), and a color story about the penitentiary at Marion and the way Fountain is regarded there ("'Part of the sad lore of

Marion': Fountain remembered at nation's toughest prison''). While not pleasant reading, the articles do justice to the topic; the presentation of the package says to the reader ''this is complex, difficult, and important for you to understand completely.''

When all is said and done, having some sense of the appropriateness of what needs to be written about a profile subject may be the most important ability you, as a profile writer, can possess. The best approach to each person you profile is to be open-minded and open-hearted. Be curious, be flexible, attempt to connect to this other human being to the best of your ability. *Be there* in all the ways that you can. Then simply describe the person you saw and understood. If the profile interview was funny, write about the subject in a way that's humorous. If it was depressing, write about the subject in a way that creates a depressed feeling. Don't consider what the journalists who have come before you and will come after you would say about this person. Just reveal to your readers what you have found, so readers can *be there* with you too.

EXERCISES

1. Most families have little stories about family members that illustrate some personality characteristic—how stubborn, vain, forgetful, hot-tempered, or whatever, they are. Create a written version of a family anecdote, revealing that personality characteristic. Or write a short anecdote illustrating some value your family holds dear, such as staying loyal, telling the truth, being stoic, or paying debts on time.
2. Find two profiles of the same person, either one profile from a newspaper and one from a magazine, or one from a current magazine and one from a magazine published 10 or 15 years ago. Compare and contrast the two profiles. What can you infer about the two audiences they were written for? How did each journalist seem to get along with the subject? Did the two accounts agree in their presentation of personality? If not, in what ways did they differ? What would you guess were reasons for the differences?
3. For a hypothetical profile subject, try to write an unusual, somewhat quirky question, such as ''What does your closet look like?'' or ''Ten years from now, what will you be doing?'' Try to write questions that would help you see a side of the subject seldom seen.
4. Read Ernie Pyle's ''Soldier Dies on a Moonlit Night.'' The lead suggests the story will demonstrate how beloved by his men Captain Henry T. Waskow was. The quotations about him in the story, however, are not very impressive: ''God damn it'' and ''I'm sorry, old man'' are not exactly eloquent tributes to someone's character. How, then, does the story (and its quotations) demonstrate that Waskow was beloved?

5. Waskow is the topic of Pyle's article, but atmosphere plays a significant role in the story. How is the reader affected by Pyle's continuing references to light or its absence, and to physical objects such as the stone wall, the cowshed, and the straw?

6. Read the Caryn James' *New York Times* profile of Katharine Hepburn. Discuss its effectiveness in the light of these two statements from this chapter:

> Readers should be able to sense ambiguities and complexities of character that make the human being seem real, and not a flat stereotype or simplistic creation of public relations promotion. Your profile should study the person inside and out, look at image and reality, so readers feel rewarded for their reading because the profile subject's character becomes clearer, is better understood, than it was before.

> Most writers of profiles try to show the difference between the subject's public persona and his or her private self. Descriptions, background, and anecdotes—as well as quotations—reveal the subject's intelligence, expressiveness, confidence, ambition, energy, humor, likeability, and general temperament.

SOLDIER DIES ON A MOONLIT NIGHT

Ernie Pyle

Scripps Howard Newspaper Alliance, *January 10, 1944*

In this war I have known a lot of officers who were loved and respected by the soldiers under them. But never have I crossed the trail of any man as beloved as Captain Henry T. Waskow, of Belton, Texas.

Captain Waskow was a company commander in the Thirty-sixth Division. He had led his company since long before it left the States. He was very young, only in his middle twenties, but he carried in him a sincerity and a gentleness that made people want to be guided by him.

"After my father, he came next," a sergeant told me.

"He always looked after us," a soldier said. "He'd go to bat for us every time."

"I've never known him to do anything unfair," another said.

I was at the foot of a mule trail the night they brought Captain Waskow down. The moon was nearly full, and you could see far up the trail, and even part way across the valley below.

Dead men had been coming down the mountain all evening, lashed onto the backs of mules. They came lying belly-down across the wooden pack-saddles, their heads hanging down on one side, their stiffened legs sticking out awkwardly from the other, bobbing up and down as the mules walked.

The Italian mule skinners were afraid to walk beside the dead men, so Americans had to lead the mules down at night.

Even the Americans were reluctant to unlash and lift off the bodies when they got to the bottom, so an officer had to do it himself and ask others to help.

I don't know who that first one was. You feel small in the presence of dead men, and you don't ask silly questions. They slid him down from the mule and stood him on his feet for a moment. In the halflight he might have been merely a sick man standing there leaning on others. Then they laid him on the ground in the shadow of the low stone wall beside the road. We left him there beside the road, that first one, and we all went back into the cowshed and sat on water cans or lay on the straw, waiting for the next batch of mules.

Somebody said the dead soldier had been dead for four days, and then nobody said anything more about it. We talked soldier talk for an hour or more; the dead man lay all alone, outside in the shadow of the wall.

Then a soldier came into the cowshed and said there were some more bodies outside. We went out into the road. Four mules stood there in the moonlight, in the road where the trail came down off the mountain. The soldiers who led them stood there waiting.

"This one is Captain Waskow," one of them said quietly.

Two men unlashed his body from the mule and lifted it off and laid it in the shadow beside the stone wall. Other men took the other bodies off. Finally, there were five lying end to end in a long row. You don't cover up dead men in the combat zones. They just lie there in the shadows until someone comes after them.

The unburdened mules moved off to their olive grove. The men in the road seemed reluctant to leave. They stood around, and gradually I could sense them moving, one by one, close to Captain Waskow's body. Not so much to look, I think, as to say something in finality to him, and to themselves. I stood close by and I could hear.

One soldier came and looked down, and said out loud, "God damn it!" That's all he said, and then he walked away.

Another one came, and said. "God damn it, to hell, anyway!" He looked down for a few last moments and then turned and left.

Another man came. I think he was an officer. It was hard to tell officers from men in the dim light, for everybody was bearded and grimy. The man looked down into the dead captain's face and then spoke directly to him, as though he were alive, "I'm sorry, old man."

Then a soldier came and stood beside the officer and bent over, and he too spoke to his dead captain, not in a whisper but awfully tenderly, and he said, "I sure am sorry, sir."

Then the first man squatted down, and he reached down and took the captain's hand and he sat there for a full five minutes holding the dead hand in his own and looking intently into the dead face. And he never uttered a sound all the time he sat there.

Finally he put the hand down. He reached over and gently straightened the points of the captain's shirt collar, and then he sort of rearranged the tattered edges of the uniform around the wound, and then he got up and walked away down the road in the moonlight, all alone.

The rest of us went back into the cowshed, leaving the five dead men lying in a line, end to end, in the shadow of the low stone wall. We lay down on the straw in the cowshed, and pretty soon we were all asleep.

. . .

KATHARINE HEPBURN: THE MOVIE
By Caryn James
The New York Times, *September 1, 1991*

Most movie stars come down off the screen for interviews. They walk into a restaurant, act at drinking a cup of coffee, then walk back into their real lives.

With Katharine Hepburn, the process is reversed. To cross the threshold of her Manhattan town house, where she has lived for 60 years, is to enter a Katharine Hepburn movie.

"Miss Hepburn is expecting you," says the woman in a modest housedress who answers the door and leads the way up a narrow red-carpeted staircase to a large but cozy sitting room. There she is, in a low chair with her feet on a footstool, precisely as you would have imagined her, only older.

Her hair is in its familiar topknot, though it is mostly gray. Her eyebrows are white; her skin is smooth but mottled as if from too many years in the sun. Her head, which shook visibly during television appearances in the late 1980's, is not trembling now, but as she talks she moves her head gracefully from the neck almost constantly, and a slight tremor would be impossible to detect. She is even wearing a no-nonsense Katharine Hepburn uniform: a navy turtleneck covers her neck, which she is said to be self-conscious about; a bright-red sweater-vest matches the red socks that fit into her white leather Reeboks; her khaki pants have been neatly but obviously mended.

Katharine Hepburn is 84, and would not be photographed for this article. But she looks spry, and her endlessly imitated, well-bred New England voice is still strong. "I've lived here since 1931; isn't that *incredible?*" she says. "Well, Spencer liked California, so when I began to go around with him I stayed in California more, but this house was always here." No one needs to ask who Spencer is, and she drops his name casually these days.

We do, after all, know a remarkable amount about her, though she has a reputation for being elusive with the press. In fact, over the years she has been accessible but cagey about her private life. "Now I'm trying to sell the book, so I'm adorable," she laughs, with precisely the disarming candor that runs through her autobiography, "Me: Stories of My Life" (Knopf). The book, whose manuscript has been as closely guarded as a state secret, will arrive in stores later this week.

In "Me" she comes clean about her real age, talks about her early marriage and discusses her love affairs with Leland Hayward, Howard Hughes and, of course, Spencer Tracy. "I don't know whether what I tell is going to satisfy people," she says. "I think they expect: I was born, I lived here, I did this, I did that." Instead, they will get a conversational ramble through the high points of her life.

She reportedly was paid $4 million for "Me" (up there with Gen. H. Norman Schwarzkopf's touted $5 million), and even the notoriously gossipy publishing world has not hinted that she had a ghostwriter. Like her 1987 memoir, "The Making of the African Queen," this one sounds just like Katharine Hepburn, full of exclamations, detours and questions to herself. Talking about the book, she is smart and witty; she is totally in command of her role as Katharine Hepburn, and

honest enough to admit that her screen persona and private personality have never diverged all that much.

On screen, she says, "I think I'm always the same. I had a very definite personality and I liked material that showed that personality. I never played with a sort of fancy accent of any kind. So, was I an actor? I don't know," she jokes. "I can't remember."

Being a Girl Was the Bunk

She has always played strong women, in films as different as "Little Women" (1933), "Bringing Up Baby" (1938) and "On Golden Pond" (1981). The stunning parallels between the tough-minded characters she played and her own willful, independent life have made her a role model for women, though she is aware that her privileged background makes her a peculiar one.

. . .

She has talked often about her intensely close family and her Connecticut childhood. Her father was a doctor, her mother a crusader for birth control. "They were a fascinating pair," she says now, "and it's too bad for you you couldn't meet them."

As an athletic little girl surrounded by an older brother and two younger brothers, she cut her hair short and desperately wanted to be a boy. More specifically, she called herself Jimmy. "I thought being a girl was really the bunk; I just nearly died," she says. "But there's no bunk about Jimmy."

Being bunkless has always been a Katharine Hepburn trait, but in "Me" this exemplar of straight-talking womanhood admits she has been lying about her age all these years. "I used to say I was two years younger than I am. Why, I don't know," she explains. "I think it must have started when 28 and 29 and then 30 raised its ugly head, and I thought, 'Oh, my God!'"

She also used to claim that her birthday was Nov. 8. "That was my brother Tom's birthday, who died," she says now, referring to one of the

great traumas of her life. When she was 14, she found her 16-year-old brother hanging from the rafters in a house where they were visiting. The Hepburn family refused to believe he committed suicide, saying he was practicing a magic trick at 3 in the morning, and Miss Hepburn writes that even now she wonders what happened. Whatever the case, it was Tom's birthday she took as her own. "My birthday was May 12, and I couldn't bear to have people know it," she says. "Now I think that's stupid. So they torture me on Nov. 8 instead of May 12!"

On Marriage: Luddy Was an Angel

Jimmy grew up to be an ambitious young woman, and during her first great success, in the 1930's, Katharine Hepburn played many ambitious young women. She won an Academy Award in 1933 for her role as a naïvely determined actress in "Morning Glory," her third film.

Only five years before, she had graduated from Bryn Mawr, become a professional actress and, for a time, a wife. In 1928 she married Ludlow Ogden Smith, the son of a wealthy

Pennsylvania family. She made him change his name to S. Ogden Ludlow, which saved her from being Kate Smith. For a while they shared the town house where she lives today, in the Turtle Bay section of Manhattan, but they led separate lives long before their divorce in 1934.

Writing about those early ambitious years and her marriage to Luddy, as he was called, she is extremely hard on herself. But when she is told that, she simply points a finger and offers a curt correction. "Accurate," she says she was. "That's all." Then she wonders, "How do you mean?" Well, she does write that she was an "absolute pig" in her marriage.

"Oh, absolute pig with Luddy, absolute pig," she says vehemently. "He was an angel. I thought of myself first, and that's a pig, isn't it? I think so, that's a pig. He was such a nice man and helped me so much. I was very lucky with Luddy because he really opened door after door after door to me, and I would have been terrified alone in New York City. We bought this house in '31, and then the minute I won the award I got rid of Luddy. So that's a pig, I would say.

"He and I were friends always. And then when he was older—his wife had died, he had two children—I tried to make up to him for the horror I had caused him. He was so generous-spirited that I don't think he considered it horror. He just considered it a kid who was wildly ambitious or something."

Did she consider not revealing such selfishness in her book? "No, because that's a very interesting fact about someone," she says. "I think most people who *arrive* are takers. They take at the beginning of their lives, then if they have

good characters they realize that they're pigs and they try to pay back some of it. I don't think I was a pig to my mother and father, but I certainly was a pig to Luddy."

'I Had Every Advantage'

Even at her fanciest, in "The Philadelphia Story," Katharine Hepburn had a down-to-earth streak. Now, when the telephone rings, she picks it up herself. It is an old black rotary-dial phone at her elbow, and she excuses herself for a brief conversation. All that is clear from her side of it is that she is talking about a television interview she had taped a day or so before; the pleasant but get-to-the-point approach might have been scripted for a Hepburn character.

"Hello, dear, I'm fine," she says. "Well, I think it went all right. I'm in the middle of doing one now, not with makeup, so I'll give you a buzz. I hope you won't have gone. . . . How are you feeling? . . . Yah. How do you mean funny? . . . Ugh, such a goddamn *bore,* isn't it? I'll call you when I finish; otherwise I'll get you later." She hangs up without saying goodbye.

It was a short break, but long enough to notice two small paintings on a far wall. One, in Impressionist style, is of a woman with a parasol on a beach. The other is a brightly colored, Matisse-like bowl of fruit. Asked about them, she says, in a voice much quieter and meeker than usual, "I did those." She points to a larger, more folksy canvas of gulls on a rock. "I did that one, too. That's the view from the Fenwick house," she says of the Hepburn family home in Connecticut.

. . .

When she accepts a compliment about her paintings, her modesty and pleasure seem genuinely un-self-conscious. "You couldn't have said anything that would please me more," she says, then recovers her firmer, Hepburn voice. "I love to paint—anything you can do alone. That's the trouble with acting; it requires other people and other places."

Being a loner and a stoic has not always worked to her professional advantage. In an often-told anecdote from her earliest theater days, when Miss Hepburn's acting teacher told her she had been fired from a play, she replied, "I'm not crying. Aren't you proud of me?"

Frances Robinson-Duff answered, "No, I'd be prouder if you were. That was the trouble with your performance last night. Too self-contained."

That criticism—that she is too cold—has trailed her for much of her career. Looking back at that early advice, she says, "I didn't analyze it. I knew what she meant, but I never knew quite why I was fired," though she was fired often in those days. In any event, she says, "I don't think I was capable of changing." It may be part of her Yankee toughness that she truly cannot envision failure. "I am terribly afraid I just assumed I'd be famous," she says.

Yet all the women who write her fan letters praising her success and independence should realize what was behind it, she thinks. "That's why I write the truth in that book—about Luddy and what a pig I was, and also that at the beginning I had money; I wasn't a poor little thing. I don't know what I would have done if I'd had to come to New York and get a job as a waiter or something like that. I think I'm a success, but I had every advantage—I should have been."

Spencer, Kate and Louise

During the 40's, Katharine Hepburn's screen persona was that of an independent and fallible woman, almost too smart for her own good. It was never more sharply drawn than in her role as a beautiful, intellectual newspaper columnist who falls in love with a sportswriter in "Woman of the Year" (1942). It was the first of her nine films with Spencer Tracy and the one that brought them together.

Tracy, as everyone knows, was married and remained so for the rest of his life. Although they never acknowledged publicly that they were more than friends, theirs became one of the legendary love affairs of our time. Tracy was ill when they made "Guess Who's Coming to Dinner," in 1967, and died soon after the movie was finished. To viewers, the Tracy-Hepburn on-screen marriage in that last film possessed an elegiac poignancy that had nothing to do with their fictional roles.

In a 1986 television tribute to Tracy, she read a long, eloquent letter she had recently written to him, in which she talked about their relationship straightforwardly for the first time. She became more candid, she says, because Tracy and his wife, Louise, were both dead. "And then Susie Tracy, his daughter, and I are friends. We met and we liked each other, so it seemed that it wasn't doing anybody any harm," she says.

. . .

She wonders in her book whether it might not have been better to have "straightened things out," as she puts it, but she says that in any case, "we would not have gotten married, because I think marriage is a strange relationship. It's very trying to be living in the same house with someone all the time if you're a grown-up person.

"When Spencer wasn't feeling too well, I began to move into his house, and then that makes sense because you're useful. But otherwise it's very difficult for two people who have money enough to be independent to suddenly say"—here she acts out in a mincing voice the deadening claustrophobia of having someone underfoot—"'Oh, do come in, yes, of course. No, no, leave the door open.' Your ways, my ways, oh, my! Relationships of male and female are certainly not easy. I don't have any solution."

She did, of course, find a solution that was perfect for her, one "in which Spencer could not have displeased me," she says. She takes a long pause before moving into an enchanted, almost girlish memory of Tracy.

"You know it isn't as if we agreed about everything, I don't think we did, but if it was an unpopular topic I didn't bring it up. I catered to him and that gave me a great deal of pleasure, just that very act itself, so it's tough, isn't it, to know what makes for a really happy relationship? I don't think we ever had a fight. And he was very Republican; I was way left of center. I really loved him—it's funny, it makes me laugh—I really did love him and I was *determined* that it

was going to work. I'm sure Spencer worked at it too, some; but he didn't have to work much because I really made it work."

• • •

She is describing a more traditional Hepburn than anyone might have guessed existed. "It is totally traditional, in that we did it his way. All I can say is it worked; that gave me pleasure. Now, I don't know whether that's a female characteristic or not. With Luddy, for instance, I don't know whether his freeing me totally and saying, 'Here, the door's open, here's the key,' whether he got pleasure out of that. In a sense that's what I did with Spencer, and that certainly is what Luddy did with me, so I've had the experience both ways. I've had the experience of Luddy loving me and I've had the experience of loving Spencer. And I liked Luddy enormously, but I mean, not the way I liked Spencer."

There are places in her book when she seems ambivalent about Louise Tracy, though. She goes out of her way to say that after the Tracy's son was born deaf, Louise understandably devoted herself to the child and the marriage crumbled. But there also seem to be hints of bitterness in her attitude toward Tracy's wife, who after his death told Miss Hepburn, "I thought you were only a rumor."

"After nearly 30 years?" she writes in "Me." "Some rumor. And by never admitting that I existed—she remained—the wife—and she sent out Christmas cards." But when asked about this angry tone, she says, with some surprise but no obvious annoyance, "You're very much mistaken. You're 100 percent off on the wrong trail. She had blinded herself totally to the facts from her point of view, you see. And I had been perfectly willing to accept the facts, from my point of view. And what the hell could she have done?" She adds, very much out of nowhere, "I did not break up that marriage. Spencer had delved around here and there before I met him."

She says of Louise: "I think she loved Spencer and it somehow suited her total self-sacrifice. I have great respect for her, and she certainly never made any difficulties at all for Spencer or for me. By the same token, I never went out in public with him in California, ever, and seldom here. So I think we were careful of each other's reputations."

Besides, she says, "I had everything *I* wanted."

Calla Lilies and Other Flowers

When she gets out of her chair to say goodbye, Miss Hepburn jumps up energetically. She stands a little stooped in the shoulders, and looks shorter than she must have been in her prime. Suddenly, she walks to the corner of the room and exclaims about a large vase of flowers, "Aren't they gorgeous? Look at the colors! Especially the ones that look like wildflowers."

Katharine Hepburn impersonators, devoted to her line (from "Stage Door") "The calla lilies are in bloom again," would kill for a moment like this. She is so enthusiastic that it seems these flowers must be from somewhere special, her garden or even Fenwick. But it turns out they are merely from "some place on Madison."

She leads the way back down the narrow stairway, sweetly calling over her shoulder, "Don't fall down the stairs." At the door she asks, "Do you have your machine?" concerned that the tape recorder might have been left behind. When she is told her book is likely to be a big hit, she says, "Well, if it isn't, send me flowers."

Who knows what she's like when no reporter is around? At the moment she is, as she promised she would be, adorable.

CHAPTER

9

Backgrounders
Giving Readers Explanations

Backgrounders explain the world to readers; they help readers understand how things operate, how and why they have developed, or in what ways they are likely to grow and change. Such explanatory articles are known by many names: they are called "insight," "analysis," or "enterprise" stories, as well as "backgrounders." These several names stress different aspects of a single story, the explanatory feature that helps readers understand a phenomenon or issue comprehensively rather than superficially.

In this textbook, the word "backgrounder" is used because it reinforces the idea of the article's depth; the word also reinforces the idea that these stories, to a degree somewhat greater than other feature stories, are second stories, stories coming *after* a preliminary awareness of a particular topic is acquired by readers. The word "background" implies a "foreground."

Backgrounders may have dual identities as other kinds of feature articles (news features, anniversary articles, lifestyle stories), but it is appropriate to discuss backgrounders as an individual kind of feature, because they represent a special type of writing characterized by depth and breadth, and by seriousness and formality of style. Backgrounders are distinctive in their instructive, explanatory nature; they teach and clarify, tell how and why, analyze and synthesize.

Backgrounders deal with readers in an intellectual, rational way. They present facts and statistics, summarize the opinions of authorities, provide historical information and experts' predictions about the future, and explain the current state of learning or research. The content of backgrounders, in other words, is much like the content of hard news stories. But backgrounders present considerably *more* information than news stories. Backgrounders try to paint their pictures on wide canvases, to portray entire landscapes rather than individual details visible day-by-day.

Like hard news stories, however, backgrounders are rather straightforward and factual. The tone of backgrounders is usually fairly formal, and their voice disciplined and organized. However some backgrounders, particularly those published in magazines that speak with their own "expert" voices, do have direct, friendly "conversations" with their readers. But generally, since backgrounders strive to be credible (if they're not, there's no sense in anyone's reading their explanations), they speak with a scholarly reserve and maintain a distance from their readers.

Some backgrounders are published because editors believe readers are curious about particular topics already familiar to them through current news stories. Reader interest has been generated by recent coverage of events.

These backgrounders give readers a much quicker comprehensive understanding of the situation than they could get on their own. Independently, they would have to do hours of research and interviewing, not to mention a great deal of puzzling over unfamiliar jargon, in order to understand the same information a backgrounder can give them in a clear, coherent summary.

Other backgrounders, however, are published because editors feel readers *need* to know more about something. Or editors may feel readers need to be reminded of a topic of concern, or brought up to date on something they may not have heard much about recently. Such stories are said to result from "enterprise." These backgrounders have to work a little harder to arouse reader interest, since no contemporary news accounts are stimulating readers' curiosity.

Backgrounders of both inherent interest and those that have to work to convince readers to read them try to make their instruction palatable. Factual content is usually enhanced by other kinds of feature material: fast-paced, suspenseful narratives; colorful descriptions; personal anecdotes or personality sketches; colorful and dramatic quotations.

But whether or not the bread of explanation is spread with the jam of more interesting feature writing, the basic purpose of backgrounders remains the same: to inform readers. Backgrounders create fair, open forums where issues can be discussed. The forums they create are generally neutral: backgrounders instruct, but do not evaluate. The writers of such articles give no overt judgments, create no biased slants. Backgrounders leave readers informed and educated, ready to reach their own conclusions.

EXPLAINING HOW AND WHY

Backgrounders typically ask questions, especially "how" and "why" a situation is the way it is, as the titles (or headlines) of backgrounders frequently reveal: "Are National Parks Endangered Species?" (*World Monitor* magazine), "How American Industry Stacks Up" (*Fortune*), or "Why Did the Germans Follow Hitler?" (*The Buffalo News*). Basically, backgrounders are useful to readers because they answer readers' questions—sometimes even before readers have thought of what questions to ask. Backgrounders help readers broaden or deepen their knowledge, or understand things more precisely.

For example, when John F. Kennedy Jr. failed the bar exam twice and was taking it for the third time, a backgrounder story syndicated by the *Chicago Tribune* explained to readers just exactly what made the law exam so difficult. The article also described the effect the exam's difficulty generally had on aspiring young lawyers.

When the state of Pennsylvania passed a new car insurance law, the third major insurance change in sixteen years, Associated Press writer Anne McGraw wrote a feature to help readers understand what the new law would mean. While the article's explanations were detailed and a variety of insurance experts were quoted, the backgrounder also told readers quite succinctly how the law would affect them:

> In a nutshell, the 1990 law reduces the amount of insurance drivers must carry, cuts rates for every driver by 10 percent and by 22 percent for those who give up their right to sue in most cases, and freezes rates for one year. The mandatory rollbacks take effect July 1.

TAKING IT APART TO SEE HOW IT WORKS

Some backgrounders go beyond answering questions, to analyzing the topic, that is, taking it apart and examining separately each component of the whole. Analytic articles try to increase reader awareness and understanding by describing what constitutes the unit, rather than explaining the process of how or why something works.

Sometimes, of course, describing what constitutes a unit ends up implying how that unit is effective or why it is efficient. A *Business Week* backgrounder about the successful joint venture of Mazda Motors Corp. and Ford Motor Co., for example, primarily analyzed the working arrangement of the two corporations. The article looked at various components of the arrangement: operating procedures, communication, mediation of disagreements, exchange of ideas, and treatment of cultural differences. Its description of individual components, however, also led to a better understanding of how the entire structure, the successful "marriage" of the two corporations, worked effectively.

CONTROVERSY AND CONFLICT

Some backgrounders use this analytic approach to examine the "parts" of a controversy or conflict. The article presents different sides of a "whole" issue—sometimes describing only two sides, sometimes more. Backgrounders explaining a conflict or controversy strive especially hard to be neutral. Readers should not be able to recognize which side of the controversy the writer is inclined to favor. The general tone of the article is one of disinterested, dispassionate inquiry, and the typical pattern of the story is to move back and forth from one point of view to the other, as different components of the situation are examined.

An article by Stuart Rothenberg in *Nation's Business* magazine on the term limitation for members of Congress is just such a disinterested inquiry. Even the title, ''Term Limits: False Hope or Cure?'' is determinedly neutral; it simply indicates there are two opposing points of view. The lead positions readers to see opposite sides of the question:

> You might find yourself facing this political situation: The U.S. representative from your area has never met a payroll and is much more interested in handing out your tax dollars to special-interest groups than in easing government burdens on small business. Seeking change, you approach someone who could represent your views forcefully and effectively.
>
> Will that individual run? No. Chances of winning are too slim, you are told. The incumbent uses the office to generate political support that assures re-election and the continuation of the cycle.
>
> Or: You might be represented in Congress by someone who reflects your views and those of other entrepreneurs and is gaining the experience and influence needed to turn those views into public policy.
>
> You want that individual to be representing you in the next century. But your incumbent is barred from re-election, and you're worried that the new member won't be as effective for a while.
>
> Those are two sides of an issue that is rapidly moving to the forefront of public-policy debate in America—whether there should be limits on the number of terms that can be served by members of Congress and state legislatures.

Rothenberg's article, like many backgrounders about controversy, moves continually back and forth, telling first one side and then the other. Rothenberg is even careful to balance his presentation by indicating that some of the opponents are Democrats and some Republicans, just as some of the proponents are Democrats and some Republicans.

A common type of backgrounder dealing with controversy or conflict is the story that describes the positions of candidates in an election (the conflict is that they are fighting for the same office), or describes the various positions of different interest groups toward a single candidate (different sides to one controversial subject).

SUMMARIZING THE SITUATION

Whether the backgrounder answers questions, explains ''how'' or ''why,'' or identifies and describes the parts of the whole, the article usually begins with a lead that summarizes the situation. One way or another, the lead makes clear to readers what questions the story answers, what condition it explains, or what phenomenon it analyzes. Sometimes the lead can be quite brief, as is this lead for a *Wall Street Journal* backgrounder by Allanna Sullivan on the conflict between the Alaskan Wildlife Refuge and oil drilling interests; the lead merely asks:

> MARSH CREEK ANTICLINE, Alaska—Should the oil industry be allowed to drill here in the Arctic National Wildlife Refuge?

Other leads take quite a while to establish the question and the dimensions of its significance, as does this opening section of a *Washington Post* backgrounder by Kathy Sawyer on the presence of puzzling hydrogen clouds in outer space:

> Today's weather in the cosmos: unbelievably cloudy.
>
> The Hubble Space Telescope has surprised astronomers by discovering that the cosmos is strewn with vast intergalactic hydrogen clouds.
>
> According to widely accepted theory of how the universe has evolved since the Big Bang, such clouds should have disappeared. There shouldn't be that much hydrogen loose in space and there is no known mechanism that would keep it clustered in such discrete clouds.
>
> "It's by far the most significant result Hubble has [produced] so far," said Edward Weiler, NASA's chief Hubble science manager.
>
> Confirmed by independent teams working with two different instruments aboard the orbiting observatory, the discovery, reported in the Aug. 10 Astrophysical Journal, has ignited what one scientist called "a small ferment" among cosmologists—those who study the large-scale structure and evolution of the universe.
>
> Before the Hubble finding, scientists had come to believe that primordial clouds of hydrogen created in the original Big Bang an estimated 15 billion years ago had long since collected into stars and galaxies, leaving most if not all of the rest of the gas to diffuse evenly throughout space.
>
> But early this year, using an unprecedented combination of advanced technology and vantage point in orbit, two spectrographs aboard the Hubble detected up to 10 times the expected number of the clouds near Earth's Milky Way galaxy. They are apparently everywhere in today's cosmos—and in the same abundance as in the young universe of 10 billion or 12 billion years ago.
>
> The mystery, scientists said, is how these clouds can exist today. Thinner by far than smoke, they presumably should have spread out into virtual nothingness long ago. So what has held them together over the eons—assuming they are not new creations?

The lead of a backgrounder story can also grab readers into a story, if it is the kind of backgrounder they wouldn't otherwise be inclined to consider reading. For example, a backgrounder can have a teaser lead, such as this lead to a *Washington Post* story by Paula Span on the conflict between the Smithsonian Institution and a New England town over the terms of a will:

> In an ordinary summer in this seaside village on Cape Ann, the most talked-about event of the season is likely to be the rescue of a pleasure boater with a balky outboard. This year, however, there were angry letters to be fired off, petitions to be signed, reporters to be stoked with indignant quotes.

Or a backgrounder can have a descriptive lead, such as this lead for the story mentioned earlier by Robert Cahn for *World Monitor* magazine on the worldwide survival of national parks systems:

> On a dirt road leading into Thailand's oldest national park, Khao Yai, we stopped to hear the ''singing'' of the gibbons, those small, long-armed apes with the distinctive musical cry. But we heard only bird calls. The gibbons had retreated deep into the park to get away from intruding villagers, said Dr. Boonsoong Lekagul, founder of Thailand's national park system, who was my companion on this trip. He explained that villagers were invading park boundaries to shoot monkeys and other wildlife for food, as well as to gather firewood and to clear land for crops.

A backgrounder can also have a lead telling about one individual who represents many people affected by a particular situation, as does this *Forbes* magazine story by Dana Wechsler Linden with Jody Brennan and Randall Land about the declining interest in hiring graduates of MBA programs:

> Don Summa, Harvard College class of '83, hasn't found his master's in business management a ticket to success. He graduated from Yale's School of Organization & Management last May, after having resigned from a glamorous job as an assistant talent agent with Triad Artists, one of the country's leading talent agencies. Two years and $60,000 worth of school bills later, he is unemployed. For whatever comfort it may bring, Summa is not alone.

Or a backgrounder can have a lead that not only piques readers' curiosity, but encourages them to identify with people in the article, as does Saul Pett's Associated Press story about the Washington bureaucracy, a story that won the 1982 Pulitzer Prize for Feature Writing:

> WASHINGTON—We begin with the sentiments of two Americans two centuries apart but joined in a symmetry of indignation.
>
> One said this: ''He has erected a multitude of new offices and sent hither swarms of officers to harass our people, and eat out their substance.''
>
> The other said this: ''The government is driving me nuts. The forms are so complicated I have to call my accountant at $35 an hour or my lawyer at $125 an hour just to get a translation.''
>
> The latter opinion belongs to Roger Gregory, a carpenter and small contractor of Sandy Springs, Md., a man of otherwise genial disposition.
>
> The first statement was made by Thomas Jefferson of Monticello.

FACTUAL INFORMATION AND QUOTATIONS

Once the backgrounder's lead presents the situation or interests readers in reading, the body of the story explains the material, using a mixture of quotation and factual information. The backgrounder is similar in its presentation to a news story, except that the backgrounder is more likely to use material gathered from texts and other written sources than the news story is.

For example, a backgrounder written by investigative reporter Ann Louise Bardach for *Vanity Fair* attempts to define "sexual sobriety" by quoting from the various literature of self-help and support groups:

> Each group has its own definition of "sexual sobriety," but S.A. [Sexaholics Anonymous] has the strictest program, outlining its goal for members as a "progressive victory over lust." . . . Sex Addicts Anonymous is considerably looser, and prohibits only "out-of-bounds sex," stating in its literature, "We cannot abstain from sexuality, because it is part of our humanity. Instead, we abstain from the compulsive, destructive behaviors that rendered our lives unmanageable." No "bottom-line sexual behavior" is the credo in Sex and Love Addicts Anonymous, which asks each member to define his or her own bottom line.

Backgrounders also use quotations in a way that is slightly different from the way news stories use quotations. Writers of backgrounders tend to summarize in their own words what they have learned from interviewing experts and doing research. Particularly in magazine backgrounders, statements explaining factual information or scientific phenomena are frequently made directly by the writer—particularly if such statements present information that is "common knowledge," that is, knowledge that can be gleaned from a variety of sources (see Chapter 18). For example, Madeline Drexler, in a backgrounder for *Lear's* magazine on breast cancer and the politics of breast cancer treatment, summarizes in her own words the basic facts about the physical make-up of the breast:

> For purposes of biology, breasts are considered merely milk factories. During pregnancy, the mammary, or milk-producing, glands, which lie behind the erectile tissue of the nipple, shift into action, prodded by two pituitary hormones: prolactin to stimulate milk production within the lobules—which are clusters of tiny sacs—and oxytocin to catalyze delivery of milk through the ducts to the nipple and the baby's mouth. Meanwhile, the areola grows larger and darker. After the baby's birth the sebaceous glands, seen as small bumps on the areola, secrete an oil that protects the nipple against chafing. It is, in fact, the infant's sucking that stimulates continuing secretion of the pituitary hormones, which, in turn, keeps the milk factory humming and explains why the longer a woman nurses the more milk she produces. Once a woman has had a baby she can breast-feed at any future time simply by letting an infant suck at her breast.*

When writers of backgrounders do use quotations, they are likely to use them almost exclusively as a way of working opinion and evaluation into the article. Since backgrounders are supposed to be neutral, when their writers *do* want to present opinions, they present them through the voices of others. This practice, of course, is not different from what news writers do, but it is done to a greater extent by backgrounder writers.

For example, when Donald G. McNeil wrote a backgrounder for *The New York Times* headlined "How Most of the Public Forests Are Sold to Loggers at

---

*First published in *LEAR'S,* July, 1991.

a Loss,'' he couldn't personally condemn the federal government's practices. But he was able to quote a retired Congressional Research Service economist about the way the Forest Service was conducting its accounting:

> "They make the savings and loan business look like an angel,'' said Mr. Wolf. "If a private business did this, they wouldn't just end up bankrupt—they'd end up in court.''

An evaluative quotation comes in particularly handy when the writer of a backgrounder wants a wrap-up statement to end the story, a quotation that will offer some sort of final assessment. For example, Janet Bingham, education writer for *The Denver Post,* ends a backgrounder—on the value of taking courses which coach students for SAT examinations—with two quotations: one from an expert and one from a person involved in the experience:

> Susie Watts, a Denver-area college consultant who offers a less expensive SAT prep course, has dealt with some students whose scores dropped after the Princeton Review.
>
> She questions a company that guarantees improvement.
>
> In any case, she said, "parents and students need to put the SAT in perspective. It is not the be-all and end-all. The most important consideration for college admissions officers will be the actual grades students have, the courses they are taking and their rank in class.''
>
> Student Garry Pfaffmann agreed. "The hardest part to overcome is the importance people put on the SAT.
>
> "A lot of students think it's the only thing that gets you into college, and they get really nervous. It's not.''

USING SOURCES AS TEACHERS

Quotations can also be used effectively in backgrounders as ways of personalizing the instruction the article gives. When a source is directly quoted, that person seems to be talking one-on-one to readers, who thus feel they are listening to a teacher give an informal lecture. The student/teacher feeling creates a sense of personal involvement with the information. In addition, if the source is a reputable authority, his or her personal instruction enhances the article's credibility as a whole.

A quotation from a "teacher" can be long and sustained, or short and simply supportive of the information the story explains. A backgrounder in *Popular Science* magazine on the next generation of computers, for example, uses many brief quotations sprinkled throughout the text to add credibility to the article and to enhance the presentation of information. The writer, P. J. Skerrett, usually describes the way things work himself, then uses a quotation from someone else to put the information in a clearer light:

> The beauty of massively parallel systems is their scalability. Need more power? Add more processors. Quadruple the size of a 4,096-processor Connection

Machine, for example, and the larger version runs about four times faster. And you don't need to alter the software or program. With microprocessor speed climbing and cost dropping, scalable systems offer a cost-effective way to provide more power.

"This is like building a computer using Lego blocks," says Reinhard Rinn, vice-president for engineering at Parsytec Inc., another teraflops [computer] competitor. "It is essential to make simple, elementary building blocks that you can then put together," he says.

MAKING THE UNCLEAR CLEAR

Backgrounders work to make clear what may be unclear to readers. Since the article's purpose is to increase reader comprehension and understanding, its success is measured in part by how well it explains what it sets out to explain. Backgrounders strive to state complicated concepts plainly. The goal is to speak economically and as directly as possible.

When you write a backgrounder, you should use straightforward sentence order and everyday vocabulary. In that sense, the style of the backgrounder *is* conversational. In another sense, however, the style is *not* conversational: you don't usually use sentence fragments, jargon, or slang.

Notice how *New York Times* writer Matthew L. Wald uses simple, uncomplicated language to explain a technical concept concerning the measurement of energy, in a backgrounder about underground heat as a future energy source:

> The standard measure of energy consumption from all sources is one quadrillion British thermal units. A B.T.U. is the amount of energy needed to raise the temperature of one pound of water by 1 degree Fahrenheit, and a quadrillion is a "1" with 15 zeroes. The United States consumes about 80 quadrillion B.T.U.'s annually, from coal, oil, gas, nuclear power and all other sources, but the estimated energy potential of hot dry rock nationwide is 10 million quads, the study found, more energy than this country uses in thousands of years.

Or consider how P. J. Skerrett, in the article for *Popular Science* mentioned above, presents a clear explanation of what the new teraflops computers can do:

> Intel is one of a dozen or so companies that are quietly racing to build the next milestone in computing power, the teraflops machine. In the blink of an eye, such a computer will be able to blaze through a *tera* (the Greek root for trillion) *flops* (shorthand for floating point operations a second, which are basically additions, subtractions, multiplications and divisions). That's at least 100 times faster than today's most powerful computers, which operate at mega- (million) or giga- (billion) flops.

Examples are also useful in making the unclear clear, because they specifically illustrate what a general statement means or implies. For a *New York Times* backgrounder on educational assessment, for example, writer Karen

DeWitt used the specific example of math testing to help readers understand what it meant when reviewers of student work indicated that students generally "did not have the sophisticated problem-solving skills that the workers of the 21st century will require":

> For example, the mathematics portfolios were assessed using seven criteria, with four levels of performance for each criterion. Four of the seven criteria were related to problem solving and three to the communication of the results. Most of the students were shown to understand the problems. . . . But in evaluating the quality of the approaches or procedures used to solve the problems, 47 percent of fourth graders and 50 percent of eighth graders were found to use effective strategies.
>
> The proportions decline further when the question is whether the student is making reasoned decisions in solving the problems; 12 percent of fourth graders inferred correctly and with certainty as compared with 21 percent of eighth graders. And students almost completely failed to synthesize, or make generalizations, from their problem solving.

Putting numbers in context is another way of making the unclear clear. It's a good idea to give readers a framework for understanding what the number means. For example, in a backgrounder about investment clubs, John Cunniff of the Associated Press discusses one club with a portfolio of $1,801,255.92. He gives a commonplace, familiar context for what that number means by telling the story of one investor, a man who is now a millionaire, but who began investing by putting $3 a week from his paycheck in the fund. Cunniff's analogy is that the small sum invested was what "a person might have saved . . . by foregoing cigarettes."

In a backgrounder about AIDS describing its effect on the small town of Belle Glade, Florida, *Philadelphia Inquirer* reporter Donna St. George takes the time to translate AIDS statistics into numbers within the reader's own frame of reference:

> To imagine an epidemic of the same scale in Philadelphia, picture a Sixers sellout at the Spectrum—with 5,665 more people lined up outside—all dying from AIDS. Or picture everybody in Upper Dublin or Deptford Townships dying.
>
> AIDS has stricken 3,247 Philadelphians. If it spread at the same rate as it has in Belle Glade, the toll would be 23,665.
>
> New York is one of the hardest-hit cities in America when it comes to AIDS. Already 39,452 people are sick or dead from it. Still, if New Yorkers were stricken by AIDS at the same rate as Belle Gladians, the toll would be 109,292.

Backgrounders present a good deal of statistical information, and must do so clearly. When you are writing with numbers in backgrounders, you should, if possible, simplify them by rounding them off: for example, don't write a percentage as 78.073 percent, write "78 percent" or "nearly 80 percent." Put numbers in terms that are easily understood: not "125,000,000 Americans," but "125 million Americans," or better yet, "one out of every two Americans."

We should add, however, that in making unclear ideas clear in backgrounders, it's important to distinguish between simplifying language and simplifying ideas. You *don't* want to strip ideas of their substance and complexity; you *do* want to express complex concepts in the clearest way possible.

TWO STORY STRUCTURES, TWO STORY SUBJECTS

Backgrounders, like most features, rarely are written according to any prescribed story structure or pattern. There are, however, two kinds of story structures particularly suited to the writing of backgrounders. The first is a backgrounder that explains things with an emphasis on time. The story is written in three sections: one of "description," one of "explanation," one of "evaluation," according to Fraser P. Seitel, *The Practice of Public Relations* (Charles E. Merrill Publishing Co.). Seitel notes that the *Wall Street Journal* particularly uses this story structure. The story describes a current situation ("description"); explains the history of the situation, that is, how things came to be the way they are ("explanation"); and discusses the future of the situation, evaluating the meaning of the information presented in the earlier sections ("evaluation"). The second and third sections of the story are usually full of quotations: experts and people with personal experience describe historical events in the second section; authorities make predictions about the future in the third section. In addition, the historical section may contain considerable factual information gathered from books and other reference sources. (Jake Hubbard of Syracuse University originally identified this common three-part D.E.E. feature structure, although he saw the structure as typical of a broad range of articles, which he identified generally as "trend" stories. His names for the three story sections are slightly different: "description," "elaboration," and "evaluation." See Chapter 13.)

Another story with a special structure is the "case history." Seitel describes the story's five steps: first, a problem experienced by one organization is presented; second, the dimensions of that problem are defined; third, a solution to the problem described; fourth, the advantages and disadvantages of the adopted solution are presented; and fifth, the experiences followed after adopting the solution are described. The article may or may not use quotations from experts and authorities to point out to readers that they ought, or ought not, to adopt such a solution.

HANDLING THE LONG STORY

Because backgrounders can sometimes be relatively long, it might be worthwhile to take a moment here to discuss handling the lengthy feature article.

Writers who have some experience in producing backgrounders and other long features seem to agree that the first step in writing them is mastering the voluminous technical material you've gathered. This mastery of material takes time. You need to spend a considerable number of hours simply reading and rereading all that you've amassed. Study your notes until they feel a part of you, until talking about the topic to someone would come naturally. Some writers suggest typing or rewriting your notes as a way of slowly absorbing the material you've assembled.

As you read (or write) through your materials, highlight the quotations you believe are particularly colorful or instructive. Also mark the factual material you feel is absolutely necessary to include in your article. Look for anecdotes and color that can enliven your story. Look for startling statistics that will compel readers to pay attention to the story's meaning.

After you've mastered the material, decide on your approach to the article, that is, on your particular way of coming at the material. Ask yourself, what really matters here? Think about how you would explain all that you now know to your friends if you were simply talking to them over the dinner table. What would you want to tell them? How would you simplify it for them?

Some writers like to create the story's title at this point, so the title can serve as a constant reminder of what they have decided is the story's focus or primary message.

The next stage in writing the long article is the same as for any feature; you must arrange your material, making decisions about what ideas are related to each other. For long articles you will simply be dealing with longer blocks of information. Some writers like to literally cut up their notes and physically order them in piles of categories. Other writers prefer making a loose outline. Of course, at this point you would also make the style decisions we discussed in Chapter 4.

The next writing stage is difficult, but most writers agree it's necessary. They advise that you sit down and write the *entire* first draft of the story, that is, *everything,* in one sitting, in one, long extended period of concentration. The point is to write nonstop, to keep going until you get most of the information out of your head and onto the computer disk.

Then leave the article alone for a while—at a minimum, 24 hours; if possible, for a few days. Do something entirely disconnected to the topic of the story, to writing in general, to journalism. When you return to the story, you'll see it with new eyes, with a fresh perspective. You'll be ready to judge it neutrally and with some distance, and see what is unclear and what needs enhancing. You'll be ready to begin the rewrite process.

Don't be surprised if the article goes through five or six more versions. Generally, as you rewrite, you strive to fill gaps you've discovered in the original draft. You'll have seen holes when you come back to the story after being away from it for a while: it will be obvious where you need more information, where you have failed to explain sufficiently, where you have not backed up assertions or presented clarification.

Rewrites also deal with deleting sentences, paragraphs, and sections of the story that fail to support the article's focus, or which dilute its impact by wasting time on superfluous, tangential material. You may also want to recast similar ideas into phrases of parallel structure to improve the clarity of your writing, and you may want to be sure that significant words and phrases are repeated to help readers keep ideas straight and to give the story coherence.

Study your long story to see whether it will hold the reader's interest. If it seems dull, even to you, you can speed the pacing by writing short sentences, and you can make the story visually less intimidating to readers if you "cut the gray" by trimming or splitting long paragraphs.

You might also consider other ways of enhancing the story's physical presentation. Are there physical effects you could use to guide your readers, for example, subheads or a row of asterisks or stars or some other printer's marks? Do you need an editor's note before the story? or a follow-up epilogue?

STORY OR SERIES

If, as you finish your long story, you discover that it's too long, and yet you feel cutting the story might ruin it, you might consider writing the story as a series rather than a single article. Backgrounders are sometimes published in several separate segments. Serial publication is particularly useful for newspaper backgrounders because of newspapers' more rigorous daily length requirements.

If you do decide to present your backgrounder in a series, be sure that each segment of the series is of equal importance, and that subsequent segments repeat the most essential information of earlier segments. The occasional Rip Van Winkle who misses the first story must still be able to understand later stories. Despite the repetition, however, each story in the series should be able to stand alone; edit the segments closely, so that no single segment derives its meaning *only* from what the previous one has said.

Writing backgrounders is challenging—and sometimes feels like a serious responsibility. You're not trying to tell a story, describe a place, or portray an interesting human being. Instead you're explaining issues and phenomena, trends and technology. If you do your work well, you can significantly aid readers in their understanding of the world around them. You can make readers better able to cope with social, political, economic, and scientific change. You can help them be better citizens, workers, and members of the community.

Their success depends to a very great extent on what they have been able to learn, and what they are able to learn depends on what *you* have been able to learn—and what you have been able to express clearly, coherently, and comprehensively in your backgrounder.

EXERCISES

1. Interview two people you know (family members, your roommates) who are having a dispute about something. Practice telling the two sides of their controversy by writing a summary of both points of view. Include quotations from each person in your summary. Don't write first all one side and then the other; discuss the various issues involved in controversy, giving both sides of each issue as you present it.

2.   a. Write a 12-paragraph story about some difficult situation around you, such as the availability of parking on campus, the number of required courses in your major, or the hours the health center is open. Use three paragraphs for "description" of the situation, five paragraphs for "explanation" of how things came to be that way, and four paragraphs for "evaluation" of what is going to happen next. You will need to interview a few authorities in order to write your story.

      b. For the same situation, write a story lead that either summarizes the significant problem related to the situation or asks a question about its difficulty.

3. Take a passage explaining a complex technological concept from a college textbook. Write a simplified version of the same concept, so that your version could be read and understood by elementary or middle school students.

4. Read Jon Franklin's relatively brief backgrounder, "A Moment of Great Opportunity," published in *Notre Dame Magazine.* Where do you find Franklin using examples? Summarizing factual information in his own words? Simplifying numerical results? Writing plainly and directly about technical concepts? How many sources did Franklin apparently consult? How many are named? Have your ideas about alcoholism changed from what you learned from reading the article? In what ways?

A MOMENT OF GREAT OPPORTUNITY
By Jon Franklin
Notre Dame Magazine, *Spring 1985*

For decades, experts on alcoholism have argued that the condition they study and treat is a disease, as physical as diabetes or cancer and perhaps as hereditary as blue eyes or red hair. Recent pioneering research has produced discoveries to substantiate these claims. Those discoveries now are coming fast and furious—alcoholism, in fact, is rapidly becoming a model for explaining how a person's genes and environment interact to cause abnormal behavior.

Perhaps the most dramatic breakthrough in alcoholism research resulted from a recent series of inheritance studies performed by a group led by Dr. C. Robert Cloninger, a scientist at Washington University in St. Louis. The Cloninger group studied several thousand citizens of Sweden who had been adopted as infants. The scientists wanted to determine if the Swedes had inherited behavioral tendencies from the natural parents they had never known. The study showed that children whose natural parents were alcoholics were significantly more likely to become alcoholics themselves, thus confirming the strong suspicion that alcoholism has a genetic component.

As the group analyzed its statistics more closely, it found that alcoholics divide into two major groups that are statistically quite different. Cloninger labeled the groups *sick alcoholics* and *violent alcoholics.*

Sick alcoholics comprised about 75 per cent of the alcoholics studied. Both male and female, they began drinking when young, but only moderately at first, and did not become alcoholic until later in life. They often eventually destroyed their own health but rarely became violent, and they usually continued to function in a marginal way in their professional and personal lives.

Sick alcoholics tended to be the children of other sick alcoholics—clearly some genes were being passed along. Genetics alone, however, did not increase a person's risk of becoming a sick alcoholic. The risk increased only when genetics and environment combined to stack the deck. For example, if a child of a sick alcoholic was adopted at infancy by a middle-class family, his risk of becoming alcoholic was no greater than average. But if that child was adopted by a family in a lower socioeconomic class, his risk was dramatically elevated.

Violent alcoholics comprised the remaining 25 per cent of the group Cloninger studied. Exclusively male, they began drinking heavily as teenagers. As their alcoholism progressed they became unable to hold jobs or sustain marriages. They also tended toward violence; they often ended up in jail for crimes involving injury to others.

The genetic component in violent alcoholism was much stronger than in sick alcoholism. In this case, a person's environment did not seem to raise or lower his risk. The son of a violent alcoholic had about an 18 per cent risk of developing the disease himself; that approaches the 25 per cent risk associated with recessive genetic diseases that are purely physical. Violent alcoholism may be the closest thing yet found to a genetic mental illness.

Cloninger also studied the daughters of violent alcoholics. These did not become alcoholics themselves, but they did tend to become severe hypochondriacs. What's more, their hypochondria was of a distinct type, both in terms of the frequency of their complaints and the location of their imaginary pain (mostly it was above the waist). Why the genetic risk should express itself so differently in males and females is a mystery, says Dr. Cloninger; the reason may be hormonal or social or some combination of the two.

However, preliminary experiments indicate that both the sons and daughters of violent alcoholics are at risk for an abnormally low production of an enzyme called monoamine oxidase, or MAO. In the brain, MAO is involved in the metabolism of the cells that process both physical and emotional pain. Scientists suspect that any defect or disease that leads to a change in a person's MAO levels might also disrupt the complex "pain filters" in his brain. These filters are believed to screen out random and constant signals of physical pain from the body and emotional pain from the brain. Without the filters, a person would feel himself to be in constant pain.

Some victims of depression experience constant (though often unconscious) emotional pain; many have been shown to have low levels of MAO. Like violent alcoholics and their hypochondriac-sisters, they seem to suffer some defect in the way their brains filter pain.

Using this idea as a base, Dr. Cloninger theorizes that violent alcoholism involves an imbalance in the brain's pain filter that is "curable" with alcohol. In this scenario, a potential violent alcoholic would be in constant pain from the moment of birth—but he wouldn't know it, since he'd never know anything else. The first time he took a drink of alcohol, the pain would cease, and the change in his mood would be dramatic. For the first time in his life he would feel . . . good. He most likely would immediately become an abuser of alcohol.

The problem, of course, is that while alcohol might effectively "treat" a person's chemical imbalance and squelch his pain, it has a broad impact on the entire brain, with serious and far-reaching side effects. Among them is physical addiction. The brain, like other organs, is genetically programmed to adapt to changing environments. If alcohol begins to appear regularly in the brain, its cells adjust their metabolisms. This means that more and more alcohol is required to achieve the desired effects. In time an alcoholic, in trying to soothe a particular, aching part of his brain, throws the entire organ out of whack. He has become physically dependent on alcohol, and if his brain is suddenly denied the chemical to which it has become accustomed, it will cease to function properly.

In a recovering alcoholic, the healthy parts of the brain readjust to a nonalcoholic environment.

However, this person still has his original problem: the unconscious ache he has suffered since birth. He knows that alcohol causes him many problems, but at least it soothes the ache. This is dangerous knowledge, because as his drinking days recede into the past, the metabolic imbalance which led him to abuse alcohol in the first place—the "ache"—remains with him always. Unless and until he learns to cope with his defect in some other way, he will fantasize about drinking. Experts believe that this "fatal vision" probably lies behind the psychological addiction that may haunt an alcoholic for life.

Other pioneering research in the alcoholism field has been done by Dr. Boris Tabakoff, chief of the intramural research program at the National Institute on Alcohol Abuse and Alcoholism. Dr. Tabakoff's research often complements Dr. Cloninger's. For example, Cloninger holds that violent alcoholics are acutely sensitive to pain. Tabakoff says that an opposite sort of defect may also lead to alcoholism: an acute sensitivity to pleasure.

Tabakoff explains that a person may inherit or acquire a brain imbalance that makes him particularly sensitive to the pleasurable effects of alcohol. For him, alcohol would be extremely difficult to resist. Tabakoff says some alcoholics may be pain-sensitive and others pleasure-sensitive; still others may be alcoholic for totally different reasons.

As their information accumulates, scientists almost unanimously have concluded that many different types of alcoholism exist (just as many different types of cancer or heart disease exist). Some kinds of alcoholism are caused by genes, others by a combination of genes and environmental factors, and still others by traditional psychological forces. For example, if a child is deprived of love during a critical period in the development of his emotional brain, the result may be a deficient production of MAO, or some other damage to the brain's pain filtration center which might be "corrected" by alcohol. This kind of brain damage would make that child a sitting duck for alcoholism.

Other research has shown that significant differences exist in the ways varying racial and ethnic groups metabolize alcohol, both in the brain and in the rest of the body. For example, some people have a genetic defect in an enzyme that breaks down a poisonous by-product of alcohol metabolism. These people are literally poisoned by alcohol; if they drink they suffer nausea, headaches and vomiting. So they tend not to drink. In a sense, their defect "protects" them from alcoholism. The defect is rare in the United States and most other parts of the world. But it is found to varying degrees in around 80 per cent of the people of Japan.

Not surprisingly, recent surveys indicate that almost all of Japan's alcoholics belong to the 20 per cent of the population who can drink without getting sick. Dr. Tabakoff notes, however, that some Japanese who are alcohol-sensitive do drink despite the violent side effects. They are compelled to do so, he theorizes, because of some powerful, alcohol-sensitive chemical imbalance in their brains—perhaps similar to the one discovered in the Swedish alcoholics. In any case, in these people the psychochemical benefits of alcohol must somehow outweigh the profound disadvantages.

Scientists also have discovered the basic mechanism by which alcohol affects the brain. It selectively alters the molecules on the membranes of cells through which the impulses of thought and emotion are transmitted. This interpretation has been given credence in the past decade as scientists have bred rat strains that are particularly susceptible to alcoholism, and other strains that are natural teetotalers. Analysis of the rats' brains has led to the identification of several specific metabolic pathways that apparently play a role in alcoholism's development.

Alcohol exerts its effect throughout the brain, but that effect is far from uniform. Some brain cells seem more vulnerable to alcohol than others. For example, the deep brain centers that control sleep seem especially sensitive to alcohol's effects. This may explain why alcoholics are particularly susceptible to sleep distur-

bances, both while they are drinking and as they go through withdrawal.

The differential effect of alcohol on various brain centers may also explain why some people with emotional problems become addicted while others do not. Both groups are suffering from chemical imbalances, but the locations of those imbalances vary; those who become addicted may be suffering from imbalances in brain areas sensitive to alcohol.

The new theory also dovetails with the general observation that addicts tend to have "drugs of choice." One addict might prefer alcohol, another morphine, still another amphetamines. Many scientists believe that such preferences should be seen as more evidence that addicts are "treating" themselves for some very specific but undiagnosed problem in brain metabolism. Presumably they select the drug which best alleviates their particular defect.

From all this, says Dr. Tabakoff, "it's very clear that alcoholism is not a single disease—an alcoholic is *not* an alcoholic is *not* an alcoholic. Genetic studies bear this out; the biochemical studies bear this out. There could be many types of alcoholism, there could be a few—we don't know yet." New types of brain scanners—capable of tracing chemical reactions in the living, thinking and feeling brain—may aid in defining the different types of alcoholism and their underlying causes. The special need now, says Tabakoff, is "to develop good criteria for [more specific] diagnosis. I think we're on the threshold of developing such criteria, both in terms of the classical methods—interview methods and such, behavioral analysis—and also biochemical methods."

The new understanding has already led to the discovery of at least one drug that in preliminary experiments seems to dramatically diminish an alcoholic's craving. The drug increases the amount of serotonin, a kind of neurotransmitter, that is available to brain cells. (A neurotransmitter is a chemical similar to a hormone by which brain cells communicate.) Serotonin has been suspected of playing a role in alcoholism for more than a decade. Tabakoff says it is not yet clear whether the drug works by fixing some preexisting chemical imbalance or by some less direct mode of action. It also is unclear whether it will help all alcoholics or just certain kinds. "A treatment that works for one group may be quite ineffective for another group," he cautions. "All the same, I think this drug offers hope."

As the various types of alcoholism are categorized and the diagnoses are made more specific, a variety of treatments may become available. Some may rely primarily on drugs to correct imbalances in the brain; others may focus more on the traditional "talk" therapies. As experts point out, psychotherapy, like drugs, changes chemical states in the brain; according to new theories, that is what "thinking" is. Whether the alcoholism treatment expert of the future prescribes drugs or psychotherapy—or,

more likely, some combination of the two—will depend on the specific type of alcoholism being treated.

Scientists like Tabakoff also hope that treatment specialists soon will be able to practice preventive medicine. In theory, preventing alcoholism is simpler than treating it. If susceptible individuals could be identified early, perhaps in childhood, many members of coming generations might avoid the development of self-destructive drinking patterns, and the secondary personality disorders that result from a drunkard's life.

"This is a moment of great opportunity," says Dr. Tabakoff. "There has been a good foundation laid, in terms of developing a basic scientific understanding of the problems. Now we have the opportunity to truly dissect this disease."

Brights
Making Readers Smile

As the name suggests, a brightener feature, or "bright," brightens up the reader's day. A bright is an article of pure entertainment, one included in publications to amuse and delight readers. A bright should elicit smiles, perhaps even produce chuckles or laughs. Really superb brights bring out a desire to share: "Listen to this," readers say, as they read aloud a bright to someone else.

Sometimes brights have a serious undertone, a message about the way life is, or a simple moral such as "look what happens when you tell a lie." But the story is not specifically told to teach a lesson or give information. It's told because readers will enjoy reading it and find in it some sunshine to put into their day.

Nevertheless, brights can perform a useful function in publications: they provide a change of pace from other stories. In newspapers they offer a welcome relief from the heavy and sometimes distressing nature of hard news. In magazines, they offer a moment's easy reading in the midst of dealing with longer, more challenging articles.

WHAT IF YOU CAN'T BE FUNNY?

Since brights elicit smiles and laughter, the first question writers beginning to write brightener features are likely to ask is "Can I write a bright if I'm not good at being funny?" The truthful answer is probably "maybe not." Most comedic writers are naturally good at thinking and writing humorously, and there seems little the rest of us can do to *force* ourselves to be funny. Certainly reading this chapter is not going to turn you into a Dave Barry or Erma Bombeck.

If you're not naturally funny, you probably won't make a career of writing brights; nevertheless, you may want to write a bright every now and then, when an appropriate occasion presents itself. It's hard to ignore a funny incident that happens to you or someone you know, when you realize that the market for certain types of brights is quite attractive: *Reader's Digest,* for example, pays $400 for brief articles used in its collections of brights.

Even if you never write a bright, however, you will still find it useful to examine their writing style. They look easy to write because they're short and a little silly, but in fact they're not produced as effortlessly as they seem. Their success depends on their being completely focused, with all superfluous words and ideas eliminated, and on their being carefully paced, with just enough information delivered at just the right time. Brights, therefore, offer good lessons in economy of language and sentence construction. And because brights typically direct their narratives or expositions toward a final humorous twist or snappy conclusion, they provide good lessons in writing *toward* a story ending that produces a particular effect on the reader.

CHARACTERISTICS OF BRIGHTS

The tight, focused language characteristic of brights evolves from their need to be brief. Why, then, do brights need to be brief?

The practical reason is that since they contain only entertaining information, they can't be allowed to take up too much expensive space in publications. Particularly in newspapers, brights provide just a *little* leaven for the full loaf of news and more informational features.

A more intrinsic reason for brights to be brief arises from the purpose of the articles themselves, from their need to produce a positive effect: a smile, a laugh, an amused reflection. Such an effect is usually created when only a single narrative line, character, or situation is developed. Presenting a variety of narratives, characters, or situations lessens the emphasis on each one, and thus diffuses the force of the article's impact, or makes its message more ambiguous.

Another reason for brevity has to do with the bright's impact: if the story is so long that the reader's attention is interrupted, the bright's mood is broken and its effectiveness lessened—just as a joke is ruined if the person telling it is continually interrupted by a well-meaning friend correcting various insignificant details.

For all these reasons, then, brights are usually kept relatively brief. The shortest are under 300 words; longer newspaper brights may be from about 5 to 10 paragraphs; magazine brights are seldom long enough to require the turning of a page. And of course, the briefer the bright, the more important it is that every word works efficiently.

Some brights have a punchline, that is, a particular statement that gives a twist to all the writing that comes before it. The punchline (which is usually the story's ending, but may come one or two paragraphs before it) may be a sentence with a jabbing thrust, a statement that's gently ironic, or a sentence containing information that explains a puzzle or some confusing situation. A bright's focused feeling can come from all the article's elements moving toward this punchline, organized to arrive there smoothly, with readers' knowing just enough beforehand so the punchline sentence is effective.

Brights are usually characterized as being warm-hearted rather than mean-spirited. Racist, sexist, and ethnic humor are avoided. Satire, too, because of its mocking quality, is not common in brights, appearing more typically in personal columns. Brights appeal to a broad audience; their humor is general and can be appreciated by almost any element of the population. If any particular person is made fun of, it is typically only the writer looking at him- or herself.

Finally, many brights can be characterized as fairly personal articles in which writers reveal their own experiences, reactions, and feelings. Whether a humorous article is considered a bright feature or a personal column depends largely on who writes it. When a feature writer writes a humorous story, we call it a feature; when a columnist known for a particular comedic voice writes it, we call it his or her column. But light-hearted, playful columns that serious columnists occasionally write—usually after a vacation or during a holiday—are, in essence, bright features, if they don't argue a point of view, don't try to teach readers anything, or don't convince readers to think in a particular way. The article is a bright when the writer simply thinks aloud on paper about something in the world around him or her, or about some entertaining experience or experiences, and those personal thoughts on paper amuse and delight readers.

TRUE-LIFE STORIES

Frequently brights evolve from unusual true-life situations. Such true-life brights are very common in newspapers, and are usually derived from wire service sources or from the public affairs reporting of police and criminal courts. True-life brights are similar to silly or light-hearted news features. The difference is that the news feature event must be reported, even if humorously, because of its minor news significance, while the bright event would never be reported at all, except for its unusual twist. The following Associated Press story is quite typical of a newspaper true-life bright:

> WARWICK, R.I. (AP)—Police across Rhode Island were put on alert after receiving a report that two women had stuffed a girl into a car trunk, covered her face with a blanket and driven off.
>
> About 20 minutes after the witness report Friday, Warwick police stopped Kristen Russell, 19, near her home. "I asked what the matter was," she said. "They said: 'Could you please step out and open the trunk.' I was shaking to death. I thought they thought I stole something.
>
> "When they saw what was in the trunk, they just started laughing. They couldn't believe it. And I started laughing too."
>
> Inside was a mannequin head that Ms. Russell used at beauty school.

It all began when Ms. Russell and her friend, Traci Wrench, went shopping with their two infant daughters. After leaving a store, they opened the trunk to stow Wrench's baby stroller and Ms. Russell asked Ms. Wrench to cover the head so the stroller wouldn't damage it.

Readers know immediately from the lead that the story is a bright rather than a hard news story, because the writer doesn't use the normal "what happened" lead. The statement "were put on alert after receiving a report" is the beginning of a narrative rather than a typical definitive news statement such as "Police found the body of . . . ." Readers continue reading the story to see what happens after the police hunt down the criminal, and the punchline tells them: "Inside was a mannequin head that Ms. Russell used at beauty school." The sense of the story rests on the explanation offered in this punchline sentence. The last paragraph ("It all began when . . .") simply unravels the narrative to clarify the situation and gives the article a sense of closure.

Sometimes an unusual true-life situation may deal with a more public event than a minor individual police arrest; such an article would still be considered a bright if it wouldn't ordinarily be published for its informational value. For example, the tone of the lead to this *New York Times* story suggests that the article is included in the paper only for readers' amusement:

HUNTSVILLE, Ala.—It was roughly 140 years overdue, but a book once owned by Thomas Jefferson was nevertheless happily received by the Library of Congress last week. The University of Alabama in Huntsville, which returned the book after finding it in a donated personal collection, was charged no fine, and the library promised that if any of Alabama's books ever turn up in the Library of Congress's book deposit, they will be returned promptly.

The writer's mock-serious language pokes fun at these two austere, grand libraries playing Marian the librarian and delinquent book-borrower. Readers can be quite sure that, literally, the Library of Congress didn't promise to return any books it might find in its book deposit belonging to the University of Alabama. The writer amuses readers by playing with the language of the common parental scolding: if-you-promise-never-to-do-it-again-you-won't-be-punished.

SLICE-OF-LIFE BRIGHTS

Some brights are first-person narratives of experiences, giving readers a brief glimpse of another individual's encounter with life's surprises and absurdities. When the personal narratives are extremely short, they are slices of life commonly found in magazines, where they serve as fillers for leftover sections of pages, or are grouped together into full-page collections of funny stories. Slice-of-life brights are generally very economical; any writing that doesn't build to the effect of the punchline is eliminated. Slices of life are also single-minded, with a sense of unity derived from their strong focus toward one point of humor, irony or reflection.

Reader's Digest is particularly well-known for its collections of slice-of-life brights; indeed, the magazine's vast popularity may well have its origin in the popularity of its feature collections such as "All in a Day's Work," "Campus Comedy," "Life in These United States," and "Humor in Uniform."

The following brights are taken from *Reader's Digest,* and reveal various humorous directions taken by slice-of-life brights. Notice that these brights are typically three paragraphs long (the maximum number of words is 300), with the last sentence bearing the punch. Notice also that all the brights are first-person narratives (they tell of experiences happening to the writer, or a friend or relative of the writer), and are thus written in conversational style, with a fairly low level of formality—though they never speak to readers directly as "you." They all begin by jumping immediately into the narrative; there's no preamble such as "Let me tell you about what happened to me last summer," nor a summarizing statement of evaluation, such as "This was the funniest thing that ever happened at University Medical School."

The following "Life in These United States" anecdote by Bryan Zwahlen derives its humor from the general absurdity of life:

> My friend Mark arrived at the airport just as his plane was scheduled to take off. The ticket agent checked his luggage and assured him he could make the flight if he hurried.
>
> Mark ran to the gate, where he found an attendant closing the door to the ramp. My friend pleaded with the woman to let him board, but she explained that the airline was promoting its "On Time" schedule and she couldn't allow any late passengers.
>
> Mark watched sullenly as the plane began to back up. After moving about 100 yards, it stopped. A small vehicle approached, and the plane's side hatch opened. Mark looked on in disbelief as his luggage was loaded on board.

The bright's humor is gentle and somewhat ironic. The story blames no particular person or organization for what happened; the airline's name is not even mentioned. The bright's humorous message is simply that stupid, silly things happen: readers smile about the ridiculous way things work.

Another slice-of-life bright, written by Elizabeth M. Dutton, from "All in a Day's Work," pokes fun at the absurdity of people; this bright is sort of an adult version of "Kids say the darndest things":

> A customer approached the service desk of the retail discount store where I once worked and, plunking down a shoe box, announced, "I'd like a refund, please."
>
> I opened the box and looked the shoes over carefully—white sandals, low heels, and showing only a little wear on the soles, caused perhaps by the woman's having tried them on.
>
> "No problem," I said. I wrote on the refund form her name, address, phone number and description of the returned item. "And what is the matter with the shoes?" I asked. "Too big? Too small? Wrong style?"
>
> "No, no," she answered. "The wedding is over."

Again, the tone of the bright is not negative; rather the writer pokes as much fun at herself as at her customer. The bright's humor is derived in part from the writer's setting herself up (and the reader) for the punchline by the slow pacing of the description of all the elaborate return procedures: her examining the shoes, filling out the forms, making the polite inquiry. Notice, too, how effectively the bright captures the customer's character. She ''plunks'' down the shoes, makes an ''announcement'' about what she wants, and corrects the clerk with a ''No, no.'' The characterization comes from just three phrases, but they work effectively to send the message that the customer is brash and somewhat imperious.

Another slice-of-life bright, written by Jason M. Rollings, creates humor out of personal embarrassment:

> New to the area, my wife and I had been invited by neighbors to join them and some other couples in watching the Super Bowl on TV. During half-time, while my wife was in the kitchen helping the hostess, the conversation turned to videos. ''We made a video of all of us in San Diego,'' one of the women told me. ''Want to see it? It's in the car.'' And she promptly ran out to get it.
>
> Minutes later while we were watching the tape of them running on the beach, my wife walked in from the kitchen. ''Those are the ugliest women I've ever seen in a commercial!'' she exclaimed, taking one look at the TV.
>
> We watched the second half of the game at home.

The bright's twist comes in the next-to-the-last line; the last line of the bright is typical of many such slices of life: it's a non-ending ending, that is, an ending that doesn't get involved in explaining every last detail of what happened. The humor is in the wife's mistake. If the bright comprehensively explained the consequences of her embarrassment (the new neighbors were angry, she and her husband had a fight, she apologized the next day, etc.), the explanation would de-emphasize the punchline and thus reduce the appeal of the bright's humor, which is universal. Readers don't really care about what happened to this particular couple; what they do enjoy is sharing a personally embarrassing moment that happened to one person, but which they know could equally well have happened to themselves.

PERSONAL REFLECTIONS

A writer's personal reflections about an experience or set of experiences can also offer readers amusement and brighten their day. Such personal reflection brights are slightly longer than slices of life—usually long enough to fill a single magazine page. Personal reflection brights generally appear only in magazines or Sunday magazine sections of newspapers. They are rarely published on daily newspaper pages, because newspapers are not comfortable with features that contain so much personal opinion. In magazines, personal reflection brights are frequently the work of free-lancers or even contributing readers.

Often a regular page is reserved for such articles, kept open for a variety of topics of interest to the magazine's readers. For example, *Family Circle* published on its ''The Flip Side'' page a personal reflection bright by free-lancer Suzann Ledbetter on a mother's frustration in dealing with shoes and children. Here's a small section:

> Therefore putting small bodies and soles together for an outing is an extremely frustrating experience for all concerned. The presence of four children means the absence of at least two matching pairs of shoes. Under-bed and toy-box searches for suitable mates take time and are often accompanied by my observation that said youngsters' heads and hindquarters might also be misplaced if not permanently attached.
>
> Once the number of shoes available equals the number of feet in need, a fork must be implemented to dislodge the aforementioned knots. This chore requires incredible patience, manual dexterity and numerous adhesive bandages to hide the self-inflicted stab wounds.
>
> Because children tend to declare their independence at the worst possible times, hurry-up pleas to ''Let me tie your shoes for you—just this once'' are met with stubborn refusal. If at first she doesn't succeed, she'll try, try again. And again. And again.

Ledbetter's article deals only with everyday, ordinary difficulties. She argues no position, advocates no cause. But her humorous, mock-legal tone helps many readers smile about a situation they no doubt endure themselves.

Sometimes personal reflection brights have a nostalgic tone, as writers reflect on the present through memories of the past. These nostalgic brights may elicit from readers not hearty laughs, but faint smiles about what was and now is, or elicit an amused feeling about the way we were long ago. In just such a nostalgic bright, Barry H. Rodrigue recalls for readers of *Yankee* magazine his Maine hunting trips with his father—in particular, a trip when he and his dad encountered a moose. Rather than hunting down the animal, Rodrigue's father hands it a cigar. Rodrigue recalls:

> The moose was as wide-eyed as I was. I don't know if it had ever consumed a cigar before, but from the way it curled its full soft lips around the stogie, you'd have thought it regularly patronized a tobacconist in the forest. The cigar and its fur were the same rich, brown color. My dad had made a friend. Matter of fact, we had an awful time trying to get rid of the moose. Pop finally had to scatter his remaining cigars around the forest as we ran off down the tote road. By the time the moose found all the cigars, we were back in the car and on our way to Mrs. Bryant's for a cup of cocoa and some homemade cookies.

Rodrigue ends his bright with a nice zapper; he says the story of the moose is a reminder ''that what you find in life is not always what you go hunting for.'' But even if the bright had no ''lesson,'' Rodrigue's colorful picture of a cigar-smoking moose is sure to bring a smile to readers' faces.

FOOLING AROUND

A final kind of bright is atypical, because rather than being short and focused, it is slightly longer and somewhat rambling. In this bright, the writer can be best described as playing around—with facts, language, images, or whatever. This playful bright more or less builds something from nothing but has so much fun doing it that readers read for pure enjoyment. A tiny kernel of news may be in the story, but the minimal news peg only provides a starting place for the writer's zany explorations of fact or history or whatever intrigues him or her.

For example, Joel Achenbach of the *Washington Post* used Daylight Savings Time as a starting point for a consideration of time in general. After telling readers that "there will come a day when the elite few individuals who totally grasp the concept of Time will be treated like rock stars" and explaining that a second is "now defined as 9,192,631,770 oscillations of a Cesium atom—approximately," Achenbach discusses Daylight Savings Time, then time in various time zones:

> Daylight Savings Time comes to an end in the fall, when we return to Eastern Standard Time, except for people who must live in some kind of West Coast Deviant Time. In between is "Central" Time—it's hard to imagine an interesting person coming out of such an area—and the obscure "Mountain" Time, which as far as anyone knows only applies to about nine families who live in cabins and trap beavers for a living.
>
> Then you have the Newfoundland problem. Newfoundland is, as you know, one of those parts of Canada that no one has ever visited, and perhaps one of the reasons is that the time there is 30 minutes ahead of (i.e. behind) the adjacent provinces. We can only presume that Newfoundland is governed by a committee.
>
> Worse yet is the situation in Guyana. This is a small South American country that has a proud and colorful history. There, the time is 15 minutes later than the country to the left of it. It is 3 hours and 45 minutes behind Greenwich Mean Time. Why the entire time system is based on a run-down hippie-dippie neighborhood in New York City is a mystery. In any case, in Guyana a "minute" is defined as the length of the king's forearm.

In another playful bright, Fred Tasker of Knight-Ridder uses soaring sales in the men's boxer underwear market to spin off some information about boxer shorts. He tells readers:

> There's a whole wall of them at Bloomie's: decorated with billiard balls for $12.95; with a big duck for $18.95; even silk ones for an astonishing $35 a pair, made in China. No wonder the Chinese call us paper tigers.
>
> And the Victoria's Secret catalog features a line of silk boxers with pictures of golden pheasants on them for up to $40 each.

An adversary of boxer-short-wearing, Tasker has fun with metaphors when he tries to convey to readers his idea of the awfulness of boxer shorts:

> Briefs are like a well-oiled, line-drive-softened old baseball glove; boxer shorts are a cracked bat. Briefs are a bar where everyone knows your name; boxers are a cafeteria with fluorescent lights. Briefs are a snuggle with your best girl; boxers are an alimony letter from your ex-wife's lawyer.
>
> They're kissing your sister, playing to a tie, oleomargarine, non-dairy creamer, decaf everything, generic anything, light beer, egg substitute, Oreos with single stuff, daytime TV.

But even without a news item to start the journalistic ball rolling, a playful writer can have fun writing brights that tell readers lots of stuff they don't need to know. Sid Moody of the Associated Press apparently got interested in "eponyms," the name of a real person given to an object. Moody's playful bright offers readers the enjoyment of learning trivial information about words they use:

> Diesel's engines make the world go 'round under his name. This is fortunate. His first patent for them issued Feb. 28, 1892, was for an "Arbeitsver fahren und Ausfuhrungsart fur Verbrennungskraftmaschinen" (combustion power engine) which is an eponym to break jaws with.

Moody's story also offers readers the fun of learning about household words. They hear in a new way names they use everyday:

> In the kitchen cupboard or refrigerator or at ladies' socials we find the works of the late Earl S. Tupper, a chemist with DuPont who was fascinated with the properties of polyethylene. . . .
>
> In the garden may bloom the Christmas plant Joel Roberts Poinsett brought back from Mexico during his difficult ambassadorship there in the 1840s. Or the yellow-blooming shrub William Forsyth returned with from China several decades before.

In another bright, Jim Knippenberg of *The Cincinnati Enquirer* spun out a speculative feature that occupied almost the entire first page of the paper's Sunday Tempo section. He considered, not words, but what sort of Olympic games could be held for ordinary people:

> Know what the Olympics needs? A lawn goose toss, that's what. And a grocery cart dash for runners, an orange barrel slalom for commuters and an airport sprint for frequent flyers. Hmmmm.
>
> Not to get all radical and wreak havoc on these venerable old games or anything, but maybe it's time for a Supplemental Olympics, say a modern version modeled after the games but still different. Say, a Lifestyle Olympics.
>
> Consider . . .
>
> Ever since the glory days of Greece, the Olympics has sailed along pretty much unchanged. Oh, there have been new events, but mostly, it remains two weeks of extraordinary people doing extraordinary things after an extraordinary life of extraordinary effort.

So how about something for ordinary people with real-life people doing real-life '90s things that reflect the times.

Knippenberg has a lot of fun describing for readers the "Long Distance Thong-Walk," the "I-275 Endurance Run" (a wait-out in non-air-conditioned Chevettes), and the supermarket "Checkout Lunge."

Playful brights exhibit a wonderful curiosity about the world, a desire to experiment with language or ideas simply because experimentation is fun. It's important to note that writers of playful brights are not on ego trips; the emphasis of their articles is not on themselves. They seek out the curious intricacies and little known facts of the world outside them—then examine that information exuberantly and humorously.

SHARING WITH READERS

Perhaps ultimately what makes brights so enjoyable to read is that when readers are done reading, they feel very much in touch with the writer. As with most kinds of humor, the success of brights depends to some extent on a sense of shared values or shared knowledge. For example, the bright on eponyms assumes that readers and writers both know the words "forsythia" and "tupperware"; the bright on time assumes that both know that time is determined from Greenwich, England, not Greenwich Village, Manhattan; and the slice-of-life bright on returned wedding shoes assumes both know that returning something after it is worn is not appropriate behavior.

The bright's sharing of all this unspoken, assumed knowledge makes writer and reader feel close; they are companions together, laughing at the world or themselves. Or, if the writer of the bright is telling his or her own embarrassing moment, the reader is drawn into a circle of shared friendship, into an inside group of people who have permission to make fun of that dear old comrade, the writer.

Perhaps this feeling of friendly sharing—as much as the humorous material in the article—is what brings the smile to the reader's face and brightens the reader's day.

EXERCISES

1. Discuss the humor in this *Reader's Digest* slice-of-life bright, written by Kimberly J. Lau. How does it make readers smile?

> My friend Bret discovered that his credit card was missing about a week after he had last used it. His initial panic was calmed when he remembered a television commercial in which a bank representative telephones to question a card holder because he notices unusual charging activity on her account.

Bret called the bank to report his missing card and to find out the status of his account. When the man on the phone reported his balance as some $4000, Bret replied, ''Why, that's impossible! My credit limit is only $3000.''

''Yes, it was,'' the representative said. ''But we noticed unusual charging activity on your card so we raised your limit.''

2. In his personal reflection ''St. Januarius: The Patron of Liars,'' Joe Ritz of *The Buffalo News* relates the essence of his situation in paragraph two. Why then, would readers continue reading? What makes readers smile? How many phrases can you find in the story describing the priest? How else do you get an impression of his character? How does Ritz' final paragraph work to wrap up the article?

ST. JANUARIUS
The Patron of Liars
By Joe Ritz
Buffalo Magazine of The Buffalo News, *May 5, 1985*

It was a warm weekend in late spring when my wife, Ann, exclaimed, "St. Januarius!" as we drove down the main street of Naples, New York. I braked to a stop and stared at the small, white building of cast cement—the Roman Catholic church with the odd name. To understand why a small church named after an obscure fourth-century Italian bishop should have excited a middle-aged couple on a drive to the Widmer Winery, one would have to know the details of a visit to a parish priest in eastern Massachusetts some twenty years earlier.

You see, I had invented a St. Januarius parish, and that simple, foolish act had caused considerable embarrassment, trouble and discomfort for both of us.

It all began when we went to make arrangements for our marriage with one of the local curates. The priest, a man in his 30s, very particular and not very friendly, asked about my religious background. To him I was a stranger, born in a distant state, reared in another, educated in several and now living more than 100 miles away. He was particularly interested in knowing the name of my parish.

As a young reporter, I was living alone in New Haven, Connecticut, only occasionally attending Sunday Mass in the chapel at Yale or whatever church was at hand.

So when the priest insisted on the name of my parish, I was nonplussed. For some reason, the only name in all the Litany of Saints that came to me was St. Januarius.

"St. Januarius," I replied through dry lips, trying to appear casual and deeply religious.

"St. Januarius?" he repeated in a doubting tone. "That's an unusual name for a church."

I laughed nervously. The priest rose and, to my horror, strode to a nearby desk and began paging through the *Catholic Directory*. He came to New Haven and looked down the listing of parishes, frowning as he did.

There was a St. Mary's and a St. Joseph's—how simple and untroubled life would have been in the next weeks if I had replied with one of those common names. But, not surprisingly, there was no St. Januarius parish in all of Connecticut.

Ann cast me a bewildered glance. She had never heard of St. Januarius. Neither, as it turned out, had anyone in her family.

Having discredited me, the priest began probing into other aspects of my past. On learning I had served in the U.S. Army, he demanded a copy of my discharge papers.

There I had a problem, for when I was discharged, a clerk had put an "x" in the wrong box and incorrectly listed me as married. It was a weekend when I was handed my discharge papers by the first sergeant and the base offices were closed.

After three years, I was relieved to become a civilian again and not particularly concerned about whether I was being discharged as a married or unmarried soldier. Reluctant to wait in the barracks until Monday, I pocketed the papers and thought no more about it.

It was these papers I handed over to the curate, whose suspicions were mounting by the minute. He quickly spotted the damning "x".

"You were married!" he said in a manner that expressed satisfaction in having found me out.

"No, Father, it was a mistake," I lamely tried to explain.

"They don't make those kinds of mistakes in the Army," he insisted firmly.

It was no surprise that he refused to marry us. When Ann's family learned of the encounter,

I began to get the kinds of looks reserved for someone who mugs old women.

Ultimately, with much trouble and correspondence, the curate's suspicions were laid to rest, and we were wed. But in all our married life, which produced five fine children and took us throughout North America—from Hudson Bay to Disney World, from Boston to Seattle—we had never found a St. Januarius Church until our trip to Naples.

It's a unique and magnificent church in a striking modern design that invites passers-by to pause for a further look. But then, I always imagined it would be.

CHAPTER

How-tos
Giving Clear, Helpful Directions

How-to articles are among the most popular of all features. They are a staple in both newspapers and magazine publishing, offering readers useful, helpful information—knowledge they can use in practical ways to make their lives easier, more effective, or more enjoyable.

As the name suggests, how-tos tell readers how to do something: how to plant bulbs in the fall, how to fertilize a lawn in the spring, how to select a wedding dress, choose a babysitter, save money on a mortgage, send a child to the right college, invest money for retirement. How-tos thus perform very particularly a service that magazines and newspapers do generally: the service of gathering information for readers. How-to articles provide very specific information about particular topics. Readers want this service, perhaps because they are themselves too shy to seek out information or too embarrassed, too busy, or too lacking in knowledge even to know what questions to ask. The how-to writer helps readers by doing the legwork for them, asking experts questions, making sense of their answers, and organizing the information into a sensible summary that can be quickly read and understood.

Magazine editors offer readers how-to information because they believe it helps sell their publications: readers buy the magazines so they can find out how to be happier, richer, smarter, or better-looking. Magazine covers are filled with titles of how-to stories, that offer solutions to readers' problems—those they know they have, and those the magazine covers can convince them they have.

Take for example, one cover of a *McCall's* magazine; it featured the following stories, all containing either specific instructions for self-improvement or general implied messages on how to improve life:

How to Find the Time for You Hidden in Your Day
Can't Talk to Your Teenager? Read This

Make Over Your Face—in 4 Minutes

Electricity & Cancer: Do You Sleep Too Close to Your Clock?

Sally Field Wises Up: Five Ways I Keep It All Together

And *McCall's* is by no means unusual. The cover of an issue of *Parents Magazine* listed these titles dealing with self-help or self-improvement:

How You Fall in Love with Your Baby

Secrets of Strong Marriages

10 Myths About Pregnancy

''But Everybody Has It'': Dealing with Kids' Envy

Treating Bumps and Bruises

Why You Shouldn't Compare Kids

How Your Child Learns to Care

Newspapers, too, publish how-to articles because they are popular with readers. Newspaper how-tos, however, are seldom used specifically to promote the publication. Instead they are part of the total package of services newspapers provide. In newspapers, how-to articles tend to be clustered together on a particular page or two, usually in the lifestyle section, though occasionally a how-to article is included in the sports section or the business section.

How-to articles in newspapers often concern hobbies or consumer interests rather than personal self-improvement; they are stories about such things as how to take photographs of children, how to buy a good tennis racquet, or how to make a backyard swing set. More recently, intense reader interest in health and fitness has led some newspapers to increase the number of their how-to articles concerning physical well-being.

ADDRESSING THE READER'S PROBLEM

Whether in magazines or newspapers, the how-to article is essentially a problem-solving article; it addresses the reader's need to know how to do something, or how to do something better. Readers may not yet have articulated, or even acknowledged, that they have that need; it may, or may not, be currently on their minds—until they see the how-to story. For example, a reader would probably not pick up the morning paper deliberately to find an article about killing weeds. When he or she is scanning the pages of the newspaper, however, an article on killing weeds may remind him or her that weeds are currently choking the lawn and something must be done about it. The feature article suggests the solution at the same time that it reminds the reader of the problem. A similar scanning process leads a magazine reader to how-tos, though he or she scans first the cover of a magazine, then the inside pages. But for both magazine and newspaper readers, the need to learn about something, to read the story, may not come to immediate consciousness until they see the story.

For this reason, both newspapers and magazines value the headlines and leads of how-to stories. These must make very clear to potential readers what problem the article solves, and remind, or perhaps convince, readers that a problem exists. If readers do not have the problem—if, for example, they have no weeds (or no yard)—then the headline and lead let them know there's no point in reading and they should turn to another story.

If you submit a how-to story for free-lance publication, you should write a title that clearly tells what problem the how-to solves. If you're a newspaper staff writer you won't write the headline for your how-to story, but you can write the lead with a clear understanding of how a how-to's lead differs from the leads of most feature stories.

While most feature leads try to hook readers into the story, using clever, original writing to enlarge the readership of the article, there's not much point in tantalizing readers into learning about something they really don't need to know, especially if the purpose of the feature is to serve reader needs. The best lead to the how-to story, then, is a lead that narrows the audience by making clear what the story has to offer, so readers can decide whether to read or not. The lead identifies readers who will most benefit from reading.

For example, the following lead for a syndicated *Chicago Tribune* how-to by Lynn Van Matre on buying pots and pans narrows the audience fairly precisely:

> CHICAGO—Maybe you're just starting out, setting up house for the first time. Maybe you're starting over—the marriage didn't pan out, and your ex got custody of the kitchen stuff. Could be that you're starting to go crazy at the thought of one more takeout dinner.
>
> Whatever your situation, the solution seems simple: Hit the stores and get some cookware. Unfortunately for most first-time cooks, choosing among the array of pots and pans—not to mention a slew of small kitchen appliances and seemingly endless heaps of gadgets—can be daunting.

Once the lead does this sorting out of who does and doesn't benefit from reading, readers who choose to stay with the story are likely to continue reading through to its end. If readers want to know about buying pots and pans, they read on; if they don't, they'll turn to another story. So the how-to article is again unlike other features because the body of the story does not have to keep using brilliant writing or exciting content to keep readers reading. If the lead finds the readers who *should* be reading the story, those readers will probably read to the end, because they're intrinsically motivated to do so.

BASICS RATHER THAN BRILLIANCE

Rather than being tantalizing, cleverly witty, or startling, the how-to story primarily aims to be clear. When readers want to solve problems or learn how to do something, they must understand the information the article presents. A solution that can't be understood is no solution at all. So the how-to's criterion for excellence is clarity. Above all, the writing should be specific and easy to understand.

Being clear is not as simple as it sounds. Writing the how-to story is a little like giving people directions for driving somewhere; before you begin, you have to think through your ideas and words carefully. You have to be clear about the sequence of actions—what logically follows what—and about the pitfalls that could exist for your followers along the way. You must use exact words in precise order. You must avoid saying anything that can be misconstrued or taken more than one way. And you must eliminate extraneous information, so that it doesn't distract from important information.

If you've ever gotten lost following someone's unclear directions, you'll understand that information that seems clear and simple to the *sender* may be confusing to the *receiver*. And you will thus understand the difficulties in writing a good how-to article.

One way to be clear is to be simple and direct, to address readers in a personal, conversational way. The how-to is typically written with a low level of formality, using the direct address pronoun "you." The writer gives advice directly, like a friend or mentor—as Bruce C. Ebert of the Newport News, Va., *Daily Press* does in this lead for a how-to on choosing a mattress:

> Unproductive as it may sound when you say it, the fact is that about one-third of your life is spent in bed.
> Think of everything you do in bed: sleep, read, work crossword puzzles. . . .
> OK, we'll stop there.
> But facts being facts, if you're going to plant yourself on one piece of furniture for about eight hours a night, you might as well be comfortable—and secure in knowing that your mattress is durable and good for your body.

EMPHASIZING THE POSITIVE

The how-to also tries to emphasize the positive—what the article will do for readers, how they will be better off for having read the story. The emphasis is never on the trials of the journalist who has worked so hard to gather this information, nor on the personalities of the experts who have given the information. Rather, the how-to article stresses how much satisfaction the reader will feel after following the story's directions or advice on solving the problem.

The beginning of the story, however, may stress the negative—the depth of the problem—in order to arrive at the positive—the benefit of learning how to do something, as does Diane Harris' lead for "How You Can Live Better" in *Money* magazine:

> You can't throw a pinpoint 60-yard touchdown pass, so forget about landing a contract worth an average of $3.2 million a year like Joe Montana's. Your acting career ended with a bit part in your high school's production of *Bye Bye Birdie,* so you'll never nab a Schwarzenegger-like fee of $10 million a film. You can't sing, can't dance, and can't even vogue, so matching the $39 million that Madonna made last year is unthinkable. And you're more likely to get struck by lightning (odds: 1 in 600,000) than you are to hit the jackpot in a state lottery (odds of winning the grand prize in New York's Lotto, for example: 1 in 12 million).
>
> Okay, so maybe you'll never be among the roughly 1.6 million Americans who need at least seven figures to count their money. But you don't have to be a professional athlete, a Hollywood star or even extraordinarily lucky to achieve a degree of financial security that exceeds the already enviable U.S. average. The crucial steps to a better standard of living: a solid education, a finely honed career strategy and a sound savings and investment program. "You won't get rich this way," says John DeMarco, senior vice president of PSI, a Tampa market research firm that studies the affluent. "But you will get the financial resources to guarantee yourself a more comfortable life style."

THE HOW-TO THAT GROWS FROM NEWS

Occasionally, the how-to article is hung on a news peg: something in the news sparks a special current interest in how to do something. The lead, or perhaps the second paragraph, alludes to that news event. For example, the Erie, Pennsylvania, *Morning News* published a how-to article about water safety following a double drowning in nearby Lake Erie. Story organization went something like this: the first paragraph referred to the news event, saying the drowning that happened "could happen to anyone"; the next paragraphs cited some statistics about the number of boating accidents in the community; the following paragraphs detailed the Fishing Commission's recommendations on how to avoid drowning, giving readers specific how-to tips concerning everything from buying proper life preservers to using visual distress signals.

Paula Voell of *The Buffalo News* wrote a how-to article in a lighter vein for the newspaper's Sunday magazine, using the local tour production of the *Phantom of the Opera* as a news peg for her story. Her how-to, on the purchasing and care of crystal chandeliers, begins this way:

> In the currently popular production of "The Phantom of the Opera," a crystal chandelier swings over the heads of the audience into the middle of the theater. It's a stage trick that draws "oohs" and "aahs."
>
> But even a crystal chandelier that simply hangs in place over the dining room table can draw that kind of admiration as it sparkles and gleams.

WHO'S THE SOURCE?

Once the how-to's lead establishes what the article will do for readers, or identifies the news situation that makes the how-to information significant, the article customarily identifies the source of the information (or advice or help) for the story.

Deciding who is the best source for your article and what research best serves your reader must be done when you first plan the article. You have to ask yourself if you know enough about the topic to be the knowledgeable expert yourself. Or is there some person of stature in the field who has a wealth of information or advice to share? Are there conflicting viewpoints on the situation, so that readers would best be served by interviews with several experts? Are there old, standard written sources which offer classic advice? Or new publications that offer information on the cutting edge of current research?

PERSONAL FEATURE OR PERSONAL COLUMN

In newspapers, if you the writer make yourself the knowledgeable expert, your article officially slides from the category of "feature" to "column," because it represents your personal opinion.

Newspaper articles dealing with such things as stamp-collecting, sewing, bridge, or antiques are considered columns rather than how-to features if the same writer writes the article regularly and speaks in a single, personal voice. Such how-to columns can be written by staff writers, local free-lance experts, or nationally syndicated columnists. They are usually identified with a standing label headline of the columnist's name or the column name above the headline of the story. Jane Bryant Quinn, who writes about financial affairs, or Alfred Sheinwold, who writes about bridge, are two well-known syndicated columnists.

The how-to column may or may not follow a typical how-to feature format. While both types of articles have the same purpose (that is, to teach readers how to do something), the column's structure may be that of a brief personal essay. And syndicated self-help columns such as Judith Martin's "Miss Manners" or Tom and Ray Magiliozzi's "Car Chat" are written in question-and-answer format and therefore are not written in typical how-to format, though, again, their columns offer helpful information similar to the information in how-tos.

Occasionally, national advice columnists write a general preamble to the question-and-answer portion of their column or a separate short piece of general guidance that is more in the style of the typical how-to.

THE MAGAZINE AS AUTHORITY

On the other hand, if you write a how-to article for a magazine with yourself as expert, your how-to will probably still be considered a feature. Magazines are much less concerned than newspapers with distinguishing stories with personal judgment from features.

Another reason your personal how-to could be identified by a magazine as a feature rather than a personal column is that your voice of expertise would likely blend with the magazine's own voice of authority. Magazines like to present themselves as experts on subjects of interest to their readers, to promote themselves as especially serving the informational needs and interests of their audiences. For example, *Seventeen* is an authority on what's "in" for teenagers to wear, *Ms.* speaks with an expert voice on the problems facing feminists, and *Ladies' Home Journal* knowledgeably advises matrons on gardening and fine dining. In contrast, it's difficult to imagine a metropolitan newspaper telling readers "We've got what you need for fall back-to-school looks" or some such similar statement.

Notice how Christine Reinhardt, in a how-to for *Working Woman* magazine, writes a lead that draws her readers, herself, and the magazine into a single, unified group:

> In recent months many of us have become conscious of the serious threat posed to our environment, and we're doing more than talking about our concerns. We're setting aside soda cans for recycling, turning off the lights faithfully when we leave a room, buying products without excess packaging.
>
> And yet, when we go to work we may leave much of this conscientiousness behind—perhaps because it seems so hard even to make a dent. But we shouldn't be thinking this way.
>
> "The amount of time we spend at work is considerable. It really represents a large part of our energy and effort," says John Javna, founder of the EarthWorks Group and creator of *50 Simple Things Your Business Can Do to Save the Earth.* "If we pretend only our time at home counts, then we're lying to ourselves."
>
> How do you turn *your* office into a model of environmental morality, even if the rest of your company still has its head buried in the sand?*

How-tos based on the authoritative voice of the magazine occasionally have no identified author. And at times the source of the expert information is unclear, with writers claiming to present information from vaguely identified sources, using the phrase "most experts agree that."

Reinhardt's article, for example, after quoting from Javna once more ("My advice to managers is, *just get started,*" says Javna. "Just do something, anything, even if it's simple. That opens the door to doing other, further-reaching

---

*First appeared in WORKING WOMAN, April 1991. Written by Christine Reinhardt. Reprinted with permission of WORKING WOMAN Magazine. Copyright © 1991 by W. W. T. Partnership.

things.''), goes on to give tips on building an environmentally conscious office; however, Reinhardt does not identify the source of this advice. She never says definitely whether it comes from Javna, herself, or the magazine editorial staff.

ONE SOURCE OR MANY

More commonly, however, you, the writer, are not the expert in the how-to story. Rather, you consult an outside expert or experts for the reader. So you must decide on how many experts to consult.

A preliminary suggestion is that you make a definite choice about whether you want one source or many: don't straddle the fence by choosing two experts as a compromise number, unless, for example, you are writing a story about how to buy a motorcycle and there are exactly two motorcycle dealers in town. Otherwise, it's best to talk to either one source or to as many as four, five, or six, so that the reader is clear about whether your purpose is to query a single person exhaustively or to survey an entire field of experts.

The choice of one source or many comes down basically to this: one expert gives your article depth, while many experts give your article breadth. If you choose one expert, that expert should have extensive credentials and considerable prestige. For an article about buying fishing equipment, for example, you shouldn't interview as your sole source the sales clerk down at the local sporting goods store. Rather, you should talk to someone who has a considerable reputation in the field, someone recognized as an expert fisherman, or someone who has written a book on the subject, taught others how to fish for many years, or done something else to gain stature in the field.

For example, Charles Fenyvesi, for his column ''The Ornamental Gardener'' in *The Washington Post,* interviewed just one person for his informative lesson on new hardier hybrid hibiscus. That one person, however, was Robert Darby, the man Fenyvesi says ''first presented'' the hardy hibiscus in 1955. Needless to say, Darby is one of the most knowledgeable sources Fenyvesi could have interviewed for an article discussing such things as hibiscus hybridization techniques, growing procedures, and the future of the shrub.

The limitation of interviewing just one person for your story is that you will get only one point of view, only a single person's opinion on how to do something. There are doubtless other points of view your article will not reveal. Since the advice you offer readers is limited, the compensation should be that the advice is particularly respected and comes from a recognized authority.

If you choose to consult a variety of sources, the benefit for readers is that you have surveyed the entire field for them; you have discovered many different perspectives and points of view. If, in addition, you include what written ''authorities,'' that is, books and pamphlets, have to say on the subject, so much the better. The length of your article, however, prohibits your using any of these sources extensively, so while readers will gain a sense of the general discussion around the topic, they will not find a thorough examination of any one authority's point of view, nor the in-depth reasoning behind any particular opinion.

Interviewing many experts would be suitable if, for example, you were writing a how-to on buying a new compact disc recorder. Your article could present information from all six local stores that sell such equipment. Readers wouldn't have to personally go to all the stores and talk to salespeople. In the comfort of their living rooms they would learn exactly the same information as if they had gone there—maybe *more* information.

When there are many experts in your article, the credentials of each one become less important. What matters is that several viewpoints are offered, so readers get a sense of the agreements and disagreements of opinion. They can then see the preliminary decisions they need to make, or what research they need to do, before they take any action.

THE SINGLE SOURCE

The source of the information for your how-to article determines the shape and structure of the story you write.

The simplest how-tos to write are derived from single sources. With one authoritative source, the story can assume, in essence, the form of an informational interview. After you write the how-to lead establishing what the reader will gain from the story, you indicate who you are interviewing and give his or her credentials (occupation, education, honors, etc.). Then you quote what the person has to say. You need not describe the setting of the interview, as you would in a personality profile, nor do you need to write creative speech tags—a simple "he/she said" is appropriate. Only the subject's knowledge on the topic is significant.

An alternative way of writing the single-source story is to give the expert's credentials after the lead, then write a statement indicating that all the how-to information which follows is a summary of what you have learned from your interview with him or her. This pattern is also frequently used when you yourself are the expert. You indicate your credentials after the lead (your personal experience or the research you have done), then go immediately to the information you have to give the reader. Obviously, you summarize the material, rather than quote yourself.

STEP-BY-STEP

When you present how-to information, you usually use one of two common formats: step-by-step or point-by-point.

Step-by-step organization is best used when the how-to story is giving precise directions—telling the reader, for example, how to bake a perfect souffle or how to get a safe suntan. Like any set of directions, the material is organized chronologically: first do this, and then do that; readers must take the first step before they take the next step. Sometimes, each step is illustrated with a photograph or diagram, as they were in a *Popular Mechanics* magazine article by Rosario Capotosto on how to prepare wood for finishing. The story was presented in a series of photos, one for each step. The caption under each photo explained to readers what the photo showed them; for example, how to remove traces of wood dust with a naphtha-dampened cloth, or how to raise the wood grain with a sponge.

The trick to writing the step-by-step how-to is to make sure you have in fact written the steps in the order they should be taken. It is also important that each step is explained separately from every other step, so that readers don't overlook one step because it's buried in another. Language is critical. You need to edit your work time and again, making sure that you are specific in everything you say. For example, you can't tell your readers to use a Phillips screwdriver unless you are certain they know what one is. If you think they might not know, explain what you mean. Before sending anything off for publication, test what you've written by having someone follow your directions without any coaching—in other words, have them duplicate what will be your reader's situation.

POINT-BY-POINT

Point-by-point is best used when the how-to story gives advice rather than chronological directions. The points organize the material in terms of categories of similar information. These categories are presented in any order that seems logical. For example, in a Knight Ridder syndicated story on home insulation, Gene Austin moves sensibly from a consideration of how much insulation is needed (first point), to the cost of such insulation (second point), to where to put such insulation (third point), to how to apply it in attics, exterior walls, and floors (fourth, fifth, and sixth points).

The separate points within a point-by-point story can at times, however, have no logical connection to each other, other than that they are all ideas around the same topic. When there is no sequence to the categories of advice, the material is often presented in a series of bullets or numbers (confusingly, sometimes called ''steps''). For example, Earl Aronson's brief article for Associated Press on how to do fall landscape clean-up lists seven tips in a series of bullets. There is no connection between each piece of advice; one idea doesn't lead to the next. There is also no chronological connection. It doesn't matter whether you do number 7 (''Consider adding a grassy mound or rock composition to relieve bareness in winter'') before or after number 3 (''Remove extended growth of ground covers that have overlapped sidewalks, driveways or patio areas'').

Sometimes, both unrelated and logically sequenced points are presented in the same story. For example, the *Working Woman* office environment story mentioned earlier uses categories in a logical sequence to organize its methods for improving the environment. Each category is a point, identified by a subhead such as ''Recycle with a vengeance'' or ''Conserve energy.'' Within these categories, however, separate pieces of advice are not connected; each one is a bullet of information that has no particular relation to advice above or below it.

A single how-to story can also combine point-by-point and step-by-step organization. For example, Jimmy Schmidt's story on how to buy and cook summer corn, syndicated by Knight Ridder, first presents information point-by-point in these categories: how to select, store, boil, crimp, roast, and grill corn. Then Schmidt gives a particular recipe for cooking corn, and thus moves into precise step-by-step organization, giving directions where each step must be followed before the next step takes place. Published recipes, incidentally, are some of the most familiar of all step-by-step how-to writing.

SEVERAL SOURCES

If you've interviewed several experts or have several sources for the how-to story, you also follow a step-by-step or point-by-point format, but the pattern is complicated by having to work into your article clear identification of your many different sources. In other words, you must weave multiple interviews through your story.

With the step-by-step, if your experts agree on the steps that need to be taken, you write the chronological steps of your article so that each includes a cluster of advice from various experts. Preferably you present the experts in the same order for every step, so that readers can keep them straight.

Sometimes, however, your experts do not agree about the number or the nature of the steps to be taken. Then you either organize your story into more than one chronological step-by-step section, with a separate section for each authority; or you go through the initial steps that all experts agree must be taken, and then write separate paragraphs for the different subsequent steps they recommend.

With point-by-point, the choice is between making the various experts the organizing points or categories of your story (you write first about what X recommends, then about what Y recommends, then about what Z recommends) or dividing the story into other categories and working into each point the experts' opinions (you write what all the experts say about A, then about B, then C, and so on).

Obviously, the second method is more complicated, because you have to blend quotations from so many different people into the relatively short writing space concerning each point. Every change of speaker requires a new paragraph, so you need to finish quoting all worthwhile material from one expert before you begin a separate paragraph for the next. You may instead want to use many indirect quotes, or to summarize material in your own words (crediting the source, of course). This way you can condense and combine information into a single paragraph, rather than write so many paragraphs (one for each expert quoted) that you create an article of unwieldy length.

SHORT AND SOLID

Generally speaking, the how-to is a fairly brief story: readers want quick, easy-to-understand tips, not lengthy historical, political, or socio-economic digressions. At the same time, the how-to should impress readers as being substantial. Readers should not get the idea that the article is simply a superficial rehash of accepted folk wisdom. They want a sense that the journalist has, in fact, done research—that what they're being offered is solid, intelligent information, representing the most up-to-date advice by the best authority or authorities available.

Because the how-to is fairly short (as little as 500–1500 words), and often written according to formula (either point-by-point or step-by-step), it's easy to get the idea that it's a fairly simple and boring story to write. Following a formula can become tedious, and how-tos don't usually walk away with Pulitzer Prizes. But if how-tos aren't dramatic, they're also not necessarily easy to write. Refining and refining each word to make sure that there's absolutely no confusion can be hard, difficult work—in some ways, very much like the labor of writing a fine sonnet (also a formulaic structure) that requires absolutely precise and careful word choice for each line written.

But whether you find how-tos difficult or easy, boring or interesting, don't underestimate their value. They are bread-and-butter features, providing readers with helpful information and welcome advice.

And no matter how much labor your how-to requires, it's important that you strive to write with enthusiasm. If you don't seem interested in *teaching* how to do something, your reader can hardly be expected to be interested in *learning* how to do it. When you first decide on your how-to topic (if you're allowed to make that choice), try to choose a topic that you yourself are interested in, either because you know a lot about it, or because you have always wanted to learn about it. If your natural curiosity is stimulated and your interest is real, your enthusiasm will communicate itself to your readers, and you'll be genuine when you promise readers that they'll profit from reading what you've written.

We should add, however, that you're free to experiment with your own way of presenting how-to information, so long as what you write serves readers by eventually telling them how to do something. You should also realize that the how-to's formulaic quality, its obvious skeleton, makes the story easy to imitate, and thus suitable for humorous parody, which can be anything from gently ironic to bitterly sarcastic. ''How to Get Mugged in New York City'' for example, or ''How to Lose Your Shirt on the Stock Market'' would send an opposite helpful message: basically, that readers should *not* do what the how-to advises. Such humorous how-tos can be highly creative—and fun to read and write.

So, if you're casting about for a way to organize material that spoofs other people or yourself, you might remember the bread-and-butter how-to. It could, because of its simplicity, provide a familiar formula useful for written flights of fancy.

EXERCISES

1. Write down three things you know how to do that you could write a how-to about. Write down three things you would like to know how to do, or to do better. Name two publications that might be interested in stories on each of these topics.

2. The following directions have some words or phrases that are vague and, therefore, would leave readers confused about what to do. Improve the directions by writing them more specifically.

    a. Put the cake batter in a pan and cook in a very hot oven.
    b. To make this flared skirt, select high quality material and thread.
    c. When buying a puppy, look for intelligence and spirit.
    d. Add enough water to make a thick wallpaper paste.

3. For a story on how to meet a member of the opposite sex, write a lead that addresses the reader's problem, speaking directly to him or her.

4. Write brief, step-by-step directions for how to do the following:

    a. format a computer disk
    b. repair a flat tire
    c. play a game like Monopoly, or keep score for a game like tennis
    d. get from where you are to a particular building within walking distance

5. With yourself as the expert, write a how-to story on a psychological topic—for example, how to get over homesickness, or how to overcome a feeling of failure. Or write a negative how-to on the same kind of topic.

6. Read Edwin Kiester, Jr., and Sally Valente Kiester's "How to Teach Your Child to Think," from *Reader's Digest*. The article takes an exceptionally long time to get to its how-to points. Why? What are the writers doing in the lead and opening section? Why do they stress that the children in question are American children? What difference does that make? Whose advice is italicized at the beginning of each of the article's points? How many experts or sources does the story mention?

HOW TO TEACH YOUR CHILD TO THINK

By Edwin Kiester, Jr., and Sally Valente Kiester
Reader's Digest, *June 1991*

Try this simple test on your child—and yourself. A laundry dryer contains ten black and eight navy socks. Without looking, how many socks must you take out to be sure you have a matched pair?

Or explain the meaning of this formula: 36b + 52w = 88k.

In the first example, the correct answer is three. As for the second, look again: it's a shorthand description of a piano—36 black keys plus 52 white.

Neither example calls for academic skills. Both demand the ability to think, to stretch the mind beyond the obvious. And thinking is an area where American children need help. Lots of help.

According to a 1983 report on U.S. schools by the National Commission on Excellence in Education, only two of five 17-year-olds could review simple statements in written material ("Swedes are Europeans. John is a Swede") and draw a logical inference ("Therefore, John is European"). And only one in five could express a point of view and organize thoughts about it into a persuasive essay. Education professor John Goodlad of the University of Washington says that students in U.S. public schools spend less than one percent of class time in discussions requiring reasoning.

"We fill students full of data," says Richard Paul, director of the Center for Critical Thinking and Moral Critique at Sonoma State University, California. "But the essence of education is to use information to address new situations and questions. We're neglecting that."

Consequently, Paul says, American kids can't apply reasonable thought to everyday situations. "A kid is much more likely to choose a bicycle by its color or by what model a friend has than to think out more relevant considerations like price, durability or perfor-

mance." More ominously, says Yale educational psychologist Robert J. Sternberg, some problems, including drug use, may occur because young people have not learned to measure actions against consequences.

Knowing how to think has never been more important to our children's future—and the future of the country. Recently, Prof. Richard Askey of the University of Wisconsin gave a math problem from a Japanese college-entrance exam to 350 freshman math students. The four-step problem required students to solve one step, then apply the answer to the next, and so forth. Most Japanese students solved the problem; none of the Americans did, and most couldn't get beyond the first step. They were skilled at computation, but couldn't apply their knowledge to new situations.

How did Americans come to neglect rational thought? The answer is complicated, but one explanation is depressingly obvious. Thinking is hard work, demanding rigor and discipline. But those virtues went out the window in the 1960s and 1970s when we let children "do their own thing." Television reinforced this by encouraging children to sit passively with their minds on idle. In too many classrooms, too little was demanded. Asks Sonoma State's Paul: "If you do everything for a child and give everything to a child, what need has he to think for himself?"

How can we nurture habits of serious, critical thought in our children? How can we help them sharpen their minds for a highly competitive future?

First, say experts, create a "thinking atmosphere" in your home. Here's how to begin:

Examine your own thinking about thinking. Don't make the mistake of believing that an intelligent child is automatically a good thinker. In fact, intelligent persons may be poor thinkers, or lazy ones, because they're able to give quick answers. Meanwhile, the slow, reflective child—the boy or girl teachers may chide for daydreaming—often produces deeper insights.

Start early. Brenda Richardson, a Pulaski County, Kentucky, mother and teacher, starts five-year-olds thinking by reading simple rhymes. Example: "If all the world were apple pie/And all the sea were ink/And all the trees were bread and cheese/What would we have to drink?"

Then she leads the children into other thought-provoking questions, such as: "If a sentence begins with *If,* does that mean it's not true?"

"You'd be surprised at the thoughts that bubble up," says Richardson. "The youngsters learn a way of reading and thinking that can last a lifetime."

Give children something to think about. Take your kids to museums, read together, watch TV side by side. Then talk about what you've seen and heard. "Don't just walk through a museum and admire the exhibits," psychologist Sternberg says. "Throw out questions. Challenge their imaginations. 'What might the earth be like if dinosaurs came back?'"

Involve the whole family. Good thinking habits can be learned best in a small group, with plenty of give and take. Even the youngest child has ideas that should be brought out and listened to. A formal curriculum isn't necessary. Dinner talk about happenings of the day can provide excellent opportunities for instruction. "Can you think of a different way you might have answered the teacher, Mike?"

Tell jokes. Humor can help teach kids there's more than one way of looking at things. A pun, for instance, gets a laugh because it looks at words from a different perspective. "Bob Hope had a disappointing Christmas," goes an old joke. "He only got one golf club—and it didn't even have a swimming pool."

Once you've established a thinking atmosphere, it's time for step two—training your kids to use the following methods of critical thinking:

Look at all sides. One technique taught by Edward de Bono, founder of the Cognitive

Research Trust program (a widely used method of teaching thinking), is the "PMI." This involves looking for the Pluses, Minuses and Interesting points about any given question.

De Bono once asked a group of 30 ten-year-olds, "How would you like to receive $5 a week for attending school?" All 30 enthusiastically voted for the idea. Then he asked them to "do a PMI." After three minutes of listing pluses, minuses and interesting points about the proposal, 29 out of 30 had changed their minds. Among the minuses: "Our parents wouldn't give allowances" and "The school would raise prices for meals." Further and deeper thought had convinced the group that the obvious answer wasn't necessarily the best.

Find patterns and threads. "How does this relate to what I learned last week? How does it fit with questions coming up?"

Fitting bits of knowledge together is the foundation of education. By identifying patterns, we avoid having to learn the same lesson again and again. Once we recognize the pattern of choices in selecting a bicycle, we also know how to go about buying a pair of jeans or a skateboard.

"Even if it ain't broke, fix it." Reverse the old axiom. The story of human progress has been one of overturning accepted ideas. People were content to light their homes with oil lamps until Edison came along. Accountants added with pencil and paper until the adding machine and then the calculator revolutionized the process.

Less set in their ways, young people are more willing to question "the way it's always been done." Parents should encourage them to make this a lifelong habit.

Ask unconventional questions. Challenge your kids with thoughts like this: "Suppose all cars were painted yellow. What would be the pluses, minuses and interesting points?" (Plus: it would be cheaper to have your car painted. Minus: you couldn't find your car in a parking lot.)

"The questions that help children think are not those with single answers, like 'When did Hannibal cross the Alps?'" says Matthew Lipman, founder and director of the Institute for the

Advancement of Philosophy for Children at Montclair State College, N.J. "They're the interesting, puzzling, problematical ones. They're open-ended."

Say what you mean. Precise words not only prevent misinterpretations but also help sharpen ideas. Is the boy down the street your son's "friend" or merely an "acquaintance"? When classmates are called "weird," what does "weird" mean? Defining terms is tough mental discipline that can help your child clarify what he really thinks.

Play this game at home: Blindfold one child, then ask another to choose one of two similar pictures and describe it aloud. Remove the first child's blindfold and ask which picture has been described. "The words used are often so vague that the blindfolded one hasn't a clue," says Richard Paul, who developed the game. "The exercise not only shows the participant how to be more precise in speech, but also to be more careful in observations."

Seek a second opinion—and a third. Children will often state their own convictions, wait impatiently for another speaker to finish and then simply repeat what they said earlier. By not listening to others, they remain ignorant of ideas that could broaden their outlook.

Get them to consider other points of view. For instance, when your child describes a neighborhood playmate as "dumb," ask a brother's or sister's opinion, which may open the first child's eyes to unthought-of possibilities. Similarly, watching and reading the news can teach the important lesson that identical bits of evidence may be interpreted in different ways.

Wear the other person's shoes. Urge your kids to try to understand how others think and feel. "That's not easy in personal matters," says Debbie Gershow, a guidance counselor at Memorial Junior High School in Valley Stream, N.Y. "It's one thing to say, 'Let's imagine how the British side felt during the Revolutionary War,' and another to hear a counselor say, 'How do you think your mother would feel if you were suspended from school?' "

Write it down. "I never know what I think," pioneer educational researcher Ralph Tyler once commented, "until I put it on paper." Encourage your child to keep a journal. "Writing is rigorous intellectual exercise," Sternberg says. "It's good practice for thinking. In fact, it is thinking."

Think ahead. Encourage children to consider short-term, mid-term and long-term outcomes. One of the most important questions a child can ask is "And then what?" Drop out of school— and then what? Cut class and miss the final exam—and then what? It's difficult for young people to think about tomorrow or next year. Yet what might happen tomorrow should affect actions and thoughts today.

Study. "Thinking is no substitute for information, and information is no substitute for thinking," de Bono says. "Both are necessary for intellectual development." You can't find a new application for quadratic equations if you haven't learned quadratic equations.

Keep at it. Young people don't develop the habits of logical thought overnight. "It's like tennis," Paul says. "The first time you play after lessons, you may forget all you've learned and just swing away. But eventually the lessons will become part of you.

"Thinking takes practice," he adds, "but it's worth it. This country needs good thinkers."

Special-purpose, Special-circumstance Stories

CHAPTER
12

News Features
Giving Timely Events
Feature Treatment

It may be misleading to devote an entire chapter to news features, because it makes them seem separate and distinct from other features. However, almost all features are news features; that is, they carry some kernel of news. Whether a story is classified as news, feature, or news feature is basically a question of degree. How much news makes news? How little news makes a feature? When is there enough news to make a news feature?

A few feature stories are almost totally lacking in news value—travel stories about very obscure places, for example, or silly, humorous brights. On the other hand, some features have a high content of hard news, meaning they have more than just a kernel of information and are closely tied to current events. The purpose of devoting a chapter to these split-personality, half-news-half-feature stories is to emphasize how closely connected feature writing and news writing can be, and to stress that you can use your feature writing skills to enhance a news story (and, for that matter, your news writing skills to enhance a feature story).

The category "news feature," is hardly exclusive. Stories described in various chapters of this text might be categorized as news features if the only criterion of their categorization were how much news they contain. For example, a personality profile of a candidate running for governor would have a high degree of timeliness and a good deal of hard news value. On the other hand, a profile about a local fellow who has an interest in old cemeteries would have little news value or timeliness. Both stories are worthwhile features; both are categorized as profiles. The candidate's profile, however, could also be identified as a *news* feature; the historian's could not.

We need to note, as we begin to discuss news features and other features in subsequent chapters, that we are now considering feature story ''types'' in a slightly different way than we did previously. Earlier, we identified narratives, color stories, profiles, backgrounders, brights and how-tos by their particular writing styles and patterns of presentation, as well as by their writers' intentions.

Now, however, when we speak of news features, travel, life-style, human interest, and anniversary stories, we are going to be discussing story ''types'' identified not so much by writing styles and patterns of presentation, as by reasons for writing the story. These stories are written with special purposes or intentions, about special situations or circumstances.

Some of the story ''types'' we have already examined may reappear in ''new'' feature story categories; narratives, for example, can be written for the special circumstances of anniversaries, and thus can be ''anniversary features.'' This chapter, too, discusses narratives, but here, because they are published for special timely circumstances, they are categorized as ''news features.''

Other ''new'' story ''types'' will emerge as blends of story types we discussed earlier, merged to accomplish a new purpose. The writing styles and patterns of presentation of color, how-to, and backgrounder stories, for example, can be blended to produce an article that helps people learn about traveling, that is, a ''travel story.''

Still other ''new'' story ''types'' will be familiar kinds of stories categorized together because they share a similarity of situation or create a similar effect. For example, a narrative and a profile can both concern the topic of a ''dying child''; thus, because they share the same situation and human interest appeal, they are both categorized as ''human interest stories.''

With an awareness, then, that we are now moving into territory where the labels we put on feature stories are not precisely like the labels we put on them before, and that the types of stories we are describing are not mutually exclusive of others we have already described, let's consider some typical kinds of news features.

A HIGH DEGREE OF TIMELINESS

As we said earlier, the characteristic that most notably distinguishes news features is their possession of the news value ''timeliness.'' News features are quite clearly tied to *current* events, which must be reported sooner rather than later.

Because of their timeliness, news features are usually associated with newspapers and weekly news magazines rather than with monthly or quarterly consumer magazines. On the other hand, special interest magazines and public relations publications, which publish infrequently, may also have news features, since their coverage of a particular topic may be the only coverage, and therefore the most timely coverage, available for their news.

News features are generally tied to timely news events in two different ways. Some news features are the *only* coverage of a particular current event or piece of news information. The news story is given feature treatment for a variety of reasons: the information is of secondary importance, of an unusual or light-hearted nature, or of interest to a small number of people. Sometimes the news is given feature treatment to keep it from being too dull.

Other news features represent *additional* coverage of timely information or news events of such interest or importance that one story doesn't seem enough. These additional stories may be published on the same day and on the same newspaper page as their related news events, in which case the news features are called "sidebar" stories. If the news features appear on subsequent days, they are then sometimes called "aftermath" "spin-off," "second-day," or "follow-up" stories.

SINGLE FEATURE-LIKE COVERAGE OF NEWS EVENTS

News features that are the only coverage of news events frequently describe events of secondary significance. These are stories with an indirect or delayed impact on a majority of readers, or they are stories of a light-hearted or comic nature.

A very common single-coverage news feature deals with the announcement of survey or research study results. Such announcements may come to the media's attention when they are made during a national conference, published in a trade or professional journal article, or released from a university or hospital public relations office. The news feature reports the findings because they have some impact on readers; however, the information is of limited current value. A survey or study, after all, is only a tentative bit of knowledge or a piece of evidence concerning a theory or speculation. And while the information is *somewhat* timely (announcements can't wait weeks to be reported), it is not so significant that readers will be upset if they don't find out about it immediately. And in a few months, of course, a new study may contradict today's results.

When research findings are reported, then, they are frequently given feature treatment, particularly in the story's lead—perhaps only in its lead. The lead may announce the findings in terms of personal impact or everyday consequences. Or it may tease readers into the story, as does this Associated Press lead for a story by Diane Duston on the federal government's study of calcium's effect on premenstrual stress:

> WASHINGTON—The best treatment for women suffering from PMS may be as close as their refrigerator.

William E. Schmidt's lead for a *New York Times* news feature about findings just published in a professional journal teases readers into a curiosity about something that normally would interest only scholars and historians:

> LONDON, Aug. 31—Once again, newspapers in London are filled with revelations of intrigue and espionage, including the unmasking of a "second man" in a spy ring operating close to the heart of Her Majesty's Government.

But this time the news is more than 400 years old and the accusations the work of a dogged British historian. He claims in the latest issue of a British scholarly journal that the philosopher Giordano Bruno, an Italian priest, was probably the spy who betrayed French and Catholic secrets to his English handlers in the court of Queen Elizabeth I.

An alternative lead might be a narrative, such as David Chandler uses for a *Boston Globe* story covering the publication of a scientific paper about the possible crash of a meteorite into Earth millions of years ago:

It was a lovely warm day in June, circa 66 million B.C., when suddenly a dark pall spread over the sky. The temperature plunged below freezing. Plants that had just flowered were frozen in mid-bloom. And the Earth was forever changed.

Chandler continues his feature treatment of the topic, summarizing what might have been obtuse scientific conclusions in casual, conversational writing. He connects ideas in his article with such feature-like transitions as "and what's more" or "but even more significant." And he ends his article with a feature-like description of pond lilies studied by the scientist:

Now, the effects predicted by that theory are seen, in concrete form, in Wolfe's fossil leaves, shriveled and crinkled in a way that happens only if they freeze.

ADDING FEATURE CONTENT

Other single-coverage news features may not use feature style to dress up the story, but feature content to enhance it. The writer uses the basic news story as a starting point for pursuing further information that saves the story from being too dull. For example, a news feature by Karen Brady in *The Buffalo News* begins with a straightforward lead announcing that a tree has been added to the "leaves" of the state's Historic Tree Register. The body of the story is also written in normal news style; it's content, however, is feature-like. The writer tells readers such things as how much the tree originally cost ($1.25) and that it still blooms each May. She continues with a list of other area trees chosen for the Register, and relates folk history about some of them; for example, she tells the lore of a Genessee County oak tree believed to have been a meeting place for Seneca Indians.

In other words, the fifteen-paragraph story contains about two paragraphs of news that *must* be told and eleven paragraphs of information that need *not* be told, and could easily be deleted if more pressing news demands space in the paper. The added folk histories and details of days gone by, however, make the original announcement about the tree more interesting and memorable.

LIGHT-HEARTED NEWS EVENTS

Single-coverage news features also report secondary events characterized by inherent silliness or some show-biz quality, such as a charity balloon toss or dancethon. Feature treatment seems most appropriate for coverage of these events; to cover them seriously would fail to convey their true nature.

For example, *Washington Post* staff writer Roxanne Roberts, covering the Rare Breed Dog Show held one weekend on the Washington Mall, treats the event with tongue-in-cheek humor. Her lead stresses the oddity of the rare-breed situation:

> Looking for a dog? Not too big, sweet temperament, doesn't shed much? Maybe the Xoloitzcuintles—better known as the Mexican hairless—is for you.

The body of the story also contains pure, fun color writing:

> It rained dogs and dogs all weekend at this show, so man and beast were nose to nose under one big tent, in jackets and doggie sweaters. The owners shouted across to each other; the dogs, more than 350 at this show, selected one tent pole as their message center. Owners dashed out in the rain, circled the ring, put the pups through their paces. Lots of doggie kisses. Muddy paw prints on everyone.

Yet Roberts' article is also news-filled and informative, containing information about the results of the show competition, the cost of an average rare breed show dog, and the debate on whether rare breeds should be recognized by the American Kennel Club.

Roberts' article, with its mixture of news and feature writing, reflects the quality of the event she is covering; the show is timely (it happened this weekend and drew a crowd) and it had certain consequences. However, it is also of secondary importance to most readers and has a slightly absurd quality. Nonetheless, since the show is serious business for a few readers, Roberts' approach cannot be *entirely* humorous, and she has to be sure her humor never becomes offensive.

ADDITIONAL COVERAGE OF NEWS EVENTS

All the articles mentioned so far are the *only* coverage of their particular news events; they accompany no other hard news story. The second large category of news features comprises stories offering *additional* coverage of particular news events. These news features tie in very closely with the news, but are not THE STORY; rather, they are supplementary stories offering other approaches to the principal news story. Of course, when we say "the story," we may in fact mean not just a single major story covering a single news event, but THE BIG STORY, many stories covering many related ongoing events reported over days or months—something like stories about the Olympic Games, or the Los Angeles riots.

News stories concerning occurrences that cause significant loss of human life—war, flood, fire, famine, explosion—seem to leave readers feeling that more needs to be said about the subject. The straight "This many people died on this day because of this disaster" doesn't seem adequate for the enormity of what has happened; the media (and its public) are not quite ready to let the story die. News features help readers slowly come to terms with catastrophes.

A news feature about THE STORY (or THE BIG STORY) can be complete in itself, appearing alone on a second or third day, or it can accompany the news story as a sidebar on the same day. For example, when Hurricane Andrew pounded Florida, Associated Press released two stories, both appropriate for front-page, same-day coverage of the disaster. Both articles were dramatic. The news story, however, delivered information about what happened in a straight way; it began:

> MIAMI—Hurricane Andrew, the nightmare storm Miami long dreaded, smashed ashore south of the sprawling city before dawn today, with walls of water and the howling terror of 160-mph-plus winds. At least two people were killed.

The accompanying news feature, on the other hand, emphasized description, showing readers what it felt like to be there:

> MIAMI—Lightning flashed an eerie tropical shade of aqua, and roads were paved in green pine needles and severed branches as the force of Hurricane Andrew hit land before dawn today.

HUMANIZING THE STORY

By far the most common supplemental way into "hard" news is by dealing with it in "soft" human terms. It's an accepted truism of journalism that people like to read about other people; the human race seems curious about fellow creatures in their village, state, nation, planet. When a news story is told through human terms, readers understand it on a personal level; they see it happening to others like themselves and envision themselves in the same situation, imagining how they would feel or what they would do. A news event in the abstract may be difficult to grasp, but a real person's actions and reactions are easy to comprehend, easy to empathize with.

The simplest way to tell the news in human terms is to lead into the story with information about a single person involved in the news. That person can be a bystander, a witness, the hero, a victim, or the person to blame (sometimes called "the goat").

Hank Ezell of *The Atlanta Journal-Constitution* leads into a story about a new Disability Act passed by Congress by telling about one person who will be affected by the new law:

> Job applicant Tom Packard already knew the catering business, and he knew a good bit about computers.

What he had to learn is just how tough it is to show up for a job interview in a wheelchair.

"I never thought it would hinder me," said Packard, a 25-year-old auto accident victim who is paralyzed from the chest down. "Hey, I'm still Tom Packard. But people look at me and see the chair first, then Tom Packard second."

Packard is lucky in several ways. He points out, for example, that he can still use his arms, while some of his friends have incurred much more severe disabilities. In addition, he entered the job market this year, just as the Americans With Disabilities Act was becoming law.

The employment discrimination section of the law goes into effect today, and for millions of individuals like Packard, now a catering manager for a restaurant chain, the act will make it easier to make their way in the work force. The act's commandment is simple: Don't discriminate. Its basic concept is clear: Look at a person's abilities, not his or her disabilities.

The individual's story can also be told beyond the lead. You can use the story as a frame: the material about the person begins and ends your feature. Framed articles are sometimes called "Wall Street Journal" stories for the newspaper that popularized their use. A framed story usually is described as having four sections: the lead, which tells about the person; the transition, which leads into the news portion of the story, saying something like "but so-and-so is only one of hundreds affected by . . ."; the body, which is the normal news story, with facts and quotations from the experts; and the conclusion, which refers again to the person whose tale began the article.

The number of paragraphs spent on the feature frame depends generally on the length of the news body: the frame is proportionally shorter. Generally the frame lead is slightly longer than the frame conclusion, since it takes more time to build readers' interest in a person than it does to wrap up what happened to him or her.

The person who provides the human interest of the frame is a typical man or woman caught in a news event—one the reader can identify with. He or she should not be an authority or expert interviewed as a source of information for the body of the story.

We might point out that framing a story, that is, putting one story inside another, is an established writing technique, scarcely unique to news features, or even to journalism. Chaucer's *Canterbury Tales,* one of the first great poems in the English language, uses a frame: the story of the pilgrimage to Canterbury surrounds the stories of the individual pilgrims.

We should also note that you can frame a news story, not just with writing about a particular person, but also with description, an anecdote, or a narrative.

ONE PERSON'S INSIGHT, ONE PERSON'S REACTIONS

Another way to tell the news in human terms is to interview an individual who has a special insight into news events, usually through personal experience or special education. For example, if you knew a musician who had studied under Aaron Copland, you might interview him or her for a news feature following Copland's death; or if you knew someone who had made a study of the czars of Russia, you might interview him or her when graves of the royal family killed in the Revolution were reopened.

A person who has been on the scene of an event that reporters couldn't reach is also a good candidate for this special insight news feature, as is a person behind the scenes of a public event—backstairs at the White House, for example.

A reaction interview stresses a person's or people's descriptions of emotions experienced as events happened, or his or her efforts in the present time to make sense of what occurred. The reaction article helps readers understand how or why someone behaved a certain way during an event.

Associated Press reporter Jay Sharbutt interviewed a 33-year-old American woman who had refused to leave her husband in Kuwait City during its occupation by Iraqi soldiers during the Persian Gulf War. Her interview, held after Americans had retaken the city, offers a personal, human perspective on the past Iraqi occupation of Kuwait:

> Iraqi troops, she said, once invaded her house, looking for resistance fighters, demanding to know who lived there. She successfully posed as a Kuwaiti.
>
> On another occasion, Iraqi deserters tried to get in to loot goods they'd resell back home, even girl's barrettes.
>
> They banged their AK-47 rifles against the reinforced steel gate of her home. She didn't reply. Frustrated, they went away, she said.

In addition to offering the drama of this woman's on-the-scene difficulties, the reaction article also offers readers the benefit of her insight, which her unique experience has given her. Sharbutt's news feature thus gives readers an alternative way to understand war politics:

> . . . [Sarrah Foley al-Gharabally] was particularly incensed at U.S. reports of those who protested the war and carried signs saying the war was a matter of "Blood for Oil."
>
> "They were completely wrong—they were off base, way off base," she said. "Because that's not what it was about." It was about Iraq's invasion and the killing and torture and atrocities that followed it, she said.
>
> "The human cost was inestimable. And it's going to go on. The scars that we have are going to last forever."

ONE PERSON'S HISTORY

Another way of telling the news in human terms is to relate one person's history (sometimes the histories of two or three people), using that person, not as someone with a unique view of news events, but as an example of what has happened or is happening to many people connected to a news story. The individual's experiences dominate the article; each time the article considers a new aspect of the story, the single person's history related to that aspect is described.

When the NFL was under attack in the news for exploiting recruits, Associated Press sports writer Hal Bock did a series concerning football players who left college within one semester of graduation to go into the NFL. Part II of the series was an article on defensive tackle Oliver Barnett, a single player representing many players. Bock's story begins this way:

> In some places, defensive tackle Oliver Barnett would have been described as a project, an academic longshot.
>
> At the University of Kentucky, though, he was the pride of the counseling department, a football player who had worked hard to make it, a student who was just nine hours from his degree in social work. On the Kentucky campus, he was a success story, a top flight athlete who was making it in the classroom as well.
>
> And then came the spring semester, the scouting combines, the tryouts, the NFL draft, the mini-camps. And that's when, after five years of classes and counselors, five years of tutors and tests, five years of working for everything he got academically, Oliver Barnett dropped out.
>
> Nine hours—not even a full semester—short of his degree.

The personal history story may or may not overtly make the point that what is happening to this single person is an example of what is happening to many others. Readers are usually quite capable of making that connection themselves. At some point, however, the number of other people involved is often stated, perhaps in an "editor's note" or "author's note," such as the "editor's note" before Bock's story:

> Almost 25 percent of the 331 players drafted by the NFL last April left college one semester or less away from a degree. This is the story of one of them. . . .

RECREATING THE STORY

Chronological re-creations of news events can be effective news features— either as a way of presenting one person's colorful and detailed narrative of what happened, or as a way of examining the role one person or several people played in a news event.

A journalist on the scene of a disaster often writes a narrative recreating his or her own experiences; indeed he or she may have been intentionally sent to the scene to send back a first-hand account. David Von Drehle of the *Miami Herald* was sent to witness Hurricane Hugo's devastation of Charleston, South Carolina; he wrote a dramatic account that is included at the end of this chapter.

After a subway train derailed in Manhattan, injuring more than 200 people, *The New York Times* published a chronological recreation of the events leading up to the accident, focusing on the train operator charged with manslaughter in connection with the crash, and the role he played in the disaster.

The writer, Robert D. McFadden, gives many details in typical crime news reporting style (''Mr. Ray has been charged with five counts of manslaughter and accused of being drunk during the accident; tests 13 hours later showed 0.21 percent of alcohol in his blood, twice the legal limit for drunkenness.''), but the story is feature-like, emphasizing narrative time, atmosphere, and personal human details:

> He began drinking in the early morning when he got home from work, just a few sunrise beers to unwind after a long night hurtling through the dark subway tunnels. But by the early afternoon, investigators said, he had switched to Dewar's White Label Scotch and he drank until after 3 P.M., when he went to bed.
>
> It was sweltering in New York that day, last Tuesday, and Robert E. Ray slept through the worst of the heat, rising at 10:30 P.M. to prepare for his final graveyard workshift of the week, eight hours in the dead of night at the controls of a train roaring up and down the Bronx, Manhattan's East Side and Brooklyn.
>
> He put on dark trousers, a pair of sneakers, a white short-sleeved shirt with a Metropolitan Transportation Authority patch on the right sleeve, a blue sweater and a blue baseball cap. Then, investigators said, Mr. Ray, a 38-year-old divorced man deeply troubled by family and alcohol problems, had a couple more quick drinks.

ADDING COLOR TO THE STORY

Hearing about someone else's experiences is not the only way to gain a supplementary understanding of what news means. Sometimes a news feature encourages readers to witness the news event for themselves. News stories that deal with significant occasions such as state funerals, inaugurations, or major sports events seem to demand color coverage. A reporter describes the scene so readers can respond emotionally to it, rather than simply learn about it.

When a Scud missile attack killed 28 U.S. servicemen toward the end of the Persian Gulf war, George Esper of Associated Press filed the following second-day account. The article includes updated casualty statistics as well as quotations from various witnesses and authorities about what happened and the damage that was done. But primarily Esper's account is a color description; it allows readers to see the catastrophe through their own eyes. He begins with physical details:

> DHAHRAN, Saudi Arabia—The soldiers' belongings were gathered from the debris of death and packed in their duffel bags.
>
> The small American flags they waved when they arrived in Saudi Arabia were tucked into the tops of some of the bags that would accompany 28 of them on their final journey home.

Esper ends his story with a strong description of the scene of the death and destruction:

A convoy of ambulances and medical evacuation helicopters carried away the wounded amid sirens that wailed non-stop through the night. A chaplain moved among the dead to pray for them and among the living to console them. Soldiers cried and embraced each other in anguish.

A soldier sat weeping near the skeleton of a building that a short time ago had been her home.

Nearby, a military policeman whispered something into the ear of a female colleague as she strapped her M-16 over her shoulder. She took a deep breath and said to no one in particular, "I have to prepare myself for this."

A bleary-eyed private walked past, his desert camouflage uniform rumpled and dirty, hair matted to his head, tears running down his left cheek.

"Try to take a break, man," a burley MP told him, offering a pat on the back.

Amidst the rubble, four pairs of boots poked out from under blankets. The charred floor was littered with sleeping bags, cots and military uniform belts. Near the body of one soldier was a letter addressed to a woman in Petersburg, Va. She would share his last moments of life.

THE UNUSUAL ASPECT

News features can also broaden readers' understanding of the story by presenting some unusual aspect of the news. A news feature can consider a side issue, an off-beat perspective, or some historical anecdotes connected to the story. For example, when Prince Charles and Lady Di were first having marital difficulties, Audrey Woods of Associated Press wrote a news feature describing some famous, and infamous, marital difficulties of other British royal couples. When Ross Perot bowed out of the 1992 presidential race, Bill Marvel and Ed Robinson of *The Dallas Morning News* wrote a story presenting some of the exit lines of famous quitters. It begins:

I've had it. I quit. Sayonara. So long. Take this job and shove it.

Some depart in style, some limp off in defeat. Some jump, some are pushed. Few quit when they are ahead.

Ross Perot was not the first to walk away from the field of battle when he dropped out of the presidential race. And he will not be the last.

His exit line: "I believe it would be disruptive for us to continue our program, since this program would obviously put (the election) in the House of Representatives and be disruptive to the country. So, therefore, I will not become a candidate."

Then the story relates "farewells and final remarks" of history's quitters, from Greta Garbo to Ingmar Bergman, from Richard Nixon to Rhett Butler.

RETELLING THE STORY

We began this chapter by saying that news features are typically associated with newspapers and news magazines, but it wouldn't be appropriate to conclude our discussion of news features without adding a qualification to that statement.

News magazines also have many stories similar to the news features described in this chapter. They too offer feature stories that are timely and present both single and additional coverage of news events and information. Magazines such as *Time, Newsweek,* and *U.S. News and World Report,* however, really exist in a category by themselves. Their news is not exactly news, their features are not exactly features, and their news features are not exactly news features.

Weekly news magazines share a characteristic that is typical of few other news publications, except the *Wall Street Journal,* the *Christian Science Monitor* and *USA Today* (and they all publish more frequently than once a week): that is, news magazines publish on the basis of being readers' second *written* encounter with the news. People who buy news magazines can be presumed to already know from local newspapers what has happened (and of course, from the broadcast media as well). Therefore, news magazines are actually *retelling* the news for readers to encounter for the second, third, or fourth time. In order to make this retelling of the news saleable, they change the nature of their news stories.

What changes do they make?

For one thing, they make the news dramatic and intense—indeed, feature-like. Consider, for example, this second paragraph in a *Time* article on the civil war between the Serbs and Croatians:

> The Serb-dominated Yugoslav military threw itself into the conflict with a will. Federal gunboats boomed off the Croatian coast as warplanes and artillery opened fire on targets across the secessionist republic. A massive column of federal battle tanks, armored personnel carriers and 155-mm howitzers set out from Belgrade to assault Croatia's eastern wing, which borders on Serbia. In another action, two columns of federal reservists marched into Bosnia-Herzegovina, shattering the tense calm of that buffer state with its explosive mixture of Serbs, Croatians and Slavic Muslims. When an oil refinery blew up under attack in Osijek, Croatia's key city in the east, it became clear that a region long dormant had loosed a volcano of passions.

The writing is full of action verbs, and the military, the gunboats, even the howitzers, all seem to have minds of their own; they ''set out'' and ''march'' apparently of their own free will. The area is described as a ''volcano of passions''—a dramatic choice of words.

News magazines also make this second version of the news worth reading by presenting it conclusively. Because they publish less frequently, they are able to wrap up a news story, give a sense of finality to it, analyze it thoroughly, and supplement it with a great deal of other material: features, infographics, commentary, photographic essays, and so forth.

It is, however, in the point of view of the story (who's telling the story) that news magazines most alter from the typical newspaper presentation. The difference begins with the identification of who has done the reporting. Articles for news magazines are typically reported by many people rather than one reporter, and those many reporters or that one reporter may not necessarily be the writer of the story. Journalistic accountability for the individual story is thus reduced even when reporters and writers are given credit at the story's end. It's still not exactly clear who's responsible for language and/or content. And since news magazines frequently use anonymous quotations, articles seem to reveal inside information, yet it's difficult to pin down precisely who got that inside information or who is responsible for its accuracy. For example, in a single *Newsweek* paragraph on a U.S. covert operation in Nicaragua, there were references to two unidentified "administration officials," "unidentified CIA records," and unidentified "aides" of Chamorro.

News magazine articles also express a point of view that is omniscient. The first paragraph for the Serbian/Croation story mentioned earlier includes an all-knowing generalization ("Not long ago, the reputation of the Balkans as the tinderbox of Europe seemed to have faded.") and an omniscient judgment of the future ("But last week that idyllic image was irreparably shattered.") A *Newsweek* news feature on the BBC network's challenge to CNN also makes omniscient statements. The second paragraph in the story tells what the magazine *knows* politicians and consumers are thinking:

> Cable News Network's legendary success has politicians and news consumers around the world worried that Ted Turner's empire is turning into a de facto American monopoly on instant news.

And the article's conclusion is also an all-knowing judgment:

> As CNN and the BBC slug it out, at least the viewers will be the winners.

What all of this means is that magazines such as *Time* and *Newsweek* don't really provide useful models of news feature writing. They certainly are worth reading and studying, but their unique style makes them poor guides for how to write a standard news feature.

It may be helpful for you to compare the news magazines' retelling of the news in the news coverage of your local newspaper, to learn how to tell a story dramatically or use intense language effectively, or to get ideas about approaches to the news that news features can take.

But be aware that, in terms of learning how to write news features, imitation of news magazine articles would not be a sure way to success.

EXERCISES

1. Your local newspaper has just run a story about four teenagers who were killed on their way to the senior prom; drunk driving is blamed for their car running off the road at 4 A.M. List five possibilities for feature stories you could research and write as follow-up news features to this accident story.

2. Attend an event of a light-hearted or silly nature and write a brief news feature reporting it. Or read a recent professional or scientific journal and write a brief news feature about information published in it.

3. Study the three leads which began the cover stories of *Time, Newsweek,* and *U.S. News and World Report* on the Senate hearings for Clarence Thomas' appointment to the Supreme Court and the accusation of Anita Hill regarding sexual harassment. How are the leads similar to each other? Different? How are they feature-like? How not?

> A painful public reunion with millions watching was not what anyone had planned: He, the self-made conservative Supreme Court nominee, defending his good name; she, the up-from-poverty legal scholar, accusing her former boss of "dirty" and "disgusting" behavior. Senate Judiciary Committee members were on trial, too, as members of a 98 percent male Senate club, accused of burying the accusations and being unable to understand the power of the charges of sexual harassment. It was a dirty circus, even by Washington standards. And when the public airing concluded, the stench lingered. (*U.S. News and World Report,* 10-21-91)

> The United States Senate is not a circus that children should attend. It is far too dangerous. Last week, as the lawmakers presided over the public evisceration of Clarence Thomas and Anita Hill, it became clear that this was a circus with an ancient history stretching back to the days when people were fed to lions. This was the kind with real victims, and no nets. (*Time,* 10-21-91)

> It pre-empted the game shows, it interrupted week-end plans of foliaging, it transfixed a nation. It was carnal, ugly, and surreal. This was the Scandal With Everything—penises, power, intense emotional pain—and millions tuned in. They watched an X-rated spectacle that was repulsive and irresistible at the same time. (*Newsweek,* 10-21-91)

4. Read David Von Drehle's story for *The Miami Herald,* "Shaken Survivors Witness Pure Fury." (The story won the 1990 American Society of Newspaper Editors Award for Deadline Writing.) What memorable physical details in the story bring home the force of the hurricane? Not only does Von Drehle's story humanize the news by showing it through one person's eyes, but it humanizes the storm as well. Where, in Von Drehle's writing, does the hurricane behave like a person? Part of the reader's reaction to this news feature is to the story itself, and part to Von Drehle's participation in the story. Would you be willing to observe a hurricane firsthand in order to write a feature about it? Whatever your answer, how do your feelings affect your perception of Von Drehle, and thus, your reaction to his story?

SHAKEN SURVIVORS WITNESS PURE FURY

By David Von Drehle

The Miami Herald, *September 23, 1989*

CHARLESTON, S.C.—It's noon on Thursday at Folly Beach, a stretch of sand raised a few inches above the surrounding tidal marsh and sprinkled with undistinguished bungalows and weathered seafood shacks.

It's gray, lightly sprinkling. Not unusual for a September afternoon. But big breakers are sending foam over the sea wall and the houses are deserted. The town has the eerie feeling of an unnaturally empty place—like a dusty street in a dime Western just before the bad guys arrive.

Hurricane Hugo is 12 hours away.

Tension grows through the afternoon. Every little gust of air, every spit of rain, every new shade of gray cloud is searched for meaning. With each new breeze, people speed their pace, tighten their jaws.

The streets empty. Traffic jams the roads out of town. Forecasters said gale-force winds might arrive by 3 p.m., but at 5, the palms and elms and oaks are still swaying gently.

At 5:30, as journalists and other thrill-seekers tour the Battery in a gentle rain, visibility drops suddenly. The famous sights from the harbor's edge—like Fort Moultrie, of Revolutionary War fame, and Fort Sumter, where the Civil War began—vanish in the fog.

Then rain comes, warm and straight and thick. The gale arrives next, driving the warm rain ahead of it. A statue honoring the Confederate war dead, a bronze nude brandishing a broadsword, confronts the storm wearing nothing but a fig leaf.

False alarm. The wind and rain die down. But they will be back.

From the television comes the news that Hugo is gaining speed and fury. This will be one of the rare Category 4 storms to hit the United States. Hugo is six hours away.

Sundown, and gray drains from the sky, leaving only black. The tension rises another notch.

In the gloaming, the trees ball and buck in the rising winds.

By 9 p.m., the gale is gusting so hard you have to lean into it to make headway, like a street mime.

Outages Black Out Area

Miami Herald photographer Jon Kral and I hope to make it to hotel rooms near the Charleston airport, 10 miles inland. As we leave downtown, a main power station gives out, and the streets become darker, more menacing.

Water swirls and snakes across the highway as we drive. The rain falls almost horizontally. Broken branches and loose garbage skid over the pavement, and the gusts are now high enough to rock the car as it creeps across Charleston's high bridges.

It's dark in all directions—power failures spread black like it was paint. The failures come quickly and rhythmically, almost as if someone were flipping a row of switches.

The manmade glow is replaced by startling eruptions of muffled light—huge lightning storms showing through the furious shroud.

A rock-and-roll station pledges to stay with us through the hurricane. "Your Hurricane Hugo station!" the DJ cries. Then he announces that the eye of the storm is just two hours away, headed straight for us—"so whatever you do, don't drive!"

Within a few minutes, the station is off the air. The storm becomes too much.

Winds Shift into Overdrive

The hotel turns out to be unprepared, but Kral produces a roll of duct tape from his bag and we strip asterisks onto each pane. At 10:30, the room lights go brown, then die, struggle back, then fail for good.

Outside, the air is screaming at the same pitch that wind reaches through a cracked window on an interstate highway. The howl is strangely pleasant, because we make the mistake of thinking that this is about as bad as it will get.

The noise halts briefly, just for a second or two, then comes back at a much higher, much more urgent pitch. After five minutes of that, Hugo clutches and shifts again to an even higher level. The winds step up like a sports car going through the gears—except that Hugo has many more gears.

With each new step, the barometric pressure drops, and we can feel the changes in our ears. At 11:30, we dress to go out into the storm, but quickly change our minds when Hugo jumps three gears in five minutes.

From somewhere inside the shrieking noise come the muffled reports of snapping trees, popping windshields, and sand hitting the windows like pellets.

Water in the toilet bowl rocks and swirls as Hugo howls through the city's sewers. Wind gusts from the light fixtures. The panes pull at their window frames.

A Sound of Pure Fury

Frightened families leave their rooms and walk nervously down darkened stairwells to the leaking lobby. At the bottom of one stairwell, we watch as the sucking wind tries to wrench open a double-bolted fire door.

First the air yanks, then slips its fingers into the tiny gap between door and door frame, then strains at the heavy steel structure until the door actually *bends.*

Then the awful clutching silence, and the wind returns, up another impossible gear.

By midnight, as the worst of the fury roars nightmarishly over Charleston, the very walls tremble and quake.

The noise of a killer hurricane has been compared to a passing freight train so many times it has become a sort of journalists' joke. "Let me guess—did it sound like a train?"

But to me, this doesn't sound like a train. It sounds like the harsh intake of a dentist's suction tube, greatly amplified and always increasing. Or the roar of a seashell a billion times over. Or Niagara, if only Niagara cranked up its volume each time your ears got adjusted to it.

Most of all, it sounds like pure fury.

One of Kral's taped windows explodes minutes after we leave the room. When we come back, it's impossible to open the door, the wind is so strong. We have to wait for a pause between gears, then drive with our shoulders.

A Tempest in a Motel Room

Thick rain is blowing horizontally through the room. Thanks to the duct tape, the shattered glass is in a neat pile on the floor. We shout over the gale.

In the bathroom, the swirling winds have pulled the Sheetrock ceiling away from the walls. For the rest of the tempest, Hugo works on tearing the room apart. Gusts of 25 miles per hour come through the ceiling. The nails and screws groan at the strain.

The winds are much wilder, much more intense than anything I have experienced before. The difference between 100-mph winds and 130-mph winds is so great that they ought to have different names.

At five minutes past midnight, the noise begins gearing down rapidly. By 12:15, it's almost still. Some of us venture outside and inspect the damage by flashlight.

A thick steel flagpole, barely anything to it to resist the wind, is bent at a 60-degree angle. An ancient Pontiac, finned and weighty, has been shoved several feet into a Saab. A Chrysler New Yorker is deposited on the sidewalk.

Along the windward side of the hotel, the windows of the cars are consistently shattered, as if by methodical vandals. "I'll sell this new Honda right now for $9,000," says a distraught owner.

Then he sees his girlfriend's matching car with matching wounds. "Two for $18,000," he says.

Complete Stillness

The ground is thick with tree limbs and glass and aluminum and shingles and bits of plastic signs. Bits of Sheraton, bits of McDonald's.

At 12:30, complete stillness. We're in the middle of Hugo's eye. It's still and silent and hot and humid on a landscape covered with debris. It feels like surfacing from a bomb shelter at the end of the world.

"I thought you were supposed to see stars when you're in the eye," someone says.

We all look up. No stars. Then we notice a highway sign, still attached to its pole, jutting up near an old Impala. The sign, we realize, must have been uprooted a quarter-mile away.

It has been driven, like a javelin, through the side of the car, and stuck there as firmly as Excalibur in the stone.

Five minutes pass. Then comes a tiny puff of breeze, so faint as to be imperceptible—except that we are waiting for it so intently. Within a few seconds, a faint drizzle follows. Half a minute after that, the breeze and drizzle are rattling shredded metal like spook-house ghosts.

Then, just before the wind resumes lifting and twirling debris, Orion's belt and a few stars peep through, low in the northern sky. Then disappear.

Wind Blows in Opposite Way

Back inside, water pours through the lobby ceiling and sloshes on the floor. Now the wind blows the opposite way, drawing the curtains out through Kral's gaping window. They snapped so hard against the adjacent panes we fear they will break, so we rip the curtains from the rods.

By 12:45 Hugo is back near peak fury. Kral points a light into the storm to illuminate the movements of the rain. It zings through the air, up, sideways, diagonally, sometimes downward. It whips and swirls, a true maelstrom.

Now a new row of cars catches the full fury, and new stands of trees. Windshields explode and trees crack like firecrackers. The noise is swallowed in the roar of the storm.

Again, the ears are popping, as the barometric pressure returns. In this respect, Hugo is a lot like flying on a jet—on the *outside.*

The backside of the storm seems to gear up and fade more quickly than the leading edge, but in fact it does not. Time is speeding up. The storm pumped so much adrenaline, and sharpened the senses so acutely, that time slowed, and now it is resuming its normal pace.

The winds drop as Hugo recedes. Almost immediately, it is hard to recall how fiercely it blew. And almost impossible to believe.

Travel and Lifestyle Stories
Exploring Distant Places and Lives

Travel and lifestyle stories are features about the way we live our lives. These stories help readers explore options and consider alternatives to their current ways of working and playing. Travel and lifestyle features describe choices readers can make about spending time (and money) so their lives are more worthwhile and fulfilling.

The popularity today of travel and lifestyle articles seems to reflect increased reader interest in the quality of contemporary American life. Readers of the '90s generally aren't living the same lives their parents lived, and since they aren't following familiar patterns, they look to travel and lifestyle articles in magazines and newspapers for guidance.

Many readers are content to simply consider the choices these articles present: they read travel stories, but never travel; they read about unusual lifestyles, but never change the pattern of their lives. Other readers, however, are eager for change, eager to exercise their options. They use travel and lifestyle features as special how-tos, that is, as roadmaps directing them to new destinations.

TRAVEL STORIES, PAST AND PRESENT

Travel stories have a long history in journalism, representing some of the best and worst in feature writing. Articles about faraway places have been written by many famous American literary writers, who worked for newspapers as "foreign" correspondents in early stages of their writing careers. You are probably familiar with "The Jumping Frog of Calaveras County" by Mark Twain and "The Open Boat" by Stephen Crane, two well-known short stories that evolved from reporting Twain and Crane did as correspondents.

Descriptive writing in such literary travel stories, and in standard travel articles of similar quality, can be exceptionally fine, with original metaphoric language, clear visual imagery, and rich physical detail. And well-written travel stories not only create vivid pictures of scenery, but also capture the mood and manners of people dwelling in far-off places.

On the other hand, travel writing has also been connected historically with some of the worst kind of journalistic boosterism: the reporter's writing of a positive, glowing endorsement of a distant location because his or her travel expenses there were paid by hotels or other travel-related businesses. Positive, one-sided stories written as a payoff for free travel may once have benefitted journalists and the travel industry, but have seldom benefitted readers.

The best travel stories are both well-written and serve readers. They paint colorful, realistic pictures of travel destinations as well as give background material about particular locations. They tell readers how to make the best decisions about where to go, how to get there, what to see, and how much the trip will cost.

Perhaps today's travel stories are more responsible to the public than ones written 50 or 100 years ago because now many more people are traveling. If you're a travel writer today, you know that a large number of your readers will already have been to places you are describing, and many more will go there soon, with your descriptions and advice in hand. If what you have written about a place doesn't match what they find, or if it doesn't match what other readers remember, then you will lose your credibility as a travel writer, and thus your audience for future travel features.

STYLES OF LIVING

Lifestyle stories, as opposed to travel articles, are relatively new to journalism, reflecting a change from the ''society'' stories of the so-called ''women's pages'' of 25 years ago, to today's feature stories written for both men and women. Lifestyle articles explore the ways people live, play, and work. Lifestyle stories, for example, might describe people who work as migrant laborers, as nannies to children of yuppie couples, or as researchers of marine life in the South Seas.

Lifestyle stories may be written about dream careers and luxurious styles of living, for readers who enjoy fantasizing about glamorous lives (such stories are more or less written versions of ''Lifestyles of the Rich and Famous''). Lifestyle stories may also be written about more ordinary employment, for readers who are considering a change in their present occupations. They may also be written about dangerous and difficult lifestyles, for readers who enjoy learning about the roles of other workers in society or who might like to compare their own comfortable lifestyle to the tough situations of other workers.

Lifestyle stories also present information about social trends, different and new ways people live, changes in government regulations, scientific discoveries, legal decisions, and the way the state of the economy affects our lives.

Let's consider first the older of the two kinds of feature stories exploring ''distant'' places and lives: the travel article.

DESTINATION ARTICLES

The most common travel article is the destination article, a feature story describing a place readers might want to visit or remember visiting. Readers can use this story to fantasize about a journey, make specific travel plans, or recall time spent at a particular place.

The destination article thoroughly describes a location, giving in addition background information and how-to advice. Just as in the color story, the writer makes readers feel they ''are there'' on the scene with their senses awakened, say, to the allure of the Aegean Sea, the smells of the Arab city, the feel of the royal velvet of a London pageant.

Some destination stories limit themselves only to description, doing little more than sketching a picture of a particular place in order to encourage readers to consider it as a vacation spot. For example, an article on Bermuda in *Elegant Bride* magazine written by Charlanne Fields is one of several brief destination articles in the magazine which merely suggest to readers honeymoon travel options. Field's article is pure description from beginning to end. The beginning:

> Bermuda is tinted in the impressionists' favorite palette—soft pastels accented with rich jewel tones. Pale turquoise water edges the scallops of her pearl pink beaches. Houses echo Nature's rainbow tints—soft-hued blues, pinks, yellow and greens—all topped with cloud-white roofs. And everywhere is a garden of gems: ruby bougainvillea, sapphire morning glories, topaz hibiscus.

The end:

> If your image of the ideal honeymoon places you in an exquisite scene captured in bits of light and color, then picture yourselves honeymooning in Bermuda. Like the splash of brilliance in Monet's famous ''Water Lilies,'' Nature has created a masterpiece here with her gentlest pastel brushstrokes.

You can see from these two excerpts how destination stories, like color stories, frequently use metaphoric language and observed physical details (such as ''ruby bougainvillea'' and ''sapphire morning glories''). And descriptive writing (as we said in Chapter 7), whether in color stories or travel articles, generally is more effective when people appear in the description, giving it life and movement. Through people observed and quoted, a sense of the personality and character of the place is conveyed.

While destination travel stories are primarily descriptive, most of them also include a great deal of information helpful to readers who are planning to travel to that location, especially if the destination is not very well known, or is a place with an unfamiliar history. For example, a *Washington Post* destination travel article written by James T. Yenckel gives readers interesting factual information on Naples, Florida:

> A winter resort from its birth in the late 1880s, Naples occupies a long, slender point of land that thrusts between the Gulf of Mexico and the many canals of Naples Bay. The city's name reflects the turn-of-the-century allure of sunny Italy, to which Florida's early promoters strove to compare the state. Until recently, the city was a sleepy backwater, and even now its permanent population is only about 21,000. But its obvious charm and year-round mild climate have sparked a home-building boom in adjacent Collier County, one of the country's fastest-growing counties.

SPECIAL ATTRACTION STORIES

Another kind of travel story is the special attraction story, which focuses not so much on a geographical location, but on a specific attraction at a geographic location, a special attraction which readers might want to visit.

In some instances, the special attraction simply provides a new angle for a destination story about a popular tourist spot, for example, the Vietnam War Memorial in Washington, D.C., or Queen Mary's Doll House at Windsor Castle in Great Britain.

In other stories, the special attraction is the only reason the location would be written about. For example, an Associated Press article on the Laura Ingalls Wilder-Rose Wilder Lane Home and Museum in Missouri focuses entirely on the special attraction, not its relatively unimportant location.

The typical special attraction story tells readers what they will see if they visit. The Ingalls Wilder museum story, for example, tells readers:

> Perhaps the best-known exhibit is the fiddle Pa Ingalls played to entertain his family on the vast, lonely prairie. . . .
>
> The building also houses manuscripts of four of the "Little House" books, which Laura wrote in pencil on Springfield Grocer Co. school tablets that cost a nickel.
>
> The display also features a sewing cabinet Almanzo made for his wife out of cigar boxes, family photographs and heirlooms, the Bible Ma and Pa Ingalls gave Laura and Almanzo on their wedding day and a nine-patch quilt made by Mary Ingalls.

The special attraction story may also give readers background information that would enhance their visit to this special place, or be worth reading even if they are not able to visit there. For example, the Ingalls Wilder museum story gives readers interesting details about Laura Ingalls Wilder's life such as these:

> Laura named their 200-acre farm, where they lived happily for more than a half-century, Rocky Ridge Farm. She and Almanzo had a successful livestock and poultry business and shipped fruit from their apple and peach orchards to markets in Kansas City, St. Louis and Memphis. . . .
> Laura boasted the most modern country kitchen in the Ozarks after Almanzo piped water from a spring through their 1908 Montgomery Ward stove and into the sink for both hot and cold running water.

We should note that the "native sons and daughters" feature which Helene Barnhart describes as a "travel profile" in *How to Write and Sell the 8 Easiest Article Types,* could also be defined as a kind of special attraction story focusing on the attraction of visiting a town and community because of its connection to a famous person. The story profiles the "character" or nature of a place in the light of how living there affected the development of that famous person.

A special attraction story can itself have a special angle, if the special attraction is one often written about or is very well-known. For example, Pamela P. Hegarty's travel article "Old Sturbridge Village in Winter" in *Early American Life,* is a special attraction story with a special angle, because Sturbridge Village is already quite familiar to readers. Hegarty narrows her focus by emphasizing what Sturbridge Village has to offer visitors in *winter* rather than in summer:

> In many ways, a crisp winter's day is the best time to journey to the 1830's, when the village wears the quiet mystique of new fallen snow. With crowds as distant as summer heat, the villagers welcome the chance to introduce guests to life in the 1830's and make them feel more like townspeople than tourists. Special "Exploration Days" offer a peek into lesser-known aspects of village life, such as storytelling, court hearings, and toymaking. Some, like schooling and candlemaking, are traditional winter activities.

An article in *USAir Magazine* about another well-known special attraction, Williamsburg, Virginia, similarly narrows its focus, telling readers (presumably business executives traveling on USAir) various pieces of information about Williamsburg as a convention site: the article relates information about its accessibility, its facilities, and its experience playing host to large gatherings.

MODE OF TRAVEL

A third kind of travel story focuses on the mode of travel. A *National Geographic* story by Richard Olsenius, for example, describes motoring on the Alaska Highway, a mode of traveling that allows visitors to see the immense loneliness of the state:

> You'll be lucky if this twisting, two-lane road lets you go as fast as 50 miles an hour along the tortuous 1,500 miles between Dawson Creek, British Columbia, and Fairbanks, Alaska. This is equivalent to driving from New York City to the middle of South Dakota, and the map, littered with settlements with cheerful names like Fireside and Champagne, gives no hint of the immense stretches of wilderness that surround you on the way to the next cup of coffee, the next human voice.

Although it's not uncommon in all travel articles for the writer to use the pronoun "I" at least once or twice (when you're describing your experience at a place, it's difficult to avoid using "I"), the pronoun "I" does appear more frequently in mode-of-travel articles, which are often written as first-person narratives. The journey becomes a kind of personal odyssey or pilgrimage. For readers, part of the pleasure of reading a mode-of-travel article, then, may be in seeing how the narrator "makes it through" to a particular destination, or seeing how he or she handles the difficulties of the chosen mode of travel.

For example, Michael Finkel's *New York Times* mode-of-travel story describes a 72-day bicycle odyssey across America undertaken by Finkel and a companion. Readers can empathize with the two men and the amateurish beginning to their difficult trip:

> To our couch-potato physiques, every incline felt like Everest as we rode up and down Oregon's forested Coast Range. And this was all before the first major climb—Santiam Pass, 4,817 feet—in the heart of the Oregon Cascades. . . . Thoughts of quitting crept into my head, and moments before Bret and I were about to make the ultimate decision we spotted the bicyclist's savior: the triangular yellow sign with a caption reading "Downgrade Ahead."

Finkel's first-person account creates a sense of immediacy that allows readers to feel they are sharing in many of his personal travel experiences—even some experiences they might never before have considered typical of that mode of travel:

> There was a steady crossing of box turtles in Kentucky, and herds of Holsteins dotted the Midwest. But Missouri stood alone as the land of dogs. Bret and I tried everything, from water guns to biscuits, to stymie their attacks; nothing seemed to work. Fortunately, neither of us got bitten, and during the daily chases an entire dog terminology evolved. There were stealth dogs (silent ones that sneak up on you), virulent dogs (those that lead especially vociferous attacks), benign dogs (chained up), and stereo dogs (more than one). They added to the excitement of the up-and-down Ozarks, where one moment I'd be braking furiously as I careened around a curve; the next I'd be standing on my pedals, straining to force one more rotation.

Finkel's story concludes with his triumphant arrival at the Atlantic coast, a triumph the reader enjoys with him because the reader has shared so much of the difficulty in getting there:

> We pedaled straight into the ocean. I dived under the waves, and it was only then, when the warm waters of the Atlantic engulfed me, that I knew we had finished. I lifted my head and looked to the horizon: for the first time in 72 days there was no more road.

INFORMATION TO HELP TRAVELERS

When you are writing destination, special attraction, and mode-of-travel articles, you will want to highlight in your stories those events and places particularly worth seeing, and mention places to avoid, or times to avoid certain places.

Generally, travel writing is positive; people who choose to travel (and write about it) are usually people who enjoy traveling, just as people who read about traveling are logically those who want to or plan to travel. And, of course, you don't ordinarily choose to write about some place that you just *hated.*

However, if a travel article is entirely, 100-percent positive in its description of a place, it is about as believable to readers as a recommendation letter that says only good things: readers know that no perfect place exists, just as employers know no perfect job applicant exists. Your praise of a place is more credible if you include in your travel article information about a few things you found to be less than ideal.

Be sure, however, that when you write something negative, you give specific opinions. Your objections (for example, it was too crowded, too hot, too expensive) may not trouble all of your readers. Some of them may be willing to endure particular difficulties in order to see something they very much want to see. And if they are willing, they will be better able to endure the difficulties if you have forewarned them.

New York Times writer Sherry Marker, for example, is very clear about the problems readers can expect if they visit Puerto Rico's seaside village La Parguera to see the dinoflagellates, "microscopic creatures that glow and sparkle like so many aquatic fireflies." She explains:

> Today the dinoflagellates are big business in La Parguera, where a steady stream of boats chugs the mile or so out to the bay year round. Throughout the lagoon, houseboats and vacation homes on floating piers are tethered to many of the mangrove islands. What with the boats churning up the water and the vacation homes polluting the lagoon, the marine life is suffering, including the dinoflagellates and the once-plentiful pargo, a red snapper from which La Parguera takes its name.

There are nights when so many tourists show up to visit the bay that some are turned away. The man who sold me a ticket for the 7:30 P.M. told me it had been canceled and rescheduled for 8:30.

When I arrived at 8:15, I was told that the 7:30 boat had not been canceled but had in fact left at 8 and that I should return at 9:30. Not eager to be left behind again, I appeared at 9:15; the boat cast off at 10, but returned to the dock almost immediately to collect a honeymoon couple.

When you are writing your travel article, include information about the times when visitors can go to see particular sights, as well as information on where they can eat and sleep—including costs, restaurant hours and dress required, information about whether reservations are necessary, and phone numbers and addresses of restaurants and lodgings. Information on the best places to exchange money and hints on tipping procedures are also useful, as is information about car and recreation equipment rentals.

Be sure, too, to consider in your article the needs of special travelers. What are the rules regarding children? Are babysitting services available? Facilities for pets? What about special difficulties for elderly and handicapped people, such as stairs or rock formations that make places inaccessible? Are there ways single people can meet others or get around comfortably by themselves? Special services or facilities available to business travelers?

ADDITIONS TO THE STORY

Since your article will be packed with a great deal of information, you might consider putting some of that information in at-a-glance boxes which list items of information as bullets (for example, names of hotels or restaurants). Consider too whether infographics such as bar charts (for exchange rates, for example) or maps (for sights to see) would save you from having to present the same information in many paragraphs of gray type. At-a-glance boxes and other infographics are also easy for readers to cut out of newspapers and magazines and carry along with them on their travels.

Your own ratings of such places as historic sights, restaurants, and hotels can be very helpful to readers. They appreciate knowing what you consider the best (and second best, third best, etc.) place to shop, the best restaurant for native food, or the most dynamic night spot for after-hours fun. But remember, as you construct a ratings list or endorse things in your text, be very clear about the meanings of the words you are using. "Expensive" can mean one thing to college students on a spring break and quite another to a double-income couple vacationing at the same location. Define terms such as "expensive" or "moderate," and give specifics, such as particular temperatures and hotel price ranges, rather than generalities, such as saying the weather will be "cool" or the hotel room rates "reasonable."

You might also consider writing two travel stories instead of the one article you had originally intended; that is, you might write a general descriptive article and then a specific sidebar story to accompany it. For example, a sidebar on the "wines of Provence" could accompany a travel story about visiting restaurants in France, or "castles in Wales" could accompany an article on historic Great Britain.

In addition to including infographics, at-a-glance boxes, or sidebar stories, you might want to include photographs with your travel article. Choose both panoramic and close-up shots, so that your photographs reveal detail as well as land- or seascapes.

We should add, by the way, that some magazines publish travel "stories" that are really photographic essays. For example, an article on the Nantucket daffodil festival in the "Traveler's Journal" section of *Yankee* magazine was essentially six photographs. Their captions, however, were detailed. They explained the origin of the festival, suggested its size and character, and offered readers information on the dates of the upcoming year's events, along with a telephone number to call for further information. A would-be traveler thus got enough from this photo package to at least *begin* considering a vacation to the Nantucket festival.

A final thought on what to include with travel articles: consider giving readers a bibliography—either within the text or in an at-a-glance box—which lists books and articles particularly useful in learning about the travel destinations. You can include in your bibliography well-known travel guides such as Fodor's and Frommer's, but you can also include texts on the history of the country, on famous people who were born there or who live or lived there, on art and architecture, music and crafts associated with the region, or anything else you think might be of interest to your readers. For many of them, travel is a hobby. They may enjoy reading to prepare for the journey, or reading about a place after they have visited there, almost as much as they enjoy the actual process of traveling itself.

LIFESTYLE FEATURES

When we turn from travel stories to consider lifestyle stories—the other kind of features written to help readers explore choices about the way they live, work, and play—we see that lifestyle stories, too, share certain characteristics with familiar feature story types. Trend lifestyle stories, like news features, discuss timely information about current ways of living life—though trend stories are a little *less* timely than most news features, since the trends they discuss are measured over longer periods of time: months, years, or decades.

Other lifestyle stories are similar to personality sketches; they are brief descriptive interview stories, portraying a person, or people, who live a special lifestyle. These stories discuss the benefits and liabilities that result from choosing that way of life.

In-depth lifestyle stories, on the other hand, are like backgrounders or personality profiles; they examine closely how a group of people living a particular lifestyle exists, and they consider how that way of life affects society at large. The lifestyle is studied, not in isolation, but in the context of the larger world of general conventional society.

THE TREND STORY

The trend story, as J. T. W. Hubbard writes in *Magazine Editing for Professionals* (Syracuse University Press) is an exciting story because it can "offer the reader wholly new insights on society and the way we live and work." Hubbard uses the term "trend" in a very broad sense, defining trend stories as informative features that cover a variety of topics, "without limit, about changes in our world."

The word "trend" can, of course, be understood that way. But the term "trend" has also been used to describe a story that tells more specifically about developments affecting the way people lead their lives: the trend toward single-parent families, for example, or the trend toward children living at home after they finish college. A trend story may describe a serious or a silly trend. It often describes the scope and dimension of the trend, explaining the history of the trend, and predicting the ways the trend is likely to continue to affect society.

Trend stories, because of their somewhat timely nature, are frequently published in news magazines. *Newsweek,* for example, presented a trend cover story on the increased concern Americans have with the concept of "self esteem." The story describes the concept of self-esteem, sketches its history (from Freud to French therapist Emile Coue, to Norman Vincent Peale, to California television preacher Robert H. Schuller), and examines the trend's impact on various social institutions such as businesses, education, and psychiatry. The article concludes by suggesting the place the concept of self-esteem is on the national agenda: " 'Lack of self-esteem is central to most personal and social ills plagueing our state and nation,' " says a California task-force. Published with this trend article were pictures of famous people and statements they have made about self-esteem, a sidebar story on a *Newsweek*/Gallup poll about how Americans feel about self-esteem, and a column by a British writer criticizing America's preoccupation with self-esteem.

Trend stories also appear in consumer magazines and newspapers. They may be informative articles, but they also may be stories that humanize the trend, emphasizing people's experiences dealing with changes in the way we live. Personal trend stories blend statistics and survey findings with interviews of people "living" the trend, and interviews with authorities and experts. Sometimes the trend story, like a travel story, takes on the tone of the how-to article—at least, it seems to give "expert" information or advice, or offers readers the comfort of knowing they are not alone.

For example, *The Daily Press* of Newport News, Va., syndicated a trend story by Jill Keech about the rising number of divorces among ''mid- and late-life couples.'' The story includes statistics and quotations from experts; it also humanizes the trend by portraying the situation of two specific women:

Barbara Besnier won't celebrate her silver wedding anniversary. Her marriage tarnished before the quarter-century mark.

''When I first realized we weren't going to make it, I was bitter,'' says Ms. Besnier, whose divorce from her husband of 19 years will be final soon.

''It was literally eating me up inside. I didn't want to be divorced at age 53.'' She and her husband separated almost two years ago.

Gloria Jean Creekmore, 57, says she never expected to wind up divorced.

''I had to go back to work,'' says Ms. Creekmore, a grandmother who was married for 37 years. She has been divorced two years.

Today both women are fending for themselves in a world that is foreign to many females of their generation. . . .

At day's end, they cook for one and sleep alone. But in another way, the two women are not alone.

''The sharpest increase in divorce is among mid- and late-life couples,'' says Anne Studner, a senior program specialist with the American Association of Retired Persons. In 1988, 35,000 30-year-or-more marriages ended in divorce, she says.

Not only are people living longer, they are playing by new rules. These days, longevity in marriage is no insurance against divorce.

Another trend story, written by Loraine O'Connell and syndicated by *The Orlando Sentinel,* discussed the trend toward an increased number of office romances occurring because more women are in the workforce. The article focused, not on any one or two individuals (though it does quote a few people engaged in office romances), but on interviews with a wide variety of experts, from management trainers, to company presidents, professors, and human relations consultants.

ALTERNATIVE LIFESTYLES

The story that most often comes to mind when we say ''lifestyle,'' however, is the feature that presents one individual or several individuals engaged in atypical occupations or unusual ways of life.

Most readers will not be likely to adopt the lifestyle described in such a story, particularly if the lifestyle is very unusual or dangerous. A feature about someone who gives up his or her job to sail around the world doesn't present a realistic option for many readers. But some lifestyle stories at least suggest a possible change of lifestyle, and some present a lifestyle choice that may be possible on a temporary basis, as in a feature about someone who takes a leave of absence from work and spends the summer sailing down the Atlantic coast.

Even if readers don't consider adopting an alternative lifestyle, however, they may discover through their reading some options they have for making minor changes in the way they live. Or they may better appreciate the good characteristics of their own style of living. At the very least, they may become more aware that life choices exist and that people can *choose* the way they live, rather than necessarily accepting a way of life decreed by family or fate.

Since most newspapers and magazines are circulated in population centers close to "civilization," a story about an alternative lifestyle frequently involves life in the wilderness. The lifestyle story uses description, factual material, and many quotations from interviews to present a picture of a way of life. An Associated Press story about a couple who built a new life in northern Alaska, for example, describes their isolation, the airplane they use for transportation, the work they do helping scientists track birds, and their garden harvest of 700 pounds of carrots and 1,200 pounds of potatoes, not to mention all their "strawberries and green vegetables—and the rows of brilliantly hued violets."

Such a lifestyle story sometimes involves multiple interviews, such as a Knight-Ridder lifestyle article about "those who turn their back on the rat race and go it alone"—in short, about those who choose to live far away from civilization.

As writer David Hawley puts it:

> In the remote wilderness of far northern Minnesota, we found six people—two couples, a single man and a single woman—who are living the backwoods life quite happily, thank you.
>
> And we learned that, while they all value solitude and the beauty of nature, their principal reason for residing in the woods is financial; they have reduced expenses to the bare minimum.
>
> By giving up their pursuit of the almighty dollar, they have forsaken some of the creature comforts of civilization. But they're not as uncomfortable as you might think.

This kind of lifestyle article does not have to be limited to describing the way of life of a person or a small group of people: sometimes it can sketch the way of life of an entire city or region. For example, a *New York Times Magazine* feature by Clifford D. May describes the way of life in Boulder, Colorado—a city where, according to the article, "Every athletic challenge seems worth the risk and going to extremes is absolutely normal." The story contains quotations from several people, but also is rich in detail and description, making concrete observations about Boulder and its citizens which are convincing as evidence that life there is indeed different from life in other places:

> Take a walk through the streets of Boulder almost any time: everyone seems to be wearing skintight Lycra and riding a bike, jogging or zipping along on in-line roller skates (more commonly called Rollerblades, the name of the most popular brand). Others are packing up their Jeeps and heading into the nearby mountains for a hike or a climb.

Go to a Boulder party and you'll find that the Democrats' chances in 1992 and similar topics get short shrift. Instead, the enthusiastic conversation might be about how the Colorado River is running.

In most parts of America, ask someone, "What do you do?" and he'll tell you how he makes a living. But in Boulder, the response is more apt to be "Well, mostly I climb and kayak, but I'm also getting into skurfing," the term used for surfing on the wake made by a motorboat." People just understand and support this kind of thing in Boulder," says Tod Bibler, a local businessman, paraglider and mountain climber (not necessarily in that order). "You go into the grocery store with chalk on your hands and the checkout lady says: 'So? Have a good time climbing today?' "

But whether the lifestyle story deals with a city, several people, or one person, the feature helps readers envision a different way of life—economically, socially, intellectually, emotionally, or whatever.

A PIECE OF THE PUZZLE

While most lifestyle stories interest readers in alternative ways of living, some in-depth lifestyle stories encourage readers to consider the role a particular lifestyle plays in society as a whole. These lifestyles features offer readers insight into how a significant element of society lives, how a certain group of individuals work and play, hate and love, live and die. The assumption underlying the story is that all elements in society are interconnected, the way pieces of a jigsaw puzzle are interlocked. For a variety of reasons, readers may need or want to have some understanding of the ways different kinds of people living different kinds of lives work to keep society functioning.

William Blundell's story for *The Wall Street Journal*, "The Fatal Fraternity of Northwest Loggers" (included in the exercises for Chapter 5), is an example of a lifestyle feature that describes one segment of society, the people who fell trees for a living. The article would be of interest to many readers simply because the loggers' lifestyle is colorful and unusual, but the story would presumably also be of *particular* interest to readers of the *Wall Street Journal,* who for the most part are workers in white collar industries where paper is consumed at a tremendous rate. These workers might benefit from knowing what some other people in society do to provide them with their paper.

John Camp's series "Life on the Land," published by the *St. Paul Pioneer Press & Dispatch,* describes the lifestyle of the American farmer and his/her family, not as an alternative way of life to the urban lifestyle, but so that city-slicker readers can gain a sense of what it means for other people in society to put food on their tables—and what it may mean to all Americans if the traditional lifestyle of the American farm family perishes. (Part I of the series, which won the 1986 Pulitzer Prize for Feature Writing, follows this chapter.)

"AIDS in the Heartland," the series that won the 1988 Pulitzer Prize for Feature Writing for Jacqui Banaszynski and again for the *St. Paul Pioneer Press,* is another example of a lifestyle story, one that focuses on a gay couple, one of whom is dying of AIDS. It is in many ways a profile of a gay man; it's also a human interest story about a person dying of AIDS. But beyond that, the feature examines the gay lifestyle and a gay "marriage." The series helps readers "see" and understand a lifestyle, perhaps in a way they never have been able to before, particularly if they live in a community where few gay people live. The story may also help readers consider the way people with AIDS live and endure, and what impact the lives of AIDS sufferers have on all society.

In conclusion, whatever you tell readers about lifestyles—or travel—the point is that through travel and lifestyle stories readers expand their horizons. They can see ways of working and playing they may never have known existed, or never have imagined existing as they do. Through your writing, readers can explore distant lands and different ways of life.

And, of course, as you prepare your travel and lifestyle stories, you will be doing considerable exploration yourself. So it is possible that the life you change may be your own.

EXERCISES

1. Read a "Frommer's," "Foder's," or "Let's Go" travel guide's description of a place where you have vacationed or visited. How well does the guidebook match your memory of the place? Was the description too positive? Too brief? Too confusing? Did the guide leave out something you thought was important? Did you learn something from the guidebook that would have been useful to you if you'd known it when you traveled to that vacation spot?

2. Read a travel article from a specialized travel magazine such as *RV Times Magazine, Cruise Travel Magazine,* or *Backpacker.* In what ways has the writer narrowed its focus so that the story suits the specialized audience? How does the article address the needs of that audience?

3. Write a column of brief descriptions of places to eat in your local area, descriptions that someone visiting could use as a guide. Include some kind of rating indicators (such as stars, asterisks, or checks) so that it's clear to readers which restaurants you consider to be of better quality and which only adequate. Write a brief explanation of your rating system to accompany the article.

4. Read Christopher Reynolds' travel article, "The Architecture Is Imposing, and the History Is Vividly Alive in England's Venerable Oxford, the World's Most Famous College Town" syndicated by and published in the *Los Angeles Times.* How does the story give readers a sense of "being there"? What information did you learn about Oxford's history and tradition? What practical information did Reynolds include to help tourists?

5. Read John Camp's story, "Life on the Land."
   a. Why does Camp begin his story with such an extended quotation? How do the first six paragraphs set the direction for and draw readers into the story?
   b. What is the effect on readers of David Benson's statement, "It's even better when you're working with horses, because everything moves fairly slowly and you don't have the tractor engine, so it's quiet. There's a rhythm to it. It's almost . . . blissful, is that the word?" and Bertha's statement, "But I remember how the lights came on, and we sat with all the lights all evening, sat with the lights on us. . . . The electricity is the best thing for farm wives. . . . Hot water is the most wonderful thing!" How does what David and Bertha value reflect on the values of your lifestyle: do you value the same things or not? What attitude do you have toward David and Bertha because of the things they value?
   c. David says, "No kid should grow up without chickens; chickens have got to be good for you." What does he mean? How do chickens affect the way a child grows up?
   d. Underlying the happy surface of the picture of the Benson family are two threats: the threat of killing the land and the threat of the lifestyle being destroyed. How does Camp make readers care whether the Benson lifestyle is destroyed or not?

THE ARCHITECTURE IS IMPOSING, AND THE HISTORY IS VIVIDLY ALIVE IN ENGLAND'S VENERABLE OXFORD, THE WORLD'S MOST FAMOUS COLLEGE TOWN

By Christopher Reynolds

Los Angeles Times, *February 14, 1993*

OXFORD, England

This is a skyline to keep you humble.

It rises from a smooth plain, an hour outside of London, and bristles with more than 600 buildings protected as national treasures. At sunset, they hurl epic shadows down on the undergraduates along High Street.

By day, while church bells toll, ancient gates scrape and beloved fountains burble, they endure the rusty leanings of 30,000 bicycles. And when exams draw near at the 36 colleges that make up Oxford University and dominate the city, I can imagine these old walls summoning genuine horror.

Fall behind in metaphysical poetry, and the 14th-century spire of St. Mary the Virgin will pierce your dreams. Overlook a subtlety of molecular biology and the bells of the 17th-century Tom Tower at Christ Church College will toll for thee.

Nearly a millennium of architectural ideas is wedged into the single square mile that holds the city's core and most of the university. It's a wonder anyone graduates.

But if Oxford were just a matter of architecture, the place wouldn't draw, daunt and seduce strangers the way it does. Oxford has tenure. Behind it stretches the longest lineage of college scholarship in the English-speaking world, spanning more than eight centuries. Row in its waters and you risk drowning by tradition and anecdote.

Here studied W. H. Auden, Benazir Bhutto, Sir Richard Burton, John Donne, T. S. Eliot, Indira Gandhi, J. Paul Getty, Graham Greene, Joseph Heller, T. E. Lawrence, John Locke, Dudley Moore, Rupert Murdoch, Sir Walter Raleigh, John Ruskin, Leopold Stokowski, Margaret Thatcher, J. R. R. Tolkien, John Wesley, Oscar Wilde and Christopher Wren—among others, including President Clinton.

Here an institution founded in 1379 still carries the nickname of New College.

Here, from the observation level of St. Mary the Virgin, a visitor may spy half a dozen langorous students in a cloistered quadrangle, not tanning, not reading, not guitar-playing, but adjusting wickets for croquet.

Here on Walton Street, the Oxford University Press publishes volumes on such small subjects as "Identity, Consciousness and Value" and "Human Morality" (two from the '92 catalog), while a few blocks away the compilers of the 20-volume Oxford English Dictionary labor to update the world's primary reference work on this language.

Where Clinton Studied

Here at University College, Percy Bysshe Shelley was ejected after writing a paper on "The Necessity of Atheism," but Bill Clinton lasted the full two years of his Rhodes Scholarship. (Moral for undergraduates: Trust in God, and don't inhale.)

Here time is told by the clock atop the 14th-century stones of Carfax Tower.

Under noon sun, watch the privileged schoolboys scamper alongside the Cherwell in their whites, pausing to chirp "cheers" as they pass, then arranging themselves on the green for cricket.

Sit above the brass section and listen as the City of Oxford Orchestra sends Schubert resounding through the 323-year-old Sheldonian Theater on High Street. The music is good, and the setting is better—a domed, airy, acoustically intimate room that was the first building designed by famed architect Christopher Wren.

Walking on High Street near the university's Examination Schools, encounter an ashen-faced young man as he steps from a 19th-century doorway. His mandatory formal wear is bunched and rumpled from neck to knees. He is a law student, and he has just performed dreadfully on the final paper of the term.

But he is an Englishman at Oxford. He neither complains nor explains, but fires up a cigarette and shuffles away, abject, unkempt, and yet somehow noble.

Offering such spectacles, Oxford does not go unappreciated. The city's annual visitors now outnumber residents 1.5 million to 100,000. The storefronts include shops like the Oxford Story, which does nothing but trade on the place's past. Dueling double-decker bus tour companies do battle in streets where once horse-drawn carriages commanded right of way. (Both charge five pounds, but the green-and-cream Guide Friday bus uses live guides instead of tapes.)

Browsing, Appraising

Some visitors browse Blackwell's, an enterprise that began in 1879 as a 12-foot-square room on Broad Street and has grown to claim nine sites around town and a reputation as England's premier bookseller.

Others appraise the considerable collection of art and artifacts in the Ashmolean Museum, England's first public museum, founded in 1683. (Also on exhibit last summer was a fine example of circuitous English logic: "Two pounds from each visitor would keep the museum open and free," suggested a sign at the entrance. Open, perhaps, but not free.)

Still other visitors line up for views from on high, seeking out St. Mary the Virgin, Carfax Tower, or the Church of St. Michael-at-the-North-Gate.

In July and August, when the place is empty of undergraduates, the tourist population peaks, and hundreds of Americans and others take up residence in college facilities to study, with widely varying intensities, in myriad summertime programs.

But in other months, the visitor shares hallowed halls with the robed dons, bowler-hatted campus police and the 14,000 students who link Oxford past to Oxford present. And while the buildings do cast a spell, it's the students who keep the place alive.

Several years ago, on my first visit to Oxford, I was assigned to interview an American graduate student there. Her name was Bonnie St. John, and she was an international relations graduate of Harvard. She was also a champion skier despite the amputation of one leg above the knee, and an African-American. Since she was a Rhodes Scholar, her fees were paid from the fortune left by the most famous of Africa's white colonizers, Oxford alumnus Cecil Rhodes.

"Sometimes," she said, "I stop in awe and just think, 'Where am I?' I live in this town with these storybook buildings, and I walk down the streets with the wind howling and see gargoyles and stained glass. It's incredible."

Then she showed me the ancient oath she swore to get reading rights at the 390-year-old Bodleian Library, led me past the dangling dead rabbits of the covered market downtown, and slipped an alcoholic gratuity to the porter at the gate of her 440-year-old campus. Nobody's 12th century plans for this university had included her, but here she was, making the place her own.

Last Look at Oxford

Sooner or later, you will have to leave.

Before you do, take another swing through town. Walk High Street on Friday evening and watch the Oddbins wine shop sprout a queue of bottle-bearing customers in college ties. While they wait, tardy undergraduates flee past on their bicycles, formal robes inflated by the breeze. When the pubs close at 11, the students will appear again, shirts limp, gowns askew.

Or stake out the Sheldonian Theater. If the month is June, a graduation ceremony may spill graduates and beaming families into the stone-walled courtyard. A young woman will adjust her mortarboard while a young man throws an arm around his father for a photograph.

Or wander south along the Cherwell. On the water, two young women balance their flat-bottomed punt, slug down Budweisers, draw slowly on their cigarettes, and ease past the cricket players. In the meadow beyond Merton College, two shirtless young men in boxing gloves spar lightly.

If this scene were on a screen, the "Chariots of Fire" theme would now swell. Instead, the sounds are bird-calls, distant shouts, slowly moving water, and the faint echoes from that humbling skyline.

. . .

LIFE ON THE LAND
An American Farm Family
By John Camp
St. Paul Pioneer Press & Dispatch, *May 12, 1985*

Part I—May 12, 1985

David Benson sits on the seat of the manure wagon, behind the twin black draft horses, reins in his hands, and he says this:

"Machinery can be intoxicating. You sit there on top of a huge tractor, rolling across those fields, and you feel like God. It's an amazing feeling, and a real one, and I think some people get so they don't feel complete without it.

"That's one of the reasons they keep buying bigger and bigger tractors, these enormous four-wheel-drives, tearing up and down the fields. Tearing up and down. They are incredibly expensive machines; they'll run you $16 an hour in fuel alone, and you can do in one day what used to take you three or four—but then the question arises, are you doing anything useful on the three or four you saved? You buy this gigantic machine with its incredible capability and all of a sudden, you're done.

"And you start thinking, 'My God, if I bought another 600 acres I could do that, too.' So you buy it, and then you find if you only had a bigger machine, you could buy even more. At the end of it, you're doing 2,000 acres on this fantastic Star Wars machinery and you're so far in debt that if anything goes wrong—and I mean if they stop eating soy sauce in Ireland—you lose the whole works, including the place you started with.

"And it's not the same as losing in the city. These people are going around asking, Jeez, what did I do wrong? They said this was the American way. You try to get bigger and take a few risks, but nobody ever told me that if I lose they were going to take away everything, my whole way of life and my children's way of life and our whole culture and the whole neighborhood and just stomp us right into the ground.

"My God, you know, people are bulldozing farmsteads so they can plant corn where the houses used to be, because there's nobody to live in these houses any more. That's happening."

David Benson. He has horses, but he's not a back-to-the-land dabbler, not an amateur, not a dilettante—he has a couple of tractors, and a barn full of machinery. But he finds a use for horses. He likes them.

And unlike a lot of farmers in Minnesota, he's making it. Making it small, but he's making it.

Go down to Worthington. Get off Interstate 90, off the state highway, off the blacktopped county road and finally go down the gravel track and into the farm land, listening to the power lines sing and the cottonwoods moan in the everlasting wind, watching a red-orange pickup a mile away as it crawls like a ladybug along a parallel road between freshly plowed fields, leaving behind a rising plume of gravel dust, crawling toward the silos and the rooftops that mark the Iowa line. . . .

A Mailbox on a Post

The landscape is not quite flat—it's a landscape of tilted planes, fields tipped this way or that, almost all showing the fertile loam of recent plowing. The black fields dominate the countryside, interrupted here and there by woodlots, by pasturage where lambs play in the fading sunlight, by red-brick or purple-steel silos, Grant Wood barns and Sears-Roebuck sheds, and by the farmhouses.

There's a turn-of-the-century farmhouse here. Gray with white trim, it could be any one of a thousand prairie homes. There's a single rural-route mailbox on a post across the road from the end of the driveway. It says Benson on the side, but the paint has been scoured by the wind and the name is almost illegible.

There is a tire swing hung from a cottonwood with a yellow rope, and a kid named Anton kicking a black-and-white soccer ball in the driveway.

The walk to the porch is guarded by lilacs and lilies of the valley and a patch of violets. A tortoiseshell cat named Yin lounges on the porch, watchfully making way for visitors; a familial tiger-striper named Yang watches from the sideyard. Just before the porch is a strip of iron set in a concrete block: a boot scraper, and well-used.

The door swings open and Sally-Anne Benson is there, navy sweatshirt, blue jeans, tan work boots.

"Hi," she says, "Come in. David is still in the field, with the oats."

From behind her come the kitchen smells of fresh bread and noodles and sauce, and blond Heather is turning to go up the stairs to her bedroom.

"We're going over to Grandpa's to do the chores," Sally-Anne says to Heather.

These are some of the Bensons. The Bensons in this house are David, 38, and Sally-Anne, 35, husband and wife, and their children, Heather, 11, and Anton, 8. Sally-Anne is small with thin wrists and curly brown hair, blue-gray eyes, a quick smile and a tendency to bubble when she's had a few glasses of white wine. She answers to the nickname "Sag" or "Sag-Oh" which is an acronym of her maiden name, Sally-Anne Greeley. David has a red walrus

mustache and the beginnings of crows-feet at the corners of his eyes, smile lines at his mouth and a story-teller's laugh. The children are blond: blonder than seems real, or even possible.

Rhythm of Work Blissful

The Bensons in the white house up the road and around the corner on the blacktop are Gus and Bertha Benson, David's parents.

Gus, 82, is mostly retired, though on this day he's been fanning oats—cleaning the oats to be used as seed—for the planting. He has white hair combed straight back, a white stubble on his pink face, and powerful, heavy hands. Bertha is 75. Her hair is a steel brown-gray, she wears plastic-rimmed glasses, and after 56 years of farming, she still can't watch when chickens are butchered. She can pick them, the hens who make the fatal mistake of not laying, but she can't watch them topped with a corn knife.

David and Sally-Anne do the bulk of the heavy farm work now. Gus particularly likes to work with the beef cattle and Bertha keeps house and recently has taken up weaving and rug-making, and cans and freezes produce during the summer; last year she got in 100 quarts of apple sauce. Heather and Anton have their chores. Together they live on 160 acres of the best land God ever made.

And they work it hard. They have the crops, the cattle, a growing flock of sheep, chickens, geese, and a boxful of tiny turkeys on the back porch.

The day started with David getting up at 6:15 a.m. and apologizing for it. "Boy, I got up earlier, but I just couldn't. . . Oh, boy, I just laid back down and the next thing I knew it was after 6. . . ."

He's planting oats, and has been hard at it for the previous two days, sitting up on top of the John Deere, first disking, then chisel-plowing a small patch of compacted ground, then hooking up a grain drill to seed the oats.

"You sit up there, going back and forth, when you're disking, and your mind goes on automatic pilot," he said. "You can think of anything, and sooner or later, you do. It's a liberating experience, really. You put in maybe 400 hours a year on a tractor, and you spend a good part of it just . . . thinking. It's even better when you're working with the horses, because everything moves fairly slowly and you don't have the tractor engine, so it's quiet. There's a rhythm to it. It's almost . . . blissful, is that the word?''

The Land Comes First

At noon, Sally-Anne brings out lunch, cheese sandwiches and fresh milk from Bluma, the milk cow, and homemade bread and a chunk of cake. David climbs stiffly off the tractor and drops down into the roadside ditch and leans back into last year's tall brown grass, out of the eternal prairie wind.

"It's just going so well, going so well," he says, looking across the barbed-wire fence toward the field. "Just need to get it in. This is beautiful weather, but I wish the wind would lay off."

He looks up at the faultless blue sky. "And we could use some rain, use some rain. Sure. We sure could."

He lies in the ditch eating, his face covered with dust, alternately eating and explaining: "We'll grow beans and corn and oats and alfalfa for hay, and the alfalfa puts nitrogen back in the soil; of course, we won't grow all those at once, we'll rotate through. You've got to be strict about it, you can't decide to knock off a little extra here and there, or you'll kill it, the land."

He's almost apologetic about the chisel plow. "Normally we don't need it, but last year we brought in some heavy earth-moving equipment to build that terrace down there, and it compacted the ground enough that disking won't do it."

He needed the terrace to correct a drainage problem. "If you don't build water structures you're going to wash ditches, and that's another way you can kill it," he says.

Kill the land. The nightmare. The land must be cared for, the Bensons say. But the land is in trouble right now. Neither David nor Sally-Anne

Benson would be considered solemn, but David will sit in his dining room chair after supper, leaning his elbows on the strawberry-patch oilcloth that covers the table, and talk like this:

"The strength of the Midwest culture was that it had a people who were developing an interest in the land, and in developing a community that had some continuity to it. Without that, we have an ethereal culture that just isn't satisfying to most people, and can't be—a people who don't really know what they want.

"We are living in the middle of one of the largest areas of fertile land on the planet. Normally you'd think that people would go to a place like that, would want to live there to form a good rooted culture, where you could form your own ties to the land and to the neighborhood and even to those people you just see driving by, but whose whole lives you know, and they know yours. . . .''

The connections between the people, the land, the crops, the food, the neighborhood, the community—they're impossible to put a hand on, but they are real. Much of its connecting web can be explained in stories of times past, of incidents that somehow hallow a particular patch of ground or even make it a place of humor, or sadness, or dread.

Gus and Bertha sit at their dining room table, at what their children call the home place, and remember it.

"Spring is always the moving time for farmers," says Bertha. "We bought this place in 1938, and we moved here in the spring of 1939, from Stanton, Nebraska. That's where Gus was born, in Stanton, and two of our children—the other two were born here. Gladys and Shirley and Marilyn and David, 17 years apart, the four of them, and we enjoyed every one . . .

"When we moved here, we couldn't tell what color the house was, it was so bad, but we were more concerned about the land. When we bought it the land cost $95 an acre, and we were trembling and afraid, because we thought if we did something wrong, we could lose it and lose everything we saved."

They had been married in Nebraska in 1929, and spent the next 10 years as renters, building up a working capital of $3,000. It all went into the new place in Minnesota.

"We moved up here because it was dry in Nebraska for so many years, you couldn't farm. We came up here on a trip and we thought it was so beautiful in Minnesota, so beautiful," Bertha says.

Unfreezing the Car

And it was cold, and windy, and the life was rough. They laugh about it now, Bertha and Gus, but at the time . . .

"When Marilyn was born, it was so cold I had to start a fire with corn cobs in a pan, and put it under the engine to get it warmed up so we could start it," Gus recalls. "She was ready for the hospital, four in the morning, and I can still remember the cold. . . ."

"And remember, when we got electricity . . ."

"Oh, yes, when we got the electricity," says Bertha. "That was in when, 1948?"

"1948, that's when it was."

"I remember," says Bertha, a glow in her face. "We got an electrician from Dundee to do the house, all the way from Dundee because all the other electricians were busy. The whole neighborhood went on at the same time. We were one of the last, because we were so close to the Iowa border, we were like in a corner. But I remember how the lights came on, and we sat with all the lights all evening, sat with the lights on us . . .

"The electricity is the best thing for farm wives. Before that, we took soft water from the cistern, and regular hard water from the well, in a pail. I think I could go back to that way of living, except that I want my hot water. Hot water is the most wonderful thing!"

"Oh, we had a wedding here, too," says Gus.

"One of Shirley's girls, Christina," says Bertha. "They had their wedding in the yard, and dancing in the corn crib, and a hay ride in the afternoon."

"They decorated the corn crib," says Gus. "They cleaned it out and decorated it and danced in there."

"We never thought David would come back," Gus says suddenly. "We thought we'd be the last. We thought he would be an engineer. He was living in San Francisco, and one day he called and said, 'Don't sell the farm, we might come back.' "

David and Sally-Anne have their memories, too—some of their courtship, in Sally-Anne's hometown of Lexington, Mass., and some of San Francisco, where they spent some time when they were in their early 20s, and many, now, of their 14 years on the farm.

Memories Grow Fast

Of walking the beans. Of haying time. Of rebuilding the aging machinery. Of David on the John Deere, dragging plow, Sally-Anne on the David Brown 990 with the disk, the wind whistling across them both, the sun beating down . . .

Sally-Anne, laughing: "You remember at a party putting those chickens asleep?"

David: "Nothing like it. Hypnotizing chickens. We had one asleep for three or four minutes I think, just stretched stone cold out on the ground . . . A rooster.

"By the way," he says to Sally-Anne, "do you see we've got another transvestite rooster coming along?"

"Oh, I saw that, he's getting big, too, he's almost as aggressive as the top one . . ."

"Well, not that bad . . ."

David explains: "We decided to get rid of all our roosters. We ate them, every one, or thought so. Then all of a sudden, here comes this chicken out of the flock. I mean, we thought all along he was a hen, but he starts getting bigger and growing some wattles and pretty soon he's crowing all over the place. He was hiding in there, pretending to be a hen. Now we've got another one coming out of the closet. He's getting bigger . . .

"I remember when we were kids, we used to chase the chickens down—chickens have got pretty good speed over the short haul, and have pretty good moves. Anyway, you'd get a rock and just chuck it at them, and every once in a while you'd lay it right alongside their heads, just throwing it at them on the run.

"And then you'd be hiding out behind the corncrib, because it'd drop over and you were sure it was dead. But it never was. It'd always get up and walk around like nothing happened. I'm not sure you can hurt chickens, to tell you the truth.

"No kid should grow up without chickens; chickens have got to be good for you . . ."

Some Memories Difficult

Some of the memories are funny, like the chickens. Some are not.

Sally-Anne: "One time we had this horse, named Belle, and that year there was an unusual mold that grew on the corn stalks, and Belle ate some of it. It turns out that it destroys your muscle control. She couldn't control the way she moved . . . like polio, in people. Anyway, we had the vet out, and he said that's what it was.

"There was nothing we could do, and David had to shoot her.

"David got the gun and brought her out of the barn, and kept backing away from her so he could get a clean shot and she kept going to him, kept trying to walk up to him, because she trusted him and she didn't know what was wrong with her. . . ."

Sally-Anne shivers as she tells the story. "I didn't want to watch. It was just awful, but finally he got back and shot her. The vet said there was nothing wrong with the meat, so David and a friend skinned her and butchered her . . . it was still pretty bad, but then, after a while, another friend came over and said, 'Ah, Taco Bell, huh?' And that made it better, somehow. God, it was awful."

A farm of 160 acres can't really support six people, and the Bensons know it. They talk about buying more land, of going into debt, the very experience they saw drag down so many of their neighbors.

In the meantime, Sally-Anne teaches at the Worthington Montessori School in the mornings, and David does casual work as a mechanic. Sally-Anne brags that he can fix most things, especially Volvos. "If you live anyplace around Worthington and own a Volvo, you probably know him," she said.

The life suits them. More land would be nice, but the spectre of debt is overpowering. The Bensons, for now, have no debt—they don't even need spring operating loans. Between grain sales, auto mechanics and Sally-Anne's job, they are self-supporting and self-financed. They're proud of their ability to survive, but there is no sense of victory when they see a neighbor fail.

Instead, there is a sense of loss. It's their community evaporating, the Bensons' along with everyone else's.

"I don't know," says David. "Maybe what we need is some kind of creative financing like they do for home mortgages. Some kind of rent-share program where younger farmers can have a chance, can move into these homesteads and take them over and work them like they should be.

"And if they fail anyway? Well, at least we tried. If we don't try, we're going to kill it, the land."

Strong stuff, deeply felt; but it's hard to stay solemn for too long at the Bensons.

"When are you coming back?" they ask the visitors at the table. "Three or four weeks? Gee, that'd be just about right time for haying."

Sure would like to see you for haying, yes indeed, they say. Bring a hat. Bring gloves. Bring beer. Love to have you.

14

Human Interest Stories
Defining the Human Condition

Human interest stories help us define our humanity. They are stories about the human condition and how we human beings deal with life. As feature stories, they are identifiable, not by a particular writing style or format (they can be any of several kinds of stories), but by their subject matter and the effect they have, or are intended to have, on readers. Human interest stories touch readers' emotions, elicit empathetic feelings for other human beings. If a human interest story leaves readers unmoved, it has been unsuccessful.

Of course, in one sense, all feature stories are human interest stories. When writing features, we constantly strive to "put people in the story" or "humanize" the information. But human interest stories emphasize the human element above all others. Their primary purpose is to create a feeling of human connection, of shared humanity between readers and subjects of stories.

The shared humanity of today's human interest stories, however, doesn't have to leave readers weeping and wailing, as their "sob story" ancestors of earlier times did. The best of today's human interest stories are restrained. They present life realistically, revealing human beings as complex, paradoxical creatures. Readers respond emotionally to stories, but also thoughtfully, with comprehension and understanding. Reader reactions may be said to be characterized more by "compassion" than "passion."

BUT FOR THE GRACE OF GOD

Much of readers' emotional response to human interest stories comes from the readers' ability to identify with the subjects of these stories, to imagine themselves in similar situations. It's important, therefore, that when you write a human interest feature, you emphasize the shared human bond between readers and subjects. Such a shared human bond, however, does not require that readers and subjects have identical lives or come from identical social, economic, or educational backgrounds. It *does* mean that stories are written so that readers can envision themselves in the situations the subjects of stories experience. When readers do this, human interest features offer at least two rewards for reading.

First, human interest stories provide a yardstick for human behavior, a yardstick which readers can use to measure themselves. Through the story they witness the actions of another human being and imagine how they themselves would have behaved in a similar situation. Would they have been as brave? As clever? As faithful? Or as weak? As vacillating? As gullible? Readers see their own images mirrored brightly or dimly in the reflection of another person's behavior.

Second, human interest stories provide readers with the opportunity to compare their lives to the life of the person in the story. Sometimes that person's life makes readers' lives seem dull and ordinary, but more often, it makes their lives seem comfortable and contented. Problems that had previously seemed enormous are reduced to mere annoyances when compared to the real disasters endured by the subjects of human interest stories.

Thus readers experience a kind of backwards pleasure; they are not necessarily pleased that another person has problems, but they *are* pleased that they themselves do not—or at least are pleased that the problems they *do* have are not serious. Sympathy for someone else is mixed with relief for themselves. Readers are able to say "There but for the grace of God go I" and be thankful for their blessings.

In addition, the best human interest stories go beyond even these two rewards for reading and offer readers something more, something difficult to define precisely but perhaps best described as a sense of awe about life. Through these stories, readers touch extraordinary people and situations, and are thus stimulated to ponder life's complexity and contradictions, to develop a philosophy concerning what it means to be alive.

And since the nature of human life doesn't change radically through the turning of days and years, human interest stories are among the most timeless of all feature articles. They can be as meaningful twenty years after they are written as they are the day they are published.

EXTRAORDINARY EVENTS/ORDINARY PEOPLE

The simplest and briefest human interest stories concern extraordinary events that happen to ordinary people. Sometimes these events are everyday disasters, sometimes a string of lucky or unlucky coincidences unusual enough to be noticed. Often such human interest stories involve chance: a chance encounter, a chance discovery, a chance piece of good fortune. Extraordinary-events stories are essentially news features that tell about average, un-newsworthy people who become newsworthy because they have experienced something the rest of us can relate to as human beings.

People who have babies in the first minutes of the New Year, people who have quintuplets, people who marry their high school sweethearts 50 years after graduation, people who run into long-lost relatives in the airport of a far-away country—people in all these situations and many situations like them are the subjects of stories describing extraordinary events happening to ordinary people.

The leads of two Associated Press human interest features illustrate the unusual experiences that such stories typically report:

> MAYWOOD, Ill.—A woman's search for the father she had never seen ended when she was sent to draw blood from a patient and discovered he was the man she had been looking for.
>
> ANNISTON, Ala.—Two women have agreed to divide the $10 million estate of a husband they unknowingly shared for nearly three decades, according to court documents.

MAN'S BEST FRIEND AND OTHER ANIMAL STORIES

Feature articles about animals have traditionally been defined as human interest stories, and that categorization may seem puzzling: the obvious question to ask is how can stories about animals help us define our humanity? But, upon re-flection, we can see that categorizing animal stories as human interest stories makes sense for several reasons. First, human beings live intimately with household animals; thus, what concerns their well-being concerns humans too. Second, human beings identify strongly with their pets and tend to personalize animal behavior. Third, people often ascribe different modes of human behavior to breeds of animals, even when that behavior is not, in fact, characteristic of the particular breed. (A teddy bear is a comforting, cuddly object; a real bear is not.) Finally, as ecological studies make clear, human beings and animals are interdependent; thus, understanding animal behavior helps people understand what constitutes their own well-being.

Man's best friend stories are popular human interest animal stories; they give heart-warming accounts of how animals, knowingly or unknowingly, be-friend or aid human beings. An Associated Press story, for example, told of an eleven-year-old boy who came out of a coma when his puppy pounced on him.

The story situation can also be reversed; for example, another Associated Press story, written by Nita Lelyveld, describes the way that human beings aid animals. In this feature, people are a "cat's best friend":

Down a winding dirt road on the edge of this quiet, rural town, 340 cats of all shapes and sizes live out their nine lives in quiet indulgence, carefully tended by a staff of eight and a local veterinarian who checks in daily.

In a row of four wooden cabins, calicos, Siamese cats and tabbies stretch out together on pillows, couches and quilts arranged for their napping comfort. Large trays of wet and dry food are within easy reach and small cat doors open onto wide, wooden sun decks.

Started in 1982 by Pegeen Fitzgerald, a New York radio personality and animal lover, the Last Post provides lifelong care primarily for cats whose owners die or have to check into a nursing home.

A newspaper reader sent a copy of the following feature story, syndicated by the *Duluth News-Tribune,* to columnist Ann Landers. The story provides plenty of evidence that animals do, indeed, create human interest.

Capt. Lenny Rouse says nothing he's done in his 25 years of firefighting compares with the attention he's received since performing mouth-to-mouth resuscitation on a kitten he rescued from a fire.

Rouse says the Superior, Wis., Fire Department has received scores of letters from people across the country praising their efforts in saving six kittens during a mobile home fire on Sept. 11.

"It's been overwhelming," Rouse said. "I never in my wildest dreams imagined that this small act would be so well-received. The common theme of what (the letter writers) said they saw is compassion. They felt as though firefighters made the effort to save a kitten because they consider pets as a part of the family and that's what made them feel so good." . . .

This was the first time he had attempted CPR on an animal, Rouse said. "I just scaled down the CPR, being it was a small creature," he said. "The technique was basically the same as for humans and the results were great. It didn't have any signs of life; it was jump limp. I stimulated the kitten by tipping it over and going with my fingernails on its spine to try to get some reaction. It started to take some breath and it actually came back to life. That was the real nice thing about it."

Rouse, captain of Engine Company No. 2, has been a little uncomfortable with the attention he's received regarding the kittens. He said the firefighters' real concern was for the six-member family that was able to escape without serious injury from the burning home. After it was determined that the family was safe, firefighters turned their attention to the kittens, Rouse said.

"A lot of people saw that picture and a lot of cards and letters were sent in my name, but firefighting or rescue is not a one-man show," Rouse said. "It's the best example of teamwork—that's what firefighting is all about."

A different kind of animal story is exemplified by an article about pandas, written by Don Lessem and published in the *Boston Globe Magazine,* then reprinted in *Reader's Digest.* This explanatory feature capitalizes on the ecological interest readers have in wild animals in general, and their concern for preserving the animal species of the panda in particular. The story describes the panda's natural habitat and its instinctual behavior. As a human interest story, it stimulates reader desire to preserve the panda's environment by describing panda behavior in a way that makes it seem similar to human behavior—or at least to certain kinds of teenage courting behavior:

> When a panda does encounter another of its kind, the animals circle each other warily. Unless, that is, it's springtime and one of them is male and the other a female ready to mate. At about age five, the female, smaller than the male, will moan, signaling she is receptive. Her call is often answered by as many as three or four males. At such times, reclusive pandas undergo a personality transformation. They moo, whine or roar. Males circle one another and engage in pushing, swatting, biting and lunging contests.

STUDIES IN HUMAN NATURE

Of course, all human interest stories are studies of human nature, but some human interest stories are particularly serious studies of human nature because they offer an unusual perspective or a unique set of circumstances with which to consider the essential character of human beings.

Articles about people living in past times can be studies in human nature if they help readers examine and consider the character of human beings in another age—and perhaps recognize a kinship with these people from another time.

For example, one *Washington Post* story reported on the discovery a history professor, Peter R. Henriques, made while searching through records held in the Library of Congress; he found transcripts of an "18th-century trial alleging the attempted debauchery of George Washington's sister-in-law by a prominent Fairfax County cleric who later became the president's physician." The story's writer, Ken Ringle, was wise enough to let most of the story of the trial tell itself. The court records described either an adolescent who was preyed upon by a "lascivious parson" or "an 18th-century Lolita tempting an upright clergyman to sin"—depending on whose account you believed.

Ringle concludes this story with factual material and a quote which remind readers how similar human nature can be, though people live in different times and under different circumstances:

> But perhaps the true measure of the suffering endured in those days was felt by Ann Fairfax Washington. Five times between her 15th and 24th birthdays she gave birth only to watch her child die a short time later. None lived past the age of 4.

Only months after her husband's death she married George Lee—a distant antecedent of Robert E. Lee, and with him had three sons. She never, however, lived to see them grown. She was dead by the age of 33.

"You know, a feminist historian could have a field day with this story," Henriques said. "You can use it to prove anything you want about the 'victimization of woman,' 'the history of sexual harassment' or whatever."

But for him, he said, the true fascination of the story is the flesh and blood it puts on those dusty names from two centuries ago, and how much closer it brings their lives. "These were obviously very strong and vital people," he said, fingering the photocopy of a fading letter. "They were all caught up in very human situations of the kind we see very much today. And most of them died so very, very young."

A quite different study of human nature was written by Libby Averyt of the *Corpus Christi Caller-Times*. Her story, which won the Edward William Scripps First Amendment Award, profiles a murderer who seems to be irredeemably antisocial. Here's how Averyt presents the enigma of the man's character:

His demeanor is quiet and polite. He avoids first names, opting to use more formal last names with courtesy titles. In high school, he was a representative to Boys State, an officer in Boys Nation, and excelled in debate.

Jemarr C. Arnold is a self-proclaimed murderer, rapist and robber.

He is accused of killing Christina Marie Sanchez, a 21-year-old jewelry store clerk, during a 1983 robbery of Greenberg Jewelers on Leopard Street. Arnold is awaiting a capital-murder trial, scheduled to begin Nov. 26.

In his cordial voice, Arnold tells stories in bloody detail, with no detectable change in tone. He shot a woman in the head. He nearly cut off a man's penis with a razor. He says he's raped about 20 women. His voice maintains an eerie calm as he recalls these incidents.

He says he feels no remorse.

He says his strongest emotion is anger. Anger to Jemarr C. Arnold is violent rage.

In recent interviews with the Caller-Times, Arnold said an execution is the only thing that will stop him.

"I have no desire to change. I'm never going to change," said Arnold, 32. "I chose to be the kind of person that I am. It was my choice, and it's going to be my choice until I die.

"I'll only get worse."

While readers probably would not have much sympathy for this particular human being, they would very likely have considerable interest in him. In general, readers are fascinated by really bad people, perhaps because they act out forbidden behaviors or exhibit scary behavior typical of nightmares and horror movies. Then too, stories about antisocial people may help readers consider whether social, political, legal, or economic systems have gone awry, creating monsters rather than redeeming human beings. But most likely the readers' human interest in people like Jemarr C. Arnold comes from their concern about whether *all* human beings, under certain circumstances, are capable of doing what he has done. And such a belief ultimately leads to a personal question about human nature: "Am *I* capable of doing what he did?"

HUMAN BEINGS DEALING WITH ADVERSITY

By far the majority of human interest stories show human beings struggling with adversity. Adversity can take different forms, and human beings react to adversity in different ways, so human interest adversity stories are not necessarily similar even when they are about the *same* kinds of adversity. Most adversity stories are interview stories, but some can emphasize narrative, description, or explanation. The mood and tone of adversity stories can also be quite different, even in stories that describe similar situations. One human interest story about a child dying of leukemia can be grim and heart-rending; another can be positive, focusing on the love of the family surrounding the child or the efforts of friends to support the family in crisis.

But all human interest stories about adversity try to elicit a sense of compassion from readers, a sense of sympathy for the struggles of their fellow human beings, and at times, a sense of pleasure when those struggles result in success.

An adversity story may describe an unexpected reversal of fortune, telling about a person on top of the world one day and on the bottom the next; or conversely, it can be about a person who is on the bottom and gets to be on top.

It hardly needs saying that reversal-of-fortune stories do not necessarily define "fortune" only as financial wealth. There are also emotional good and bad fortunes, and reversal of those fortunes as well.

An Associated Press story by John Nadel about a soldier fighting in the Persian Gulf War, for example, tells about a positive reversal of fortune:

> LOS ANGELES—In less than two months, Army Spec. Nick Lozenich has gone from the dust of Operation Desert Storm to his own personal "Field of Dreams."
>
> Ken Minyard, co-host of a morning talk show on KABC radio, got the ball rolling after seeing Lozenich featured on ABC News from Saudi Arabia on Feb. 16.
>
> "They showed this kid who stood out in the sand for two hours every afternoon with a pickax handle, throwing up rocks, and hitting them," Minyard recalled Friday. "You could tell he had a nice swing. He indicated that his dream after the war was to come back home and be a big-league ball-player.
>
> "I thought anybody who had that kind of dedication was entitled to a look."
>
> And that's what Lozenich will get today when Los Angeles Dodgers manager Tom Lasorda pitches batting practice to him before a night game between the Dodgers and San Diego Padres at Dodger Stadium.

Many adversity stories focus entirely on ill fortune, that is, on human beings who are down on their luck, constantly enduring adversity with little hope of the situation being changed. Even today these stories are likely to be called "sob stories" because of the sad feeling they create in those who read them. Down-on-luck features are about people experiencing eviction, homelessness, or unemployment; about people whose homes have been burned down or their money stolen; about people who have been beaten or abused, or who have felt the pain of loneliness, poverty, or old age. Sometimes the stories emphasize the role that various social agencies play in alleviating the subject's distress—or in contributing to it. Another, secondary message in such articles may be that readers should vote to change government policy, send contributions, investigate wrong-doing, or do something—whatever it takes—to end such suffering.

Another kind of adversity story focuses on the situation of a human being learning a tough lesson from life. Sometimes this lesson-in-life story studies the character of the person experiencing misfortune. Did the person make choices that the rest of us can avoid? Can we learn the same painful lesson without experiencing the pain?

An anonymous first-person narrative in *Mademoiselle* magazine, for example, details the mistakes the writer made in having intercourse with someone without using condoms or having any "deep meaningful discussion about our sexual and intravenous-drug histories." Her final words express the writer's regrets, but they also express an indirect admonition to readers to learn from her mistake:

> If I had to do it all over again—and if only I could—there are a lot of things that I would do differently. I would practice safe sex from the beginning and have my boyfriend go with me to get tested before I stopped using condoms (or better yet, before we had sex). I would also make sure I knew everything possible about that person's past. Sometimes, when I lie in bed at night, I kick myself for being so stupid. For thinking that it could never happen to me. For having to find out how wrong I was.

Dave Finkel of the *St. Petersburg Times* was a finalist in the 1988 American Society of Newspaper Editors competition with a story describing a controversial drug addiction treatment program. His explanatory piece is dominated by the human interest story of one young man who is facing up to the lesson he has to learn. Finkel begins the article by describing the youth and his parents coming to a decision about the treatment:

> Sitting tensely in a chair, he is a young man not to be messed with, a coil of barbed wire. His mouth is in a sneer. His eyes could burn holes. His name is Paul Kulek, and he's doing his best to look as if he's in control.
>
> But in truth, he is just a 15-year-old boy with skinny arms, and when the clipboard with the admission form is handed to him, he begins to cry.
>
> He is on the verge of entering a drug rehabilitation program called Straight, an intensive, high-pressure program that could take a year of his young life to complete. His parents think he has been smoking too much marijuana, and they want him in.
>
> But he is scared.
>
> He looks at the clipboard, and the words blur. He looks up, and there are his parents. His mother is crying. His father is biting his lip.

Already, they have heard their son admit he not only has smoked pot, but he also has swallowed speed, inhaled gasoline, and toyed with the idea of shooting himself.

"You qualify for our program," Steve Knowles, an official with Straight, had said after the last of those revelations.

Other human interest adversity stories concern situations in which human beings are experiencing a loss—most frequently the loss of their own life or the life of a loved one, although sometimes the loss is of physical well-being or good health.

So-called dying child stories are published so frequently that we even have that cynical name for them, but no matter how often they are published, the pathos of a child dying is appealing as a human interest feature. Readers identify with the parents; they also pity the child facing death; they feel an awesome awareness of the injustice of someone's dying before he or she has lived a full life.

A slightly different version of the dying child story is the "last wish" story, a feature about a family, community, or celebrity fulfilling the last wish of a child before he or she dies.

Of course adults facing death are also subjects of human interest stories, which frequently focus on the personality of the adult—on his or her individual courage, generosity, or religious faith. These adversity stories can sometimes send a message to the public about the disease that causes death. A story about someone dying of lung cancer, for example, can also give information about the signs and symptoms of the disease and can send a message about the dangers of passive smoke.

A rather unusual story dealing with loss-of-life is a feature written by Rose Post of *The Salisbury Post* in North Carolina. It tells, not of one individual dealing with loss, but of an entire town attempting to come to terms with the loss of one man's life:

> "He didn't have to shoot him," a neighbor said. "If he'd asked, Raymond would have given him anything he wanted."
>
> So folks in this tiny Iredell community where Raymond Niblock's Gas and Museum is not only The Square but the whole downtown aren't really scared by his murder two weeks ago—even if they do think about locking their doors now.
>
> Somebody who didn't know Raymond must have done it. Somebody who came in off the interstate to get gas. Or somebody from some other part of the country. Or another county.
>
> It's not fear that's gripping the people here. It's sadness, and anger. And loss. Their friend is gone. Their father, their grandfather, their mayor, mailcarrier, teacher, grademother, paperboy, repairman, practical prankster, who came home again and gave Cool Spring back its soul.
>
> Like he gave everybody everything else—his time, a laugh, a quarter for a cold drink, gasoline for the car.
>
> Bob Horne remembers the story his stepson told because he was at the Gas and Museum when it happened.

"This man stopped in from West Virginia, and he needed to get home," Bob says, remembering, "and he told Raymond, 'I don't have any money, but I'll give you my wristwatch for a tank of gas.'

"And Raymond said, 'Fill up your gas tank and go on. I don't want your watch.'

"So the man filled his tank and left and that's all there ever was to it."

(Post's story won the 1989 Ernie Pyle Human Interest Writing Award in the Scripps Howard Foundation National Journalism Awards competition.)

THE TRIUMPH OF THE HUMAN SPIRIT

Some human interest stories about adversity particularly emphasize the positive actions or attitudes of individuals who have overcome obstacles. Their victories over disease, injustice, hardship, or any loss or difficulty inspire readers, confirm a belief in the possibility of triumphing over life's trials. The winner of the 1990 Pulitzer Prize for Feature Writing was Dave Curtin's human interest feature for the Colorado Springs *Gazette-Telegraph* about a family that recovered from a devastating explosion that gave third-degree burns to the father, son, and daughter. The story is titled with the names of the children, "Adam & Megan," but the subtitle indicates its positive human interest message; the article is "The Story of One Family's Courage."

An Associated Press story by Joan Sanchez also tells the positive story of someone who has overcome an obstacle, a soldier who survived the Vietnam War but was "horribly wounded." The surgeon who saved the soldier's life—but amputated both his legs and could not save his sight—spent twenty-three years wondering whether he had done the right thing in saving nineteen-year-old Kenneth McGarity. Finally, he decided to find McGarity and see if he had in fact been condemned to a "life of dependence and misery." Instead, the surgeon found a life of accomplishment:

"I expected to find him in a VA hospital, neglected, bed sores, psychotic, pitied," Swan [the surgeon] said.

After three years [of searching], he found a disabled veteran who has worked hard to adjust. McGarity has attended college, learned to scuba dive and wants to earn a degree to help others cope with debilitating injuries.

Another example of a story revealing adult courage and spirit in overcoming adversity is this personal narrative from *Ladies' Home Journal* written by a woman who suffered the loss of her leg in a car-pedestrian accident, after she saved her baby son by pushing him out of the path of a swerving car. Phyllis Churchill describes what clearly has been a difficult time overcoming a handicap:

Early this year, however, the reality of what had happened finally hit me: This was permanent. Since the accident, I'd been so busy that I hadn't allowed myself to think about losing a leg. Now I began to grieve; unexpected feelings of sadness washed over me, and I cried easily. Even though I knew the doctors hadn't had a choice, I'd ask myself, Why didn't I tell them to try saving my leg?

Last spring, we took a family trip to Mexico, and I refused to sit in the sun or wear a bathing suit for fear that others would stare at me. Joe and the girls were very understanding, though, telling me how proud they were of me. Their support and the natural healing of time have helped me adjust to loss.

I'm happy to say that more than a year after the accident I'm enjoying an active life again. I walk normally on flat surfaces, I drive, I use our home treadmill and stair machine—I even dance. Slopes will always be hard for me because I can't flex the prosthetic ankle or foot, but I can manage them if I go slowly and hold someone's arm.

I'm still self-conscious about revealing my leg, but I know I'll get over that in time. If people stare at me, it's their problem, not mine. . . .

I'm making the most of every minute of Carr's [her son's] growth and development, because I know now how unpredictable life is and how close I came to losing him. I thank God every day that he took my leg and not my baby. I can live with that.

Human interest features with a slightly different triumphant tone are stories about people who have been more or less defeated by disease or adversity but have managed somehow to turn the evil of their misfortune into something that does good for others. The generous acts of defeated people affirm the goodness of the human spirit and speak to the reality that, at least for some human beings, physical defeat does not necessarily mean spiritual defeat.

A human interest story about a woman who worked for what she saw as justice despite her fatal illness creates such an inspirational sense of the strength and indomitability of the human spirit. John Donnelly of Knight-Ridder begins his feature this way:

WEST PALM BEACH, Fla.—For more than a week now, spectators have filled the benches in a Palm Beach County courtroom directly behind William Kennedy Smith. They watch him greet each potential juror in his rape trial. They watch him take notes. They watch his expressions.

But one seat away, another drama is unfolding, a private one. Cathy "Cat" Bennett, 40, a nationally known jury selection expert who is dying of cancer, is spending what may be her last professional effort to get Smith acquitted.

For 5 1/2 years, Ms. Bennett, a former high school cheerleader, has battled breast cancer. Two months ago, she learned the cancer had spread to her stomach and colon, and her Houston doctor recommended she be hospitalized for chemotherapy.

But for a woman who turned a psychology degree and an uncanny ability to "read" people's minds into a career that some say changed the course of criminal law practice, there was another job to do. Ms. Bennett checked herself out of the hospital a week before jury selection began.

Her mother, Jimmie Ellis, could see that she had made up her mind. . . .

"She's fighting for her life right now," said Ms. Ellis. "I've often wondered how that little 100-pound person could do so much."

That 100-pound person now weighs about 80. Her face is pale and drawn. She took a half-day off recently when her pain became unbearable. And yet no one in the courtroom seems as focused.

A human interest feature in *The Pittsburgh Press,* part of a series on organ transplants, also emphasized the generosity of the human spirit. Reporters Andrew Schneider and Mary Pat Flaherty spoke with families who struggled to turn their personal sorrow into other people's joy, to turn their negative experience with death into someone else's positive hope for new life:

> None of the families asked about the sex, race, age or residency of the potential recipient. The single most frequently voiced concern was: "Will they [the organs] go to someone who really needs them?". . .
>
> "Our only concern was, could part of Joshua help someone else," says Chris Lamison, who donated the kidneys and corneas of his 29-month-old boy who died after his spinal cord was severed in an automobile accident in Armstrong County in January 1983.
>
> "It didn't make any difference who got it. We trusted them (procurement people) to make the best decision. In the tragedy, the hope that Joshua's death would help another was the only bright spot we could grasp."
>
> Lamison, a 31-year-old surveyor from Kittannig, says both of his child's two tiny kidneys were transplanted into a 17-year-old boy from southwestern Pennsylvania.
>
> Mary Lou Harbulak donated her husband's organs.
>
> "At first I only said they could have my husband's kidney, then Brian Broznick (the procurement coordinator) told me that in another hospital a 30-year-old man with two kids needed a heart desperately or he'd die. I told Brian to take Paul's heart," says Mrs. Harbulak, whose 25-year-old husband died of a ruptured vessel in his brain in August 1982.
>
> "I didn't know Brian before that night but I believed him when he said Paul's organs would save someone's life. You grasp for trust in a situation like that, without it you can't cope with anything," she says.

SERIOUS STYLE

When you're writing the human interest story, *you are* often dealing with solemn topics and are writing to elicit serious emotions from readers. No matter what style or format you choose for your story, you must control its emotional tone carefully.

Most feature writers agree that a human interest story, to be effective, should be fairly restrained, even understated. At the first hint of the pathos or joy of a story being pushed beyond reasonable limits, the reader will withdraw emotionally—and snicker or snort at what should be sad, or shrug at what should be happy.

The best advice, then, is to let the story tell itself. Don't interject a lot of material designed to hype emotional impact. Avoid sentimentalized descriptions, melodramatic overstatements, and sweeping generalizations. Don't write statements you can't support, things like ''Her courage will live in memory forever'' (forever is a long time) or ''His generosity is an example to us all'' (every single one of us?).

Particularly avoid summing up situations or drawing conclusions, such as ''so-and-so revealed courage and discipline in the face of excruciating pain.'' Instead, let the person's courage and discipline be revealed through his or her actions, or described through quotations from people around him or her.

Finally, avoid using clichés or making statements that reveal clichéd thinking about human emotions, such as ''if it's meant to be, it will be'' or ''hope springs eternal in the human breast'' or ''there's no love like a mother's love.''

In addition to being restrained—or perhaps as part of being restrained—limit your story to one strong emotional tone. Before you begin writing, decide what basic emotion characterizes the situation, then strive to capture its essence. Of course, life is confusing and human beings are complex. Your story shouldn't oversimplify things just to produce a single emotional message. But you should strive to eliminate *unnecessary* material that doesn't sustain the emotion you want. And keep the article reasonably short, so your reader's concentration remains unbroken.

No matter how tempting, however, don't yield to the impulse to omit a *necessary* piece of information because it contradicts the mood you want to create, or to change a bit of the story here or there to make it just a little bit more pathetic, a little bit more rags to riches. Tell the story with honest detail, description, and dialogue. Most of the time, readers can sense when something's phony and when it ''rings true.'' You'll actually earn *more* emotional response when you write something honest—despite its contradictions and ambiguities—than when you write something fictionalized.

And if the point of the human interest story is to help readers define their humanity, it really makes little sense to try to fool them with exaggeration or falsehood. You serve them better if you simply tell them the truth.

EXERCISES

1. Write a brief personal narrative of several paragraphs telling about an unhappy experience you had. Then write two different endings for your narrative. In one, cast the experience in a positive light; in the other, leave the unhappiness of the experience unresolved. In both endings, try not to *tell* what you feel about the experience; rather, *show* what you feel by giving information about what happened next, by presenting facts summarizing the impact of the experience, by describing other people's reactions, or by any other way you can imply rather than overtly state the meaning of the experience.
2. Students often feel they have ''nothing to write'' about human interest subjects. To help you discover story subjects, brainstorm with a group of people. Sit down together and try to come up with a list of all the kinds of adversity,

bad and good luck, and situations of stress you can think of. Then see how many people you know who are in those situations. How many of those people would be willing to share their experiences? Under what conditions and circumstances?

3. Read Doug McInnis' story from *The Columbus Dispatch,* ''Violence put a price of $50 on young man's life.'' How does McInnis restrain his writing style? What effect does his restraint have on your reactions to the story?

4. Read the series ''Mother's Drug Habit Turns Baby into Victim,'' written by Terrie Claflin for the *Mail Tribune* of Medford, Oregon. Claflin won the 1990 non-deadline writing award from the American Society of Newspaper Editors with this series. Discuss these questions:

   a. If human interest stories provide a ''yardstick for human behavior which readers can use to measure themselves,'' how do you measure yourself against Carole White? How do you think most readers would measure themselves against her? What characteristics of her life seem most admirable to you? What characteristics are difficult to understand, or would be difficult to emulate?

   b. If human interest stories help ''define our humanity,'' what did this series teach you about human beings and their behavior?

   c. What overall feeling did you experience when you finished reading the series? Did you have more than one emotional response? To which elements in which stories?

VIOLENCE PUT A PRICE OF $50 ON YOUNG MAN'S LIFE

By Doug McInnis
The Columbus Dispatch, *April 10, 1991*

Michael Burks Sr. yesterday condemned the nationwide violence that now counts his son among the victims.

"We live in a city, in a country, surrounded by crime," he said. "It was published that for all of Great Britain, there were only 80 homicides last year.

"Here we are (in Columbus,) and it's only four months into the year, and we already have 50."

His 18-year-old son, Michael Jr., was No. 50.

He died Thursday night during an apparent robbery at the East Side pizza shop where he worked.

He was found dead by police, who had responded to a 911 call that Burks was in trouble.

He was killed by a gunshot that traveled through his right arm and into his chest.

Both lungs and his spine were damaged by the impact.

No arrests have been made in the case.

Yesterday, his father sought to work his way through the emotional tangle that violent crime leaves in its wake, while trying to find a way to tell his 5-year-old daughter that her brother was dead.

At the same time, Burks made it clear that his son's case would not be allowed to drop from sight before it was solved.

"I want something done," he said. "Instead of building new jails and fancy buildings, why don't we put more cops on the street?

"Why don't we break up these gangs? I don't want to see the file closed on this.

"I'm not going to let this die. If I have to bang on City Hall's door. I will do it. I want some answers.

"If they can tax us to build a new convention center, why can't they use that money to put another 30 or 40 police on the street?

"I know the police do what they can. There's just not enough of them."

Michael Jr. was working at Little Caesars Pizza, 3685 E. Livingston Ave., when he was shot.

His father said Michael had been working at another Little Caesars, at Livingston and Parsons avenues, but had sought a transfer because of problems there.

"He didn't like the area," Burks said. "He told Little Caesars to transfer him or they could consider it his resignation.

"So they transferred him, and he was only there two days . . .

"The same thing I think he was afraid of (at the first store) happened here."

Burks said he moved his family to this area from Youngstown five years ago when he foresaw that the collapse of that city's steel industry would eventually affect his own steel-related job.

He settled in Grove City.

His son loved cars, he said. "His hobby was his car. Every car my son ever had, he tried to make it perfect."

Michael Jr. also worked long hours at Little Caesars.

Then he became another statistic on the nation's homicide log.

His father learned of his death from the radio.

Now he is preparing to bury him Monday, next to his grandfather in a suburban Youngstown cemetery.

Burks is angry and bitter.

"My son was trying to make something of himself, and he's dead because somebody was trying to make $50 the easy way," he said.

"His life was worth more than $50."

. . .

THE TENTH CHILD
By Terrie Claflin
Mail Tribune (Medford, Oregon), November 12, 1989

Mother's Drug Habit Turns Baby into Victim
July 19, 1989

She is, in many ways, a china doll. Skin like snow, eyes like sky, a tiny body rigid and cool to the touch. Her cheeks are rosy, her face expressionless, unchanging. The world swirls in color and motion around her, yet she does not perceive it. For like a china doll, within her tiny head, behind those ice-blue eyes, Rachel has no brain.

Rachel was born Jan. 2, 1989, at a hospital here in southern Oregon. The birth was premature, only three weeks before the due date, but there were severe complications apparently caused by the mother's drug use. The placenta had detached from the uterine wall. The baby was without oxygen for God-only-knows how long.

God only knows how, or why, she lived. It wasn't until days later that computerized tomography scans showed that the baby's seizures and strokes were so intense inside the womb that most of her brain tissue had turned to a watery consistency.

There was nothing the doctors could do. They kept Rachel in the pediatric unit at Rogue Valley Medical Center for a month before they decided she might be better off at home. The baby needed a mother who could rock and hold and comfort her 24 hours a day, if that's what it took. Rachel's own mother, however, wouldn't do.

For one thing, she lived too far from the pediatric center and the specialized care the baby would need. For another, before Rachel's mother left the hospital, both she and the baby tested positive for marijuana metabolites, amphetamines, and cocaine.

Carole White, a foster care provider, holds the baby in her lap, rubbing the fuzzy blond head, wrapping the tiny fingers around her own.

"I've picked up a lot of babies from the hospital, but I think they (hospital workers) were more upset about this one than I've ever seen before," she says.

Maybe it's because she's so beautiful, Carole says. And maybe it's because Rachel is going to die.

Rachel seems perfect, but at 6 months, she's so tiny. Rachel weighs only 9 pounds. She looks and acts like a newborn, spending most of her hours eating or sleeping. When she's awake, she either cries or looks blank, confused. She never smiles. She can see images and hear certain sounds, but can't make sense of it all.

Rachel's brainstem keeps her heart thump-thumping under her little flannel pajamas, Carole says. It sends hunger signals to her belly. And it allows her to feel pain—and comfort.

"She definitely knows the difference between lying in her crib and being held," Carole says. "Let's just say we've spent many an hour right here in this rocking chair, watching the sun go down and then come back up again."

Carole is a foster care provider for the state Children's Services Division. Just as the doctors suspected, Rachel is a 24-hour-a-day job. Since she came home from the hospital in February, she had lost the ability to suck, so Carole has to feed her formula and sedatives every few hours with a syringe. The baby has frequent seizures—arching her back and contorting her body, howling and gasping for breath. Carole says that even Rachel's sleep is less restful than it was.

She changes every day, seldom for the better.

"Actually, she's doing pretty well, considering. They didn't think she'd live four months," Carole says, looking at the sleeping baby in her lap. "We're proving them wrong, though, aren't we Rachel?"

Carole and her husband, Charlie, live in a big farmhouse in the hills north of Central Point. The gate on the little picket fence out front has a latch on it, but it's seldom closed—not with all the comings and goings.

The Whites' two oldest children, Jon and Tracy, are married, but they spend almost as much time here as they do at their own homes. The youngest daughter, Susan, is in high school, a cheerleader with friends and boy-friends who fill in whatever empty chairs might be found at the dinner table.

"I decided to start providing foster care when my son left home," Carole says. "I guess I was feeling a bit empty-nested."

That was four years ago. The family supported her decision, and six months later she was certified by CSD. She requested small children, not over the age of 5, and they began showing up regularly on her front porch, sometimes asleep on a police officer's shoulder, sometimes with nothing on but a T-shirt and diaper.

"I provide a place for children to go when their parents need some time to work out difficulties in their lives," Carole says. "It's usually short-term—sometimes for just a few hours. I bathe them and feed them and put them in sleeping bags on the floor."

More than 80 children have spent anywhere from a night to a couple of years with Carole and her family.

"These are children who are unbonded and lost," she says. "They don't seem to care that they are at a stranger's house. They just move right in. And we just make them part of the family. Even if we have them just for a night, I feel we can still make an impact on them. Maybe they'll know what's possible—they don't have to be beaten, they don't have to live in filth, they don't have to be hungry. We can show them that 'home' can be a secure place, that people can love one another, and that they are loved.

"The hardest part has been sending them home, wondering if their natural parents are going to take care of them the way I would. . . ."

The hardest part got even harder two years ago. When Carole filled out her original foster care form with CSD, she said specifically that she did not want children with "special needs." Then came a little 11-month-old on a heart monitor. After that a baby addicted to heroin, then babies who were battered, babies who were neglected.

She took them all. Then, she decided she would take only kids with special needs. Rachel is the most recent.

"I guess sometimes you don't know yourself as well as you think you do," Carole says.

Violet has bright red hair and a way of crawling into just about anyone's lap. She is 3. She came to Carole's house when she was 7 months old—possibly the most severely battered child ever to survive at Rogue Valley Medical Center.

She would like to draw a picture, but she has trouble picking up a pencil. Two tries, three tries, and she has it between her stubby little fingers. She wrinkles her nose and grins. "I can do it."

Violet was born with fetal alcohol syndrome, caused by her mother's abuse of alcohol. She was beaten by her mother's boyfriend because he was tired of hearing her cry. She has had so many brain surgeries and come close to dying so many times that Carole has lost count. The CT scans show that large parts of her brain have died, and doctors are still unsure how that will affect the rest of her life.

While Violet has problems with speech and fine motor movement, Crystal appears to be a perfectly normal, curious, hey-look-out-world 4-year-old. She was never battered, Carole says, but she was neglected.

When Crystal arrived at the Whites' house at age 16 months, she crawled around looking for crumbs of food under the furniture. She couldn't speak and wouldn't look at Carole no matter how hard Carole tried to reach her.

It took months, but finally the love came back. Eventually, both of the girls were declared well enough to be adopted. So that's what Carole did—she adopted them herself.

"I had worked so hard building up a trust in them," she says. "How could I give them away?"

Carole would have adopted J. J. too, if she could have. She walks to the bookshelf and picks up a photo album, its cover showing a baby boy with light blond hair, and eyes and a smile that seem to go in two different directions at once.

J. J. was a heroin baby. He cried 24 hours a day for three months. The drugs had left him blind in one eye and severely retarded. He wasn't supposed to live, but Carole says she willed him to anyway. In the next 2–1/2 years she willed him to feed himself, walk, run, laugh, and learn sign language.

He was doing well in February when Carole agreed to care for Rachel, to rock the baby until she died.

Then one night last March, J. J. died in his crib.

The baby who had been given a new lease on life was dead. The baby that was supposed to die, Rachel, was still alive.

The doctors said J. J.'s death was somehow linked to the heroin his mother had taken before he was born, but no explanation could soften the shock for Carole and her family.

With renewed determination, Carole began willing Rachel to live.

Foster Mom Struggles to Cope
September 18, 1989

"I didn't want to do it, really I didn't. I wanted to keep things as normal as possible, as long as I could. I just wanted to do what's best for Rachel."

Carole White sits in a softly lighted room in Rogue Valley Medical Center's pediatric ward. She rubs the dark circles under her eyes.

"Putting the feeding tube down her nose will be easier for her—and for me as well," she says.

The tiny cocaine baby had taken a turn for the worse.

August is still a blur in Carole's weary mind. The baby began having seizures over and over again, crying and contorting for three long, awful weeks. Carole refused to sleep. Her 17-year-old daughter, Susan, began noticing that Carole couldn't complete a sentence anymore. A therapist who comes to the house and works with Carole's 3-year-old adopted daughter, Violet, contacted Children's Services and suggested that Carole take a vacation with her family.

She did, reluctantly, leaving Rachel with a respite care volunteer. The family went to Disneyland—and came back a week early. Carole just felt that Rachel needed her.

Now the seizures are under control; the baby is on an almost adult-level dosage of Phenobarbital, a sedative. But she's having trouble breathing. And she's lost the ability to swallow. Over the weekend Carole had to resort to an eyedropper to get any formula down her. She brought Rachel here to the hospital two days ago.

Medical staffers inserted the feeding tube, which drips baby formula from an IV unit, but not without much discussion, Carole says. How far can they, or should they, go to keep this baby alive?

The room is quiet. Crystal, Carole's other adopted daughter, watches cartoons from a chair in the corner. The nurses hustle in and out with charts and hushed words of encouragement. They have just replaced the tube and Rachel's newbornlike squalls have turned to sobs.

Carole rocks, endlessly, in a well-worn recliner. She manages a smile as Rachel opens her eyes.

"Are you going to be all right now?"

September 27, 1989

Carole needed a friend—someone who understood what she was going through. Someone who wouldn't ask "why" she chose to take care of this baby. She has found that kind of friend in Christina Smith.

Christina is a respite care volunteer for Easter Seals. Every third night she takes Rachel to her home, a few miles away in Medford, so that Carole can get one good night of sleep a week and do some of the things she used to do with her family—such as go to high school football games to watch her Susan cheer, or go out to dinner with her husband, Charlie.

Rachel and her condition are no shock to Christina. If anything, the baby is a bright spot in her life.

Two years ago Christina's mother-in-law had a series of strokes and had to move in with Christina and her husband. Like Rachel, she was a round-the-clock commitment. Like Carole, Christina had no one to turn to.

"I know how desperate you get for some kind of respite," she says. "So this has become a special ministry to me. When I went through the hurt and anger of not having help, I knew I needed to do this."

The two women talk a lot on the phone. They laugh as much as they cry. This morning at 3 A.M., Christina called Carole in panic, afraid Rachel was about to die.

"She was just coughing so hard, she turned so limp, so blue, I thought I'd lost her," Christina says.

They took Rachel to the medical center, where the doctors determined that the convulsions stemmed from a crimp in the feeding tube. They also diagnosed a slight ear and sinus infection. They put Rachel on antibiotics, replaced the tube, and sent her home.

Lying in her crib, Rachel is carefully propped on Boris the Bear, a gift from the hospital's nurses. She looks as if she's doing better. The tube has helped her gain a few pounds. Her color is pink, her body no longer rigid. The warm and snuggly position on the bear helps her breathe. She sleeps peacefully as Christina and Carole talk about their lives and the fragile life in the crib.

"People react so differently to this baby—she touches them somehow," Christina says. "Sometimes there are tears or anger. Sometimes they have no compassion at all."

Carole tells about an encounter she had in a fast-food restaurant last week. She and Crystal and Violet, plus a 4-year-old autistic foster care child who lives with the Whites, had been at the hospital all morning and needed lunch.

Carole put Rachel in her special infant seat and set her near the table. A woman eating nearby came over, saying rather loudly that the baby was obviously very sick and Carole had no business bringing her there.

"It happens more often than I wish," Carole says. "People don't want to deal with it. They say it's just too hard. They couldn't do it. They think maybe these children should be put away in a nursing home.

"And it's NOT easy. But it IS easy. It's not easy because we might lose her and we love her so much. But it IS easy because we love her so much."

Carole's lap is just big enough for the three children who are trying to climb into it. But if another was to come along, somehow she'd find room.

"These are special children; they have a glow about them that so-called normal children don't have," she says. "There's potential here. There's a message for all of us here."

It's a message both painful and promising, Christina says. Take one of them in your arms. Hold her close. You'll feel it.

"She makes you feel so special, like you're holding a gift from God."

Loving Hand Guides Infant During Ordeal
October 2, 1989

6 p.m.—Susan and Tracy are clink-clank-clearing the dinner dishes. Tracy's husband, Jon, is telling a story at the kitchen counter, Carole is mixing up a new bag of formula in the sink, Charlie is jangling his keys on the way out the door to a Camp Fire meeting, the three little kids are rolling and romping and wrestling on the living room floor.

A few feet away, Rachel sleeps through it all.

"We've tried everything," Carole says, measuring the formula and pouring it into the plastic pouch. "We thought maybe it was too quiet, so we left the radio on all night. We tried keeping her up all day and she ended up staying up for 49 straight hours.

"Nothing works. She still sleeps all day and stays up all night. That's just Rachel."

Susan says she's going to go get a movie. Carole suggests that it not be a tear-jerker. Not tonight. It's been a long day.

Rachel and Carole have been fighting a battle of body temperature all afternoon. Because Rachel has no brain, she has no thermostat. Her temperature can drop to 92 degrees in 20 minutes. If it gets down to 90, her systems will start shutting down.

The woodstove blazes in the middle of the room. A cat curls up under Rachel's crib. A little vase of roses withers on a table nearby. The heat is almost tropical. Most of the family runs around in shorts.

8 p.m.—Carole and Tracy set up a bathtub assembly line, plopping one kid in the tub, then passing him on to be dried and dressed, kissed and tucked under the covers. Violet has fallen asleep in a chair. As Tracy carries Violet upstairs, Carole sinks into her soft blue recliner. But before she can kick off her shoes, Rachel is stirring in the crib.

Carole shakes her head.

"Timing," she says.

9 p.m.—You can tell when Rachel is awake. Her breathing sounds like a drip-coffeemaker, gurgling, pop-popping, sniffing, fluids moving through airways, clogged. She starts to cry— long, soft, newbornlike waaaaaahs, followed by a cough, then an ooh-ooh-ooh and a pout. Carole picks her up, kisses her on the cheek, then lays the baby belly-down over her knees. With cupped hands she begins beating on the baby's back like a bongo drum.

"This is supposed to break loose the phlegm or whatever it is that's in there," Carole says, settling into a rhythm. "She likes it. She thinks it's fun."

Indeed, Rachel holds her head up high, eyes as wide as they've ever been. After a few minutes, she's quiet, alert. Happy.

11:45 p.m.—Having finished *Gorillas in the Mist,* a tear-jerker after all, most of the family and visiting friends have wandered home or to bed. Rachel sits in her infant seat, eyes half-open. Each breath comes hard. Tracy has one more lunch to pack before she pours another cup of coffee for her mom, softens the lights, turns down the TV, and disappears up the stairs.

"This has definitely disrupted my family," Carole admits. This summer the weeds in Carole's garden grew right alongside the vegetables. A lot of tomatoes never made it into jars, the camping equipment gathered dust in the garage. Besides the vacation to Disneyland, the family had a few outings—mostly without Carole. Because of Rachel's condition, Carole is afraid to get too far from home. Two nights out of every three she doesn't even get to sleep with Charlie. She usually just picks a place on the couch and takes short, restless naps. If she's lucky.

"You have to have a pretty strong marriage to do something like this," she says. "Even my mother doesn't understand. She thinks I'm putting myself and my family through too much by taking on this kind of commitment.

"I don't think I'm putting myself through too much."

But she does worry, out loud, about her family.

2 a.m.—The family has already been through one death this year: J. J.'s was a nightmare that came with no warning. Carole hopes that this time, this death will be better.

Doctors and nurses have told her that Rachel could die three different ways: She could have massive convulsions and not come out of them, she could get pneumonia and not recover, or she could slip into a coma and die in her sleep.

"The coma is definitely the easiest of the three," Carole says. "That's what we're praying for now. I've finally got it through my head that we're not going to save her. I finally understand and accept that."

Rachel is considered a "no code" with local emergency service agencies. That means that rescue workers are not to resuscitate her if she is in a life-threatening situation. She is not to be saved. Even the feeding tube was a question of possibly "going too far" to extend Rachel's life, Carole says.

Rachel coughs and cries and refuses to sleep.

"Look at her; she's not a happy baby. When she's awake, she's miserable. But someday," Carole says with a smile, "she'll be happy and whole and run and play. . . ."

3 a.m.—The way Carole sees it, God has given her a chance to be a caretaker for these children while they are here on earth.

"Maybe that's arrogant for me to say, but I feel that's my job in life, my purpose," Carole says. "I feel, in my own way, I'm Rachel's caretaker and someday I'm going to hand her over to God."

Of course, some people would take one look at Rachel and wonder if there is a God at all. Why would He create this baby? Why would He put her, her real family, her foster family, her doctors, and her caseworkers through so much pain?

Carole shakes her head. She believes Rachel has her own purpose. It could be just to tell her story, to show people—in a painful, but powerful, way—what happens when pregnant women take drugs.

Or it could be to prepare Carole for the children yet to come. If the experts are right, if America sinks deeper and deeper into its drug problem, there will be many more Rachels for the Caroles of the world.

She would take another one in a minute. But she knows she can't take care of them all.

"There are so many children out there who need homes—not just foster care, but adoption," she says. "These are children with rough histories—babies from Medford, babies from our neighborhoods. Cocaine babies, heroin babies, battered children.

"But look at Crystal and Violet. I mean, they're coming out okay. If we had let the thought that Violet had permanent brain damage or that Crystal had been severely mentally abused . . . if we had let those things keep us from adopting them, think of the joy we would have missed."

Rachel yawns, a big yawn for such a tiny mouth, but her eyes refuse to close. The hands on the clock nudge closer to 4.

"If you really want to help, if you love kids, then there's no excuse," Carole says.

"Even Rachel. With all the hardships she's caused in our family—not being able to go anywhere, staying up all night, the fear that hurts so badly in your stomach when you think you're going to lose her—even with all that, she's such a blessing. After she's gone, that's what we'll remember."

4:30 a.m.—After a half-hour of seizures, Rachel's body finally relaxes. Her eyes close. Her breathing is peaceful, silent.

Carole adjusts the drip of the feeding unit, covers the baby with a blanket, and makes her way through the darkness to the couch.

5:30 a.m.—Tracy's husband, Jon, moves through the room on his way to his job at the mill.

6 a.m.—Charlie throws another log on the fire, grabs his lunch out of the refrigerator, and closes the door quietly behind him.

6:30 a.m.—Rachel is choking. Tracy, still in her pajamas, gropes in the darkness to pick Rachel up and hand her to Carole. The baby's breathing is fast, hard, loud, then muffled.

The house is silent.

At the bottom of the stairs, a soft pink shadow with a Cheshire Cat grin fades into view.

"Good morning!"

6:35 a.m.—Carole heads into the kitchen to make a fresh pot of coffee, hugging the tiny figure at her side.

"Good morning, Violet. Did you sleep well?"

Carole Fights Fatigue as Rachel Weakens
October 9, 1989

Carole could have gotten a night's sleep. But she couldn't sleep. Yesterday evening at 6, Rachel had a terrible spell. She coughed and gagged and turned purple. Charlie "whomped" her, as Carole puts it, until the baby started breathing again. Then she went to sleep.

"She's been gone ever since."

It's noon on Monday and Rachel is sleeping blissfully in Christina's arms. She's still the color of china, but her body acts as if it's made out of rags, limp, fingers uncurled, arms outstretched. Her tiny head is tucked in a little pink stocking cap. The face below it is puffed, blotched, unresponsive. Christina kisses her until there's slight reaction—a yawn, a soft cry, a flutter of eyelashes.

Then she's gone again.

"It's a blessing," Carole says. "This is the way we hoped she would go, but now that it's happening, it's happening too fast."

Nancy Gish knocks on the front door, but no one hears it. She comes in anyway, as she has so many times before, carrying a country doctor's black bag with a city doctor's beeper attached to it.

Nancy is a nurse for the home health program at Rogue Valley Medical Center. She was working in the neonatal intensive care unit 10 months ago when Rachel was there. Now it's her job to continue providing that care, that comfort, from the office within her car.

"Rachel was such a beautiful baby; I remember her well," Nancy says. "But within 24 hours, you could tell there was something different about her. You'd look in her eyes and there was nothing there.

"Nothing."

She holds the baby in her lap, taking a temperature reading, listening with her stethoscope to the short, sharp breaths. As the canary in the corner starts to sing, Rachel's eyes open. Then they close again.

"It certainly looks like a semicomatose state to me," Nancy says, gently. Carole asks the nurse what will come next and Nancy explains that more than likely, Rachel's systems will start to shut down. A damaged brain simply lacks the capacity to keep things working the way they should.

As that happens, Rachel will become more lethargic, her heart will speed up and then start slowing down.

"She's going to sound worse, but it will be easier on her," Nancy says. "That's what we're hoping for."

Nancy stops to dab at a tear with her finger and smiles at the baby.

"Are you getting at peace with everything?" she asks softly. "Is that what's happening?"

October 11, 1989

Carole debated whether it was too early to buy Rachel a new dress, her last dress, and a little band with a bow to put around her head. She decided it wasn't.

"I just felt like it was too soon—like I'd be rushing things to start making her final arrangements," Carole says as matter-of-factly as she can. "But everyone says it will be easier if I do. So I am."

Today Rachel has an appointment with her pediatrician, Alan Frierson. Carole knows that there's not much he can do, but she still wants to know what he thinks about Rachel's new condition.

They undress her except for the little white bow stuck to her thin blond hair, weigh her (14 pounds), and wrap her up in blankets while they wait for the doctor. He arrives, does a quick exam, and asks that everyone else leave the room so he can talk to Carole.

Out in the waiting room, mothers wait with their healthy babies—babies that kick and coo and toss their rattles and think and feel and respond.

When Carole finally emerges from the office her jaw is set, her brown eyes sharp and round.

"Do you want to know what he told me? He told me that despite what everyone else says, he doesn't think we're dealing with a dying baby. He says she may just be slipping into a 'happy sleep.' That she may be this way for 20 years."

With Tracy's help, Carole carries the baby out to the car, buckles Crystal into the back seat, then stands in the parking lot with empty hands.

"In a way, I'm relieved; in another way, I'm disappointed," Carole says, looking up at the sky. "I know that sounds awful. I hope you understand. It's just not fair to Rachel."

She had planned to make the funeral arrangements tomorrow.

"I'm just so incredibly confused . . ."

Dr. Alan Frierson is a long, lanky man with the thought pattern of a pinball machine. His ideas bounce off the top of his head and ricochet around the room, seemingly faster than he can say them.

One idea stands firm.

"I absolutely think Rachel is going to be 40 years old someday, lying somewhere in a nursing home unable to move and unable to speak," he says sadly. "(What is left of) her brain has kept her alive this long; it should be easier to stay alive all the time."

As she ages, the airways will get bigger, making it easier to breathe. The organs will mature. Her body will set itself on automatic pilot. There will be no one visible at the controls.

"My biggest problem is burning out Carole. She's a valuable resource for Medford and I'd hate to lose her," Frierson says.

October 13, 1989

You can only balance on an ethical tightrope so long. After a while, you either fall or jump. Today Carole has decided to jump. She's weighed the professional opinions in one hand with her gut feeling in the other—and made an appointment at Conger-Morris Funeral Directors for 2 p.m.

"Wednesday (the day of the doctor's appointment) was the hardest day yet," she says. "I was devastated. And then I was so guilty for feeling devastated. How could hope make me feel so bad?"

Rachel is dressed in soft pink pajamas. She gurgles in Christina's lap as the funeral director, Chuck Loyd, goes over the details. He remembers Carole from J. J.'s death seven months ago, so he skips most of the paperwork.

The state will provide $304 for the burial. But whatever Carole wants, Conger-Morris is willing to make up the difference. A marker on the gravesite will cost at least $300 more. Carole says it will be marked one way or another.

Loyd is curious about the baby. He asks questions, delicately, which Carole answers, honestly. She tells him the whole story, right up to her decision to make these arrangements.

"I think an animal is an animal. We've raised rabbits and sometimes these baby rabbits are born and they don't do very well and I'd work and work and try to save them." Carole fingers the chair. "She reminds me of these baby rabbits. No matter what I do, she's going to die."

October 17, 1989

Steven Morris of Conger-Morris calls and offers to pay for the gravesite marker. Carole wonders aloud how one tiny baby can have such a big impact on so many hearts. Rachel is sleeping well, she says. It's a good day.

October 27, 1989

Rachel was in a complete coma for 14 hours four days ago. She's come out of it, but she hasn't been the same since. She's not tolerating her feedings well, her diapers are dry as if nothing is going through, and she has serious problems breathing when she is awake. The day after she came out of the coma, she stopped breathing. Carole says she panicked, and revived Rachel.

"Not yet," she says. "It's not right yet."

Carole says she catches herself wishing, sometimes, that Rachel would drop back into the coma. Then it would be easier. Then they could talk about stopping her feedings. But then, Rachel and God have their own plans, she says.

Carole has decided to keep Rachel at home and not send her to Christina's every third night as she has. Christina comes over and helps Carole catch an occasional nap, and tends to the baby so Carole can tend to her family.

While the baby sleeps bundled in her crib, Carole and her oldest daughter, Tracy, are cleaning house. The younger ones, Crystal and Violet, try to stay one step ahead of the vacuum, scattering crayons in their wake. Carole's husband, Charlie, and her youngest daughter, Susan, should be home soon. No one is sure what's for dinner. Carole looks out the window at the darkening clouds and laughs about this compelling urge she has to go out and walk in the rain. Without an umbrella.

That's what she used to do, back when she was younger, in high school, she says with a grin. She'd break up with a boyfriend or have some other major event happen in her life, and she'd step out into the rain and walk until she was drenched.

When she got back, everything would be better.

Tracy shakes her head, grins, and goes back to helping the kids color.

Oh, by the way, Carole says, she and Christina found this wonderful saying that they want read at the funeral. It was on a coffee cup and Carole copied it down on a piece of lined paper. It says:

Some people come into lives and quickly go.
Some stay for a while and leave footprints on our hearts,
And we are never ever the same.

There is less sadness than joy in Carole's face. "It says it, doesn't it? It says it all."

Rachel: A Final Journey
November 12, 1989

Rachel died on Wednesday, just four days ago, at 5:34 p.m.

Carole was holding the baby in her arms, in the recliner where they had spent so many hours, when Rachel opened her eyes one last time, took a deep breath, let it out, and left the world, with all its pain and suffering, behind. . . .

Oregon State Police officers met with District Attorney Bill Juba on Thursday morning to discuss possible prosecution of Rachel's mother. Upon handing over the case to the district attorney, Lt. Del Hussey said, "The OSP is behind it. We'd like to see it prosecuted and I have committed any resources I have available to get it prosecuted."

Juba said no decision had been made. The state has one year from the date of the "crime" to file charges. Since the damage to the infant occurred by birth, Jan. 2, 1989, a decision must be made by Jan. 1, 1990.

"We are still in the stages of investigation," Juba said, "not only in the investigation of this particular case, but from the entire legal perspective as well.

"No decision is forthcoming at this time."

Services for Rachel will be held at 11 a.m. Monday at the Conger-Morris Chapel in Central Point. Carole considered burying Rachel with Boris, the bear she snuggled with in her crib, but it is the only thing Carole has that was truly Rachel's. Instead, Carole plans to buy a new teddy bear to place in the casket "so she won't be alone."

An interment, at Memory Gardens, will be attended only by Carole and her family.

Rachel's mother, who declined to be interviewed for this special report, is due to have another baby in December.

Holiday, Anniversary, and Seasonal Stories
Participating in the Ritual of Recurring Events

Stories that mark the coming of the holidays, the recurrence of anniversaries, and the cycle of the seasons are stories set apart from other features in a special way. Not particularly special in terms of the types of features they are, holiday, anniversary, and seasonal articles can be almost any of the usual kinds of feature stories we have discussed in this text so far. And anniversary stories (we'll use the term ''anniversary'' story for holiday and seasonal stories as well as anniversary stories) simply perform, in one sense, an obvious journalistic function: they mark the occurrence of particular days and times of the year.

In another sense, however, anniversary stories play a special role unique in journalism. Anniversary features—written, published on paper, and distributed widely—mark the occurrence of significant days and times in a permanent and public way. If newspapers and magazines failed to publish anniversary stories, then festive celebrations, somber commemorations, and the yearly return of the seasons would seem less significant, because less recognized.

Readers, through reading anniversary stories, participate in a small way in this public written ritual marking the recurrence of special events. They take note of holidays and consider how to observe them; they honor memories; they mark the changes in the natural world. Thus anniversary stories do something we seldom think of feature articles as doing: they sustain societal and religious values by commemorating the days symbolizing those values, and reinforce the sense of the cyclical nature of human life by noting the regular return of each season.

Any particular anniversary story may not seem or even be especially significant, but anniversary stories as a collective, continuing group of feature articles are therefore special—or at least special to those who choose to read them.

FRESH IDEAS AND STORY TIMING

Of course, the significance of anniversary stories as a whole is in contrast to the often tedious and repetitive process of writing individual anniversary stories. The very regularity of their publication makes writing such stories a task filled with frustration and feelings of inadequacy. Year after year newspapers and magazines publish stories about various anniversaries—New Year's and Fourth of July, Halloween, Washington's Birthday, spring fashions, and fall leaves. So, staring the would-be anniversary feature writer in the face is the prospect of adding yet one more article, done 100 times before, to the existing multitude. The challenge is finding a fresh topic or improving on one already published.

Adding to the difficulty is the forced timing of the story's publication. If you're a newspaper writer, you don't typically have the luxury of seeing, hearing, or reading something interesting and having it suggest an anniversary story to you. Instead, you are reminded that such-and-such a date is approaching and you have to "write something" about it. The stereotypic situation is the editor pushing the cub reporter out into the snow December 24th, with an uncharitable growl not to come back until he or she has a story that conveys the spirit of Christmas.

Of course, last-minute, rabbit-out-of-the-hat stories often turn out wonderfully: adrenaline kicks in and you produce a brilliant piece of writing (or maybe the spirit of Christmas descends after all). But, on the other hand, being pushed to write a story sometimes means you produce something phony and artificial.

If you're a free-lance writer, your calendar rather than your editor reminds you that special anniversary dates are approaching. For you, the difficulty of forcing yourself to "write something" is compounded by the fact that you need to write that something so it will be in the mail approximately six months before a particular anniversary date. Magazines generally work well in advance of major holidays, and plan, for example, their Christmas issues before July. *Writer's Market* magazine entries frequently list special advance deadlines for major holiday magazine issues, so you should check its entries if you're uncertain whether you have enough time to submit an article. If you're a slow starter, you may have to begin gathering story ideas almost a year in advance, to give yourself time to research, report, write, and rewrite, and still meet a magazine's six-month advance deadline.

Obviously the problem with such advanced deadlines is that it's hard to sustain an appropriate mood while you write. It's disorienting to try to conjure up an atmosphere of pine trees and egg nog for your Christmas article when you're sweating over a computer in a mid-summer heat wave. Some of your disorientation and detachment may communicate itself in your article.

SOME DOS AND DON'TS

The point, then, is that the two major difficulties in writing anniversary stories are finding fresh story ideas and overcoming the forced nature of the assignment.

There are, however, some other difficulties to consider. One is the tendency to think that because you've lived through so many anniversary dates and times, you, as a personal historian, can sit in your chair and simply spin an anniversary feature out of your head. Throw in a few references to turkeys and pilgrims and you'll have a Thanksgiving feature, or explain that the name ''Halloween'' is derived from All Hallows Day, and conclude that you're telling readers something new and interesting.

Of course, anniversary stories full of such stale generalities do get published, so we can't claim that stories written this way never see the light of day. But the best anniversary stories result from solid research and strong reporting, not from the writer's spouting forth familiar platitudes. Good reporting is as necessary for anniversary stories as it is for all other features. Anniversary stories should be filled with observed detail, accurate and significant information, colorful quotations, and clear explanations. Reading an anniversary story may be the way readers participate in a ritual of recurring events, but that ritual shouldn't be meaningless or simplistic.

Another difficulty concerns the emotional tone of anniversary stories. The anniversary article's tone should correspond to whatever occasion it's commemorating. April Fool's Day stories, for example, usually have a clever and silly tone; Valentine's Day stories a sentimental and romantic tone; Memorial Day stories a solemn and dignified tone. At the same time, when you're conveying the appropriate tone, you must be careful that descriptive writing doesn't run away with the article and pull too many of the reader's emotional strings. Anniversary stories, like human interest stories, work best when they are simple, straightforward, and restrained.

Another ''do'' to remember is to keep the story's language familiar to your readers. Anniversary stories appeal to memory, nostalgia, and a sense of community, and so are most effective if their language is traditional and unpretentious. The story should use words with universal meanings and the common touch.

Since many anniversary stories are given special layout treatment and presented as major stories with attention-getting headlines and large photos or graphics (often on the front page of newspaper lifestyle sections or on covers of magazines), do have some idea of your story's visual potential. Pursue ideas that will result in attractive layouts and write your stories in a way that makes it easy for an editor to envision their presentation on special pages.

SOMETHING FROM NOTHING

Sometimes the pressure to "write something" forces the writer to produce one of two kinds of relatively meaningless anniversary features. The first collects information that is basically unrelated and forces it together into a story, because something must be written to fill an appropriate number of newspaper column inches on a significant day. The lead for an Associated Press story, for example, shows how the article patched together various events to create a Christmas Day story, although the events were unrelated in significance, style, or symbolism:

> The "Cadillac Santa" handed out 500 $10 bills to the homeless in Los Angeles, recently freed American hostages are spending their first Christmas in years with their families, and 27 Haitian children being raised by an Indiana couple became U.S. citizens in a Christmas Eve ceremony.

Another Associated Press story, written to observe the tenth anniversary of the death of actress Natalie Wood, illustrates the second kind of meaningless story, a nonstory contrived from virtually no information, because the reporter must "write something"—anything—in order not to leave an anniversary unobserved. The only new fact in this story is that fresh flowers are left on Natalie Wood's grave every week. Other than that, as this excerpt reveals, the reporter has only *nonquotes* by *nonsources* about what folks around the harbor *won't* say:

> The drowning is often discussed among yacht owners at Doug's Harbor Reef resort at Santa Catalina's isthmus, 25 miles off the Los Angeles Harbor breakwater, said a resort operator who wouldn't give her name.
> "Nobody here on the island has any comment to make," was the terse response from Randy Bombard, whose father runs Doug's Harbor Reef.

The article also includes the assertion of the investigator from the Sheriff's Department that there's *nothing* to the homicide allegations, and citations from a book saying there's *no truth* to rumors about the drowning.

FAMILIAR STRUCTURES AND STYLES

When you are straining for a topic for an anniversary story, or trying to discover a fresh way to write about a recurring event, you may find some inspiration in remembering common feature stories we've already discussed.

A brief factual news feature can be an anniversary story if it is pertinent, of interest to readers, and concerns the holiday. One Associated Press brief published on the day after Thanksgiving, for example, simply brought readers the information that more than 7,000 cooks nationwide had called the Butterball Turkey Talk-Line on Thanksgiving Day to ask questions about cooking their birds.

Another anniversary news feature, published at Christmas in *The Boston Globe,* reported on a study by a British scientist, who claimed that from "astronomical and historical evidence" he was able to give a precise date for the birth of Jesus Christ.

A *Washington Post* news feature reporting a nearby bird-watching event became an anniversary story when the reporter, Robert O'Harrow, Jr., described the activity in a way that reminded readers of the change of seasons:

> The bird slipped above the treetops on the Blue Ridge Mountains faster than the breeze. In a moment Kerrie Kirkpatrick had to tilt her binoculars straight back to figure out just what it was. . . .
>
> Nearly every day since Sept. 1, Kirkpatrick and other suburbanites have gone to the place called Snickers Gap to keep tabs on hawks and other migrating raptors, which pass over the Washington area by the thousands each fall.
>
> There have been golden eagles, bald eagles, harriers and thousands of red-tailed and red-shouldered hawks this fall. The birds have rocketed over 40 mph and drifted in spirals. They have hunted other birds and pestered one another, as hawks sometimes do.

HOLIDAY HELPS

Another familiar story, the how-to, surfaces frequently as an anniversary feature, particularly during the days before family holidays involving food preparation. Numerous articles offer readers help in making family feasts delicious or pleasant, sometimes giving recipes for traditional dishes.

For example, a *Seattle Times* holiday how-to by Larry Brown begins with the typical direct address lead presenting the reader's problem: "When the holiday too-much-to-do and too-little-time-to-do-it stress syndrome strikes, you need some handy antidotes." His article then identifies its expert information as coming from "wit and wisdom gleaned from various cookbooks," and presents pieces of advice in a series of bullets, advising the reader, for example, to stack silverware at the end of the buffet table, so that cutlery doesn't burden guests while they are filling their plates (the source: *The New Basics Cookbook* by Julee Rosso and Sheila Lukins).

You can almost imagine Brown, forced to "write something," leafing through cookbooks on a library's shelves, trying to come up with a feature idea. But the resulting how-to isn't bad; his study of a variety of sources *does* aid readers, because it presents information from research they probably don't have time to do. The resulting tips are helpful—particularly to readers planning holiday get-togethers for the first time.

Other anniversary how-to stories may be less directional, but also help readers deal with anniversary events, advising them on such things as controlling holiday drinking or depression, avoiding family arguments, or coping with painful memories of past holidays.

A Universal Press Syndicate story by Patricia McCormick, for example, gives parents serious information about telling their children the truth about Santa Claus, summarizing for parent-readers the advice of various experts:

> [Bruno] Bettelheim urged parents not to tell children the truth about Santa too soon. Rather, he said, parents should allow such myths to undergo a "slow disintegration" under the child's ever-growing intellect.
>
> This process generally begins around age 6, according to John Condry, professor of human development at Cornell University, who, along with Cynthia Scheibe, a graduate student there, studied the beliefs of 700 children. "Almost all children believe in Santa at 5; very few do by 8," Condry said. . . .
>
> But parents needn't worry too much about the influence of their child's doubting or non-believing peers. "Through age 6, when belief is very strong, a child can seldom be shaken, no matter what other children say," according to Louis Bates Ames, director of the Gesell Institute for Human Development in New Haven, Conn. "They might become a bit suspicious, but they're not going to give up believing."

NOSTALGIA STORIES

Both narratives and color features can be used as anniversary articles, particularly when they strive to develop in readers a feeling of nostalgia for a past event or time. Narratives are particularly useful for recreating a sequence of past events, and color stories are effective for recreating past atmospheres. In both narrative and color anniversary stories, readers experience a feeling not unlike the feeling they would get from looking through an old scrapbook or family photograph album. There's a pleasure in recalling times gone by.

Sometimes color and narrative writing are both emphasized in a single anniversary article, as in the following *New York Times* story written by Ray Robinson on the fiftieth anniversary of the great baseball summer of 1941. (Consider the writer's originality in this story idea: not everyone in the summer of 1991 would conceive of writing a story about 1941 baseball.) Robinson begins his anniversary feature with an anecdote about Joe DiMaggio and spring training, then writes a paragraph stressing the importance of the anniversary:

> DiMaggio's elegant presence and 56-game hitting streak were hardly the only reasons that 1941 merits inclusion in any baseball time capsule. That summer, as the United States edged toward entry into World War II, the game produced a blend of grand-scale heroics from Ted Williams and his .406 batting average, Bob Feller, Lefty Grove, Bucky Walters, Pete Reiser, Tommy Henrich, Whitlow Wyatt, Cecil Travis, Country Slaughter, Johnny Vander Meer, Leo Durocher, and Dixie Walker.

His third paragraph adds color, stimulating readers' nostalgic memories of a time long ago:

> That summer, in the waning days of the Great Depression when more than nine million remained unemployed, baseball seemed to provide a cocoon for many

Americans amid lingering economic woes of the past and Hitler's ominous conquests in Europe. The basic nourishment at ball parks was the nickel hot dog, and, after the game, a full-course dinner at a good restaurant could be eaten for half a dollar. Tickets to the ball park ranged from 50 cents for a perch in the bleachers to $1.10 for general admission to $3 for the best seat in the house.

The article continues narrating its chronology of baseball events of the summer of 1941, with the story's final event the World Series. The story's last paragraphs set the historical context through which readers can appreciate the baseball season's poignancy, whether fans or not:

> Less than two months later, on Dec. 7, the Japanese navy rained bombs down on the Hawaiian island of Oahu. The attack on Pearl Harbor, a place unknown to most Americans, cost 2,280 American lives and wounded more than 1,000.
>
> In recalling that time, the author William Manchester would write: ''It had been a fine, golden autumn, a lovely farewell to those who would lose their youth, and some of them their lives, before leaves turned again in a peace-time fall.''

Sometimes the nostalgic sense of the past is developed through contrasting it with the present: a reader's memory of what happened *then* resonates against his or her sense of how different things are *now*.

Fred Hiatt of the *Washington Post* Foreign Service syndicated an anniversary story about the Nov. 7, 1991, Revolution Day celebrations in Moscow. His then-and-now contrast emphasizes the magnitude of the changes in Russia since the downfall of communism:

> In the past, Revolution Day was hailed as a time to renew one's faith in the inevitable triumph of socialism. In day-care centers, children memorized stories of Grandpa Lenin. A few days before the parade, approved slogans were distributed to workplaces so marchers could prepare appropriate banners. And on the day itself, thousands of tanks and artillery pieces and missile batteries roared through Red Square, solid proof of Soviet might.
>
> But in the last few years, fewer and fewer believed, and the parade turned into an opportunity for leftists and rightists alike to jeer Soviet President Mikhail Gorbachev with a disrespect shocking at the time.
>
> Last year, a confused gunman fired a shot into the air and was wrestled to the Red Square cobblestones. This year, for the first time, the parade simply did not take place.

Hiatt gives a color description of what he sees today—a pathetic contrast to past Revolution Days:

> Nearby, a small crowd of mostly elderly Christian Democrats gathered in front of KGB headquarters to mourn the victims of Stalinism and to celebrate a brief Russian Orthodox Mass. Katya Kotava, 56, listened and cried for the relatives she lost in brutal, frigid labor camps, for her mother who died in Siberian exile, and, she said, for her own 36 years of labor that have left her with nothing but the clothes she was wearing and the boots on her feet.
>
> Across the Moscow River, a few thousand die-hard Communists and Russian nationalists, most of them elderly, gathered to celebrate the Bolshevik Revolution

of 1917, even though Russian President Boris Yeltsin had issued a final ban
Wednesday on all activities of the Communist Party. Democracy, said a worker
from the Hammer and Sickle machine factory, means "the rule of poverty, and of
speculation that now is called 'business.' "

THE HUMAN INTEREST ANGLE

Often anniversary articles are written with a human interest angle; the special
event is presented through one person's, or several persons' viewpoints. George
Esper's Associated Press story on the twentieth anniversary of the May 3
anti-war demonstrations at Kent State University considers the past through
interviews with the families of the students who were killed, and with one
student who survived the shooting but was paralyzed by a bullet wound:

> Dean Kahler has only to look down to remember that day. A rifle bullet made
> him a paraplegic and put him in a wheelchair for life.
> "I know why I'm sitting in it," Kahler said. "I'll never really forget Kent State."
> Kahler, then a 20-year-old freshman from Canton, Ohio, had worked nearly a
> year in a steel mill to help pay for school. When rifle fire crackled over the shouts
> of his fellow students, he fell to the ground to take cover. He felt a sensation like a
> bee sting; it was a bullet ripping into his spinal cord.
> Kahler, a conscientious objector, was the most seriously injured of the nine per-
> sons wounded. He finished school seven years later, then built a career in state
> government, working for the secretary of state and attorney general. He was
> elected an Athens County commissioner in 1984 and re-elected four years later.
> Kahler, divorced in 1984, married a counselor he met in a pub last August. He
> frequently drives the 340-mile round trip to Kent State for sports and alumni
> events. He is a guest lecturer for a regularly offered course that examines the Kent
> State shootings and their aftermath.
> "Kent State is not something I carry around as a burden," he said. "Just be-
> cause I had one bad day at Kent doesn't mean the whole university should be
> condemned. . . . To me what's more important is the county budget . . . and my
> family and the rest of my life."

An Associated Press story, written by Robert M. Andrews and syndicated
on the twentieth anniversary of the death of president John F. Kennedy, artfully
mixes a wide variety of individually remembered incidents to relive the day of
the assassination. The story lets us see the event through people's eyes—both
famous people and not-so-famous people. The article is deliberately chaotic,
jumping from one person's remembered actions and statements to another's; the
chaos recreates the mood of those historic moments. Through the story, young
readers can experience these chaotic moments for the first time; older readers
can relive them through sharing in the memories of other people and recalling
their own personal memories:

> WASHINGTON—The first dreadful flash from Dallas clattered across bell-
> ringing teleprinters in newsrooms across the country at 1:34 p.m., Eastern time.

The news raced to car radios and street-corner transistors, then to television. . . .

Even now, 20 years later, people who have trouble remembering details of a wedding or the birth of a child can recall with remarkable clarity exactly where they were, and what they were doing, when they first heard that John F. Kennedy had been assassinated. . . .

Across the country, shoppers began weeping and praying together in the aisles of department stores. Traffic came to a halt. Courts closed in the middle of hearings. Racetracks shut down, bewildering bettors. The telephone system blacked out in Washington, D.C., under an avalanche of calls.

Richard J. Daley, the tough mayor of Chicago, burst into tears at lunch with associates. NBC anchorman Chet Huntley went on television but was too stunned to speak. . . .

In Chicago, a husky black construction worker on lunch break in a tavern knocked a glass of whiskey from the bar. ''For God's sake,'' he said, and rushed out. A bartender in Harlem, pondering Lyndon B. Johnson as the new president, told a customer: ''Let's see what your cracker president is going to do for you now.''. . .

Housewives came to the door sobbing when postman Fred Tracy of Greenwich, Conn., appeared with their mail. Misthopoulis Georges, a Greek-born barber in New York, said, ''I feel he was a very good boy. I cry.'' . . .

When the *New York Times* hit the streets that night, it contained 22 paid obituary notices lamenting the death of John F. Kennedy.

GRANNIES AND GRAMPS

When you're trying to ''write something'' about an anniversary, often you're advised to ''find a granny''; that is, to find someone in whom other human beings would have an interest, who can describe meaningfully and colorfully what it was like to live through D-Day, freedom marches with Martin Luther King, or the Depression. If this ''granny'' or ''gramps'' creates vivid word pictures, you simply quote her or him extensively, without interruption, so your story creates in readers the feeling they are sitting at the knee of a wise, experienced elder, listening to him or her give a firsthand version of what events were really like.

An example of an anniversary story which includes the personal reminiscence of a ''gramps'' is an article written for *National Geographic* by freelance writer Cameron Thomas on the fiftieth anniversary of the World War II London blitz. Thomas interviewed his old London friends and neighbors; in this excerpt, you can see how he quotes his expressive ''gramps'' without interruption:

> ''I remember that we'd been in the shelter for a long time, and it was very hot and stuffy,'' he recalled as we sat in his garden last year. ''Then the bomb hit the house. First we heard the swish as it came down. You knew it was near if you heard the swish. We heard an explosion, and at the same time the shelter heaved up and down and filled with dust and smoke. We could see flames. Then the house must have collapsed because we got covered in bricks and stuff.

"We tried to get out," he went on, "but the entrance was blocked with bricks and rubble. We started to dig our way out with our hands. A lot of the rubble was too heavy to move, and I thought we were going to die there. After a little while we heard a rescue squad, and we yelled to tell them we were still inside. There was just a space where the house was earlier on that day, and a lot of the other houses had gone too.

"My dad decided to take us to my uncle's. It took us a long time to walk there, and a lot of times we had to find shelter again because the bombs kept coming all night. When we got there, they were all in a street shelter, so we went in too. About four in the morning a bomb hit really close. After the all-clear we went to my uncle's house, but it wasn't there any more. We'd been bombed out twice in the same night."

Len looked up with a rueful smile. "It's a pity we weren't in the rubble business then," he said in his gentle way. "We'd have made a fortune."

SEASONAL BACKGROUNDERS

An anniversary story can also be a backgrounder, explaining a seasonal natural phenomenon, or teaching readers how some physical or biological reality has evolved or operates, such as a summer sunburn's effect on the skin, how Canada geese migrate in the fall, or causes of winter avalanches.

The New York Times syndicated a seasonal backgrounder by Jane E. Brody on the singing of birds. Her story has as its news peg the coming of spring:

> From woods and meadows, yards and city parks, a chorus of avian melodies announce the arrival of spring. But many researchers who study bird songs are staying indoors.

The article includes a wealth of information written in understandable language, informing readers of little-known facts such as these:

> Song birds raised in isolation in the laboratory without having heard their species sing develop an incomplete and abnormal version of the song. . . .
>
> Deaf birds, on the other hand, never come close to singing the right song. . . .
>
> As for the sequence of song learning, the findings show that birds are very much like human children. As fledglings they babble a so-called subsong of nonsense syllables. . . .
>
> Birds can even recognize and remember their neighbors' voices. . . .
>
> If a song the bird knows is transposed up or down an octave, the bird fails to recognize it. . . . In other words, birds respond to absolute pitch (as do only about 5 percent of people) rather than relative pitch.

A seasonal backgrounder can also explain something in nature apparently gone awry, that is, nature being unnatural. For example, a feature by Joel Achenbach of *The Washington Post* explained the failure of leaves to turn colors in the fall of one year. His article teaches readers how the process of seasonal color change in leaves occurs and reports on some of the theories of climatologists regarding global warming and its environmental effects on the natural phenomenon of leaf color change.

EXPLAINING ANNIVERSARIES

Backgrounder stories can also be written to explain the meaning and significance of certain anniversaries, particularly those associated with political or economic events. *The New York Times Magazine,* for example, published a backgrounder by Steven R. Weisman a month before the fiftieth anniversary of the bombing of Pearl Harbor. Weisman's backgrounder analyzed *how* the Japanese were dealing with their memories of Pearl Harbor and *why* their attitudes could have effects on the United States and other Asian countries.

The story helps readers view the American Pearl Harbor anniversary from an unfamiliar perspective, and thus gain a broader understanding of the anniversary:

> The "date which will live in infamy," in President Roosevelt's words, is seen in Japan as a relatively unimportant event. There will be no Pearl Harbor ceremonies in Japan this year. There are none any year. Indeed, only a tiny percentage of the 1.4 million Japanese tourists visiting Hawaii each year bother to go to the Pearl Harbor Memorial. . . .
>
> The dangerous paradox of the war [World War II] for Japanese is that while emotions remain high, so does ignorance. A restless new generation is waiting to assume leadership of the most powerful nation in Asia. Yet in contrast to German textbooks, Japanese textbooks whitewash the war. Some 20 million people died in the Pacific war, and Japan itself lost 2.5 million lives, had 10 million men under arms and forced millions of prisoners into hard labor. But after Emperor Hirohito died in 1989, grainy footage of the Japanese occupation of much of China amazed young television viewers, who had not known about it.

HISTORICAL ORIGINS

If few feature stories can be identified solely as anniversary stories (except by topic), some stories *do* treat holidays and anniversary events in special ways. One of the most common is the backgrounder article that explains the origin of a holiday or an ethnic, national, or religious custom. Historical origin stories reveal how particular events came to be celebrated, or how they came to be celebrated in the way they are. These features may also explain the derivation of different aspects of the celebration, such as why eggs and rabbits are associated with Easter, or jack-o-lanterns with Halloween.

This Associated Press story by John Barbour is typical of the holiday origin story (and was perfect for its December 24th publication). Its narrative lead begins:

> NEW YORK—It was Christmas Eve 1822, and snow lay heavily over old New York, the downtown streets and the farmland that occupied most of the island of Manhattan. Sleigh bells jingled through town, but would not inspire ''Jingle Bells'' for another 35 years.
>
> Clement Clarke Moore, a 43-year-old teacher at an Episcopal seminary, had been at work for weeks with his quill, crafting a secret present for his six children. Now it was done.
>
> Earlier that day Moore rode out in his carriage on Christmas errands with his servant, Patrick, and returned home to his four-story brick farmhouse with the largest turkey he could find in the Washington Market's crowded pens at the tip of the island.
>
> After Christmas Eve dinner, the family retired to the parlor in front of the hearth, with its warming fire. And now Moore unveiled his Christmas gift. His children—Margaret, Charity, Benjamin, Mary, and Clement Jr.—sat at his feet. Infant Emily was in her mother's arms.
>
> He began to read:
> '' 'Twas the night before Christmas, when all through the house
> ''Not a creature was stirring, not even a mouse . . .''
>
> When he finished, ''Happy Christmas to all, and to all a good night,'' there was silence and then exultation. The children prevailed on him to read it again and joined in with lines they remembered. Bedtime interrupted their pleas for a third reading.
>
> But ''A Visit From St. Nicholas'' was born, and with it a vision of Santa Claus, the sainted gift-giver to children that would decorate the American Christmas, its street corners and department stores, its trees and cards for decades to come.

The key to successfully writing a historical origin article is willingness to do in-depth research. You can't simply retell what most people vaguely remember from television specials and book introductions. While the excerpt of the article quoted above gives only the opening paragraphs of Barbour's story, the full article tells much, much more. It details the first publication of the St. Nicholas story (in the Troy, New York, *Sentinel*) and gives the history of the poem's growing popularity, including an explanation of why it took fifteen years for Moore to publicly acknowledge his authorship.

But even the lead of Barbour's article reveals interesting details concerning the historical time connected to the origin of the American Santa Claus: the article notes that Manhattan is mainly farmland, the crowded pens of turkeys are at the tip of the island, and *Jingle Bells* would be published in 1857.

The Associated Press ran a full-length version of ''A Visit From St. Nicholas'' with Barbour's story, so newspaper readers who didn't have a copy at hand, or couldn't afford to buy one, were given a gift, a free copy to enjoy and share on the night before Christmas.

DEBUNKING HISTORY

Another anniversary article reveals the truth about commonly held misconceptions concerning historical anniversary events. Stories that take the bunk or humbug out of history reveal what *really* happened long ago, correcting exaggerations, and perhaps revealing sordid or dull reality rather than pleasant myth.

Scott Thomas' anniversary article debunking history, written for the *Buffalo Magazine of The Buffalo News,* reveals the unpleasant side of Christopher Columbus. Thomas' story begins:

> Christopher Columbus discovered America.
> Christopher Columbus, a brave and true leader of men, made his historic voyage for the glory of God and the queen of Spain.
> Christopher Columbus made a success of himself.
> Lies, lies, lies.
> But they're lies that have become legends, and legends die hard. So generation upon generation of Americans have grown up thinking nice thoughts about the Great Admiral, the Discoverer, the "greatest dead-reckoning navigator of all time." You'll have to forgive the descendants of the people whom Columbus and his henchmen cheated, enslaved and murdered if they beg to differ.

Thomas' article goes on to give many details about the *real* Columbus: the discoverer of America never gave his poor old father any money, he had a mistress, he negotiated with Queen Isabella for a noble title as payment for undertaking his voyage, and his log entry summarizing the new, never-seen-before race of men he found in America, says only, "They ought to be good servants."

It should be added, however, that readers generally don't like to have history debunked when that history is connected to deeply held religious beliefs or significant ethnic or national traditions. Therefore stories that give the "lowdown" about a particular anniversary event usually are written only about historical legends people don't take too seriously; for example, George Washington's cutting down the cherry tree, or Betsy Ross' creation of the flag.

And no matter which commonly held misconception the story corrects, you need to be sure that your writing doesn't have a tone that seems superior to, or mocking of, readers. Readers should share in the fun of learning the truth, not be made to feel stupid because they haven't known it all along.

PARTICIPATORY EXPERIENCE

Another kind of story, the participatory journalism story that we usually think of as related to investigative reporting, can be used in a particular way for holidays and anniversaries.

When done for an anniversary story, the participatory experience involves taking part in a situation or condition that is not permanent, but rather lasts only as long as the holiday or anniversary celebration. The ''investigation'' is done in order to give readers insight into some person's role in the holiday, perhaps to enable readers to more fully appreciate the anniversary event. The idea is to focus on unknown, unsung heroes of anniversary events, on those people whose performances go beyond the ordinary in order to ensure that the rest of us have happy holidays. For example, a feature writer might pose as a mall Santa Claus or a New Year's Eve bartender, to be able to tell readers what those people do to serve the public during these holidays.

The classic participatory experience story, of course, involves two reporters, dressed as Joseph and a very pregnant Mary, who seek ''room at the inn'' by applying to twentieth-century hotels and motels. How people treat them sheds some light on the spirit of Christmas alive today.

The idea of the participatory experience, of course, can be modified so that the writer is not personally experiencing a holiday situation, but observing someone who does play a part in it. Such a day-in-the-life-of story, for example, might have the journalist witnessing a flagmaker's days before the Fourth of July or a candy maker's days before Valentine's Day.

FINDING IDEAS FOR ANNIVERSARY STORIES

Much of the advice given in Chapter 2 about finding ideas for feature stories is also applicable to finding topics for anniversary stories. You need to get up from your desk, go outside, and stop, look, and listen to preparations going on around you for the holiday or anniversary, or to signs of seasonal change. As always, follow your natural curiosity about what you see. Try to consider events from new, unusual perspectives. Consider roles people are playing in connection with an anniversary; think how you could enable readers to understand or share in what they do.

Talk to people in agencies and businesses who sponsor anniversary events, or talk to people who actively work on committees organizing commemorations. Speak also to people who are on museum staffs, who serve on chambers of commerce or fund-raising committees, or to owners of small businesses or restaurants. All of these people may have stories to tell about preparing for and celebrating anniversaries.

Library research can also help you produce good anniversary stories. Look for anniversary stories in publications different from the ones your audience customarily reads, and look through out-of-town publications and very old publications. Use the stories you find for inspiration. Recycle them with new, original treatment. Update them, localize them, or give them a different slant.

If you're a free-lancer (even if you're a staff writer), as a special project, do research on a particular anniversary so you become something of an expert on it. The following year, study another anniversary. Repeat the process each year and fairly soon you'll have considerable knowledge (and material in your notebooks) that can serve you for a long time, helping you generate many stories.

Cultivate sources for your anniversary stories. Throughout the year, as you interview people for other articles, be alert to those you meet who are old enough to have lived through certain events, and interesting enough to tell appealing stories about them. Keep a list of potential ''grannies'' and ''gramps.'' Also, public relations offices of many universities keep lists of scholars willing to be sources of information for media stories. Scan the list to find unusual areas of expertise, particularly in history and the social sciences. These people may help with historical origin stories, or with seeing things from a historical or cross-cultural perspective.

USING CALENDARS

Calendars can suggest story ideas and help you avoid some of the difficulties caused by the forced nature of the anniversary assignment. Construct a personal calendar of anniversary dates and keep adding to it as you discover new anniversaries. Use this ''tickler'' calendar to keep yourself reminded of upcoming anniversary events, to keep you prepared to submit free-lance features well in advance of deadline, or to be one step ahead of your newspaper editor.

Bruce Garrison in *Professional Feature Writing* (Lawrence Erlbaum Associates) says that specialized or theme wall calendars, topical or theme appointment books, and state travel department calendars can bring to your attention less well-known anniversaries, such as Secretary's Day or Earth Day. Try collecting an assortment of such specialty calendars.

Write to travel bureaus or chambers of commerce for their calendars of the upcoming year's events. Acquire almanacs as well; they will give anniversary dates of general interest. And don't forget to include on your calendar local anniversaries and special city and county holidays.

Whether you use a personal calendar or another method of organization to keep special dates and story possibilities at your fingertips, when you consider your anniversary story topics, keep in mind what you are doing with your story. You're marking recurring events in the cycles of your readers' lives. You're helping readers appropriately observe holidays, anniversaries, and seasonal change. You are also, with each individual story you write, participating in a ritual created through the public, written medium of journalism.

EXERCISES

1. What are two or three holidays celebrated in your area that are not observed nationally? How could you write about them so that they are of interest to a national readership?
2. Spend an hour or two substituting for someone who plays a role in a holiday celebration, or who works to make a holiday festive. Write a brief narrative of your experience.

3. Imagine you are planning your first family Thanksgiving feast or Fourth of July picnic. What are three things you would want to know to help you successfully play host at the event?

4. Interview a ''granny'' or ''gramps'' you know about a historic event that happened more than twenty-five years ago. Build a brief story, extensively quoting her or his remembrances.

5. Read the following lead from an anniversary story about the Eastern European tradition of artistically decorating Easter eggs. (The story was published in a weekly neighborhood newspaper.) If you were writing a full-length feature for a national audience about what the lead discusses—the connection between eggs and spring rituals and Easter traditions—what more would you want to know? Or what would you want to know more specifically? Find the answers to your questions, then write a story from what you have learned.

> Many ancient cultures believed the world began as an egg which divided into the various elements of the Earth. The egg was often an integral part of spring rituals. Often, colored eggs were presented as gifts.
>
> So it was hardly unusual that early Christians adopted the egg, long a symbol of the continuation of life, to represent Christ's resurrection from the tomb. To this day, the egg continues to be strongly associated with Easter traditions.
>
> The ancient Egyptians, Greeks, Romans and Persians are known to have colored eggs, but there is no record that egg decorating was practiced in Western Europe prior to the 15th century. Missionaries or knights may have brought them from the Crusades.
>
> Once the practice was introduced, the people of Eastern European communities developed egg decorating into distinct—and often elaborate—forms.

6. Read ''The Resurrection of Richard Hauptmann,'' written by Jay Maeder for the *Daily News Magazine* of the *New York Daily News*. Why is the story appropriate for its Easter Sunday publication? How does the story make meaningful to its 1988 readers the anniversary of events that happened fifty-two years before its publication? (The story won first place in the 1988 New York State Associated Press Awards, Features Division, and third place in the 1989 Sunday Best competition of the Sunday Magazine Editors Association.)

THE RESURRECTION OF RICHARD HAUPTMANN

By Jay Maeder

Daily News Magazine of the New York Daily News, *April 3, 1988*

April 3, 1936. 8:45 P.M. Trenton.

"I believe in one God the Father Almighty," the ministers murmured.

The condemned man said nothing. He didn't look at the churchmen. He didn't look at the witnesses. He didn't look at the warden. Wordlessly, he walked to the chair and seated himself.

"Maker of heaven and earth."

The black mask was slipped over his face, the leather cap fitted over his shaved skull, the straps buckled, the electrodes clamped. He said nothing.

"And of all things visible and invisible."

Briefly the lights dimmed.

"And in One Lord Jesus Christ."

In her hotel room, Anna Hauptmann tore herself from the arms of her friends and fell screaming to the floor. *Ach, Gott. Ach, mein Richard.* She screamed for most of the night. *Ach, Gott, why did You do this to him?*

On the street below, the extras were selling briskly. "Bruno Is Dead!" the newsboys sang.

Bruno the Hun. Bruno the baby killer. He was the most despised man on earth, the beast who had stolen Col. Charles Lindbergh's laughing infant son one storm-stricken night in March 1932 and with his dirty foreigner's hands had crushed out the little life. Outside the old Flemington, N.J., courthouse where the Crime of the Century was tried five decades ago, there roared thousands of good citizens maddened by the scent of his blood. *Kill him!* they screamed. *Kill Bruno the Hun!*

But his name was Richard, and no one but his prosecutors had ever called him Bruno in his life, and 52 springtimes after he went stonily into the hereafter he is—like Leo Frank, like Sacco and Vanzetti—increasingly a nettle in the American memory as more and more freshly uncovered evidence casts darker and darker shadows over the confluences that sent him to his grave.

And he does not perish from the earth.

"Richard didn't do it. Period." This is the assertion of the man who would redeem the name of Richard Hauptmann, criminal attorney Robert R. Bryan of San Francisco, who some weeks ago came back to Trenton to file another massive amendment to his massive civil action in re the Wrongful Death of Bruno Richard Hauptmann on behalf of his client, the widow Anna Hauptmann of Yeadon, Pa., formerly of 1279 222d St., the Bronx, N.Y.

She is nearly 90, a frail and tiny woman clawing at the time, twisting anxiously at Richard's silver wedding band on her finger. *The lies. The lies. In the court I want to scream, I want to cry out you are lying and you know you are lying. How can they lie like this, every one?* Anna Hauptmann closes her eyes and there it is all over again, the bewildering bright lights and the shoving newsreel crews and the interminable parades of witnesses attesting to things she knew could not be so because she knew that on the night of March 1, 1932, her husband was at home with her and it was as simple as that.

The Crime of the Century. *No. No.* The Trial of the Century. *No.* The Story of the Century. *Ach, Richard, Richard.* "All that I want is to go before a jury," says lawyer Bryan. "This should be laid to rest. A lot of wrong occurred here." Bryan's suit has been dismissed on technicalities several times over seven years; it has never yet been heard on its merits, and he always refiles, with ever more attachments and addenda, always alleging new proofs of the state conspiracy to convict hapless Richard Hauptmann at any cost: Most recently he has uncovered thousands of papers in the private files of the late New Jersey Gov. Harold Hoffman—who deeply distrusted his own police officers and was convinced Hauptmann was innocent—and on the basis of these papers, Bryan alleges specific instances of witness tampering and fraud by former New Jersey Attorney General David Wilentz and former officers of the New Jersey State Police.

Bryan has turned up a great deal more documentation and is now working to get it before a court of law, hard evidence the Hauptmann jurors never saw:

Damningly, through what at the time was a dazzlingly sophisticated piece of forensic comparison, it was established that one plank of the ladder the baby-snatcher had used to climb to the child's window had come from the floor of the attic of Hauptmann's home. This is so. It had. What the jury didn't know—what nobody but New Jersey authorities knew for years thereafter, until the confidential documents came to light—was that Anna Hauptmann had given up the house to a new tenant shortly after her husband's arrest. That tenant was Lt. Lewis Bornmann of the New Jersey State Police, and it was he who reported the discovery of a missing plank in the attic floor—after, according to unsealed police files in Bryan's possession, the attic had already been searched, nine times, by at least 37 police officers, who found nothing amiss with the floor.

Jurors were told by a handwriting expert that Hauptmann certainly wrote the series of ransom notes that stunned the nation in March and April 1932; they weren't told that, until shortly before the trial, he had just as emphatically insisted Hauptmann had not.

Jurors were told that no fingerprints were lifted from the first ransom note found in Baby Lindy's bedroom, that the kidnapper had craftily worn gloves—but they never saw U.S. Division of Investigation Laboratory report No. 1948, dated Sept. 22, 1934, which flatly states that prints were in fact taken and that they demonstrably did not belong to Richard Hauptmann. "That's how brazen this thing was," snaps Bryan. "They knew from the beginning they had the wrong man."

Even given the hysteria of the time, Bryan insists, "Richard would have gone home on evidence like this. This case is a defense attorney's dream." Perhaps, and perhaps not. A man like Bruno the Hun—an illegal immigrant, a fugitive ex-convict, a hard-eyed workingman of stumbling English and a brusque Germanic demeanor—did not stir public sympathies.

It will be later this year before the District Court even considers hearing Bryan's most recent trial-irregularity charges. He has grown accustomed to lengthy waits; his suit is scarcely a popular one in New Jersey, whose current chief justice is prosecutor Wilentz's son. Realistically, he concedes the possibility that Anna Hauptmann will not live to see her husband's name cleared. "This is all that's been keeping her alive, but she's been disappointed many times," he says softly. "Mrs. Hauptmann doesn't have a lot of time left."

In Yeadon, Pa., it is Easter Sunday, and the widow Hauptmann is twisting Richard's ring on her finger, and she is closing her eyes, and it is the same thing again and again: *No. No. No.*

Annie, he said, don't worry, Annie, the truth will be known, I am in a terrible place, but soon I will be home with you. It is not the end, Annie, someday I go home with you and we will continue.

He was a chubby blond baby, an uncommonly pretty child, not quite 2 years old, first-born son of the nation's foremost conqueror, the little living symbol of everything that was good and golden and bountiful about America. His father heard the crack in the night as he read in his study. For an instant, he thought a tree had snapped in the storm.

In a moment the household stirred. Upstairs the little crib was empty. "Anne, they have stolen our baby," Lindbergh cried to his horrified wife.

The case was the ghastliest of circuses from the beginning. Jailed Chicago crimelord Al Capone immediately sent out intimations that he could find the child in exchange for his freedom.

A prominent Virginia shipbuilder named John Hughes Curtis announced himself to be the kidnap gang's go-between. So did Bronx schoolmaster John F. Condon, an eccentric who took to communicating with the gang in code in the classifieds of the Bronx Home News.

The frantic Lindbergh, the extremely careful man who had weighed out his trans-Atlantic fuel to the ounce, pinned most of his hopes on "Jafsie" Condon, but still elected to deal with practically everyone who approached him, including a bizarre collection of spiritualists who shut fast their eyes and called forth visions of the baby's whereabouts.

Six weeks later, the body of a child was found in the Sourland Mountains' forlorn spring leaves less than a mile from the Lindbergh's Hopewell home. The flier and his son's nursemaid made their grim identifications on the basis of cursory physical inspections. There was no autopsy. There could be no fingerprinting. The little corpse had no hands.

Shortly after that, Lindbergh's butler, Oliver Whately, suddenly died—of peritonitis, it was said.

And shortly after that, Violet Sharpe, a serving girl in the employ of Anne Morrow Lindbergh's mother in nearby Engleswood, swallowed poison.

Later it began to appear that both Whately and Sharpe seemed to be linked to a Harlem spiritualist group whose leader, one Peter Piritella, had been a marginal figure very early in the investigation. Later still, it began to appear that John F. Condon may also have been linked to the same group. The connections were never firmly fixed. Richard Hauptmann was already tried and convicted and executed in any event, and the case was closed.

In recent years at least two men have publicly claimed to have been the real Lindbergh Baby, the handless corpse in the woods having been a ringer. One of them says he was raised by the Capone gang. A related yarn holds that Lindbergh's noisy pro-Nazism of the 1930s was a direct result of his son's hostage status. Another theory somewhat less than gallantly avers that Lindbergh masterminded the snatch himself.

It is convenient to say that no one will ever know the truth. But that is not necessarily so.

"The fingerprints are real," says lawyer Bryan. "Someday they're going to be identified."

Two and a half years after the Lindbergh Baby evaporated, Richard Hauptmann, whose fingerprints the ransom-note prints were not, was charged with the crime. Police called him Bruno. As long as he lived, he was never Richard again.

Beyond the fact that the single alibi witness attesting to his whereabouts on the night of March 1, 1932, was his wife, who kept insisting that the two of them had spent a quiet evening at home—this she remembered, or course, because the next day's newspapers had reported Baby Lindy's kidnapping, a colossal news event that served to fix the previous evening in her memory—Bruno Richard Hauptmann was confronted with not entirely inconsiderable circumstantial evidence against him as he went spectacularly on trial for his life in January 1935. He had been arrested after buying gasoline with marked Lindbergh ransom money, and police had thereupon found nearly $15,000 in identifiable currency hidden in his garage. His explanation was howled at from coast to coast: His sometime business partner Isidor Fisch, he said, had stored some boxes in his closet in late 1933, then sailed for Germany, then died there. Later he found money in the boxes; Fisch had owed him money; he kept the windfall and hid it, without telling his wife, in order to someday surprise her. "Why should I make my wife excited?" the simple German carpenter asked on the stand, puzzled that such an everyday decision should be in question.

"It had to be a secretive fellow!" Wilentz thundered to the jury. "It had to be a fellow who wouldn't tell his wife about money, who would conceal the truth from her . . . type of man that would hold up women at the point of a gun, women wheeling baby carriages!"

It is true that Bruno the Hun was a thief, a man who had once robbed a woman pushing a baby carriage on the street. Nobody explained to the jurors that in broken postwar Germany, every *hausfrau* trundled a pram, that the woman he had robbed had no baby in the carriage, only groceries.

Ja, he stole a loaf of bread. That is the kind of criminal was my Richard. Hauptmann had slipped out of Kamenz in 1923, bread thief and jailbreaker, and he had stowed away on a liner to New York. The young girl Anna Schoeffler processed through Ellis Island one year later, found work in a bakery, mingled with the close-knit emigre community. *I met a woman, I could speak German with her, Richard was there one day when I go up, she had told me about a young man who was living there with. Ach, he was so nice. And he walked me to the subway.*

Oh, and the summer came. And my girlfriend asked me have I ever gone to Coney Island, and she told me all about. I said, oh, I would like that. Oh, you never saw anything like that. And we were walking there and she said oh look who's here. And Richard is sitting in the sand. More than 60 years later she still blushes. *Now isn't that something.*

They were married in October 1925. *We would go for walks, and one day he had to tell me something, about what he had done in Germany, that he was in jail there. I wanted to work, he said, there was no work, Annie, I has holes in my shoes. He was ashamed, he said how can you tell this to your mother. I said this is behind, let us never talk about it again, we are going to be married.*

Oh, he worked so hard. He would come home and his shoulders were bleeding from carrying beams to those high buildings. We did not go out to big parties. We saved our money, so we have something to get older. We never wanted big things. I will buy you a nice house, Annie, he said, and we will have a garden and a few children.

Yes, I see him working in the garage, and I say, oh, I'm going to peek in. And then I say no, he is making a surprise for me, I will spoil everything.

"Let me ask you," Wilentz snarled, stabbing at Bruno the Hun with a finger, "when you found $14,000 or more in gold, did you say anything, did you holler out, Anna, look what I found?"

"No, I did not," the defendant mumbled.

"Didn't she work and slave in a bakery and bring to you her earnings and her savings?"

"That has got nothing to do with them $14,000 at all," Richard Hauptmann said indignantly.

"Didn't she do that? Please answer."

The prisoner looked at the floor. "Yes."

Oh, it looked so bad. The people, yes, I put myself in their places. Suppose I hear this, suppose I read this in the newspaper, you see, and I know nothing else but this. What am I to think?

"That's the type of fellow!" Wilentz declared. "Public Enemy No. 1 of this world . . . Bruno Richard Hauptmann!"

My neighbor said to me, didn't your husband go to work today, I hear somebody talking upstairs. I said please hold the baby.

I went upstairs and there is Richard and there is my shoes and everything was thrown around, I said oh my God what is this. Take that woman out of here, they said.

I had no idea, to me it was just. . . . I thought there had been an accident, maybe there is somebody hurt. I thought maybe somebody find out about his hunting rifle, Richard came to this country illegal, he wasn't supposed to have rifle, I think if he had only listened to me this would not happen. The men are talking about the Lindy kidnapping, Richard did this, oh my God, there is money in our garage. All I hear them say, oh, he's going to burn for this, he's going to burn.

I said no no no, at the police station. I said I want to see my husband, I want to see what this is all about. Richard is . . . and Richard is all black and blue, and he is looking at me. Annie, he says, the snake plant, Annie, you said Richard someday you must put it in a bigger pot, the roots are coming out . . . I spilled some soil on the floor, Annie, and I wanted to clean it, I go to the closet for the broom and, Annie, there is Isidor's box. Annie, do you know what I find in Isidor's box?

Isidor Fisch's role in the Lindbergh case has been a matter of much imaginative speculation for many years. Recurring scenarios have put him alive and well in South America, both with and without the baby in tow. Some more moderate theorists believe that petty wheeler-dealer Fisch merely bought hot ransom money off the street; others remember that late in the 1930s, the inquiry into Peter Piritella's spiritualist church turned up another name alongside those of Whately and Sharpe and Condon. That connection was never firmly fixed either, but the name was Isidor Fisch.

What if Fisch had come back, he wants his packages, how different it would be. . . . What if Richard had never met him?

Scratch one lurid theory, find another. It is Easter Sunday today in Yeadon, Pa., and none of the lurid theories makes any difference at all to the widow Anna Hauptmann, formerly of the Bronx, N.Y., who remembers only that on this day 52 springtimes ago, her husband, Richard, walked wordlessly to the electric chair in the New Jersey State Prison, looking like a man already dead. He had seen enough fabricated evidence, he said, to convince him that nothing would now save his life. "Up to the present day," he had earlier written Gov. Harold Hoffman, "I have no idea where the Lindbergh house in Hopewell is located."

It does happen. Yes, it does happen. Let it be a warning, what they did to my husband.

It cannot be the end, it will not be the end, I ask God why did You let it happen and I have no answer. I ask the priest why did God let Richard die and he has no answer. Mrs. Hauptmann, he says, we must not ask God these questions.

The pity I feel for the people who do this thing. Ach, they stoop so low. How must they feel thinking, ach, I was the one who sent that man to his death. Because they know. They know. They all have to die, and with all their money and with all their titles they will go the same way, and when their hour comes, they will be afraid.

I am not afraid.

PART

The Publication Process

16

Markets
Considering Where Features Flourish

If you become a newspaper staff writer, you probably won't need to worry too much about where your feature articles will be published. For the most part your job will be to consult with your editor about article possibilities and to write the stories assigned to you. On the other hand, if you become a free-lance writer (or if you decide to do free-lance writing on a part-time basis), you will need to have some sense of the market for feature stories, of where feature stories flourish.

Studying the markets where features frequently appear will help you gain a definite idea of which kinds of features are popular and in what kinds of publications. You'll also gain a clearer sense of the different purposes for which features are written, as well as a clearer picture of the different audiences that might be judging your writing.

The general notion of the process of free-lance feature writing is that the writer comes up with the initial story idea, the seed sprouts, the story grows, and *then* the writer worries about where the story will be published. A better process, however, would be for you to discover where the soil is fertile before you let your ideas germinate. See which publications buy a good many free-lance articles, and which deal with subjects that interest you. Analyze potential publications to see who reads them and why. *Then,* when you know for whom you may be writing, begin brainstorming.

After you're a big success at feature writing, perhaps you will be able to afford the luxury of following an idea any old place it leads you, without a care for who will publish the final written product. But as a beginner, you're better off studying markets so that your story ideas have a reasonable chance of being accepted by editors—and of being well-received by readers.

DAILY NEWSPAPERS

Daily newspapers can be a good starting market for free-lance writers, although large metropolitan papers are less likely to publish free-lance work than are small-town newspapers. Most of the time newspaper feature writing is done by regular staff members, but daily newspapers have a greater "news hole" (space left after advertising fills the pages) to fill than do weekly newspapers or monthly magazines; editors may turn to free-lance feature writers to help fill the hole. Then, too, during summer vacation time and holidays, editors may be short-handed, and thus more willing to publish free-lance writing. Also, if you have a particular specialty or area of expertise, or live in a hard-to-reach geographic location, you could be a valuable, if occasional, free-lance resource for an editor to call upon.

Newspapers often enlarge their daily lifestyle sections around holidays, adding pages for special anniversary stories, which may be written by free-lancers. And newspaper Sunday supplement sections concerning travel, fashion, and entertainment also offer free-lance opportunities. Many newspapers publish separate Sunday magazines; these magazines are generally more positive about using free-lance work than are the daily newspapers associated with them. For example, the *Washington Post Magazine* and the *Boston Globe Magazine* are both nearly 50 percent free-lance written.

Newspaper payment for free-lance articles is not generally high, but the low pay is to some extent compensated for by the "payment" of being published in a reputable publication. A clipping you earn from a daily newspaper, especially from a paper with a large metropolitan circulation, is impressive.

Newspaper magazine features are frequently published with pictures or art, so effective photographs or graphic material accompanying submissions may help sell the story.

To identify newspapers publishing in your area or in any geographic area you feel might be receptive to one of your articles, consult the *Editor and Publisher International Yearbook,* called "the encyclopedia of the newspaper industry." This annual yearbook lists names, addresses, corporate offices, and some editorial staff of U.S. newspapers, both dailies and weeklies, and of syndicates.

WEEKLY AND SPECIAL INTEREST NEWSPAPERS

Smaller suburban and rural newspapers, special interest newspapers, and so-called "alternative" newspapers (those taking positions outside the political or social mainstream), which publish on a weekly rather than daily basis, are usually friendly markets for beginning feature writers. Such papers often have more limited budgets for full-time reporters and can frequently be short-handed. They may welcome well-written submissions that save their reporters' time.

Weekly newspapers and special interest publications generally pay very poorly, but they offer exposure and a chance to gain publishing experience. Writing for them can also help discipline your ability to narrow a story's focus to suit a particular audience.

Alternative newspapers have a reputation for being more willing to take risks in story style than conventional daily newspapers. Their sense of experimentation originates in their striving to be different: if they're just like standard newspapers there would be no reason for anyone to buy them. So if an idea for an article seems a bit adventurous (not to mention anti-establishment), you might find that alternative papers offer a favorable market. *Alternative Press Annual* (Temple University Press) gives selections from alternative newspapers, and the *Directory of Small Magazine Editors and Publishers* (Dustbook) gives names and addresses.

CONSUMER MAGAZINES

When people think of magazines, they tend to think of large national consumer publications: *Life, Time, Seventeen, Sports Illustrated, Ladies' Home Journal, Esquire, The Atlantic Monthly, Money.* Clearly, if your work is published in these magazines you have achieved first rank as a magazine article writer, just as you have achieved first rank if your features are published in the *Los Angeles Times, The Washington Post, The New York Times, The Wall Street Journal,* or *The Philadelphia Inquirer.*

Magazines with enormous national circulations, however, are typically difficult markets for writers who are not well-established. As a beginner, keep in mind that features flourish equally well in large- and small-circulation magazines. Both need stories, but smaller, special interest publications may be more receptive to submissions of free-lancers who are starting their careers.

WRITER'S MARKET

Whether you consider large- or small-circulation magazines, you will find that the best publication resource for considering free-lance markets is *Writer's Market.* Published annually by Writer's Digest Books, *Writer's Market* can be purchased in most bookstores and found in library reference sections. It lists American and Canadian book publishers, small presses, consumer magazines, trade journals, syndicates, greeting card publishers, and script-writing markets. For free-lance writers, the sections of the book devoted to consumer magazines, trade journals, and syndicates are the most helpful.

Writer's Market has entries for both large-circulation and small-circulation magazines; they are listed together in one section titled "consumer publications," which is then subdivided into specific units identified by headings that describe a publication's content or readers. *Life, Time,* and *The New*

Yorker, for example, are listed under "general interest," *Esquire* under "men's," *Ladies' Home Journal* under "women's," *Seventeen* under "teen and young adult," *Sports Illustrated* under "sports," and *Money* under "business and finance."

Entries in each section are full of helpful information: they may tell you the percentage of articles in the magazine that are free-lance written, how long it takes the magazine to publish an article after it is accepted, the kind of articles the magazine is looking for, and how much it is willing to pay. Entries will also tell you how to submit your work and to whom to submit it—and a host of other things as well.

Some well-known magazines are not listed in the *Writer's Market,* usually because they did not supply that publication with information. Sometimes their names and addresses are listed, but the entry contains a statement that the magazine requested not to be included in the book. A magazine's omission in *Writer's Market* or a statement that it does not wish to be listed means it is not interested in receiving submissions from free-lance writers (and that you'll be wasting your time if you send them anything). Of the major magazines we just mentioned, *Time, Sports Illustrated,* and *Money* have entries in the 1993 *Writer's Market* that give only their addresses and the statement that they did not want to be listed.

Esquire's entry, on the other hand, indicates it is 99 percent free-lance written. It adds, however, that the magazine depends " 'chiefly on solicited contributions' " and stories from literary agents. *The New Yorker*'s entry doesn't indicate whether it is interested in free-lance work and says, "Long pieces are usually staff-written"; *Life*'s entry says that it is only 10 percent free-lance written and "prefers work with published/established writers."

After reading such entires, you would no doubt consider some of the *other* publications we mentioned as better markets for your free-lance submissions. *Ladies' Home Journal,* for example, indicates it is 50 percent free-lance written and pays average fees of $1,000 to $3,500 for certain articles. *Seventeen*'s entry says it is 80 percent free-lance written, will work with "a small number of new/unpublished writers each year," and pays $650 to $1,500 for a nonfiction article.

If, however, you're willing to consider writing for a magazine with a circulation of 20,000 rather than the 1.9 million circulation of *Seventeen,* you will also find in *Writer's Market* an abundance of entries for special interest magazines. For example, in the "health and fitness" section, *Accent on Living* (for disabled persons and rehabilitation professionals) indicates that it is 75 percent free-lance written, "eager to work with new/unpublished writers" and interested in publishing how-to and interview articles, as well as articles about vacations, places to go, sports, self improvement, and personal adjustment if the stories are all—"related to physically handicapped persons." The pay is 10 cents a published word, with stories averaging 250 to 1,000 words.

Or, if you like history, you could try an article for *True West:* circulation 30,000, 100 percent free-lance written, buys about 150 manuscripts a year, pays 3 cents to 6 cents a word, and wants reliable research on historical topics.

Not every special interest magazine or smaller publication will be a good match for your interests and expertise, but it's worth your while to skim through all the entries in the *Writer's Market* as you begin your free-lance efforts. It will give you a good idea where features flourish and help you match yourself to the particular markets in which you can reasonably hope to succeed.

TRADE JOURNALS

The *Writer's Market* includes a second large section of magazine entries titled "trade journals." Trade journals are magazines written for readers in a particular occupation or industry. They are, in other words, special interest magazines, but for an interest related to the reader's way of earning a living. Trade journals, like most special interest magazines, tend to have smaller circulations. Writing for them may seem less glamorous, but as *Writer's Market* argues, in terms of successful free-lance writing, the market deserves to be considered:

> Perhaps because they are often overlooked, trade journals offer writers more security. They tend to be more stable markets, not bought and sold as much, and continue to publish after achieving an acceptable level of success in their niche. Payment is rarely as high as $1 per word, but it is also rarely less than 10 cents a word. Also, trade journals are often actively seeking freelancers to add to their stables of regularly contributing writers.
>
> Consequently, trade journals do not deserve a second-choice status among writers. Sure, maybe our non-writing friends will not be as greatly impressed by a clip from a trade journal. A professional writer, however, will recognize it for what it is: a published article that earns income and builds credentials. The stability, rate of pay and opportunity for regular contribution offered by trade journals make them a market too good to be overlooked.

Trade journal feature articles are usually more technical than articles for general consumer magazines. Informative sources and factual information are important to a story's worth. Readers of trade journals want lots of material packed in shorter articles; they don't want just a rehash of conventional wisdom.

You're especially attractive as a writer to editors of trade journals if you have expertise or experience in their particular fields. If you don't have this expertise, however, you can still be attractive if you are willing to do solid research and to contact many sources. Don't underestimate your writing ability as a valuable commodity to trade journal editors: many people know their fields of work, but can't write about them. If you can take their knowledge and translate it into your feature—a feature that can be helpful to a large number of working people—you've performed a significant service. Editors are willing to buy that service because it sells magazines.

The magazine HOW (subtitled ''The Bottomline Design Magazine'') is a good example of a trade journal. Its entry in *Writer's Market* indicates it has a circulation of 35,000, is 75 percent free-lance written, pays $250 to $600 for a nonfiction article, and is interested in interviews, profiles, and articles on how to run a profitable studio and new products. The magazine's statement of tips for interested writers encourages them to show that they can relate the magazine's step-by-step approach in an '' 'interesting, concise manner,' '' that they have studied the subject, have an awareness of detail and can '' 'go beyond' '' asking questions that everyone else has already asked.

SYNDICATES

Many features are marketed by syndicates such as King Features Syndicate, Inc., and the Los Angeles Times Syndicate. Syndicates act as agents for free-lance writers, paying them a fee or splitting commissions with them. Syndicates are regarded as a difficult market for beginning free-lancers; syndicates generally prefer to syndicate the work of established writers. If, however, you live in, or happen to be at, an unusual or remote geographic location when something happens, or if you have a connection to a person no one else can interview, you might be able to sell a story to a syndicate. You will probably write for the syndicate on what is called a ''one-time basis''; syndicates are not likely to have permanent contracts with writers who don't already have numerous clippings of published articles.

Nonetheless, there are syndicates that seem to have a favorable attitude toward buying stories by free-lance writers. For example, American News Features Syndicate, according to *Writer's Market,* syndicates one-shot free-lance features to newspapers, paying $35 to $200 for story ideas, and up to $400 for a 1,000-word article. The syndicate advises free-lancers to forget about ideas that have already been written about in major national publications, but tells writers if they have an idea about something that happened locally or has been written about only in local publications, then they '' 'have a real shot,' '' at having an article accepted.

In its *Writer's Market* entries, American Newspaper Syndicate indicates that 50 percent of its articles are written on a one-time basis; Allied Features Syndicate and Continental Features both claim to be 30 percent written by writers on a one-time basis. The *Editor and Publisher Syndicate Directory* lists syndicates and contact names, and *Writer's Market* devotes a section to syndicates, with entries similar to entries for magazines and trade journals.

PUBLIC RELATIONS PUBLICATIONS

We couldn't conclude our consideration of where features flourish without mentioning that features appear in a wide variety of public relations publications.

Internal publications (those going to personnel within an organization) and external publications (those representing the organization to outside audiences) both include a wide variety of features. Because public relations newsletters and newspapers publish infrequently, even their news is often presented in feature style or with feature additions to make it more appealing and readable.

Universities, hospitals, arts organizations, charities, and large businesses all produce public relations publications which use features to tell their stories to the world, to tell what the organizations do and what services they provide. These organizations also produce internal publications which attempt to make employees feel better about the organization and themselves.

Public relations publications are usually staff-written and so are not an especially good market for free-lance submissions. In fact, at times public relations practitioners are competing with free-lancers for outside markets. For example, a university public affairs writer may be attempting to place a feature article about a new college research program in the same newspaper Sunday magazine that a free-lancer is hoping will buy a travel article on holidays in Aruba.

On the other hand, some publications you would expect to be off-limits to free-lancers are not: the magazine *Modern Maturity,* which is sent by the American Association of Retired Persons to its members, is, according to *Writer's Market,* 50 percent free-lance written. *USAir Magazine,* which USAir distributes to its passengers, is 95 percent free-lance written.

LOOK AROUND YOU

The point to be made, then, is that features flourish *everywhere.* Look around you, and you'll find a feature—whether it is in the metropolitan newspaper delivered to your door, the neighborhood weekly, public relations newsletter in the mail, the consumer magazine you pick up at the doctor's office, the special interest magazine you see at the mall hobby and craft show, or the professional trade journal you receive where you work. The large number of features currently published can, in fact, be almost overwhelming. It's not so much a question of whether there are any opportunities for you to publish your stories, as it is a question of what market opportunities you should explore first, what opportunities best suit your ability to report and write.

While generally this chapter has advocated starting with easier markets, there are, of course, two schools of thought about where to begin submitting your work. Some people believe you might as well start at the top and work down—''who knows what might happen,'' ''you never know until you try,'' ''you might strike it rich,'' and so forth. Other people believe you should start where you can be successful—''begin publishing where you know your work will be welcome,'' ''don't program yourself for rejection and failure,'' ''start small and gain experience,'' and so forth.

Which approach you embrace is really up to you—up to your temperament and your ability to handle rejection, and to the demands of your pocketbook and your ability to wait a long time for a paycheck.

But whichever procedure you choose, a major mistake is to waste valuable time. If you're going to fight the odds, at least improve them by studying thoroughly whatever market you choose, so you're aiming at a reasonably high goal, not a ridiculously inappropriate one. Know what sells, what's wanted and needed, and what suits readers' needs and interests, so you know how to shape your story to fit the market you seek.

ANALYZING PUBLICATIONS

Looking over the general market, perusing the *Writer's Market,* examining features published in a particular magazine or newspaper will all help you understand whether the feature you want to write has a chance for publication. But an additional way to consider feature markets is to analyze prospective publications carefully, studying not only their feature articles, but also other aspects of their publication.

For example, study the publication's advertising. What does it tell you about who buys it? After looking at the ads, what would you guess the age, sex, educational level, and income of its readers are? Can you speculate about the money and time they have to spend? About their values, their sense of family? Their commitment to work, friends, or community?

Or consider the staff organization of the publication as revealed in its masthead (and be sure it's a *current* masthead; magazine staff organizations change frequently). Are most of the top editors women or men, or are both sexes represented fairly equally? Is the magazine or newspaper published in Manhattan or Iowa? Are there lots of staff writers or only a few?

Or study the method of article presentation. How are articles laid out? Do they fill one page or several pages? Are stories jumped to later pages? What kinds of titles or headlines announce their contents? Is headline typography conventional or sensational? Do stories have bylines? Do stories have many accompanying photographs or graphics? Are they presented with lots of color?

Finally, consider editorial content generally. What styles of writing are in evidence? What tone do most of the writers take? What types of leads begin stories? What length are most of the stories? Does the publication seem to have favorite themes or subjects that appear over and over? Are there any topics that seem definitely taboo? Is there a clear political or social slant to the publication? Can you tell what values the editors believe in, or what values they believe their readers believe in?

In seeking to discover the identity of a publication and what kinds of stories a magazine wants and needs, you can also send for its guidelines for writers, enclosing with your request a self-addressed stamped envelope and a small payment fee, if such a fee is requested (check *Writer's Market)*. Guidelines for writers make specific and clear statements about a publication's editorial policy: they indicate what its editors want to publish.

The initial image you have of a magazine may make it seem a favorable market, but a close analysis may encourage you to reconsider and search for a more suitable publication, or your analysis may simply confirm your sense of the magazine's suitability for your feature.

Even if you decide against submitting to a particular publication, your time analyzing it is seldom wasted. Months later, you may find that all you've learned comes to mind when you're trying to think of a market for another story. In addition, each understanding you gain of a specific magazine, newspaper, or other publication contributes to your general intelligence about the publishing industry—intelligence that can serve you well in many ways.

It should be added that you need to *regularly* consider where features flourish. For example, as you begin writing free-lance articles, you should examine various places where feature stories are published. Then, after you've done some free-lance publication, you should examine the markets again. At that time you'll have a better awareness of subtle differences in articles, and you'll see more clearly why a particular article suits the style of a particular publication.

Even after that, keep surveying the markets for feature articles. You'll not only continue to discover where the fertile soil for your stories lies, but you also may experience some good cross-fertilization. Seeing what others are writing and reading, considering where other writers are publishing, discovering new publications with new audiences—all can enliven your own sense of what's possible for you to accomplish. The stimulation can encourage the growth of a hardy, abundant crop of new features.

EXERCISES

1.   a. Make a list of the stories in your local newspaper on a particular day. Then make a list of the features you find for the same day in a large metropolitan paper in your section of the country, a paper such as *The Boston Globe, Seattle Times, Miami Herald,* or *Cleveland Plain Dealer.* What kinds of stories do *both* newspapers have? Do you find any differences in the kinds of stories they publish? What might have caused any differences you find?

   b. If there is a regional magazine or a newspaper's magazine published near you, compare and contrast its presentation of material to a similar publication from another section of the country.

2. Find an entry in *Writer's Market* for a magazine you think would be interested in publishing a how-to article on the purchasing and care of fine pearls, or of antique automobiles, or of cross-country skis. Then summarize what you have learned from the entry and estimate your chances of having an article accepted. How might you shape and focus your article for submission to the magazine you have chosen?

3. Identify five special interest magazines you believe would be most receptive to publishing articles on subjects of interest to college students. What might the subjects of some of those articles be?

4. Using the questions in the ''analyzing publications'' section of this chapter, analyze a magazine found in the *Writer's Market* consumer magazine section under the category of ''men's'' or ''women's.'' Describe what you think the magazine's typical reader is like.

17

Query Letters
Offering Ideas to Editors

After you have studied feature story markets, come up with a feature article idea, and finished preliminary research on the topic, you need to decide how you want to handle the article's submission to a publication's editor. You have three choices: you can write a query letter at this time, suggesting your article idea to the editor; you can keep working on the story, sending a more detailed query letter, article proposal, or memo to the editor when ideas and research are more developed; or you can wait still longer and delay submission until you're ready to send a completed manuscript.

TO QUERY OR NOT TO QUERY

When deciding whether and when to query, your first consideration is the prospective publication's expectations of free-lance writers. If the magazine's *Writer's Market* entry indicates that its editors prefer query letters rather than the submission of finished manuscripts, your decision is made for you: send the query. You won't go far with your feature story if you fail to follow the guidelines for submission outlined in the *Writer's Market,* or for that matter, in any guidelines for writers issued by the magazine.

Next, you need to consider your personal situation, to think about whether you can afford to spend most of your time developing one particular story, or whether you need to move on to other story ideas. Generally, free-lance writers who need to make a stable and continuing income from their writing must have many articles in different stages of development. While they are researching some articles, they are making queries about others, writing still others, and waiting to hear from editors on yet another set of articles.

If financially you need to be working on several ongoing projects in order to keep your income constant, then writing query letters is very likely a good idea. It can save you from investing time and energy in any one feature until you have some definite positive response from an editor. While you're waiting for that response, you can work on other features and other story ideas.

When deciding whether or not to query, you should also consider the nature of the feature article. Is the article very brief? Will its appeal be based primarily on subleties of style or humor? If a prospective article will eventually be the same length as a query letter, you may be better off putting your energy into writing the article rather than the query. Then, too, if an article depends entirely on stylistic characteristics or on a special kind of humor, it may be better to send the article, rather than trying to *describe* in the query letter what will make the article special and unique.

On the other hand, if the article is very long, or if it is about an extremely specific topic only suitable to one publication's readership, you're definitely wiser to write the query. You would be foolish to spend time and energy on a highly individual, one-shot submission that may never work out.

APPEARANCE COUNTS

If you decide, after all this deliberation, to go ahead and send a query letter, you need to write it carefully, putting almost as much effort into composing it as you would toward writing any brief article. A query letter sells two things: the idea of the article, and the idea of you as its writer. *What* you write in the letter convinces an editor that your feature is publishable; *how* you write the letter convinces the editor you are the person to write the story.

At a minimum, the letter should be neat and professional looking. It should contain no typographical errors, inaccuracies, or grammatical mistakes. Your letter's format for margin and spacing should conform to the standards for business communications (see figure 17.1). It should be typed single-spaced (with double-spacing between paragraphs) and typed or printed on white, standard-size (8 1/2 by 11 inches) business stationery of good quality. It should not be typed on erasable bond typing paper (it smudges) or printed on thin computer printout paper (it's difficult to read). If you are using a computer printer, be sure it is capable of letter quality printing or, better yet, is a laser printer.

Include your phone number with your return address. Many busy editors prefer to respond to queries with phone calls rather than written responses.

In your letter's inside address, use the editor's full name (first name, middle initial, and last name) followed by a comma, then his or her correct business title. If the title is very long, omit the comma and type the title on a separate line under the editor's name. In the salutation ("dear so-and-so"), use the editor's last name preceded by the correct courtesy title (Mr., Miss, Mrs., or Ms.).

```
               Letterhead

Date


Editor's name, Editor's title
Teen Magazine
8490 Sunset Blvd.
Hollywood, CA 90060

Dear Editor's name:

Full block style is considered the most
formal of business letter styles; it is
usually used with letterhead stationery.
Every element of the letter is flush with
the left-hand margin.

Paragraphs are single-spaced, with double
spacing between paragraphs. Paragraphs
are not indented.

Sincerely,

[hand-written signature]

Your name, typed
```

```
                        Your street address
                        Your town, state, zip code
                        Phone number with area code
                        Date


Editor's name, Editor's title
Fishing World
51 Atlantic Ave.
Floral Park, NY 11001

Dear Editor's name:

In block form, some elements of the letter
are moved to the right. These elements are
flush to an imaginary line, so that they
appear to all begin the same distance from
the left of the page.

Paragraphs are not indented. They are
single-spaced, with double spacing between
paragraphs.

                        Yours truly,

                        [hand-written signature]

                        Your name, typed
```

Figure 17.1

Diana Hacker describes these business letter formats in *Rules for Writers: A Concise Handbook* (St. Martin's Press). She also gives these directions:

The inside address includes the full name, title, and complete address of the person to whom the letter is written. (This information is repeated as the address on the envelope). The inside address is typed flush left, a few lines below the return address heading. The salutation, or greeting, is typed two lines below the inside address. A colon follows the salutation, and the body of the letter begins two lines below the greeting.

In the salutation use *Ms.* if you are writing to a woman whose title or marital status you do not know or if the woman prefers this form of address. . . .

Common closes are *Yours truly, Very truly yours,* and *Sincerely.* (Note that only the first word of the close is capitalized.) . . . The name of the writer [in the signature] should not be prefaced by a title or followed by an abbreviation for a title or position. This information can be included in a separate line under the typed name. . . .

The letter (which should be about the same width as the envelope) is folded in thirds.

```
                        Your street address
                        Your town, state, zip code
                        Phone number with area code
                        Date


Editor's name, Editor's title
Indiana Business Magazine
6502 Westfield Blvd.
Indianapolis, IN 46220

Dear Editor's name:

   Semi-block form is considered the least
formal of the three business letter formats.
In semi-block form, certain elements
continue to be flush to an imaginary line.

   Paragraphs are indented five spaces,
single-spaced, with double spacing between
paragraphs.

                        Very truly yours,

                        [hand-written signature]

                        Your name, typed
```

Do not use the editor's first name. If you are unsure whether the editor is a man or a woman, use both first and last names, and no courtesy title. If you're not sure whether a woman is married, use "Ms."

You can discover the editor's name and correct business title from the *Writer's Market.* Be sure, however, that you use the most current edition of the book; editors change jobs frequently, and their titles change too. To be 100 percent sure of the editor's name, its spelling, and his or her title, call the publication's office and verify your information with the switchboard operator or editor's secretary. Also, be sure to proofread your typing of the editor's name; a letter which misspells the editor's name is sure to be poorly received.

Strive to limit your query letter to one typed page—or if absolutely necessary, to a page and a half. Editors are busy people; they receive many, many query letters. Show some awareness of how busy they are by not detailing every bit of your article over several typed pages. Chances are, if you can't interest an editor in your idea in a page and a half, you won't be able to interest him or her in two or three pages either.

THE QUERY "LEAD"

Most experts recommend writing a beginning section to your query letter that is similar, if not identical, to the lead you will write to the article itself. (The beginning of a query letter is sometimes even called its "lead.") You should "hook" the editor into reading your letter in the same way the lead for the story will hook readers into reading.

If the lead you consider writing is unusually startling or puzzling, you may want to precede it with a more neutral opening statement, something like "I'd like to propose an article on 'Planning a Trip to Las Vegas' for your magazine." Be sure, too, that the lead paragraph you write is not so snazzy that it's inappropriate to the tone and content of the intended article, or to the magazine to which you are submitting the story idea. A lead paragraph in a query letter to *Modern Maturity,* for example, would not be racy, glib, or filled with teenage slang.

Lisa Collier Cool in *How to Write Irresistible Query Letters* (Writer's Digest Books) gives many examples of query letter leads; here are two dynamic ones she's written:

> Confession is good for the soul—and the bank balance. Last year, confession magazines paid out nearly $1 million for new stories. At the current rate of 3 to 5 cents a word, this works out to $150 to $250 per story—money that could soon be accruing in your savings account once you understand the simple formula used in this type of writing.

> 11:30 A.M. Outside Click Model Management, the Kimberlys, Jennifers and Ericas clutch snapshots or portfolios, hoping to break into New York's $150 million modeling business, where a beautiful 15-year-old can earn $3,000—or

more—for a day's work. It's the monthly "open call," where anyone who thinks she's got the right stuff can audition with Click booker Bonnie Tayar. Precisely at noon, Bonnie steps out into the crowded hallway, announcing "Anyone under 5'8", please go home." Two girls slink off.

Cool advises query letter writers to write leads that arouse interest and provide specifics (especially startling statistics), and that close with a key point. She also advises query letter writers to avoid leads that use dictionary definitions, quickly dated references, technical language or jargon, lengthy historical background or descriptive material, and bad puns or weak jokes.

Hiley Ward, in *Magazine and Feature Writing* (Mayfield Publishing Co.) suggests that query letters, rather than beginning with a "lead," begin with a brief opening statement, something that directly asks the editor, for example, "Would you be interested in an article on raising SAT scores?" The next statement would then suggest to the editor how you are especially qualified to write the proposed article, saying something like "As teacher of a course on improving SAT scores, with 30 years experience coaching pre-college students, I am interested in writing an article about 20 steps students could take to prepare for this test."

SUGGESTING THE ARTICLE'S APPROACH

Whatever your lead, after the letter's opening section you give the editor some sense of the article's approach or focus and its intended structure, form, and length. If the time or date when the article would be published contributes to its effectiveness (for example, if it's a holiday submission), you need to mention its completion date as well. As you're describing what you intend to do, try to reveal to the editor that you have done your homework and that you understand precisely how your article will suit the magazine's readers and the magazine's editorial philosophy. Don't, however, *tell* the editor how the article will benefit his or her readers; he or she may take offense at being instructed by you about the magazine's readers.

This middle section of the query letter might also be a good place to describe photographs that would enhance the story's presentation, or graphics or artwork you could supply to illustrate your feature. (Remember, however, that you will not submit original photographs with your query letter; you should wait until an editor expresses interest, or until you send the completed manuscript.)

In most cases, you will also sketch out the lines of inquiry you intend to pursue in further research for writing the article. Give the identities of experts you will consult, or of people you plan to interview. Indicate what data you have yet to collect, or what places you intend to visit. Be sure that as you make these statements, it's clear to the editor that you have already done preliminary research: you are past ground zero and have thought about what information will complete your article, what will make it meaningful and informative. Your specificity in describing your intended research will convince the editor that your idea for the article is more than a vague, general concept.

YOUR CREDENTIALS

The next section of the query letter *briefly* indicates to the editor your credentials as a writer (that is, if you haven't followed Hiley Ward's suggestion mentioned earlier). If you have some publications to your credit, you should mention a few names of magazines, newspapers, or journals that have published your work—particularly those publications that are most like the publication you are querying. The more publications you have to your credit, the more you can be selective about which ones to mention. Don't indicate every last one of them. Modesty is the best policy.

You can include with your query letter clippings of some published work, particularly if the clippings are of stories similar in style or format to the feature article you are currently proposing to write. Again, don't swamp the editor. Don't send your entire clippings file.

If you have no publications to your credit, give information about what makes you the appropriate person to write the article. Perhaps you have some personal experience, or geographical proximity to certain kinds of information or sources of information. Perhaps you are able to take special photographs, or have special training or background in the field, or more education about the subject than most other writers possess.

If you can think of nothing to say that would argue for your capabilities as the writer of this article, omit a credentials statement and showcase your writing abilities in the excellence of your letter; also showcase your research capabilities by discussing your proposed article with intelligence and forethought.

Don't feel compelled to ''confess'' to being a student. Writers are as mature and adult as the work they write. You don't have to apologize for being a student if you take your work seriously and do professional-level writing. Remember, just like you, many ''professional'' free-lancers have yet to complete their college degree requirements.

CLOSING THE LETTER

End your query letter with a simple, short statement to the effect that you are hoping for a positive response from the editor. Don't elaborate or overdo the closing, and don't try to be cute or coy or assertive. The closing paragraph is another place in the query letter—if you didn't mention it earlier—where you can indicate the proposed article's length and its approximate date of completion.

Don't end your query letter by discussing finances or fees; you will sound presumptuous if you assume at this time that your article will be commissioned. And don't offer to write the article for less than the normal fee; you will sound unprofessional, if not unethical.

In your concluding paragraph, try to express confidence without seeming arrogant. Try not to be too tentative (''It seems that this article might appeal to some of your readers.'') or negative (''I know that many of your readers might not be interested in this topic, but my article will encourage them to reconsider.'').

Be sure to keep a copy of your query letter, or preserve your computer file of it on a disk. Some experienced free-lance writers, who keep many query letters and manuscripts circulating, advise that you keep records of all query letters and manuscripts sent out. Write down on 3-by-5 cards the names of the editors and the publications to which you have sent a query. When you receive a response, note its date and content before sending a query out again. If your records are accurate, you'll know at any given moment where all your queries or manuscripts are and how long they have been there. You'll also, over time, have an idea of how successfully you have fared with individual ideas, stories, editors, and magazines.

OTHER ETIQUETTE

Don't confuse the editor by submitting several story ideas in one query letter. Send individual letters at separate times for each feature article you hope to write. And always include with any unsolicited correspondence to editors a self-addressed, stamped envelope (SASE) which they can use for their responses. Once an editor has agreed to buy your article, however, you no longer need to include an SASE with your correspondence.

You should receive a response from an editor in a reasonable length of time; experts say anywhere from two to eight weeks, but six weeks is probably the most ''reasonable'' time period. If you don't hear in that time, it's appropriate to call the editor's assistant, or write again to the editor, asking for a response to your query.

THE ARTICLE PROPOSAL AND THE ARTICLE MEMO

Bruce Garrison (*Professional Feature Writing,* Lawrence Erlbaum Associates) and Myrick E. Land (*Writing for Magazines,* Prentice-Hall) suggest two options other than query letters for offering article ideas to editors, options you might want to consider.

Garrison suggests that an article proposal is more effective than a query letter if the story idea is in a later stage of development. A proposal, he says, can give a more detailed outline of the story. It is longer (about 500–750

```
Your legal name
Your address
Your town and state with zip code
Your phone number with area code
[in final manuscripts, your social security number]



                    TITLE OF ARTICLE IN CAPITAL LETTERS

                                    by

                Your name as you want it in your byline



        After the byline, drop down two double spaces before you

    begin typing the story. The entire text is double-spaced.

    Leave wide margins, particularly at the bottom of page. On

    subsequent pages, include your name and page number at the

    top of the page; the text starts on the normal top margin

    (about two double spaces down). Type "the end" three double

    spaces below the end of the story. When possible, avoid

    splitting paragraphs at the bottom of any page.

        For final manuscripts, indicate in the upper right corner

    of page one the story's approximate word count and the rights

    offered, and give the copyright notice if you have a copyright.
```

Figure 17.2
Format for article proposals and manuscript submissions.

words), typed double-spaced in article manuscript format (see figure 17.2), and sent to an editor with an accompanying cover letter indicating the writer's credentials and other material normally included in the query letter and not included in the proposal. Information that is in the proposal is not repeated in the cover letter, and the cover letter ends as a query letter ends, with a request for a response from an editor.

According to Garrison, the article proposal contains these things:

1. Summary of the idea and the approximate word length
2. Examples or cases to illustrate your focus
3. Primary expert sources you plan to interview
4. Facts/statistics from authoritative sources
5. Time factors affecting freshness of material
6. Outline of the article and tentative title (if possible)
7. Availability of photographs and other graphics.

Land favors the article memo. He says a memo is more direct and attention-getting than a query letter. In addition, the memo forces the writer to conceive of the article's title before writing the story. The article memo, according to Land, should have the writer's name, return address, and phone number in the upper left-hand corner of a standard 8 1/2-by-11-inch page. Below that, and centered, comes the article's title, followed again by the name of its writer. Below the title are several single-spaced paragraphs that give the story's lead, tell the editor what the article is about, give an indication of sources for the story, and describe the writer's qualifications.

MANUSCRIPT FORMAT

If you decide not to query, but to send a completed manuscript, follow the manuscript format indicated in figure 17.2. The writer's social security number is usually included on the title page of completed manuscripts, so that the payroll office has this information. If you have a copyright for your story (see Chapter 18), you should include this data on the manuscript's title page as well.

Follow all the guidelines we've previously discussed in regards to paper size, and paper and printing quality. Be sure to mail your article flat, not folded (use a large manila envelope), and to include an SASE if you want it returned.

With your submission include a cover letter. The cover letter may include a brief statement about your credentials, but otherwise should be kept simple and short. It should give only a courtesy statement to the effect that you hope the editor will consider your article for his or her magazine. You may want to indicate your willingness to modify the article if the editor has suggestions for improvement.

THE USEFULNESS OF WRITING TITLES

Both the article proposal and the article memo require that the story's title be written before you write the article, or at least before you complete the article. The idea of writing a title before you write is a useful one. Creating a title can force you to stop and think about the appeal of your story, to consider how the article will be perceived by readers, and what it will encourage them to expect from the story. A title can also serve as a reminder to you, when you're writing, of the intended focus of the article. If your thoughts stray, the title brings you back to your original angle.

You should understand, however, that any title you write will not necessarily be used when the story is published. Magazine editors decide the final title of your article and, of course, newspaper editors write headlines. The title you have written, however, may influence their decision or at least initially get them seriously interested in reading your article.

As you start creating titles, try to imagine each title you consider on the cover of the intended magazine. Does it seem appropriate there? Would it encourage readers to buy the publication?

You also want the title to be appropriate to the tone of your story. Don't, for example, write a catchy, casual title for a story about eye surgery. And don't write a title so full of pizzazz that it misleads editors and readers about the kind of story you've written.

Finally, you want to create a title that reflects your particular approach to the topic. If possible, the title should reveal how your story is different from others on that subject.

You can choose from several title formats. Perhaps the most common is simply a topic label (a noun), preceded by a single adjective or several adjectives:

- ''4 Chic (but Cheap) Wardrobe Basics'' (*Mademoiselle*)

Instead of adjectives, a prepositional phrase may come *after* the topic label, modifying it:

- ''Medical Tests for Healthy Women'' (*Good Housekeeping*)
- ''The Lifestyle of the Drifting Continents'' (*Scientific American*)

Another common title format uses a topic label created from a verb, that is, a ''gerund'' (gerunds usually end in ''ing''). A gerund title emphasizes action:

- ''Rearing a Child Therapy Dog'' (*Dog World*)
- ''Building a Better Backyard for Kids'' (*Parenting*)

A third kind of title format begins with the words ''how'' or ''why,'' emphasizing the story's explanatory purpose:

- ''Why Women Are Better, Smarter, Stronger, Than Men'' (*Cosmopolitan*)

An article's title can also ask readers a direct question:

- ''Should You Try to Change Your Guy?'' (*Seventeen*)
- ''Are You a Wimpy Mom?'' (*McCall's*)

Or give a command:

- ''Get On Top of Your Bottom Line'' (*Modern Maturity*)

In slightly longer titles, the topic label can be followed by a colon, then by a phrase or clause which asks a question or makes a statement:

- "Keck: World's Most Powerful Telescope" (*Popular Science*)
- "Raising Figs: You Can Do It Anywhere" (*Organic Gardening*)

TITLES AND SUBTITLES

Double titles (titles with subtitles) generally fall into two groups: those titles for which the subtitle is optional because it simply expands on the title, and those for which the subtitle is necessary, because without it, the meaning of the title would not be clear.

Optional subtitles specify the story's focus:

- "Health Care: Building the System We Need" (*Fortune*)
- "TB: Why It's Back, How We Can Protect Ourselves" (*Newsweek*)

Necessary subtitles, on the other hand, solve an enigma or clear up the confusion created by the title:

- "First Things First: One More Writer's Beginnings" (*Harper's*)
- "Designing Women: Coco Chanel—Fashion's First Feminist" (*New Woman*)

Many titles for feature articles, whether single or double, are creative and clever:

- "Ivana Be a Star: Ms. Trump's Literary Debut" (*Vanity Fair*)
- "Real Fake Shells" (*Natural History*)
- "Such a Nice Young Man: The Making of a Serial Killer" (*Mirabella*)

But no matter how creative and clever feature titles are, they should not be so obscure that editors and/or readers can not understand what the story is about. A title should entice editors and readers into reading, not leave them puzzled about, or uninterested in the story's content.

EXERCISES

1. Take two or three feature articles currently published in magazines. Imagine that you, as a free-lance writer, were writing the query letters that originally sold editors these article ideas. Write one or two sentences you would have written in your query letters to outline the approach of the article.
2. Write a one-paragraph biography listing your publishing credits, or giving information that could serve as evidence to an editor that you are a capable and talented writer and researcher. Polish the writing of this biographical paragraph so you could use it in your next query letter.

3. Do this exercise with another free-lance writer: both of you consider a feature article you have written. Write a query letter and an article proposal you could have originally written to offer the article idea to an editor. Now exchange all three documents. Discuss with each other which approach—the query letter, the article proposal, or the manuscript—most effectively and positively represents to an editor what the article says and does?

18

Professional Ethics
and Legal Issues
Preparing for Publication

When you submit a feature article for free-lance publication, you are entering a professional world governed by legalities and ethical considerations. You would be wise to gain a preliminary understanding of how this professional world operates, so that when you enter it, you act with competence—and also save yourself from decisions you might regret.

Many beginners are hesitant to raise questions with editors about contracts or other legal issues. But the best advice is: educate yourself as much as possible about journalistic law and ethical practices regarding free-lance publication; then, if you still have questions, *ask them*. What does it matter if an editor, or some other authority, doesn't think you're a man- or woman-of-the-world? You'll gain the knowledge you need to make important decisions carefully.

COPYRIGHT

One legal decision that worries many starting free-lance writers is whether they should copyright their work. Obtaining an official copyright is not really a great concern, however. The Copyright Revision Act of 1976, in effect since January 1, 1978, protects the copyright on whatever anyone writes from the moment he or she writes it. So whether you officially register for a copyright or not, your creation is protected by an automatic copyright. This copyright will last for your lifetime and 50 years beyond.

You should understand, however, that *general* ideas are not copyrighted. Only the individual expression of ideas is protected. And that expression must definitely be your own original creation and must be "fixed in tangible form."

If you still would like to secure a registered copyright for your articles, you can write to the Copyright Office of the Library of Congress in Washington, D.C., to request a copyright application. You will pay a small fee in order to obtain a copyright, and you must submit copies of the final version of your work.

Magazines and other publications apply for their own copyrights to protect their entire publications. If you publish in a copyrighted magazine, then, you also have a secondary protection through its copyright.

THE RIGHTS YOU SELL

The major difficulty in the issue of article ownership is what rights you are selling when you sell your feature article to a magazine. What you would prefer is to sell only the rights for the *first* American/Canadian magazine publication ("First North American English-language rights—one-time use only"). When you sell those rights, the rights revert to you after that first publication; if the article is printed again, you are entitled to fees or royalties.

Magazines, obviously, would prefer that they retain the rights to subsequent printings, and so may offer you a contract stipulating rights with some variation of wording that indicates you are signing away subsequent rights as well as first rights. The contract might say "all rights" (the magazine would own every right except copyright); "all publishing rights" (the magazine would own publishing rights; you would own rights to movie, TV, or video); "all periodical rights" (the magazine would own rights to all periodical and newspaper publications; you would own other rights, including book and dramatic rights); and "English-language serial rights" (the magazine would own the rights to publish in English; you would own rights to publish in foreign languages).

Basically, it is your decision which rights to sell. With some articles, signing away all rights is not much of a loss: some stories are very unlikely to be reprinted or resold. Or you may decide that you would rather sign away some rights than risk not having a story published. Even with an article of great resale potential, you may be willing to give up rights in order to be published, especially if you've never been published before. After you've done some publishing and established a credible reputation, however, you will probably more rigorously limit the rights you are willing to sell.

WORK MADE FOR HIRE

Another phrase that you will hear used regarding selling the rights to articles is ''work made for hire.'' ''Work made for hire'' normally describes work written by staff writers, that is, those writers specifically hired to write permanently for a publication. Whatever they create is copyrighted, not in their name, but in the name of their employer. (The publication is considered the author, and the employee loses all rights to what he or she has written.) In essence, hired writers give up publishing rights in exchange for employment.

A provision in the Copyright Act about ''work made for hire'' does allow employer and employee to negotiate ''a written instrument signed by them'' that would allow an employee to retain his or her rights to what he or she has written. If you were a staff writer and retaining rights to a particular article were extremely important to you, you might consider negotiating such a ''written instrument.''

As a free-lancer, you might be offered a ''work-made-for-hire'' agreement. It means that you are being asked to permanently give up all your publishing rights to an article, including your copyright, to someone else. It is an agreement generally considered the least desirable of all rights agreements, one you should avoid signing.

You also should avoid signing any contract with an indemnification clause, that is, a clause that states that you indemnify, or hold harmless, the publishing house from any loss or expenses incurred in legal suits brought about by the publication of your article.

CONTRACTS AND LETTERS OF AGREEMENT

One definite piece of advice about selling an article is ''get it in writing.'' Never rely on oral contracts.

Larger publishing houses will likely offer you a standard contract which they have already drawn up and use for all their writers. Be sure to read it carefully. If you object to any of its provisions, don't sign it. Discuss the changes you want with the editor. Then, when you and the editor have come to some kind of agreement about revisions to the contract, ask for a new contract to be written, or cross out provisions on the old contract that no longer pertain and initial the strikeouts or changes you have made. The editor should initial the changes as well.

If a publishing house does not send you a contract, you should write a letter that will serve as a ''letter of agreement'' between you and the magazine. Put in your letter all the oral understandings you have reached with the editor. You should include statements about the rights you are selling and the amount of money you are being paid to sell those rights. Also mention the topic of the article, your treatment of the topic, the deadline you have agreed to, and the approximate length of the completed manuscript.

An editor who offers you an unfavorable contract may believe that you are uninformed, or so desperate to publish that you will sign whatever is offered. You may decide to sign an unfavorable contract for a variety of reasons (perhaps you *are* desperate to publish). But sign knowingly, after you have asked questions and taken time to rationally assess all aspects of the sale.

GIVING OTHERS CREDIT

Probably the second most significant area of legal concern for feature writers is copyright protection for people other than themselves, that is, for people whose written work they quote. You need to know when you must obtain permission from other writers to use their words and when you can use their words without permission.

The term used frequently regarding permissions is "fair use," which means that you can use a brief quotation from copyrighted material when you are criticizing, reporting, teaching, or doing research. What makes "fair use" difficult is the definition of the word "brief": five lines of poetry might be considered brief, but it is not brief, and therefore not "fair use" if the entire poem is ten lines.

Consider two things when you want to use someone else's published words: first, whether you are using a high *proportion* of the total amount of written material, and second, whether your use of the material will reduce the likelihood that someone else will buy the original. If either is the case, then you are probably harming the original writer and, therefore, you are not entitled to claim fair use protection.

Probably the safest procedure is to ask for permission whenever you're in doubt. When you write for permission, include with your letter a copy of the exact words you wish to use, and indicate where you intend to submit the article, or the name of the magazine that has already accepted the article for publication. Keep a copy of the letter for yourself. Send a self-addressed, stamped envelope with your request.

In addition, if you send photographs with an article submission, have signed permission forms from the people in those photographs. Any private citizens photographed in a private place must give their permission to have their photographs published. If you fail to get these permissions, you could be liable for an invasion-of-privacy lawsuit. People photographed in public places, however, cannot sue for invasion of privacy.

Also, be careful not to use photographs from a previous situation in an article about a new and different situation, or to use photographs that make someone seem to be doing something he or she is not. Private individuals portrayed in a way that misrepresents their actions can sue for a kind of invasion of privacy known as "false light."

COMMON KNOWLEDGE

Of course, you must identify in your article all sources of ideas and theories not your own, and sources of most information. But certain information is considered ''common knowledge,'' that is, material available from a variety of sources. For example, information about the number of square miles of the state of Texas, or the length of the Mississippi River, would be common knowledge. You can use generally known facts such as these without identifying the source of the information. However, if you copy the exact words of a written text to relay the information, then you must identify the source and seek permission to use the words.

A final point: material in U.S. government publications is not protected by copyright. Such publications are considered to be ''in the public domain''; therefore, you can quote from them freely without having to obtain permission.

WHAT EDITORS CAN EXPECT FROM YOU

A good deal of what concerns writers and editors, however, has to do with ethics rather than legalities, because, sometimes the line between what is ethical and what is legal blurs. In an ethical situation, there's no basis for a lawsuit. An editor can't sue if you fail to live up to certain obligations; you, on the other hand, can't sue if an editor fails to live up to your expectations. One reason you're advised to get conditions of your article's sale in writing is so that you're legally protected, not hurt should an editor turn out to be unethical.

By the same token, you should realize that an editor who feels you have acted unethically in the sale of an article is *not* very likely to buy another article from you.

The ethics code of the American Society of Journalists and Authors is included at the end of this chapter. It's worth reading carefully, because it outlines, from the perspective of free-lance writers at least, what constitutes ethical behavior on the part of editors and writers.

What can an editor expect from you?

First and foremost, the editor has a right to expect that your writing will be accurate. Magazines often have fact-checkers to help ensure accuracy in their published work. Newspapers do not normally have fact-checkers on staff. Neither newspapers nor magazines in principle should have to. You are responsible for seeing that your facts are correct in every way. If not, and a magazine editor finds you consistently in error, you can be fairly sure that he or she will not purchase an article from you again.

The editor also has the right to expect that you have not plagiarized anything in your article. In addition, you are responsible for seeing that nothing in your writing is libelous; i.e., none of your statements damage a person's reputation, causing him or her hatred, contempt, or ridicule in the eyes of a substantial and respectable group.

A topic that requires particular vigilance with respect to libelous statements is criminal activity. Anyone charged with a crime is innocent until a court of law has proven him or her guilty. In your writing, therefore, you must treat that person as innocent, whether indicted or not.

If you are worried about writing something that might be libelous, keep in mind the following defenses commonly used for libel suits, and ask yourself if any one of them could be used to defend your words.

The best defense against libel suits is the truth: material that is provable and substantially true is not libelous (which is why magazines and newspapers regard accuracy as having such importance).

If you do err, and write something false, you are in less danger of a lawsuit if you have made the mistake about a public official or public figure. These individuals have to prove, not only that what you said is false, but that you said it with "actual malice" and a "reckless disregard for truth"; that is, you knew the statements were false, but you wrote the material anyway in order to damage the person. Private individuals, on the other hand, need only prove that you made an error that a "reasonable person" in the same position would not have made.

Another libel defense is the argument that material relating to the work of public officials in their public lines of duty is protected by what is called "privilege." Privileged documents, so long as a journalist uses them accurately and representatively, cannot be used as the basis for libel suits. The Congressional Record, for example, is a privileged document, as is a police arrest report. Court transcripts of trials are also privileged.

You must be careful to check, however, that you are, in fact, using the exact document covered by privilege. An arrest report is privileged; off-the-cuff comments by the arresting officer are not; court transcripts are privileged; courtroom comments struck from the record are not.

The third defense for libel, "fair comment," means that the person about whom you said negative things willingly submitted him- or herself to public criticism and evaluation. Someone who gives a concert, publishes a short story, opens a restaurant, markets a product, or offers artwork to public review is considered to have asked for judgment, and therefore is not entitled to sue if that judgment is not positive.

Editors and their magazines have legal departments that can advise you on appropriate ways to handle potentially libelous material, but you must first ask them. You are responsible for taking that initial step.

In addition to accuracy, editors can also expect that you will deliver your story on the agreed-upon deadline, and that the article will be substantially as it is described in the original contract or letter of agreement.

SIMULTANEOUS SUBMISSIONS

It is not clear whether editors have the right to expect you not to engage in "simultaneous submission"—that is, in submitting your article idea to several editors at the same time. Editors, as might be expected, generally are opposed to simultaneous submissions. They argue that they invest a good deal of time considering an article and shouldn't be asked to make that investment only to have some other editor beat them to the punch. Free-lance writers, on the other hand, favor simultaneous submissions because it allows them to have, in a shorter period of time, more possibilities of positive responses.

The issue is not yet resolved, and so the decision about submitting simultaneously is up to you. What you have to keep in mind is that if an editor gets "burned" by your work being accepted by another editor, that editor may not give your work much consideration in the future.

You also have to keep in mind that this circumstance is fairly unlikely to happen.

Some editors suggest that if you intend to offer your article simultaneously to several editors, you should at least inform them of your intentions. The difficulty with this procedure is that an editor's knowledge that you're submitting your article to other editors may prejudice him or her against your work.

Most experts do agree that you can follow this practice: if you don't receive a response from an editor in a reasonable amount of time (particularly if an article you have submitted will lose its value if it is not published by a certain date), then you can write again to the editor, advising him or her that while you are still hoping for a positive response, you are going to go ahead with submitting your article to another publication.

Simultaneous submissions are not quite the same thing ethically as double-duty articles. These are several distinct articles generated from one experience, or one stint of research, or one set of interviews. It is not considered unethical to try to create *different* articles from one reporting project. These multiple articles, however, must be substantially dissimilar in their approach and offered to magazines with substantially different audiences.

WHAT YOU CAN EXPECT FROM EDITORS

As a free-lancer, you too have a right to expect certain kinds of ethical behavior from editors. You have a right to expect, for example, that editors will give you the opportunity to make revisions to your own article—that they won't cut and slash your work without your knowledge and permission. You also have a right to expect that they will give you a byline to your story, since a byline enhances your reputation and thus is a kind of payment, different from money, but nonetheless valuable. You can also expect editors will send the payment for your article shortly after delivery of the finished manuscript, and not upon the article's publication (which may not occur for several months). And you can expect editors will publish your story in a reasonable length of time—generally no later than a year.

While these are all reasonable expectations, it is advised nevertheless that you include statements about conditions of payment and rights to make changes in the story in your contract or letter of agreement.

KILL FEES

If a magazine, after receiving your query letter, indicates that it wants to review your manuscript "on speculation," the editor is giving you no assurance that your article will be purchased. The editor is not obligated to pay you any fee. If, however, your article has been commissioned and a letter of agreement or contract signed, then the editor ethically is obligated to pay you what is called a "kill fee," if, after receiving your finished manuscript, he or she decides it is unsatisfactory. The kill fee is a partial payment to compensate you for the effort you put into preparing the story. Kill fees typically are in the neighborhood of 30 percent of the original agreed-upon price for the article.

Terri Brooks, in *Words' Worth: A Handbook on Writing & Selling Nonfiction* (St. Martin's Press), describes the following circumstances as situations when an article is killed through no fault of the writer; she argues that in such no-fault cases, the writer deserves full, rather than partial, compensation:

- your editor left, and the new editor wants to use his/her own writers
- the owner left, and the new owner is aiming for a slightly different market
- the editors couldn't make a timely decision on the story, and now it is too old to use
- the editors like the story, but a superior will not run it for political reasons
- the editors like the story, but they hadn't realized someone else was working on a similar piece
- the editors like the story but feel—for some vague reason—it is just "not right" for them (this is usually a camouflage for one of the above)

Kill fees give writers some protection from the whims of editors (although, of course, it would be better to receive the entire payment), and paying kill fees rather that full payment protects magazines from shoddy work being done by free-lancers. Neither side is particularly happy with the arrangement. But the important point to make here is that kill fees should be negotiated in the original contract or letter of agreement. It's reasonable to expect a kill fee. A contract or letter of agreement, however, ensures that you will get a kill fee. *After* the magazine has decided it doesn't want the manuscript is not the time to negotiate whether or not you'll be reimbursed for your time.

EXPENSES

Another unclear issue is what you can expect from editors for the expenses of preparing an article. The code of ethics of the American Society of Journalists and Authors asserts: ''Unless otherwise stipulated by the editor at the time of an assignment, a writer shall assume that normal, out-of-pocket expenses will be reimbursed by the publisher. Any extraordinary expenses anticipated by the writer shall be discussed with the editor prior to incurring them.''

It may feel strange to you to ask an editor to reimburse you for ''normal, out-of-pocket expenses,'' and perhaps as a beginner, it's not appropriate to be too demanding about either kill fees or expenses. But the point is, people write articles to make money; the expenses of writing them shouldn't be more than the fee they earn. You may feel that publication of your story is all the payment you want or need, but if you settle for much less than your efforts deserve, you help lower the compensation standards for all free-lance writers, and thus harm professionals who can't afford to work for free.

So, you have the right to expect that you will be reimbursed for reasonable expenses; the difficulty comes in determining what is ''reasonable.'' Reasonable expenses might include transportation costs, computer search charges, long-distance telephone charges, or unusual submission expenses made necessary through a request of the magazine editors, as with fax fees or express mail charges. You and your editor should discuss expenses to clarify what is reasonable, before you sign the contract or send a letter of agreement.

AGENTS AND PROFESSIONAL CONTACTS

If all these legal and ethical issues feel like a lot to consider, you may be tempted to lay them on the shoulders of a literary agent. But you should know how to handle your own affairs before you hire someone else to do it for you; that's the only way you can know if the person handling your affairs is doing it properly. Keep in mind, too, that most agents aren't very interested in representing magazine article writers; the payment for published articles is typically too small to make it profitable for the agent.

At any rate, having an agent is not a professional ''must''; many writers succeed perfectly well without one. If you do hire an agent, you'll probably pay a fee of between 10 and 15 percent.

Instead of seeking an agent to help you, you might consider finding support among your colleagues. Look for professional organizations you can join, such as the National Writers Union (open to anyone seeking to publish writing), the Society of Professional Journalists (open to newspaper writers and broadcasters), and the Public Relations Society of America (open to those in public relations). When you have published eight bylined articles in general magazines in the past four years, you will be eligible to join the American

Society of Journalists and Authors. In the meantime, you can send for *The ASJA Handbook: A Writer's Guide to Ethical and Economic Issues.* (Contact the organization at 1501 Broadway, Room 1907, New York, NY 10036.)

If you are professionally employed on the staff of a newspaper or a university, you might seek your institution's financial support for attending seminars for writers, such as those sponsored by the Poynter Institute for Media Studies or the American Press Institute.

Another way to gain professional support is to enter professional writing competitions. Recognition for your writing excellence gives you encouragement and looks impressive in your query letter's credentials statement. The *Writer's Market* gives a listing of contests, fellowships, and writing festivals in which you can participate. *Editor and Publisher* also annually publishes a list of competitions. If you educate yourself about which contests are suitable to your work, you can ensure that your best articles fit deadline and eligibility requirements.

Working as a professional may at first seem an awesome undertaking. You're sailing in what are, for you, uncharted waters. But others have been on this course before. They have found the waters navigable, and in time you will too. You may even come to enjoy testing your skill and fortitude.

But before you master the seas, you must leave shore. So raise the anchor of your inexperience and set the sails for professional expertise: write that first query letter, submit that first manuscript. You may experience some rejection—but hold the course. You'll discover that the winds and waters of free-lance feature writing can be favorable.

EXERCISES

1. Go to the *Media Law Reporter* volumes in the reference section of your library and look up these cases in communication law:
   a. New York Times vs. Sullivan (1964)
   b. Time, Inc. vs. Hill (1967)
   c. Butts vs. Curtis Publishing (1967)
   d. Cantrell vs. Forest City Publishing (1974)
   e. Gertz vs. Welch (1974)
   f. Time, Inc. vs. Firestone (1976)
   g. Pring vs. Penthouse International (1982)

Discuss with other journalists in your class the implications of these decisions.

2. Assume hypothetically that an editor of a particular magazine has expressed willingness to buy one of your articles; however, the editor has not sent you a contract. You want to write a letter of agreement to send to the editor. Compose a rough draft of the letter you would send. Share it with class members or other journalists for their critical review and discussion.

3. Do some role-playing with members of your class or other journalists. Take turns being editor and free-lance writer; have a conversation discussing publication rights, rights to revise the article, deadlines, kill fees, and expenses.

A P P E N D I X
ASJA CODE OF ETHICS
AND FAIR PRACTICES

Preamble

Over the years, an unwritten code governing editor-writer relationships has arisen. The American Society of Journalists and Authors has compiled the major principles and practices of that code that are generally recognized as fair and equitable.

The ASJA has also established a Committee on Editor-Writer Relations to investigate and mediate disagreements brought before it, either by members or by editors. In its activity this committee shall rely on the following guidelines.

1. Truthfulness, Accuracy, Editing

The writer shall at all times perform professionally and to the best of his or her ability, assuming primary responsibility for truth and accuracy. No writer shall deliberately write into an article a dishonest, distorted, or inaccurate statement.

Editors may correct or delete copy for purposes of style, grammar, conciseness or arrangement, but may not change the intent or sense without the writer's permission.

2. Sources

A writer shall be prepared to support all statements made in his or her manuscripts, if requested. It is understood, however, that the publisher shall respect any and all promises of confidentiality made by the writer in obtaining information.

[In 1991, the U.S. Supreme Court ruled that a source whose name had been revealed contrary to a promise made by a journalist was entitled to sue, even though the agreement was not a written contract.]

3. Ideas and Proposals

An idea shall be defined not as a subject alone but as a subject combined with an approach.

A proposal of an idea (''query'') by a professional writer shall receive a personal response within three weeks. If such a communication is in writing, it is properly viewed and treated as business correspondence, with no return postage or other materials required for reply.

A writer shall be considered to have a proprietary right to an idea suggested to an editor.

[A beginning writer should enclose a self-addressed, stamped envelope (s.a.s.e.), to be used for the magazine's reply, along with an article proposal. *All* writers should enclose such envelopes when submitting *unsolicited* manuscripts; no magazine can be expected to assume the cost of returning material it has not assigned or invited. If the material is stored on a computer disk, the writer may wish to advise the magazine that an unwanted manuscript need not be returned. . . .

4. Acceptance of an Assignment

A request from an editor that the writer proceed with an idea, however worded and whether oral or written, shall be considered an assignment. (The word ''assignment'' here is understood to mean a definite order for an article.) It shall be the obligation of the writer to proceed as rapidly as possible toward the completion of an assignment, to meet a deadline mutually agreed upon, and not to agree to unreasonable deadlines.

5. Conflict of Interest

The writer shall reveal to the editor, before acceptance of an assignment, any actual or potential conflict of interest, including but not limited to any financial interest in any product, firm, or commercial venture relating to the subject of the article.

6. Report on Assignment

If in the course of research or during the writing of the article, the writer concludes that the assignment will not result in a satisfactory article, he or she shall be obliged to so inform the editor.

7. Withdrawal

Should a disagreement arise between the editor and writer as to the merit or handling of an assignment, the editor may remove the writer on payment of mutually satisfactory compensation for the effort already expended, or the writer may withdraw without compensation and, if the idea for the assignment originated with the writer, may take the idea elsewhere without penalty.

8. Agreements

The practice of written confirmation of all agreements between editors and writers is strongly recommended, and such confirmation may originate with the editor, the writer, or an agent. Such a memorandum of confirmation should list all aspects of the assignment including subject, approach, length, special instructions, payments, deadline, and guarantee (if any). Failing prompt contradictory response to such a memorandum, both parties are entitled to assume that the terms set forth therein are binding.

All terms and conditions should be agreed upon at the time of assignment, with no changes permitted except by written agreement signed by both parties.

9. Rewriting

No writer's work shall be rewritten without his or her advance consent. If an editor requests a writer to rewrite a manuscript, the writer shall be obliged to do so but shall alternatively be entitled to withdraw the manuscript and offer it elsewhere.

10. Bylines

Lacking any stipulation to the contrary, a byline is the author's unquestioned right. All advertisements of the article shall also carry the author's name. If an author's byline is omitted from the published article, no matter what the cause or reason, the publisher shall be liable to compensate the author financially for the omission.

11. Updating

If delay in publication necessitates extensive updating of an article, such updating shall be done by the author, to whom additional compensation shall be paid.

12. Reversion of Rights

A writer is not paid by money alone. Part of the writer's compensation is the intangible value of timely publication. Consequently, reasonable and good-faith editors should be made to schedule an article within six months and publish it within twelve months. In the event that circumstances prevent such timely publication, the writer should be informed within twelve months as to the publication's continued interest in the article and plans to publish it. If publication is unlikely, the manuscript and all rights therein should revert to the author without penalty or cost to the author.

13. Payment for Assignments

An assignment presumes an obligation upon the publisher to pay for the writer's work upon satisfactory completion of the assignment, according to the agreed terms. Should a manuscript that has been accepted, orally or in writing, by a publisher or any representative or employee of the publisher, later be deemed unacceptable, the publisher shall nevertheless be obliged to pay the writer in full according to the agreed terms.

    If an editor withdraws or terminates an assignment, due to no fault of the writer, after work has begun but prior to completion of a manuscript, the writer is entitled to compensation for work already put in; such compensation shall be negotiated between editor and author and shall be commensurate with the amount of work already completed. If a completed assignment is not acceptable, due to no fault of the writer, the writer is nevertheless entitled to payment; such payment, in common practice, has varied from half the agreed-upon price to the full amount of that price.

14. Time of Payments

The writer is entitled to full payment for an accepted article within 30 days of delivery. No article payment, or any portion thereof, should ever be subject to publication or to scheduling for publication.

    [Writers are strongly urged to reject agreements that specify payment at any time later than this.]

15. Expenses

Unless otherwise stipulated by the editor at the time of an assignment, a writer shall assume that normal, out-of-pocket expenses will be reimbursed by the publisher. Any extraordinary expenses anticipated by the writer shall be discussed with the editor prior to incurring them.

16. Insurance

A magazine that gives a writer an assignment involving any extraordinary hazard shall insure the writer against death or disability during the course of travel or the hazard, or, failing that, shall honor the cost of such temporary insurance as an expense account item.

17. Loss of Personal Belongings

If, as a result of circumstances or events directly connected with a perilous assignment and due to no fault of the writer, a writer suffers loss of personal belongings or professional equipment or incurs bodily injury, the publisher shall compensate the writer in full.

18. Copyright, Additional Rights

It shall be understood, unless otherwise stipulated in writing, that sale of an article manuscript entitles the purchaser to first North American serial rights only, and that all other rights are retained by the author. Under no circumstances shall an independent writer be required to sign a so-called "all rights transferred" or "work made for hire" agreement as a condition of assignment, of payment, or of publication.

> [See the ASJA Statement of Position on Work Made for Hire, p. 75 in *The ASJA Handbook*.]

19. Reprints

All revenues from reprints shall revert to the author exclusively, and it is incumbent upon a publication to refer all requests for reprint to the author. The author has a right to charge for such reprints and must request that the original publication be credited.

20. Agents

An agent may not represent editors or publishers. In the absence of any agreement to the contrary, a writer shall not be obliged to pay an agent a fee on work negotiated, accomplished and paid for without the assistance of the agent. An agent should not charge a client a separate fee covering ''legal'' review of a contract for a book or other project.

21. TV and Radio Promotion

The writer is entitled to be paid for personal participation in TV or radio programs promoting periodicals in which the writer's work appears.

22. Indemnity

No writer should be obliged to indemnify any magazine or book publisher against any claim, actions, or proceedings arising from an article or book, except where there are valid claims of plagiarism or copyright violation.

> [See the ASJA Statement of Position on Blanket Indemnification Clauses, p. 79 in *The ASJA Handbook.*]

23. Proofs

The editor shall submit edited proofs of the author's work to the author for approval, sufficiently in advance of publication that any errors may be brought to the editor's attention. If for any reason a publication is unable to so deliver or transmit proofs to the author, the author is entitled to review the proofs in the publication's office.

> [In the past, magazines have sometimes pleaded time constraints, with turnaround within hours, to explain failure to submit proofs. With the advent of the fax machine, a publication's inability to transmit proofs to the author, or to some facility in the author's vicinity, would be extremely rare.]

CREDITS

Chapter 1

Page 15: Reprinted by permission of Associated Press. **p. 16:** Peter Marks/*Newsday.* **p. 20:** © 1990, *THE WASHINGTON POST.* REPRINTED WITH PERMISSION.

Chapter 2

Page 23: © *The Baltimore Sun,* 1985. **p. 23:** Copyright © 1992. From *Coaching Writers: Editors and Reporters Working Together.* By Roy Peter Clark and Don Fry. Reprinted with permission of St. Martin's Press, Incorporated. **p. 24:** William Ruehlmann, *Stalking the Feature Story,* © 1977, Random House. **p. 28:** Myrick E. Land, *WRITING FOR MAGAZINES,* 2e, © 1993, p. 19. Adapted by permission of Prentice Hall. Englewood Cliffs, New Jersey. **p. 38:** *St. Paul Pioneer Press.* **p. 48:** *Knight-Ridder/*Tribune News Service.

Chapter 3

Page 63: *The Milwaukee Journal.*

Chapter 4

Page 73: © 1992, The Boston Globe Newspaper Co./Washington Post Writers Group. Reprinted with permission. **p. 73:** Taken from the ''On the Right'' column by William

F. Buckley, Jr. Reprinted with permission of Universal Press Syndicate. **p. 75:** © 1988, *THE WASHINGTON POST.* REPRINTED WITH PERMISSION. **p. 78:** Reprinted with permission by *The Philadelphia Inquirer.* **p. 78:** Truman Capote, *In Cold Blood,* © 1965, Random House, Inc. **p. 79:** Reprinted by permission of Associated Press. **p. 80:** The (Danville, Ill.) *Commercial-News.* **p. 82:** By Richard Aregood, Editorial Page Editor, *Philadelphia Daily News.* **p. 83:** Reprinted with permission of the *St. Petersburg Times.*

Chapter 5

Page 91: © Copyright 1992, Chicago Tribune Company, all rights reserved, used with permission. **p. 92:** Copyright 1991, *USA TODAY.* Reprinted with permission. **p. 92:** Reprinted by permission of Sterling Lord Literistic, Inc. Copyright © 1991 by Bob Drury. This article was originally published in *Vanity Fair.* **p. 93:** Reprinted with permission of Associated Press. **p. 93:** Copyright 1991, *USA TODAY.* Reprinted with permission. **p. 93:** Copyright 1991, *USA TODAY.* Reprinted with permission. **p. 93:** Copyrighted 2/19/1989, Chicago Tribune Company, all rights reserved, used with

permission. **p. 94:** Reprinted by permission of Associated Press. **p. 95:** *Yankee Magazine,* Dublin, NH. **p. 95:** Ellen Byron, journalist and playwright. **p. 96:** Copyright © 1991 by The New York Times Company. Reprinted by permission. **p. 96:** Christopher Knowlton, *FORTUNE,* © 1991 Time, Inc. All rights reserved. **p. 96:** Reprinted with permission of *The Seattle Times* from an article by Carey Quan Gelernter, October 1, 1991. **p. 96:** Copyright 1990, *The Buffalo News.* **p. 97:** *The Fort Collins Coloradoan.* **p. 97:** Reprinted with permission by *The Philadelphia Inquirer.* **p. 98:** Reprinted by permission from *The Christian Science Monitor* © 1987 The Christian Science Publishing Society. All rights reserved. **p. 98:** Reprinted with permission, *The Denver Post.* **p. 99:** Copyright, 1991, *Los Angeles Times.* Reprinted by permission. **p. 99:** Debra Kent. **p. 99:** Reprinted with permission of the *St. Louis Post-Dispatch,* copyright 1993. **p. 100:** Reprinted with permission from *MODERN MATURITY.* Copyright 1991, American Association of Retired Persons. **p. 100:** Copyright © 1991, by The New York Times Company. Reprinted by permission. **p. 100:** *Knight-Ridder/*Tribune News Service. **p. 100:** Copyright 1991, *USA TODAY.* Reprinted with permission.

p. 101: Michael Maxtone-Graham.
p. 101: Copyright © 1991 by the New York Times Company. Reprinted by permission. p. 102: Copyright © 1991 by The New York Times Company. Reprinted by permission. p. 102: Copyright © 1991 by The New York Times Company. Reprinted by permission. p. 102: Copyright 1991, USA TODAY. Reprinted with permission. p. 102: Knight-Ridder/ Tribune News Service. p. 103: Copyright © 1980 by The New York Times Company. Reprinted by permission. pp. 103, 104: Reprinted with permission of Associated Press. p. 104: Reprinted by permission of Wall St. Journal, © 1981 Dow Jones & Company, Inc. All Rights Reserved Worldwide. p. 106: Mike Capuzzo is a feature writer with The Philadelphia Inquirer. Reprinted with permission by The Philadelphia Inquirer.

Chapter 6

Pages 116, 130: Copyright 1990, Des Moines Register and Tribune Co. Reprinted with permission. p. 118: Copyright 1988, The Buffalo News. p. 118: Reprinted by permission of Associated Press. p. 119: George Weller, reprinted with permission from the Chicago Sun-Times © 1992. p. 123: TOM WEBER, SENIOR WRITER, BANGOR (MAINE) DAILY NEWS. p. 124: Reprinted by permission of Associated Press. pp. 125, 126: Reprinted by permission of Associated Press. pp. 127, 128: Copyright © 1982 by The New York Times Company. Reprinted by permission. p. 128: Scripps Howard Newspapers.

Chapter 7

Page 135: Mike Bartell, the Toledo Blade. p. 136: © 1991, THE WASHINGTON POST. REPRINTED WITH PERMISSION. p. 137: Knight-Ridder/Tribune News Service. p. 138: By Dan Luzadder of The Fort Wayne (IN) News-Sentinel. p. 138:

Reprinted with permission from The Tampa Tribune. p. 139: SMITHSONIAN, June 1990 by Mary Anne Weaver. p. 139: Reprinted by permission of The Philadelphia Inquirer, March 17, 1978. p. 141: Charles N. Barnard. p. 142: © 1987, THE WASHINGTON POST. REPRINTED WITH PERMISSION. p. 143: Copyright 1989, The Buffalo News. p. 144: © Copyright 8/4/35, Chicago Tribune Company, all rights reserved, used with permission. pp. 145, 146: Copyright © 1958 by The New York Times Company. Reprinted by permission. p. 146: Copyright © 1991 by The New York Times Company. Reprinted by permission. p. 149: Copyright © 1945 by The New York Times Company. Reprinted by permission. p. 150: Greta Tilley, "Dorothea Dix Hospital Series" Part III published beginning May 1, 1984 in the Greensboro News & Record, Greensboro, NC 27401.

Chapter 8

Page 159: © 1979 THE WASHINGTON POST. REPRINTED WITH PERMISSION. p. 160: © 1991 THE WASHINGTON POST. REPRINTED WITH PERMISSION. p. 160: Copyright © 1991 by The New York Times Company. Reprinted by permission. p. 161: Greta Tilley, "Suicide at Age 16" published 2/7/82 in the Greensboro News & Record, Greensboro, NC 27401. p. 162: Reprinted by permission of Associated Press. p. 162: Angela Wright, The Burr, Kent State University. p. 162: Copyright © 1991 by The New York Times Company. Reprinted by permission. p. 163: Reprinted by permission of Associated Press. p. 163: Reprinted by permission; © 1991 Barry Paris. Originally in The New Yorker. All Rights Reserved. p. 164: © Copyright 1990, Meredith Corporation. All Rights Reserved. Reprinted from LADIES' HOME JOURNAL magazine. p. 165: Knight-Ridder/Tribune News Service.

p. 165: © 1991, THE WASHINGTON POST. REPRINTED WITH PERMISSION. p. 166: Knight-Ridder/ Tribune News Service. p. 167: © 1991 THE WASHINGTON POST. REPRINTED WITH PERMISSION. p. 167: Knight-Ridder/Tribune News Service. p. 168: By Marcia Froelke Coburn. From Rolling Stone, May 16, 1991. By Straight Arrow Publishers, Inc. 1992. All Rights Reserved. Reprinted by Permission. p. 169: Knight-Ridder/ Tribune News Service. p. 170: Reprinted with permission of The Pittsburgh Press. p. 174: Scripps Howard Newspapers. p. 175: Copyright © 1991 by The New York Times Company. Reprinted by permission.

Chapter 9

Page 182: Reprinted by permission of Associated Press. p. 183: Reprinted by permission, Nation's Business, November 1991. Copyright 1991, U.S. Chamber of Commerce. p. 184: Reprinted by permission of Wall St. Journal, © 1991 Dow Jones & Company, Inc. All Rights Reserved Worldwide. p. 184: © 1991, THE WASHINGTON POST. REPRINTED WITH PERMISSION. p. 184: © 1990, THE WASHINGTON POST. REPRINTED WITH PERMISSION. p. 185: Robert Cahn. p. 185: Reprinted with permission from Forbes. p. 185: Reprinted by permission of Associated Press. p. 186: Ann Louise Bardach, Investigative Reporter. This article was originally published in Vanity Fair. p. 187: Copyright © 1991 by The New York Times Company. Reprinted by permission. p. 187: Reprinted with permission, The Denver Post. pp. 187, 188: P. J. Skerrett, free-lance science and medical writer. p. 188: Copyright © 1991 by The New York Times Company. Reprinted by permission. p. 189: Copyright © 1991 by The New York Times Company. Reprinted by permission. p. 189: Reprinted with permission by *The Philadelphia Inquirer.* **p. 194:** Jon Franklin, University of Oregon School of Communication *Notre Dame* Magazine.

Chapter 10

Page 200: Reprinted by permission of Associated Press. **p. 201:** Copyright © 1991 by The New York Times Company. Reprinted by permission. **p. 202:** Reprinted with permission from the August 1991 *Reader's Digest.* Copyright © 1991 by The Reader's Digest Assn., Inc. **p. 202:** Reprinted with permission from the November 1991 *Reader's Digest.* Copyright © 1991 by The Reader's Digest Assn., Inc. **p. 203:** Reprinted with permission from the November 1991 *Reader's Digest.* Copyright © 1991 by The Reader's Digest Assn., Inc. **p. 204:** Reprinted with permission of Suzann Ledbetter. **p. 204:** Barry H. Rodrigue. **p. 205:** © 1991, *THE WASHINGTON POST.* REPRINTED WITH PERMISSION. **pp. 205, 206:** *Knight-Ridder*/Tribune News Service. **p. 206:** Reprinted by permission of Associated Press. **p. 206:** *THE CINCINNATI ENQUIRER.* **p. 207:** Reprinted with permission from the November 1991 *Reader's Digest.* Copyright © 1991 by The Reader's Digest Assn., Inc. **p. 209:** Copyright 1985, *The Buffalo News.*

Chapter 11

Page 213: © Copyrighted 9–9–91, Chicago Tribune Co., all rights reserved, used with permission. **p. 214:** *THE DAILY PRESS,* NEWPORT NEWS, VA. **p. 215:** Diane Harris, Senior Editor, *MONEY* Magazine. **p. 215:** Copyright 1990, *The Buffalo News.* **p. 224:** Reprinted with permission of Edwin Kiester, Jr. Reprinted with permission from the June 1991 *Reader's Digest.*

Chapter 12

Page 230: Reprinted by permission of Associated Press. **p. 230:** Copyright © 1991 by The New York Times Company. Reprinted by permission. **p. 231:** Reprinted courtesy of *The Boston Globe.* **p. 232:** © 1991, *THE WASHINGTON POST.* REPRINTED WITH PERMISSION. **p. 233:** Reprinted by permission of Associated Press. **p. 233:** *The Atlanta Journal-Constitution.* **p. 235:** Reprinted by permission of Associated Press. **p. 236:** Reprinted by permission of Associated Press. **p. 237:** Copyright © 1991 by The New York Times Company. Reprinted by permission. **pp. 237, 238:** Reprinted by permission of Associated Press. **p. 238:** Reprinted with permission of *The Dallas Morning News.* **p. 239:** Copyright 1991 Time Inc. Reprinted by permission. **p. 241:** Copyright 10/21/92, *U.S. News & World Report.* **p. 241:** Copyright 1991 Time, Inc. Reprinted with permission. **p. 241:** From *NEWSWEEK* 10/21/91 © 1991, Newsweek, Inc. All rights reserved. Reprinted by permission. **p. 242:** Reprinted with permission of *The Miami Herald.*

Chapter 13

Page 247: ''Bermuda Brushstrokes'' by Charlanne Fields, *Elegant Bride* Magazine, a publication of Pace Communications, Inc. **p. 248:** © 1991, *THE WASHINGTON POST.* REPRINTED WITH PERMISSION. **p. 248:** Reprinted by permission of Associated Press. **p. 249:** Reprinted with permission from *Early American Life,* a Cowles Magazines publication. **p. 250:** Richard Olsenius, *National Geographic.* **pp. 250, 251:** Copyright © 1991 by The New York Times Company. Reprinted by permission. **p. 251:** Copyright © 1991 by The New York Times Company. Reprinted by permission. **p. 255:** *DAILY PRESS,* NEWPORT NEWS, VA. **p. 256:** *Knight-Ridder*/Tribune News Service. **p. 256:** Copyright © 1991 by

The New York Times Company. Reprinted by permission. **p. 260:** Copyright, 1992, Los Angeles Times. Reprinted by permission. **p. 262:** *St. Paul Pioneer Press.*

Chapter 14

Page 269: Reprinted by permission of Associated Press. **p. 269:** Reprinted by permission of Associated Press. **p. 269:** Reprinted by permission of Associated Press. **p. 270:** Reprinted with permission of the *Duluth News-Tribune.* **p. 271:** Don Lessem, author and journalist. **p. 271:** © 1990, *THE WASHINGTON POST.* REPRINTED WITH PERMISSION. **p. 272:** *Corpus Christi Caller-Times.* **p. 273:** Reprinted by permission of Associated Press. **p. 274:** *MADEMOISELLE,* MARCH 1992. **p. 274:** David Finkel, *St. Petersburg Times,* May 3, 1987. Reprinted with permission of the *St. Petersburg Times.* **p. 275:** By Rose Post of *The Salisbury (N.C.) Post.* **p. 276:** Reprinted by permission of Associated Press. **p. 276:** © Copyright 1991, Meredith Corporation. All Rights Reserved. Reprinted from *LADIES' HOME JOURNAL* Magazine. **p. 277:** *Knight-Ridder*/Tribune News Service. **p. 278:** Reprinted with permission of *The Pittsburgh Press.* **p. 281:** Doug McInnis, *The Columbus Dispatch.* **p. 282:** From the *Mail Tribune,* Medford, Oregon.

Chapter 15

Page 294: Reprinted by permission of Associated Press. **p. 294:** Reprinted by permission of Associated Press. **p. 295:** © 1991, *THE WASHINGTON POST.* REPRINTED WITH PERMISSION. **p. 295:** Reprinted with permission of *The Seattle Times* from an article by Larry Brown, November 6, 1991. **p. 296:** Universal Press Syndicate. **pp. 296, 297:** Copyright © 1991 by The New York Times Company. Reprinted by permission. **p. 297:** © 1991, *THE WASHINGTON POST.* REPRINTED WITH

INDEX